D1294012

# THE BIG GAME ANIMALS OF NORTH AMERICA

OUTDOOR LIFE

# The Big Game

FULL COLOR PAINTINGS AND BLACK AND WHITE DRAWINGS BY DOUGLAS ALLEN

SCIENTIFIC ANIMAL PORTRAITS BY Alexander Seidel

# Animals of North America

by JACK O'CONNOR GUN EDITOR OF OUTDOOR LIFE MAGAZINE

with Natural Histories by George G. Goodwin ASSOCIATE CURATOR OF MAMMALS, AMERICAN MUSEUM OF NATURAL HISTORY

OUTDOOR LIFE • E. P. DUTTON & CO., INC.

NEW YORK

LIBRARY OF CONGRESS CATALOG CARD NUMBER 61-17292

MANUFACTURED IN THE UNITED STATES OF AMERICA

DESIGNED BY BEN FEDER

# CONTENTS

# THE BIG GAME ANIMALS OF NORTH AMERICA

CHAPTER 1

# THE DALL SHEEP

WHEN I awoke that August morning in a flimsy little tent beside Moose Horn Creek in the Yukon not far from the Alaska border, I felt the same sort of a pleasant and exciting glow that used to come over me when as a child I first drifted into wakefulness on Christmas morning. This was it! This was The Day. With luck I'd get a good look at some Dall sheep within a few hours. Possibly I'd even get a crack at a good ram.

I could hear the crackle of a willow-wood fire outside the tent and as I slipped on my long-handled underwear, the warm and comforting smell of coffee began to steal into the tent. A moment later I was fully dressed and outside with the smell of willows and dawn and glacial water. Our little French cook was squatted by the fire frying bacon, and Field Johnson, my Indian guide, was having his first cup of coffee. I washed in the frigid water of the creek and made a stab at combing my hair. A few minutes later, while the ptarmigan flew out of the willows around us and up to the caribou barrens to feed, I was devouring hotcakes.

Then my large and amiable friend, Myles Brown, joined me as I squatted on a pack pannier.

"Think we'll see sheep today, Field?" he asked.

"You bet. Maybe so. This is good place. We get him, that fella!"

The plan, Field told us, was for his half-brother Johnny and Myles to hunt the slopes of tremendous, ice-sheathed Mt. Natazhat back of camp while Field and I made a long circle over the caribou barrens and hunted the basins above the Klutlan Glacier, the source of the Generc River.

It was a long haul—up over the barrens where the dwarf arctic birch was beginning to turn scarlet from the early frost, down a precarious trail into a deep canyon that ran into the Generc. Then we pulled out and rode up a series of grassy benches far above timberline. Finally we tied our horses to stones and began our climb.

Sheepy-looking country this—cliffs and slide rock for refuge, and good grass for feed. We climbed on a heavy used trail beaten deep into the turf, clear cut across the slides. Tracks and droppings were fresh.

The first basin we looked into produced nothing, but when we poked our heads over the ridge to scan the second we immediately saw snow-white ewes and lambs—slender, lithe, and beautiful. Before this I had hunted desert sheep in Sonora, Rocky Mountain bighorns in Alberta, British Columbia, and Wyoming, but this was my first good look at the wonderful northern sheep.

I could have watched longer, but Field was impatient. "Come on," he whispered. "Let's look in next basin. Maybe we see rams."

Again we saw ewes and lambs. A dainty ewe walked out of a cave in the dark lava and stood silhouetted glittering white against the green of the lush grass. A moment later a lamb joined her. About a dozen more popped up on a ledge of a black cliff at the head of the basin where they had been lying.

We scrambled down the steep slope and jumped a little creek that was born in the snowfield above. We had started up the other side when suddenly, over-poweringly, I smelled a ram—the oily, sweetish odor that all sheep hunters know.

"Field," I whispered, "I smell a ram."

"If you do," he said, "you got nose like wolf."

Above us a long ridge of black volcanic rock projected out from the cliff into the center of the basin, and the cold air from the ice fields above was rolling gently downhill. If there was indeed a ram around he'd have to be on that ridge.

Apparently a ram had seen us from his bed on the ridge as we came into the basin. He had remained quiet until we stopped. Then, just as deer often do, he had decided he had been seen. I got a momentary glimpse of his chunky snow-white body and his curling, golden horns when he jumped off the ridge and out of sight.

"Big one. We see again. Shoot!" Field yelled.

Knowing that the ram couldn't stay behind that ridge all the way up the hill, I worked the bolt of my .270 to put a cartridge in the chamber and flopped into a prone position. When he came out running hard I was ready for him. The dot reticule in the scope found his rump, and I squeezed the trigger. Abruptly the ram stopped and stood weaving. Another shot beside the first tipped him over, and with that he started rolling gently downhill.

A few minutes later I was standing beside my first Dall ram. He was snow-white, his eyes were amber, and his horns the color of dried lemon peel. His ears were short and round like those of the bighorns from Alberta, his horns slenderer than any I had previously seen on a mature ram. But they were long. Both were slightly broomed, but they swept up above his nose and made a good deal more than a complete curl. I didn't have a tape with me and I guessed that they'd go a little over 40 inches. When I got back to camp I found the longest horn measured 38½. The annual rings on his horns showed him to be about twelve years old. He was definitely smaller than the bighorns I had shot, and about the size of the average large desert ram. I had read that Dall sheep stained their white coats badly in the summer, and I had also read that all Dall sheep showed black hairs along the backbone and in the tail. But this lovely ram hadn't a single black hair and was as clean in his short summer coat as a fresh-washed kitten.

Incidentally, I have often read that during the early fall hunting season, old rams are never found near ewes. Like many generalizations, that one doesn't always hold. As we have seen, this first Dall ram of mine was bedded down alone right in the midst of a basin full of ewes and lambs, and on another occasion I saw over eighty ewes, lambs, and yearlings in a big basin, and on a ridge above —not over half a mile away as the crow flies—was a herd of about ten old rams.

Although they may be near each other, rams and ewes generally stay in separate bands and don't pay any attention to each other. But even that rule doesn't always apply. In late August, 1956, I saw, stalked, and photographed a herd of about forty ewes, lambs, yearlings and about eight or ten large rams. When I saw them the following day, the rams had left the ewes, but the first time I spotted them they were feeding and traveling together.

A wonderful animal, this Dall sheep, one of the two land animals in the world that is white the year around. The other, of course, is the Rocky Mountain white goat. Oddly enough, this snow-white sheep is a first cousin of the Stone sheep, the darkest of American sheep, and so closely are they related that the Stone is considered a subspecies of the Dall—*Ovis dalli stonei,* whereas the Dall is *Ovis dalli dalli.*

Dr. Ian McTaggart Cowan, professor at the University of British Columbia and authority on North American sheep, believes that the ancestors of all North American sheep migrated from Siberia in remote times. Then when the glacial ice came down, they were split into two groups. The ancestors of the brown bighorns were driven south of the ice into what is now the United States. They gradually moved as far south as Sonora, Chihuahua, and Lower California. Then as the ice receded, some of them worked north to occupy their ancestral ranges in the Rocky Mountains of the northern United States and Canada.

The ancestors of all the so-called thin-horned sheep, the Stones and the Dalls, managed to survive north of the glaciers, up in the Arctic where the light, dry snow does not form into great masses of ice. As the ice receded, these sheep worked south. Those in the southern part of the range gradually evolved into the dark Stone.

The Dalls are found from the arctic ranges of Alaska south to the chain of lakes that is roughly on the border of the Yukon and British Columbia.

The most serious wild predator of the white sheep, particularly in the Arctic, is the great northern wolf.

East of the lakes the sheep are mostly white. A few may show a scattering of dark hairs in the tail, along the spine, or on the bridge of the nose. Now and then one with a suggestion of a gray saddle will be shot, but almost all are snow-white Dalls.

As soon as one gets south and east of the Yukon River and below the chain of lakes some very dark sheep, true Stones with black-brown saddles, are seen. When Bill Rae, the editor of *Outdoor Life,* and I were hunting sheep around Prospector Mountain in the western Yukon in 1956, most of the sheep looked snow-white, but a few had black tails. Many of them, upon close examination, would show dark hairs, and two young rams we saw had the gray saddles of light-colored Stones. Even in the Tanana Hills of Alaska, a saddle-back sheep shows up now and then, and I understand that many of the sheep have black tails.

In the arctic ranges, on the Kenai Peninsula, and in the southwest Yukon, the sheep are pure-white Dalls. There are snow-white Dall sheep in a limited area in extreme northwest British Columbia just south of the Yukon border northwest of Skagway, Alaska, the same as the other sheep found in the St. Elias Range in the Yukon. They are also found in the Northwest Territories.

Wild sheep are restless and wide-ranging animals, and in one form or another they have adapted themselves to everything from the subzero winters of the Arctic to the searing summer heat in the deserts of Arizona and northern Mexico. If feed conditions are poor, or if they are much bothered by human and animal predators, they will leave a mountain range and go great distances to another. In the Yukon, I have seen sheep tracks many miles from a mountain, and in Sonora I have seen sheep far out on sandy flats traveling from one mountain to another. The white goat sticks to high, rough mountains and is found no farther south than the Salmon River country of Idaho, but the restless, adaptable sheep can get by anyplace he has feed and where there are rough cliffs or slides to help him get away from his enemies.

No wonder that a restless Stone ram will wander now and then into white-sheep country and leave little saddle-back lambs the next spring—or that a snow-white Dall ram with golden horns will head south to make love to the darker ewes.

Like all wild sheep, the Dalls vary in size from locality to locality, and they likewise vary as individuals. I have hunted them in several areas of the Yukon, have shot a good many trophy rams, and have seen many hundreds of sheep. In general, my observation is that they average somewhat smaller than the Stones and much smaller than the enormous Rocky Mountain bighorns of southwestern Alberta and southeastern British Columbia, where the North American sheep reach their greatest size.

I have often read that they run small and are the smallest of the North American sheep, a generalization that I take with a grain of salt. The ram I shot on Pilot Mountain in the Yukon in 1950, a ram which was number twelve on the white-sheep list in the 1952 edition of *Records of North American Big Game* and number nineteen in the 1958 edition, measured on a straight line from the top of the shoulder to the bottom of the brisket 22 inches and from his chest to his rump 44 inches. That is a large animal, larger than all but the very largest mule deer. When I got home after that trip I checked the measurements of the big ram with those of an *Ovis poli* from Central Asia as given in the late William J. Mordin's book, *Across Asia's Snows and Deserts.* They were exactly the same. The *poli* is not as large as some of the other members of the argali group, but it is one of the world's largest sheep. Since my 1950 Dall ram was shot in early August, he was in his thin summer coat; what I measured was mostly solid meat.

The largest white ram I have ever measured was an enormously fat old-timer shot by Bill Rae near Prospector Mountain in 1956. He measured 24 and

Prone and ready, O'Connor lined up on the spooked ram when it came running out from behind the ridge.

46 inches and had a back as broad as a pen-fed beef steer. I hesitate to guess at his weight, but it was plenty.

A Yukon Indian who used to hunt sheep for the market before commercial hunting became illegal in the Yukon told me that in the area where he hunted, big rams averaged about 175 pounds field dressed. He hunted in country not far from Whitehorse, where the sheep are large and grow large horns. In many other sections they would run a good deal smaller.

In the *Wolves of Mount McKinley,* a study of the wolf-sheep relationship in the Mount McKinley National Park, Adolph Murie, biologist of the U. S. Fish and Wildlife Service, says that mature Dall rams average about 200 pounds. This would mean a field-dressed weight of 160 to 165 pounds. Some rams would be much heavier since wild sheep, like most human beings, alas, tend to increase in weight with age and, as long as their teeth and health hold out, get heavier. The eleven- and twelve-year-old rams are much chunkier than the more active middle-aged rams of seven or eight. I have occasionally seen thirteen-year-old rams that were fat and had good teeth, but along about that time most of them start going downhill and few seem to survive their thirteenth and fourteenth winters. One fourteen-year-old Dall had a magnificent head, but even in August in the time of lush and plentiful feed, he was very thin and his teeth were so bad I could pull out with my fingers some of those that remained.

Rams likewise vary greatly in size, even in the same locality. Twice I have been badly fooled by small rams. Once near the Alaska border in western Yukon I stalked a ram that was lying alone. He was an old-timer with broomed and blunted horns that came well above the bridge of his nose—a close-curled, massive-looking head of the bighorn type. My excellent guide and I both guessed that it would go around 38 inches on the curl and the base well over 14. When I shot him we discovered he was a dwarf ram. Head and body were in perfect scale, and his annual rings showed him to be thirteen years old. His body was small, his skull small, and his horns measured only 35 inches long and about 12½ around the base. But it is a beautiful head, and I still have it in my trophy room. I have given much larger heads away, but I keep that not only as a memento of a great hunt but to look at whenever I get to thinking I am a red-hot judge of sheep heads.

The other time I got badly fooled by a wonderful-looking head on a small ram was in 1956. Things had got loused up and I had to take a running ram at around 300 yards. I had only seconds to make up my mind, but the head was one of the argali type that comes in close and flares out. I made a mental note, as I dropped my binoculars and picked up my rifle, that it would go around 44 inches. It measured only 40¼. It is still a beautiful and exceptional head, and in the pictures I took that day it looks enormous. But it was, of course, another dwarf ram. It had a small body and a skull 1½ inches shorter than the ram Bill Rae got on the same trip. A sheep head is necessarily judged in comparison with the size of the animal, and a good head on a small animal looks as large as a tremendous head on a big animal.

The glory of the Dall ram and the reason he is such an outstanding trophy is his wonderful horns. Because horns are made of hair material and vary in color with the color of the hair around the head, the horns of the Dall are very light. Sometimes they are stained by dirt and by the sap of plants, but generally they are a light grayish-yellow, lighter than the horns of most Stones, and much lighter than the dark-mahogany brown horns of the Rocky Mountain bighorn.

Generally they are more nearly triangular in cross-section and have an overhanging ridge on the upper outside edge. The annual rings are strongly marked. There are three types of horns among North American sheep—the close curl, the wide spread, and the argali type, in which the horns pinch in close to the face and then flare out. Possibly because the Dalls are closer to the Asiatic argali-type sheep than their more southern relatives, they show, I believe, a higher percentage of the beautiful argali-type heads. I have two Dall heads like this, but

I have never shot a Stone or a bighorn of that type. The Dalls also occasionally produce rams with very wide spreads. In 1950 I watched part of the stalk that resulted in Herb Klein's shooting a superb fourteen-year-old ram with an argali-type head that measured 47½ inches when he brought it into camp that night, but which eventually shrank together, and the other had horns with the widest spread of any ram I have ever seen. I was about a mile away watching it through a 20X spotting scope, and those wonderful horns flared out like those of a Texas longhorn steer.

However, as is the case with any species of North American sheep, most common type of head among the Dalls is the one with a fairly close curl; but the extremely close curl common among bighorn and desert sheep is never seen among the Dalls. On average, the horns of the Dall are somewhat slenderer than those of the Stone and much more slender than those of the bighorn. It is not uncommon to find horns of Dall sheep that go 40 inches or more around the curl but less than 13 inches around the base. The world-record Dall shot in the Chugach Mountains of Alaska in 1956 is 49½ inches around the curve of the longest horn, but only 14 inches around the base. Nevertheless, some massive heads turn up. My own best Dall ram has a base of 14⅞ inches, a husky base even for a bighorn.

Because many Dall horns begin the upward curve well above the point of the jaw, it is easy for the man used to bighorns but hunting Dalls for the first time to misjudge the heads. Often I have seen Dall horns that went up well past the nose and made more than a complete curl but did not go over 36 inches. One of the first things for the trophy hunter to check is whether the horns come down below the point of the jaw. If they do and, in addition, look massive and make more than a complete curl, the head is probably a very good one.

Because Dall horns generally do not make the close curl which blocks side vision, white sheep do not rub and broom the points of their horns to the same extent bighorns do. It is common to find horns of very old Dalls with perfect points—something almost never seen with old bighorn rams.

In the past fifteen years or so, the best Dall heads have been coming out of the southwestern Yukon from the relatively low mountains in the general neighborhood of Aishihik and Kusawa lakes and from the Chugach Mountains of Alaska. The world record is from the Chugach and the No. 2 from the Yukon. Big-head areas are generally mountains with a lot of limestone in their composition, and they are also areas that are not hunted hard since it takes from eleven to thirteen years to produce a really outstanding head. Any area where the rams are shot off when they are from seven to nine years old won't produce records, and neither will any area where the forage is deficient in lime and other vital minerals.

I have never hunted sheep in Alaska and so I would not hazard a guess as to how serious the hunting pressure is there. But I know that in the arctic ranges Eskimos kill many sheep, and I also know that the Alaska Dall sheep are heavily hunted in areas not far from large centers of population where sportsmen can fly in, land on a lake, and then hunt. One chap told me he flew to a mountain lake in Alaska two days before the season opened and by the time it was legal to start sheep hunting nine other planes had landed on the same lake.

I do not believe the hunting pressure amounts to much in the thinly populated Yukon. Fur prices are low and I doubt if there are as many trappers in the bush as there were twenty years ago. Many of the Indians who used to live on game have moved into Whitehorse where they can get steady employment or close to the Alaska Highway where they can pick up a job now and then.

Many Yukon ranges are almost never hunted. Pilot Mountain is only half a day's pack from an automobile road, but when I went in there in 1950 I do not believe a trophy hunter had tried it in many years. The only trails we found were made by Indian trappers with pack dogs, despite the fact that from the ridge above the spot where I shot my ram I could, with binoculars, see the Whitehorse airport.

Incidentally, that ram—the largest Dall I have ever taken—came as a result of one of the easiest sheep hunts I have ever been on. My guide, Moose Johnson, and I found four rams well over a mile away in less than an hour out of camp the first morning we hunted. We set up a spotting scope. Three of the rams were ordinary. The head of the big one was partly concealed by the lie of the ground, but from what we could see it looked massive enough to bear investigation.

The stalk was easy. We dropped out of sight, led our horses up a steep hillside, then got aboard. Keeping a ridge between us and the sheep, we made a wide circle. Then we tied our steeds to some willow brush, made a short and easy final stalk, and found the rams directly below us and not over 50 yards away. I sat up on the ridge drooling over the ram for about five minutes, until one of the four happened to look around and see me. Then they all ran, and I cut the big fellow down.

Some lambs are taken by eagles, mostly when

they are quite small. Sheep are also killed occasionally by wolverines, and, in years of rabbit shortage, by starving and desperate lynxes. Coyotes that have invaded some sheep areas from the south also kill sheep, but rabbits are their principal prey. The most serious predator of sheep is the great northern wolf. A few years ago wolves were on the increase in the Arctic and subarctic, and Dall sheep numbers were down everywhere, but there has been some wolf control in the Yukon and a great deal of it in Alaska. The wolves, from what I hear, are now on the bottom of a cycle, and in most areas sheep have been increasing in the past few years.

In years of few wolves, sheep move into low and rounded mountains where food is good and life is easy but where escaping the gaunt, gray predators would be difficult. Then when the wolves increase or move back into that country, the sheep are killed off or driven to the cliffs and slides where no wolf has much chance to catch them. A wolf will never turn down an opportunity for juicy mountain mutton, but his natural prey in the far north is primarily the caribou and secondarily the moose. Generally, the wolves follow the migrations of the caribou, and if there are no caribou in a country there are few if any wolves.

In the area around Pilot Mountain and the Sifton Range, I saw not a single wolf track and heard not a wolf howl. The Indians told me that a score of years before, the country had been full of caribou—and also wolves. Then the caribou moved out and for a time the wolves lived on the sheep and drove them out of all the low, rounded hills. Then the wolves moved out or died off, and the sheep increased and started moving back into the low hills.

Books and stories about hunting Dall sheep in Alaska and the Yukon written about the time of World War I tell of more white sheep being seen than one sees these days. Apparently the sheep were then at the top of a cycle. One book I read about a hunt around the head of the White River in the Yukon told of several hundred sheep being sighted at one time. I hunted the same area twenty years later and saw nothing like that many sheep. Why? Wolves got the blame.

Another factor limiting sheep populations is heavy snowfall, particularly if the snow is wet. Then the sheep cannot travel in search of food, and in their weakened condition are easily killed by wolves and other predators. A bad winter is particularly hard on both young and old sheep. An early and heavy snow is particularly rough on old trophy rams that are getting weak and stiff, and they go into the winter thin from the rutting season.

It has been the history of sheep herds studied in the United States that if animals become too plentiful, disease breaks out and thins them down. Little study has been made on the prevalence of disease among northern sheep. Lung worm has been found among white sheep, and in bad winters it no doubt weakens them so they die or are taken by predators. Sheep also suffer from what natives call "lumpy jaw" and what scientists call necrotic stomatitis, a fungus disease that attacks the bones of the jaws so that the teeth fall out. To my layman's eye, the condition looks much like a bad case of pyorrhea in a human being. Happily, white sheep seem free from scabies, a disease that bighorns catch from domestic sheep when they use the same range and that has decimated them in many areas.

In the days when the sheep were hunted for the market in the far north, great numbers were killed. Murie tells of finding a pile of horns from over seventy rams shot by a couple of market hunters before establishment of McKinley National Park. In the gold-rush days, sheep were almost exterminated in areas close to mining camps. Trappers and Indians not only killed many sheep for food but also to feed their dogs.

One trapper I knew in the Yukon told me that he and a partner killed about one hundred sheep in a year, mostly for dog food. A sheep is just about a one-day ration for a team of sled dogs. Another trapper told me that he once caught a bunch of ewes, lambs, and young rams crossing in deep snow from one mountain to another and killed every one of them, a lucky break, he said, which saved him no end of time and trouble.

The flesh of a fat ram taken before the rut is the most delicious meat in the mountains. In Whitehorse, when market hunting was legal, it used to sell for fifty cents a pound, whereas caribou and moose meat brought about half as much. Generally, though, the Indian or the trapper would prefer to kill a moose or caribou.

Trophy hunting has no effect on sheep numbers since sportsmen shoot rams, and generally old ones that would die in a few months. Sheep are highly polygamous, and in regions of large sheep populations the removal of old rams should actually be beneficial to the herds.

Like most sheep, Dalls go into the rut about mid-November, but the season is at its height in early December. Single births are the rule, but occasionally twins are born.

I cannot but believe that with anything like wise management, Dall sheep will continue to furnish good hunting and beautiful trophies for the foreseeable future. The country they inhabit has too short a growing season and is too cold for grazing of domestic stock, and the land is not suited for agriculture. Future economic exploitations most likely will take the form of water-power development and more mining. Populations will undoubtedly increase. Even so, it is difficult to see how the sheep can be affected in most areas. Wise wolf control will have to be practiced, and, in hunting, the use of such modern gadgets as helicopters will have to be forbidden. A machine that can land on top of a mountain doesn't give the sheep a chance—and the climb is one of the best things about sheep hunting.

The head of a fully mature Dall ram that goes 38 inches if unbroomed, 35 if heavily broomed, is one of the finest hunting trophies in the world, one that stands near the top of the list of North American trophies in the world, and ranks far above any but the very rarest of African antelope. European sportsmen, incidentally, nearly always regard the Dall as the number one trophy on this continent—even above the Alaska brown bear. In the Yukon, the grizzly and the white sheep are considered the two top trophies, but I'd rather line my sights up on a Dall with a head over 40 inches than on any grizzly that ever walked.

Going after a trophy Dall takes the hunter into some of the most beautiful country on the globe—a land of snowy peaks, and frigid crystal brooks, of lush mountain meadows, of caribou barrens red from frost, and gray slide rock—a big and unspoiled land where the northern lights sweep across the sky and where chill winds blow on the ridges.

One sheep hunt I'll never forget was near the source of the St. Claire River in the Yukon. My old friend and guide Field Johnson and I had left the main camp not far from where Harris Creek runs into the Generc, and for a week we had been wandering through beautiful sheep country. We had two saddle horses and a packhorse loaded with a little tent, our bedrolls, and some grub.

One morning we made a long climb almost to the top of the lofty ridges on one side of the river. We hunted a dozen basins and saw many rams, but nothing special. Then about 2 p.m. we discovered a bunch of rams on the shoulder of a great mountain across the river and probably three miles away as the crow flies. We had no spotting scope, and we knew they were rams only because they looked large and there were no small sheep with them.

It was a bad day. Very cold. Dirty clouds swept low over the peaks, and occasionally a snowflake spiraled down. But we decided to look this new bunch over. Tough from a month of walking and climbing, we ran down the mountain and stripped naked to the waist to wade the freezing St. Claire.

On the other side we thawed out our frozen feet, dressed, and began the climb, going as fast as our laboring lungs would permit, fighting against snow and approaching darkness. By the time we got to the level where the sheep were, it was snowing so hard

Perched on a ridge 50 yards above the rams, O'Connor took an easy shot at the biggest of them.

that we often could not see 50 yards. The storm had moved the sheep, but we finally found them bedded down in the lee of a dark cliff.

We had made our final approach behind a knife-sharp ridge, and I squirmed into a comfortable position for glassing and shooting. The Yukon game laws allowed two rams to the license then, so Field and I tried to pick out the two best. One was off by himself at the right of the bunch, an old-timer with heavy, broomed horns that made more than a complete curl and went up well past his nose. The other we decided on had perfect points and plenty of curl.

I took off my down jacket, placed it in a notch, settled down behind my rifle, and laid out five extra cartridges on a rock shelf in case I'd have to do a lot of shooting. Just as I was about ready to cut loose, the snow thickened and blotted out the rams. Then when I could see them again I found that the objective lens of the scope was plastered with snow and I had to wipe it off.

I guessed that the rams were about 300 yards away, so I held just under the backbone of the ram to the right. Field, who was watching with the glasses, called my first shot—just under. The ram jumped to his feet and stood there. I held my next shot just over his back. The ram stood still for a moment and then slowly keeled over.

Now the whole bunch was running for a ridge behind. I held up between the horns of the second ram and shot. Field called a broken leg. I shot again and the ram limped over the ridge and out of sight.

We scrambled down through a draw and ran across the rock under the cliff where the sheep had been lying. Half a dozen rams were humping up an almost vertical cliff on the other side, but the big fellow was down at the bottom of the canyon.

By this time it was very late in the afternoon and a heavy snow was falling. Quickly we took off the rams' heads, loaded ourselves down with meat, and set out for camp. By the time we got to the river we were plowing through snow a foot deep, and we were so wet and cold that we didn't even bother to take off our boots. Instead we simply plunged into the waist-high, frigid water and fought our way across. It was so dark that if we hadn't been guided by the neighing of our picketed horses, we could have had a hard time finding camp.

Once there we changed into dry clothes that we had rolled in our beds, and while Field hobbled the horses and turned them loose to graze, I built a fire, fried some bacon, heated some beans, and pan-broiled slices of backstraps from one of the rams. As I finished up the meat Field made some bannock.

Neither of us had eaten since breakfast. We had made two climbs of over 2,000 feet. We had been empty and cold. But hot rum revived us, and with the fire and the dry clothes we were deliciously warm.

We wound up with a little rum and a lot of sugar in cups of hot tea. It was snowing heavily, but we didn't mind a little thing like that. We sat on the pack panniers before the cheering fire. We could hear the mellow tinkle of the bells as our horses fed on willows. Our bellies were full of the finest meat in the world, and under a nearby willow bush lay two fine ram heads.

# THE STONE SHEEP

I GOT my introduction to the Stone sheep one afternoon in late August in a deep canyon in northern British Columbia. Two and a half days before, the pack outfit had left the Alaska Highway, and we had been stumbling through forest and muskeg toward the foothills of the Rockies and the country where the mysterious Stone sheep were to be found. Shortly after noon we led the packhorses down into the canyon of Neavis Creek and planned to follow it down until we camped that night on the banks of the Besa River.

Up there in the subarctic forest, the sun had been hot, but the depths of the canyon were cool and shady, filled with the voice of running water and the chill mist of waterfalls that came cascading down from the heights in little side canyons. We hadn't gone far when we began to see sheep tracks in the sand.

Then, as I came around a bend ahead of the packstring, I saw my first Stone rams. All were big old fellows with massive heads, but to my surprise no two were alike. As I sat down on the sand to look them over carefully with my binoculars, I saw one with a head and neck so light he looked like a Dall ram that had been lightly sprinkled with coal dust. He was altogether the lightest ram in the bunch, and his coat was a medium gray. The darkest of the rams looked, at 300 yards, to be coal black except for his white rump patch and underparts and the gray bridge of his nose. His horns looked bright yellow against his black neck.

Coloring of the other rams ranged somewhere in between. Some had very dark saddles, but heads and necks that were very light. The most common pattern in the area, and the type most common in that little herd, was a neck and face of medium gray and a very black body. I was later to find that the ewes averaged much lighter than the rams, and that even in that area—which is fairly far south—some of the ewes were so light they could have been mistaken for Dall sheep, at a distance. The bighorns are always brown and the Dalls white, but the Stones vary enormously.

To the south, the Stone sheep are cut off from the brown bighorns by the Peach and the Skeena rivers and a belt of heavily wooded country of deep snows where, in historic times anyway, there have never been any sheep. Theoretically, there has never been any contact between the Stone sheep and the brown bighorn. But, to the north, the Stone gradually fades into the snow-white Dall until no one can precisely say where one subspecies begins and the other ends. Indeed, the Stone is closely related to his white cousin, and his scientific name is *Ovis dalli stonei*—or the Stone subspecies of the Dall species.

The wonderful Stone sheep is the most isolated and least hunted of all North American sheep, and he was also the last one known to science. Many hundreds of years ago the Spanish saw and described the desert variety of the brown bighorn in Lower California, and the explorer Coronado saw them in Sonora and Arizona. The Canadian bighorn was first collected in Alberta more than 150 years ago. The white Dall sheep became known to science in 1884, but it wasn't until 1897 that the mysterious Stone was first recognized and named for Andrew Stone, the Missoula, Montana, man who shot three on the Stikine River in British Columbia and donated them to the American Museum of Natural History in New York.

The home of the Stone is in the wildest section of this continent—the northern part of British Columbia north of the Peach and Skeena rivers, east of the tremendous glaciers of the Coast Range, and east to the foothills on the east side of the Rockies.

For many years a hunt for Stone sheep was a major expedition. The first sportsmen to go after them went into their country by taking a steamer to Wrangel, Alaska, then going up the Stikine River by gas boat to Telegraph Creek in interior British Columbia and outfitting from there. A little later, Stones were hunted out of Atlin in the extreme northwest corner of British Columbia. Parties would go by steamer from Vancouver, B. C., to Skagway, Alaska, take a train to Carcross, Yukon, then a lake boat to Atlin.

O'Connor and guide Frank Golata had to sweat out half-hour scrutiny by two curious rams.

In the late nineteen twenties, a number of parties began to penetrate the Stone sheep country on the east side of the Rockies by taking the railroad from Edmonton, Alberta, to Dawson Creek, B. C., and then packing out of there or Ft. St. John to the land of great sheep heads in the mountains toward the sources of the Muskwa and the Prophet rivers. At that time a six-day trip was about a minimum for a good Stone-sheep hunt out of Ft. St. John. During World War II, the building of the Alaska Highway opened up a great deal of black-sheep country that had previously been almost impossible to get to. Some of the winter sheep range is very close to the highway—so close that a hunter I know spent his nights in a cabin right on the highway and hunted Stones back in the hills during the November days of 1953.

But most of the wilderness of northern British Columbia is still almost as wild as it was when Columbus landed. There are fewer human beings in the area than there were fifty years ago. The hunting Indians that used to live off game are moving out to the highway where they can pick up odd jobs and buy luxuries more easily. Only a few families now live in Telegraph Creek. Atlin, which was at one time a roaring boom town of thousands of people, is almost a ghost town. Its big hotel is a bat roost, and its once-palatial lake steamers are rotting at the docks. With the price of fur down, there are not many trappers in the area, and most of those who prospected for gold are also gone.

In addition to the beautiful Stone sheep, some of the largest moose in North America stalk through this country. There are grizzlies and white goats, and the great Osborn caribou with towering, palmated antlers. I have never seen such wonderful caribou heads as those that are worn by the great bulls of the magic Cassiar.

Some Stone sheep are found in very rough country, but as one goes north the Rocky Mountains that are so rugged and so cliffy near the United States border break up and round off. Black sheep are found in many areas where they can be hunted almost entirely from horseback. A bit of Stone-sheep country that is little visited, but is yet famous among those who'd rather hunt sheep than do anything else, is Table Mountain in northern British Columbia. It is a big plateau, or mesa, as it would be called in the Southwest, with a gently rolling top and steep sides. The sheep feed up on top and seek refuge from the wolves in the cliffs. When they are not bothered, they'll bed down right up on top in such easy country that a horse can be galloped over much of it.

But the greatest of all the Stone-sheep countries is not precisely easy to hunt. This is the area around the upper Muskwa and Prophet rivers, the areas of the Besa River, Richards Creek, Keily Creek, and Redfern Lake. It was there, on a hillside overlooking Lapp Creek, a tributary that flows into the Prophet River 10 or 12 miles from its source, that L. S. Chadwick in 1936 shot the number one Stone sheep in the world records. It was a ram with the longest horns ever taken on a North American sheep —50⅛ inches for the right horn, 51⅝ inches for the left. This wonderful head is now in the National Collection of Heads and Horns in New York. I have seen the place where the great ram was camped, and sat on the stump on which the great head was photographed when it was brought triumphantly in from the hills.

This is the area of big heads and big rams, a land of enormous, shouldering mountains of solid limestone. The grass and browse is rich in lime and other minerals. The old rams are tremendous, and the moose have heads that have to be seen to be believed. Of the first fifteen Stone sheep heads in the 1958 edition of *Records of North American Big Game,* all except one came from this general area. The Stone sheep of the Cassiar district across the mountains to the west often have very long horns, but they are not as massive as those of the Prophet-Muskwa sheep, and the animals are not as big.

As a rule, the northern sheep average smaller than do the bighorns, but in favorable country some of them grow very large. I believe the largest-boned and heaviest sheep I have ever shot was a great Stone I took from the Prophet. I would estimate that he was slightly larger than the largest bighorn ram I have ever seen dead, and he was a good deal heavier than the largest buck mule deer I have ever shot. If he didn't weigh well over 300 pounds field dressed, then I'm a poor guesser indeed.

The dark Stones and the snow-white Dall sheep, the darkest and the lightest of American sheep, merge almost imperceptibly in color. In the southern part of the Stone range, most of them are quite dark. As they go north they become, on the average, lighter, but anywhere east of the Yukon River and south of the big lakes like Teslin, Atlin, Bennett, Tagish, and Gladys—which form a barrier for sheep migration between northeast British Columbia and southwest Yukon—the hunter is apt to run into some very dark sheep.

In 1951, in the mountains off Eva Lake just south of the Yukon border, my son Bradford and I hunted sheep and got one ram that could be called a fairly typical Stone with light-gray head and neck and very dark, black-brown body. We also got one with a very light-gray saddle and a head and neck that are white except for a scattering of dark hairs around the eyes and on the bridge of the nose. North of the lakes and west of the Yukon River, the typical sheep becomes the snow-white Dall, although in some areas a few may have black tails, and a careful search will generally show black hairs along the spine, around the eyes, and on the bridge of the nose.

At one time these intermediate sheep were thought to be a different subspecies and were called Fannins. The term has persisted, and in Stone-sheep country the light ones are generally referred to as Fannins. Stone ewes always average lighter than the rams, and—in the areas where I have hunted sheep of the Fannin type—many of the ewes appear snow-white at a distance.

Since Stones are sheep of the wilderness, and are hunted only in the more easily accessible portions of their range, they are subject to cycles of abundance and scarcity. In some ranges they have been shot down badly by hunting Indians, trappers, and prospectors. When Atlin was a boom town of thousands, market hunters killed off the more accessible sheep, and prospectors lived on game. But now the mining district is pretty well played out and the sheep have come back. They are still subject, however, to heavy predation when wolves are plentiful, to diseases, and to hazards of deep, crusted snow.

It is often said that northern sheep have much more slender horns than the bighorns, and in the main that is true. The heaviest base I can find listed for a Rocky Mountain bighorn is 17⅛, and the heaviest base for a desert sheep 17. One hears of sheep horns with 18- and even 19-inch bases, but they do not turn up in the record book. However, all large sheep heads shrink somewhat as they dry out, often as much as an inch, both in length and circumference. These 17-inchers may well have measured 18 inches when killed.

The largest recorded base of a Stone sheep is 15 6/8 inches; it may have gone nearly 17 inches around the base when it was taken.

The closer you get to the bighorn country, the more the heads of the Stones appear to approach bighorn type. I have one fine old Stone with the big, massive, round-based horns that, except for being lighter in color, are dead ringers for the horns of a typical *Ovis canadensis.* On the other hand, the farther north you go, the more nearly triangular in cross section the sheep horns are. The Stones and

Dalls have close relatives in eastern Siberia—the Kamchatka bighorn of the Kamchatka Peninsula and the Clifton bighorn, which dwells in the mountains between the Lena and Yana rivers in eastern Siberia. Both are gray sheep with large areas of white. Their horns are so much like those of the Stone and Dall sheep that no one but a scientist could tell one from the other. It isn't difficult to see that these North American and east Siberian sheep are pretty much the same breed and share common ancestry. They are far more like each other than they are like any of the other kinds of Asiatic sheep.

Because of the wide varieties in color of the Stones found there, one of the most interesting places on this continent to hunt is the belt of country beginning at Atlin, British Columbia, and running north and east through mountains great and small—the Pellys, the Glenlyons, the Rose mountains, the Ogilvie Rockies. This is the strip where the Stone and the Dall come together, and where no man can tell just what sort of a ram he's going to get. It's the country where the mythical Fannin was generally supposed to live.

Almost fifty years ago Charles Sheldon, a wealthy man and a dedicated sheep hunter, spent his own money and his own time studying the sheep in that area, and he wrote a book called *The Wilderness of the Upper Yukon*. He proved that the Fannin sheep was not a separate species, but simply an intergrade between Stone and Dall. His charts showing the markings of the sheep in the various ranges, and his comments on sheep horns and sheep habits, are so accurate that they have never been improved upon.

Over this tremendous area a few trappers and Indians wander. The Alaska Highway cuts through a little piece of it, and the Canol Road, which leaves the Alaska Highway at Johnson's Crossing in the Yukon and runs to Norman Wells in the Northwest Territories, was pushed right through the middle of the Pellys. But the road has been abandoned and is going back to wilderness. Just how much of it is passable today I do not know.

The most fantastically lucky day I have ever had in hunting Stone sheep was much farther south than this transitional country and right off the Prophet River not far from where it is crossed by the old Klondike Trail made by gold-seekers trying to get to Dawson from Edmonton, Alberta. When the trail crosses the Prophet, it goes over a high ridge between that river and the Muskwa—a ridge that forms a migration route for the Stone rams that have summered in the cool country around the glaciers in the very crest of the Rockies.

The animals' fat white rumps were bouncing out of sight as O'Connor scrambled up to the top of the ridge.

As summer dies and the frosts come, the aspens on the hillsides turn into masses of shimmering gold and the dwarf arctic birch to scarlet, and as fluffy new snow dusts the peaks, the rams begin to move down toward the winter range, toward the lower and easier country where most of the ewes and lambs have spent the summer. Almost always, when sheep are plentiful, the rams of similar age, like human beings, flock together—young with young, middle-aged with middle-aged, old with old.

There on the Prophet, the mountains are built on so tremendous a scale as to confuse even an experienced mountain man. I grew up in mountains, and I have climbed around in them all my life. Yet when I was in that Prophet country I could never grasp emotionally the tremendous heights and distances. One day in 1946 Frank Golata and I stood above timberline on a point jutting out above camp. The air was so clear and so still that we could hear the cook and the horse wrangler talking, hear the crack of the ax against wood. With 9X binoculars I could see the dishtowels fluttering in the breeze by the cook tent. I would have sworn that I could be in camp in minutes, yet I knew we were about 3,500 feet above our tents and somewhere between 2½ and 3 miles away.

Above our camp was a big, black, limestone mountain streaked with snow, cut by gorges, and sprinkled with rock-slides. Because the Indians who dwelt there once thought their gods lived on it, some unimaginative surveyor has given it the hackneyed name of Mount Olympus, or the Mount of the Gods. The local guides and trappers simply call that whole high area the Prophet Bench.

When Frank Golata and I first climbed up on the bench, autumn was not far advanced. The first frosts had turned willow and aspen yellow and had painted the dwarf birch scarlet. All over the valley of the Muskwa the fall colors flamed. That day on the heights brought us the sight of many rams, but almost all of them were young or middle-aged. Many of the heads were long, but they were clean, and slender, and unbroomed. We didn't fire a shot.

We packed up the next day and went clear to the head of the Prophet and saw where it has its origin in a dying glacier that has strewn the whole upper valley with the rubble of its dead moraine. We hunted the mountains around the tributary Lapp Creek where the world-record Stone came from. Then we took the whole pack outfit over lofty Muskwa Pass and saw sheep, but nothing outstanding.

Almost three weeks later, when most of the golden leaves were off the aspens, the yellow off the willow, and the red from the dwarf birch, and the country had the gray, pinched look of approaching winter, we were back on the Prophet Bench once more, and this was it—this was the jackpot. There were rams all over the mountain, so many rams that it was difficult to stalk any one of them without frightening others. When you climb up on the bench, you first go through a forest of spruce and fir, then through a great aspen grove where the trunks shine clean and white, and golden leaves spin softly down. The next zone is shoulder-high willow. Finally there is a steep shoulder covered with rich, ankle-high grass. Frank and I had left camp so early we could barely see, and frost shone white on the grass. But by the time we pulled up the last slope and onto the rolling, grass-covered plateau it was midmorning.

We sat down to glass the undulating points and ridges, and almost at once we saw rams—one here, three there, five lying down together. Rams, rams, very dark rams with black necks and horns that looked bright yellow against them, rams with heads and necks so light they looked white at a distance, rams with heads of medium gray. As we lay there we could see rams with massive, close-curled horns that were as heavily broomed as those of an old bighorn, rams with wide flaring horns, one ram with horns that pinched in close and then flared out like those of an *Ovis poli*.

I was like a kid in a candy store, a kid with greed in his heart but only one nickel. First of all I wanted a ram with a head that would go 40 inches or more. I wanted a very black Stone, a medium Stone, and a light Stone. I had one permit.

Frank and I set up a 20X spotting scope on its little stand and watched the rams. By this time the bright fall sun in the clear sky was hot where we lay sheltered from the wind. Our wool underwear made us itch. The sun brought mirage dancing up off of the grass and moss and lichens that carpeted the sheep pastures, and the rams that showed tiny and unreal in our spotting scope were fuzzy with distance, grainy with mirage. Finally, though, we decided that the two best sheep we could see on the mountain were a couple of light-necked rams bedded on a ridge about a mile away.

We started to stalk. Every time we came around a point we would see more rams. Since we didn't want to frighten them and have them spook the others, we'd drop low to pass them. Finally we wound up with much of our precious altitude lost and were clear down into the belt of willows.

We cut back into the mountain along the side of a big black canyon filled with sheep beds and trails. Once we had to sit for half an hour while a couple of rams we had blundered into looked us over, decided we were nothing very formidable, and then moved off.

When at last we were in a position to strike over toward the two big, light-necked rams, I picked up another bunch of big rams with the binoculars. They were about a mile away lying down in a pass right at the head of a side canyon. A couple of them looked pretty good. I set up the spotting scope, took one look at them, and flipped! There in the clear field of that wonderful optical instrument was the largest sheep head that I had ever seen at that time and possibly the largest I have seen to this day. Frank and I both looked it over carefully. Even the conservative Frank admitted it was a dilly—and when he does that you can shoot the works.

So we turned our backs on the two rams we'd been after. Instead of going over the ridge, a maneuver that would have brought us into shooting position on the big fellows we had first begun to stalk, we kept on up the canyon, then cut up the side over a great rock-slide filled with boulders from the size of baseballs to the size of very large houses.

By this time we had been without water since early morning. Here I was in the subarctic and dying of thirst. I had on long wool underwear, two wool shirts, and a pair of wool pants. We were out of the wind and right on the slide where the sun was reflected blindingly from the light-gray limestone. I could hear the tantalizing tinkle of water far below in the rocks, and I was miserably thirsty. We had planned to cut over the slide, hit a side canyon, and toil up to the head of it. Then I would ease myself up to the ridge overlooking the saddle where I had seen the great Stone ram, and cut loose.

But the gods had other plans for me that day and

Getting back to camp after dark, O'Connor and Golata had to measure the horns by lantern light.

other plans for that great ram. Instead of achieving immortality of a sort by getting his head mounted, winning me a Boone and Crockett Club award, and then adorning my trophy room, that old ram was fated to wear his head some time longer—until he was pulled down by wolves, poached by a meat-hungry Indian, or until, weakened by the cold and the deep snow, ill-fed and thin because of the bad and loose teeth that old rams get, he simply bedded down some winter night in the boreal cold and went gently to the land where pastures are always lush and even wolves are friendly.

Our companions, Colin McGuire and Dr. Wilson DuComb, were on the bench that day. The original plan had been for them to hunt the other side, but they had made the top a good deal later than we had. The rams they glassed were nothing special, so they had cut right over the top of the bench toward where we were. Suddenly Mac happened to look down as they came to a drop, and below them were bedded around forty big rams. Recognition was mutual and instantaneous. Doc had to pick out a couple of good heads and shoot fast. He did.

Over in the next canyon I heard the shooting with a sinking heart. If the big fellow was spooked it would practically kill me. As fast as I could make it I scrambled to the top of the ridge to see if the bunch was still in the saddle. I made it just in time to see their big, fat, white rumps bobbing away and out of sight.

Right then I was the sickest person in northern British Columbia. I would have wept if I hadn't been so old that I had forgotten how.

"Don't feel too bad," Frank comforted me. "Maybe something good will come around this way."

He had hardly spoken when we saw a ram come over the skyline from the direction of the shooting. He was perhaps 500 or 600 yards away. He was trotting, but when he got on our side of the ridge, he slowed to a walk. Then another ram showed up—and another. Presently there were seven or eight rams in sight, slowly picking their way along the opposite side of the canyon.

All of the rams were dandies, and among them they ran the whole gamut of the Stone's colors, from very dark to fairly light. Two intrigued me. One was a typical Stone with a medium-gray head and neck, massive horns that were well broomed at the ends but that yet came up over the bridge of his nose for a complete curl. The other was a strapping ram with horns that looked heavy and made more than a complete curl. Since he had a very light-gray head and neck, Frank and I decided that he was one of the two we had started to stalk that morning.

I kept looking at the two, fairly sure that I would take one or the other, but as yet undecided. Then another ram, which I had thought of as being not much smaller than the big Fannin-type ram, walked up beside him. Instantly I could see that the big fellow was a tremendous sheep, a ram with a heavy, big-boned body at least one-fourth larger than that of his companion. He was a beauty.

Since I had plenty of time, I slipped my upper arm into the loop of my sling and drew the keeper up tight against it. My left hand was hard against the swivel. I could see the big ram sharp and bright in the 4X scope on the .270. I followed the ram along with the crosswires on his brisket to give a little lead. When I shot, he stopped, and Frank told me that his front leg on the far side was swinging. He did not go down until I had fired four shots. When we got over there we found that all had struck low but in a group about the size of my palm. They had gone in behind the right front leg and had so nearly shot the left front leg off that it was hanging by a single thread of skin. Only one shot had touched the lungs. The rifle had shot low either because my tight sling had warped the barrel down, or the ram was farther away than I had thought.

With the ram down, I began to have misgivings. Had I taken the best ram? Should I have waited and than come back the next day on the off chance that I'd see again the big one that got away? As I crossed the canyon to the spot where the big ram lay, I was as apprehensive as a horse player who has just laid the grocery money on some nag's nose.

But I needn't have worried. As soon as I got up to the ram I knew I was correct in assuming that he was a tremendous sheep with a great head. I had forgotten my steel tape, so we couldn't measure those wonderful horns until we got back to camp. I could scarcely keep my eyes off them.

It was 3:30 when we got the head skinned out and the meat cut up. Frank took the two hind quarters, which were a grueling load. I carried the great head, the backstraps, the front feet, my rifle, camera, and binoculars. I had been in the mountains almost a month then. I was hard. We walked fast and rested but once, then only for five minutes. It was after seven o'clock when we hit camp, and it was so dark I couldn't see my own feet as I walked.

We measured the head by lantern light on the table of the cook tent. Bases were about 16 inches and the longest horn was 42½. But all sheep heads shrink. When the head finally got down to Denver, Coloman Jonas, the taxidermist, measured it and found the longest horn to be 42 inches. Some months later when it was officially measured by the Colorado Museum of Natural History, it came out 41½ and the bases were 14⅞. My second-choice ram was a pretty fair sheep—number ten in the 1952 and 1958 editions of *Records of North American Big Game*. I didn't know that at the time, and likewise I didn't know that shooting the ram had made me one of the few people then who had ever shot all North American wild sheep—bighorn, desert, Stone, and Dall. At that time those who had done so could be counted on the fingers of one hand.

The big one that got away? I hate to think about him even today. I'll always feel I was within a couple of hundred yards of a ram that would have been an easy number two in the records. But there are other big Stone rams on other big mountains, and there will be, I hope, forever. That wild and wonderful wilderness should be furnishing great Stone-sheep hunting for our children and our children's children.

# The Natural History of the Dall Sheep

[OVIS DALLI]

## DESCRIPTION

The difference in color between the typical snow-white sheep of Alaska and the blue-black Stone sheep of British Columbia is so gradual that it is difficult to draw a line where one subspecies stops and the other starts, yet the extremes are so distinct that they could not be confused. In the mountains of Alaska, the Dall sheep is all white except for its hoofs and horns, which are yellowish-brown. In the northern Yukon, the white sheep have a few dark hairs on the tail, and farther south the tails are all black. Still farther south the sides of the animal gradually become dark gray. Southward in British Columbia the color gradates from blue-gray to almost black.

As a typical member of the order *Artiodactyla,* or even-toed, hoofed mammals, the Dall sheep's third and fourth toes are well and evenly developed, with the tips encased in a horny sheath which is the hoof. The second and fifth toes are small, indicated externally by small, lateral hoofs which serve as brakes when the animal travels on steep mountain slopes. Like all sheep, it is digitigrade and travels on the extreme tips of its toes. Its hoofs are equipped with soft, rubber-like, shock-absorbing pads that grip and hold fast on slippery rocks.

The Dall sheep's coarse, brittle hair is about 2½ inches long, cellular or pithy in texture, and sealed with a smooth outer covering. The air locked in the cells of the hair acts as an insulated blanket to conserve body heat and keep out the bitter cold of the arctic winters. An herbivorous, ruminant animal, the Dall has a compound stomach, as is the case with all cud-chewers, and has no teeth in the front of its upper jaw.

When walking, the Dall sheep places its hind foot close behind the track left by the forefoot. The tracks resemble those of the bighorn but are smaller on the average.

## HORNS

The Dall sheep has relatively long, slender horns, somewhat triangular in cross-section, broad at the base and tapering to flaring tips. The formation of the horns is a loose corkscrew-like spiral. They consist of a hollow, horny sheath growing over a solid bony core, which continues to grow throughout the animal's life, and is never shed. Only the rams have large horns; those of the ewes are short, slender, and flattened, never exceeding 15 inches in length. The record length for a ram horn is 49½ inches along the curve, with a circumference at the base of 14 inches, and a spread from tip to tip of 24½ inches. Any ram with a horn length of 40 inches or over is considered exceptional.

## ORIGIN

While the Dall sheep is of Euro-Asiatic origin, it must have reached America at a different time and with a different group of immigrants than the bighorn. Furthermore, it does not have any close relatives living in Asia today, as does the bighorn. None of the mountain sheep ever found their way to the mountains of eastern North America, nor did they migrate south to Central and South America.

## RANGE

The Dall sheep and its allies inhabit the mountainous regions through most of the peninsula of Alaska and east to the Mackenzie River, and south in British Columbia to about latitude 55 degrees. They occupy the upland meadows among the slide rock well above timberline, but are not necessarily found among peaks and crags of the highest ranges, the home of the Rocky

Mountain goat. The Dall's home range is governed largely by local conditions. Undisturbed, a flock of white sheep may stay within a radius of one mile for several weeks when food is plentiful. It feeds during the early morning and evening and again for a short period shortly after noon. Dall sheep normally retire for the night soon after sunset. However, they can, if necessary, make a fast getaway under cover of darkness. The sheep have regular resting quarters, usually situated on small elevated hills with a view commanding all directions. Each sheep scrapes out a small depression in the ground with its forefeet before settling down to rest. The feeding ground may be half a mile away.

There are three subspecies of Dall sheep (*Ovis dalli*): The Dall, or White, sheep is found over most of the mountainous country in the peninsula of Alaska and the Yukon east to the Mackenzie River. It is a comparatively small, all-white sheep.

The Kenai White sheep is an all-white sheep similar to the Dall, but smaller and restricted to the mountains of the Kenai Peninsula, Alaska.

The Stone sheep, Blue sheep, or Black sheep is a handsome and distinct subspecies. It is larger and more sturdy than the White sheep but the horns are similar, triangular in cross-section, slender, and curve strongly outward. Its color varies according to locality and ranges from almost black to a soft blue-gray and almost white. The horn sheath is dark brown instead of amber, as in the typical white Alaska sheep. Its range is from southern Yukon south to northern British Columbia.

Other species now considered synonyms (not recognized by science as a separate subspecies but only as a geographical variation) of the Stone sheep are the Black sheep from the headwaters of the Skeena River; the Saddle-back sheep from near Dawson City, Yukon; the Mount Logan sheep; the Liard sheep from the Liard River region; and Millais sheep from the Samilkameen Mountains.

## HABITS

The Dall sheep loves the company of its kind. The herds of rams may number from four to twenty-five individuals; flocks of ewes and lambs are larger and may number as many as thirty or forty. There are a few solitary old rams that travel alone and are very irregular in their habits.

About 95 per cent of the food consumed by the Dall sheep is grass and it rarely ever browses on twigs or leaves of shrubs and bushes. All sheep are partial to salt and make regular trips to any salt licks in their neighborhood and drink water every two or three days.

The Dall sheep has sharp eyesight, equal to a man equipped with high-powered binoculars. Its sense of smell is equally well developed and it can never be approached down wind. Though they have a good sense of hearing, the white sheep do not pay much attention to sound, as they are adjusted to the continuous rattle of sliding shale and rocks loosened from the mountain sides by frost and water.

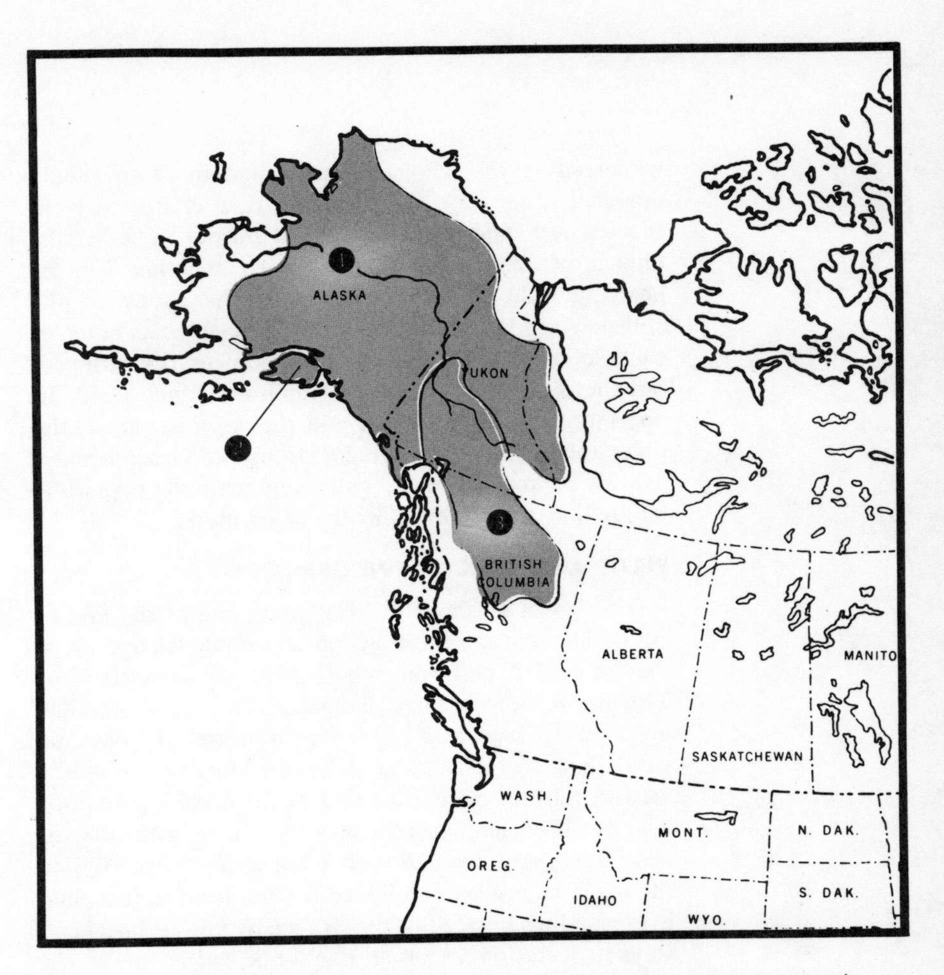


Distribution of races of Dall sheep *Ovis*: 1. Dall sheep, 2. Kenai white sheep, 3. Stone sheep.

## VOCAL

The white sheep is usually silent except for the few snorts or grunts uttered by the rams during the rutting conflicts, and a few low "blatts" and "baas" made by the ewes and small lambs.

## ENEMIES

The Dall sheep has few natural enemies. Wolves may occasionally get an individual when the animals descend into a valley and pass the edges of timber moving from one mountain range to another. A wolverine hard-pressed for food may successfully stalk and kill a sheep, and the lynx will get a limited number during years when the rabbits are scarce. Now and then a golden eagle manages to carry away a newborn lamb left unguarded by its mother.

## MATING

Early in October in the cold northern latitudes, the rams that have lived in friendly association together all summer begin to eye each other with distrust and suspicion. By the middle of November the mad season is at its height, and with necks swollen and eyes flashing, the battling rams fight for possession of the ewes. Male aspirants are satisfied with a harem of from four to seven females. Some harem masters are not too offensive to a lone male poaching on his preserves, but other rams will not tolerate the presence of a competitor and furious battles may result.

Mountain sheep put on the most amazing show ever

witnessed in the whole animal kingdom. Two evenly matched rams back off 20 paces, then charge with all the strength and power they can muster. The terrific impact of the heavy horns coming together can be heard a mile or more away, and the shock of the collision sends a shivering ripple through the body of each animal. Both animals are momentarily stunned, but the procedure is repeated time and time again. In one month the rut is over, and the sexes separate, the rams congregating in bachelor groups of about twenty-five each, and the ewes gathering with their yearling lambs into flocks of up to thirty or more.

**BIRTH AND EARLY DEVELOPMENT**

The lambs are born in May, or as late as the first of June. The nursery may be on a secluded ledge or at the base of a cliff somewhere high above timberline. The ewe leaves the flock and seeks a place—a secluded ledge or the base of a cliff—that is sheltered from cold winds and storms and at the same time commands a view of all the approaches that might harbor predators. The newborn lamb comes into the world with its eyes wide open, and covered with snow-white fleece. Within the hour the mother has licked it from head to foot, and it is standing unsteadily on its feet to nurse. The lamb stays in seclusion for about one week and in two weeks it has joined the main herd with its mother. The lambs are nursed until the first days of winter but have learned to help feed themselves long before this.

Forming a loose spiral curve, the Dall sheep's slender horns are never shed and continue to grow throughout the animal's lifetime.

The horns of young rams up to the second year are curved and as slender as those of the female. Each year the growth of the horn is indicated by a ridge around the base of the horn; during the early stages these ridges are widely spaced but in later years the ridges come closer together. By counting the ridges the age of the animal can be roughly estimated.

## Popular and Scientific Names of the Dall Sheep

**ORDER:** *Artiodactyla* | **GENUS:** *Ovis*

**FAMILY:** *Bovidae* | **SPECIES:** *dalli*

**SUBSPECIES**

| | |
|---|---|
| Dall sheep | *Ovis dalli dalli* |
| Kenai white sheep | *Ovis dalli kenaiensis* |
| Stone sheep | *Ovis dallis stonei* |
| Black sheep | *Ovis dalli niger* |
| Saddle-back sheep | *Ovis dalli fannini* |
| Mount Logan sheep | *Ovis dalli cowanii* |
| Liard sheep | *Ovis dalli liardensis* |
| Millais sheep | *Ovis dalli samilkameenensis* |

CHAPTER 2

# THE BIGHORN

OF ALL the superb trophies found on this fortunate continent of North America, I'd put the wild sheep right at the very top of the list. And of all the wild sheep, I'd give first place to old *Ovis canadensis,* the brown bighorn, that monarch of the crags and canyons. Right behind him I'd put his first cousin, the desert sheep, and in a dead heat for third I'd list his second cousins, the pure white Dall and the gray-faced, black-bodied Stone sheep.

The bighorn is not as large as the moose, as swift as the antelope, as ferocious as the grizzly, as beautiful as the caribou, or as cunning as the whitetail. But generally the taking of a fine, old ram with burly neck, Roman nose, heavily broomed and blunted horns that chronicle the twelve or thirteen years of his loves and battles, his feasts and famines, requires more work, more patience, and more sweat than the taking of any North American game animal. He is hunted for the most part in the Rockies, up around timberline, in the most beautiful country ever trodden upon by unworthy man. Anyone who has the head of an old Rocky Mountain bighorn ram has the very cream of all American trophies.

The sheep hunter himself is as special a breed as the game he goes after. With the great increase in Canadian hunting, and with more Western states now open to the pursuit of sheep, there are more sheep hunters than there used to be. In the days before World War II, when Wyoming and Idaho were the only two American states open to sheep hunting and when only a handful of Americans hunted in the mountains of northern Mexico and in the Canadian Rockies, I believe I knew most of the dedicated sheep hunters in this country. I also believe I knew every one of the first ten men ever to shoot all varieties of North American sheep.

Sheep hunters come in all sizes and shapes—tall and short, lean and plump, old and young. It is the toughest hunting in the world, but one of the most enthusiastic sheep hunters I know is a tycoon who is fond of fork and bottle and who would dress out at 275 pounds.

But all sheep hunters are romantics who love high places and solitude. To them the wild ram embodies the mystery and magic of the mountains, the rocky canyons, the snowy peaks, the fragrant alpine meadows, the gray slide rock, the icy, dancing rills fed by snowbank and glacier, the sweet, clean air of the high places, and the sense of being alone on the top of the world with the eagles, the marmots, and the wild sheep themselves.

The sheep hunter is willing to climb until his

lungs are bursting, to walk until his legs are dead weary, to grow hungry and thirsty for great rewards. There is no half way. After his first exposure a man is either a sheep hunter or he isn't. He either falls under the spell of sheep hunting and sheep country or he won't be caught dead on another sheep mountain.

Since the war many new areas in the West have been opened up to sheep hunting, and many persons have had an opportunity to try the sport for the first time. The majority find it too rugged, and they would rather stick to the easier elk, deer, and antelope. Generally when a state is opened to sheep hunting on special licenses for the first time there is a great rush for permits, but after two or three years they usually go begging.

Going after the bighorn is no game for the weak-kneed and faint-hearted. Hunter success is not high, not because there aren't enough sheep but because there aren't enough people with the temperament to become sheep hunters. Herds in the West are now generally increasing or holding their own. Native hunters who are more interested in meat than trophies quickly decide the hard work involved isn't worth it. I think anyone who really wants to get a ram trophy in the United States now has an excellent chance for a permit and a head. Wyoming, Colorado, Idaho, Montana, Arizona, New Mexico, and Nevada, all have sheep in huntable numbers.

The very best bighorn country is in the southern Rockies of Canada. In the limestone ranges of Alberta, where there are an estimated fifteen thousand bighorns, sheep reach the greatest bodily size and have the finest horns. The world record bighorn is an Alberta ram, and seven of the top ten heads in the 1958 edition of the Boone and Crockett Club's *Records of North American Big Game* are from Alberta, as are sixty of the one hundred heads listed.

Charlie Ren of Sonoyta, Sonora, and I once weighed an enormously fat desert bighorn shot in the spring. He went 225 pounds field dressed, and from what I've seen of Wyoming and Idaho sheep I'd say one that went much over that would be large. The monster Alberta sheep commonly dress out at 300 pounds or so, and I have a record of one great ram shot by Bert Rigall, dean of Alberta sheep guides who led Martin Bovey to the present world record. It dressed out at 365! The Rocky Mountain bighorn ram will weigh about what a very large mule deer will weigh, plus the weight of the heavy horns. The skull and dry horns of a big ram will weigh about 40 pounds. I once carried a sheep head and scalp down a mountain and weighed it. It went 46.

A bighorn does not stand as high as a deer, but he is a broader, chunkier animal with heavier bones and a more solid look. He is a brown animal with a small black tail and a dingy white rump patch and belly. His nose is white and his ears small. Rams are usually darker than the ewes, and old rams are darker than young ones. Sheep are darkest in the late summer or early fall when they are growing their new winter coats. In the spring, when the coats are bleached by the sun, they often fade to a khaki so light that at a distance they look almost white. Color varies with individual sheep and with the subspecies. An albino ram was killed in Nevada a few years ago, and once I saw a melanistic desert bighorn with all the brown replaced by coal black.

The crowning glory of the trophy ram, and the things in which sheep hunters are most interested, are his big curling horns. They are different from the horns of the Stone and Dall sheep in that they curl closer to the face, are somewhat more massive, darker, and are more nearly round in cross-section. The horns of the sheep grow as long as he lives. At the time of the late November and December rut the rams stop feeding and horn growth ceases. In spring, as abundant feed becomes available, growth is resumed. The result is an annual ring, deeper than seasonal rings, which tells the animal's age. Apparently the life span of the bighorn is about twelve or thirteen years. I have shot several rams with thirteen rings, but I have only seen one with fourteen.

The horns of most old bighorn rams are broomed off at the end, whereas the horns of the Stone and Dall sheep often have perfect points. Why does this happen? The answer lies, I believe, in that the horns of the brown sheep often curl close to the eyes and block the side vision. When this happens the sheep rub the tips against rocks to wear them off.

I have heard that sheep wear the points down by using their horns to dig roots. I don't believe it. I have seen many hundreds of feeding sheep in my day. I have never seen one digging roots or seen any sign that they dug roots, but I have seen several rubbing their horns against rocks. To me the most logical reason for this rubbing, or brooming, is to clear the vision.

In my trophy room I have the heads of a dozen North American sheep, and in every case where the side vision would be blocked by continued growth of the horns, the points are rubbed, and in every case where the points are perfect the tips do not block the side vision. Because the big, massive, heavily broomed horns with their close curls are typical of the bighorn, I much prefer horns of this type in the brown sheep to those with perfect points.

The bases of the horns of the brown sheep average larger than do those of the Stone and Dall sheep, but horns that measure 16 inches at the base after the head is thoroughly dry are very large. In the course of a year or two a big sheep horn will generally shrink about an inch at the base and about that in length. One base measurement for bighorns in the record book, for example, is $16\frac{7}{8}$ and one desert ram has a base of 17 inches. Each of these, when first taken, would have gone around 18. A bighorn head, well broomed with a length approaching 40 inches and a base of 16, is a prize beyond compare and will have a good solid place in the records. The famous Simpson head from British Columbia, number three in the records, has one horn $49\frac{1}{8}$ inches long. It is now in the American Museum of Natural History in New York. Horns of Stone and Dall sheep that go 15 inches at the base when dry are very large, and I have one fine Dall with a curl of over 40 inches that has a base less than 13.

Hunting any wild sheep is an entirely different proposition from hunting deer, and that is why many good deer hunters have a tough time when they start hunting sheep. A deer is generally jumped, but a sheep is stalked. The deer is generally concealed and the hunter does not see it until it moves. The sheep, on the other hand, likes open country, and the best way to hunt him is to see him a long way off before he sees you. Then you must figure out a way to approach down or cross wind and out of sight. Anyone who tries to hunt sheep by barging around in sheep country hoping for a ram to come dashing out of some brush to get shot is in for some disappointment.

The deer's primary means of protection are his nose and his ears. The sheep depends mostly on his wonderful eyes. These are at least as good as the human eye aided by an 8X glass. Many times I have located sheep with binoculars—sheep I could not see with the naked eye—only to find them on their feet and watching *me*. The ears of sheep are small, and since sheep live in rough country where rocks are always rolling they don't pay too much attention to what they hear. Their sense of smell isn't as keen as that of a deer or moose, but if a tricky air current carries the hunter's scent to a wary old ram he is long gone. Many claim that sheep pay no attention to what they smell, but I have proved to myself many times that they do by deliberately giving them my scent. They don't like it.

The sheep hunter's most useful tool is not his rifle but a pair of good binoculars supplemented by a spotting scope. Then, if the head is what he wants, he makes the stalk. The spotting scope of from 20 to 25X is not an absolute necessity, but it will save the hunter many long and fruitless stalks for rams that he will decide not to take when he gets a good look at them.

Old rams join the ewe herd before the rut begins in late November and stay with it until lambing time in the spring. Then they go off by themselves, generally in small bands of rams all about the same age. Sometimes old rams are found close to the ewes and lambs during the fall hunting season, but often they are found many miles away, as they gen-

Sheep in areas not often hunted show no great fear of man. Once six rams stood around and watched O'Connor dress out one he had shot.

erally like to summer in higher and rougher country. In a stretch of good sheep country 15 by 15 miles (225 square miles) there may be two or three very large bunches of ewes and lambs, several bunches of young rams from two to seven years old, a couple of bunches of fairly good rams from seven to ten years old, and a couple of small bunches of very old rams with fine trophy heads. Now and then an old ram with decayed teeth, and probably a bad disposition, will go off and live by himself until he dies some bitter winter night or is killed by wolves or mountain lions. Usually, however, the ram is a gregarious animal. If you find one in your glass you'll generally see others.

Even in the best sheep country it often takes a lot of work to locate the trophy rams. The old-timers of the Rockies like to find a basin where feed is good, and clear, cold water is close by. They like to be near shale slides or rocky cliffs so they can escape predators. Often they will spend a whole summer in a few square miles, sometimes in one basin. They have their places to feed, their places to rest during the middle of the day, and their places to bed down at night. The more restricted their range, the harder they are to locate. The hunter may look into twenty basins, see many ewes, lambs, and fair rams. He may be ready to say there isn't a trophy head in the whole country, and then find a dozen busters in the twenty-first basin. Sometimes rams will come back to the same basin every summer, and that's one reason why a guide who knows the country and the habits of a particular herd is a great asset.

Rams are up and feeding at daylight. They are usually afoot for two or three hours, but as the sun gets high they go to some place where they can paw out beds, where it is cool and comfortable, and where they can look out for enemies over a lot of country. Along about noon they generally get up for a bite of lunch. Some of the rams may feed only a few minutes. Others may feed an hour. Then they lie down once more until late afternoon.

The time to locate the rams is when they are afoot. Bighorn country is generally rougher than country in which Stone and Dall sheep are found, and the brown bighorns are better camouflaged. A stationary sheep lying on shale or slide rock about the same color is pretty hard to see. Often, particularly early in the season when it is warm, the rams will bed in the shade of scrubby, timberline trees. A herd of rams on a boulder-strewn hillside is also difficult to glass. I have often searched a wide area for hours without finding anything, and then suddenly become aware that a ram was on foot feeding in a place I would have sworn held no sheep. Then I'd see another—and another.

When rams are located, the next step is to set up a spotting scope and look the heads over. Unless it is still so early that the hunter can be assured the rams will be on foot for considerable time, or they are not far off, it is usually wise to watch the sheep until they bed down. Then one can be sure they will stay put for several hours. Often the feeding ground and the bedding ground are some distance apart, and if the rams have moved when the stalk is in progress they will have to be located again.

When the hunter has found a bunch of rams and has decided it contains one he wants, he should look over the lay of the land to find a way he can approach them from behind ridges and up ravines without being seen. If he can stay completely out of sight he is lucky. He may find that part of the stalk must be made across a piece of ground where he must inch along on knees and elbows, flattening out and lying still each time a ram looks his way.

At all times the stalker should look over each new area thoroughly with his binoculars before he exposes himself. Many a fine ram has been lost because the hunter was too intent on his quarry, moved too fast, and spooked a straggler from a bunch he hadn't seen. Now and then the hunter will run into a ram that at one time has had a bad scare and that will get up and look over the ridge from which the hunter had planned to approach. Very often one sheep will go off by himself and lie down where he can see country that his companions cannot see. If the hunter does not have this sentinel located, his sheep hunt will blow up.

The final stage of the stalk should be made with the greatest caution. Not only should the hunter keep an eye peeled for the sentinel ram, but he should also remember that sometimes a bunch of rams will move a little way and lie down again. Possibly the sun is too hot, or the shade too cool, or they simply decide that the shale on the other side of the hill is softer.

Once I was out with two companions and an impatient, neurotic Indian guide. My amigos were out for heads, but I carried only binoculars and a camera and tagged along at the rear. We had located two big rams right on the top of a mountain, and the Indian charged right up a deep canyon out of sight of the two sheep. At the head of the canyon there was a little bench lying just below the peak. The Indian did not stop to look this over, but scrambled up on the bench with his eyes and mind on the peak where we had seen the bedded rams. While we had been climbing, the two rams and seven others we had not seen decided the peak was too windy or something and had moved down on the bench. They saw the guide and the hunters first and took off fast. My two hunters got excited, fired a fusilade, and never got a sheep hair.

The grandeur of a sheep trophy and the rugged beauty of the country in which wild rams are found make sheep hunting a fascinating sport. Another factor is the long-lasting suspense. I know of no other hunting that will keep the hunter keyed up so long. Often he will see a ram in the afternoon too late to make a stalk, find him again about 8 o'clock the next morning, spend the day making the stalk, and then get his shot late in the afternoon. All that time, if he's been bitten by the sheep bug, he is excited, a little breathless, living at a high pitch, fearful that something may make the stalk go wrong, and wondering how his nerves will be when the chips are down.

I saw the best bighorn I ever got early one morning after my guide and I had made a climb of about 1,500 feet out of the canyon of Muddywater River in Alberta. He and another ram were bedded on a long point overlooking tributary Chocolate Creek. Keeping out of sight, we dropped down 1,500 feet into the Muddy once more and worked up to where Chocolate Creek runs into it. Then we sneaked up through the timber-fringed bank of Chocolate Creek on the opposite side from the ram. When we got to the spot from which I had planned to shoot, I found that I could see only the head of the ram about 200 yards away and 300 feet above us. I didn't want to ruin the scalp, and I also didn't want to chance a miss. We then sneaked through the timber until we got to a bend out of the ram's vision, stalked back, and finally climbed up the side of a little canyon to the top of the next point. When at last I thrust my head over, the old ram was lying facing away from me, chewing his cud.

The sight of that blocky brown body and those broomed and massive horns made me shake for a few seconds, but he was not much over 100 yards away and the knowledge that he was mine calmed me down. I waited until I had my wind back and had stopped shaking. Then I let him have it. When we finally got to camp it was long after dark, but I was a very happy sheep hunter.

Ewes, lambs, and young rams are not very wary, as the sheep has to learn to fear men and rifles and is not instinctively spooky the way a deer is. Once a companion and I, by keeping in sight and moving slowly, managed to get close enough to a herd of 87 ewes, lambs, and young rams to take some good pictures. Even mature rams in an area that is

Rams use rocky cliffs and shale slides as escape routes. Hunters must negotiate open spaces on elbows and knees.

not hunted often show no great fear of man. Once in a wild and lonely section of British Columbia I was stalking a goat when a herd of seven mature rams came over a ridge—apparently headed for the lick where the goat was. I shot the largest ram and went up to dress it and skin out the head. The remaining six rams stood around watching me. I don't think they had ever heard a rifle shot or seen a man.

But where the wild ram is much hunted he quickly becomes one of the wariest animals in the mountains. He beds down where he can keep an eye peeled for danger, and when his incredible vision tells him a man with a rifle is after him he takes off. A deer that has been shot at will go around the side of a hill a quarter of a mile away and lie down. A ram will leave the country, generally heading for the highest peaks and the rockiest ridges.

And it doesn't take much to spook the wary old monarch of the crags. If he sees the glint of your binocular lenses, the top of your hat sticking over a ridge, or notes that you are headed generally in his direction up a canyon that will be out of his line of vision, he is gone. If a ram definitely sees you and is on his feet, the smart thing to do is stay in plain sight and walk away from him. Then maybe he'll decide you're not a sheep hunter and get over his fright. Permanent camp should never be made right in sheep country, as the sound of the axes and the horse bells will move the sheep back over the ridges.

Once a companion and I were hunting sheep and had located five big rams lying right at the foot of a cliff at the head of a big basin. They were in such a position that we could not get closer than 400 or 500 yards. We crawled behind the cut bank of a little creek to a point below where we could watch them through the branches of some stunted Alpine firs—called shin-tangle in the Canadian Rockies.

The slope below was a beautiful Alpine meadow, and we hoped that when the rams got up to feed they'd come our way. Along about two o'clock I got hungry and decided to eat a sandwich I had in my shirt pocket. Just as I unwrapped it a little breeze snatched the waxed paper and sent it sailing out from behind the clump of shin-tangle. Instantly every ram was on his feet. For ten minutes they stood looking right at us, and I think they could see right through the branches. Presently they turned, and with great dignity marched single file out of the basin, over a ridge, and out of sight. Try as we would, we could never locate them again.

If the stalk is properly executed, shots at rams are generally easy. If all is well the hunter has time to get his wind back and get over his jitters. Usually he can shoot from prone or even with a rest. I have made a few long shots at sheep and a few running shots, but most of the sheep I have killed have been lying or standing within 200 yards. I have never lost a wounded sheep in North America, and most I have killed with one shot. The last bighorn I shot was just 35 yards away.

The sheep rifle should, above all things, be light and relatively short of barrel. A heavy rifle becomes a fearful burden, and a long barrel is awkward to climb with. I like a rifle with a 22-inch barrel weighing about eight pounds complete with scope and sling. A good 4X scope with crosswire reticule is exactly right. Even though most shots at rams are short, the sheep hunter occasionally may have to take a long one, and he should select a cartridge with a reasonably flat trajectory. A .250/3000, a .243, a .244, or a .257 has plenty of power for sheep, but since sheep are often hunted in grizzly country a cartridge with somewhat more power is a good bet. One of the finest of all ways to run into a grizzly is to hunt sheep.

I have shot rams with the .270, the .30/06, and the 7 mm. All are excellent and all have enough soup for big bears. Generally I use the light bullets —130-grain in the .270; 150-grain in the .30/06, and 140-grain in the 7 mm. With a well-placed shot any of these will almost always kill a ram instantly. And one should take care to place that shot and to do everything he can to avoid wounding and losing this grandest of American game animals.

Whether he is hunted in the Colorado Rockies, the Middle Fork of the Salmon River in Idaho, the Wind River Range of Wyoming, the Sun River country of Montana, or the wonderful limestone mountains of Alberta and British Columbia, the pursuit of the brown bighorn is the cream of mountain hunting. The old bighorn will lead the hunter into the most beautiful country he's ever seen. He'll wear him out, give him buck fever, and break his heart; but if the hunter is the type that's susceptible to sheep fever he'll never be completely happy hunting anything else.

# THE DESERT BIGHORN

THE TOUGHEST hunting I have ever done has been for the desert bighorn sheep. In hunting other types of sheep in North America, horses can be used much of the time to take the hunter right into ram country. On a Wyoming hunt for Rocky Mountain bighorns, a companion and I actually camped on a plateau at 11,000 feet and grazed our hobbled horses higher than the head of the canyon.

But in Sonora, Mexico, where I have done my desert sheep hunting, it is all foot work. Most of the sheep mountains are so rough and rocky that a horse couldn't get 50 feet up the first slope. Many of the mountains are vast piles of solid rock, full of deep canyons, knifesharp ridges, and precipitous drops. The mountains do not go very high, but they rise sharply from low country. Among the toughest ranges I have ever hunted are the Cubabi Mountains south and somewhat east of Sonoyta, Sonora. The highest peak is only 4,480 feet above sea-level, but it rises sharply from a plain about 1,200 feet in elevation, and when anyone climbs to the top and back in a day, he knows he's been somewhere.

The Cubabis are solid granite, much of it worn as smooth as glass by rain and weather. The Pinacates, below the Arizona line in northwestern Sonora, are a series of lava fields, volcanic craters, and cinder cones. The highest of these, Pinacate Peak, is about 4,500 feet high. Cerro Viejo (properly Cerro del Viejo, or the Mountain of the Old Man) is weathered limestone so sharp that a few days on it will tear the soles off the stoutest shoes. To me the toughest mountains of all are those of decomposed granite, so steep and unstable that every chunk of rock is ready to roll. A sheep hunter makes three steps upward and slides down two.

Once in the San Franciscos I had spent a fruitless day looking for a big ram, and in the late afternoon I decided to take a shortcut back to camp. The ridge I was on ended in a very steep cliff, but the one across the canyon, although very steep, looked like a feasible route. But to get there I would have to cross a slanting shelf worn glass-smooth by water. It was 40 feet or so wide, but it dropped off about 200 feet to the bottom of the canyon. The slant was so steep that I was afraid to try walking across, and I didn't have enough nerve to run across and let my momentum carry me forward. I decided I could safely edge across by lying face down with my rifle strapped to my back. So I started out.

For the first few feet the friction of my body, the toes of the basketball shoes I was wearing, and my bare hands kept me from slipping. My progress, though slow, was sure. But about halfway across, the angle became a bit steeper, and I started to slip down toward the precipice. Every time I wiggled a foot to the right, I'd slip 6 inches down. The farther I went, the closer I got to the cliff. I sought for depressions I could dig my fingernails and my toes into, but the whole slanting ledge was smooth and slick. When I finally made it across and grabbed a piece of solid rock to arrest my slide, I had about an inch between my toes and a 200-foot drop.

Desert sheep not only are found in the toughest country, but they are the hardest of the sheep to see. They are brown or gray-brown, and so are the rocky hills where they are found. At a distance, these hills look as bare as the face of the moon, but most of them have just about enough desert vegetation on them to break up the outlines of the sheep and make glassing difficult. During hunting season the snow-white Dall sheep is conspicuous against almost any background—high grassy pastures or slide rock.

The Stones, with their light-colored heads and necks, are also easy to make out. Even the brown bighorn of the Rockies generally stands out plainly against grassy ridges and green basins. But the desert sheep lives in a land of neutral-colored rocks and neutral-colored vegetation. If it weren't for his rump patch of dingy white he'd be even harder to find than he is.

To make the desert sheep an even tougher trophy, the fantastically rough country where he lives is both dry and hot. The hunter of the northern sheep can generally find an icy little rill to quench his thirst, or he can even pick up a handful of snow. But the hunter of desert sheep must carry his water with him. In the fall and winter most men can get by on a couple of quarts, but in the hot months they will come back with all their water gone, and their mouths dusty dry.

In some sheep mountains the rain water collects in basins worn out of solid rock. The Mexicans call them *tinajas*. Generally they are full of the droppings of sheep and those of the whitewing dove, and long streamers of moss float on the surface. The water looks like the devil, but it's cool and wet. I have drunk gallons of it.

Many of the best sheep ranges have no open water whatsoever. In the areas of broken granite and lava rock, any rain sinks in the instant it falls. This absence of open water does not seem to bother the sheep, however. They obtain sufficient moisture from the dew that comes in from the Gulf of California, from the water-filled fruit of various cacti, and from water-storing cacti like the *bisnaga* (barrel cactus), and saguaro and *sahueso,* both forms of giant cactus. Down on the Sonora desert bordering the Gulf of California, all the game has learned to survive for long periods without water. Not only many sheep but many desert mule and whitetail deer live and die without ever having tasted water.

The task of collecting a desert ram is often made more difficult because many of the sheep ranges are right above the blue and tantalizing gulf, and limpid, cool-looking water is always in sight. It is a trying experience to be so thirsty that every cell in your body is crying for water and yet to be within sight of thousands of square miles of it.

Unless he is fortunate enough to camp near a *tinaja* or close to a well that has been developed by some rancher, the hunter of desert sheep has to carry all his water with him. Once, in the springtime, some friends of mine and I camped beneath a paloverde tree that was a mass of yellow bloom and singing with a million bees. We had two 25-gallon water tanks of galvanized iron. We finished one and started on the other. As soon as we started drinking it we became aware that it smelled. We squeezed limes in it, and we made tea out of it; but even when we used it for coffee it still stank. Finally we found that the faucet had inadvertently been left open and thousands of bees had crawled up the spout and drowned.

On another occasion I lived for ten days on flood water that came down an arroyo after a violent thunderstorm. It was full of silt so finely suspended that it never settled, and it had a curiously repulsive taste. But it was wet. I'll never forget how passionately I longed for a drink of water that tasted good and didn't stick to my teeth.

It is a harsh and bitter land, this desert sheep country, so dry that often it doesn't rain for months or even years, so dry that tracks made months before look but a few days old. One late December, with my wife and one of my sons, I made camp at the same place in the Serol Mountains in Sonora south of Puerto Libertad, right near the shore, where a friend and I had been hunting sheep in April. The tracks still looked fresh. The cigarette butts looked as if they had been smoked within the hour, and a tin can that was sitting under a stone had not a particle of rust on it.

Hunting the desert sheep is made the more difficult because the animals are not plentiful. Once, on a lofty mountain above the Prophet River in northern British Columbia, I saw at least eighty big Stone rams in one day, but in the desert a man might hunt hard for six months and never see that many. The sheep are not only scarce but they are highly migratory. To survive they must move from range to range searching for succulent vegetation. Particularly in the summer the rains are very spotty, and one range may be green but another 20 miles away may be bone dry. When the country dries up, the sheep move on. When a good rain falls on a mountain the sheep appear to harvest the quick-growing vegetation that follows the moisture.

Once in February I was in the San Franciscos after the local winter rains had been good. There was plenty of green stuff—and plenty of sheep. Two months later the country had dried up. There was not a sheep, nor even a fresh track. Another time a friend and I spent ten days looking for sheep in the mountains along the coast between Cape Lobos and Tiburon Island. Not a single sheep did we see. Apparently all the sheep had left the coastal ranges for those inland.

The range of the wild sheep forms a great semicircle that goes halfway around the world. It embraces the aoudad of the rocky hills that rise from the Sahara desert, the red sheep of the Middle East, the urial of India, Iran, and Pakistan, the goatlike bharal or blue sheep of the Indian frontier, China, and Tibet, the *Ovis poli* and other great argalis of central Asia, the Clifton and Kamchatka sheep of eastern Siberia, then the Dall, Stone, bighorn, and desert sheep of North America.

In its wanderings in various parts of the world, the genus *Ovis* has assumed many different forms—the odd-looking Barbary sheep of Africa and the bharal, both of which are about as much goat as sheep, the little mouflon of the islands in the Mediterranean Sea, the small red sheep that are generally considered their ancestors, the medium-size urial, the large argali-type sheep, some with horns having bases as large as 19 inches and some with horns over 6 feet long. The sheep of eastern Siberia are so closely related to the North American sheep that British zoologists lump them into one species along with those of North America. I have seen the heads of these Siberian sheep in the Kensington Museum in London and I am inclined to agree with them. It would take a more discerning observer than the average sheep hunter to tell the horns and skull of a Kamchatka bighorn from those of an Alaska Dall.

Sometime early in the Pleistocene era the ancestors of the American wild sheep crossed from Siberia to Alaska on the land bridge which was in existence off and on for a million years and which was finally covered with water only twelve thousand years ago. It was also used by such other animals of Asiatic origin as the elk, the moose, and the Rocky Mountain goat and by the American bears as a means of entering Siberia.

One theory is that all North American sheep had a common ancestor, but that the sheep were split into two groups by an ice age, with the ancestors of the Dall and Stone sheep surviving north of the glaciers and those of the Rocky Mountain bighorn and desert sheep south of them in ice-free areas of the United States. Another theory is that the ancestors of our sheep came in two waves. The first, the brown bighorns, were driven south by the glaciers, and then, when the ice receded, the ancestors of the Dall and Stone came over to populate the northern ranges.

At any rate, it is a reasonable theory that when the ice drove the brown sheep south, they moved in the course of the centuries from range to range. As the ice withdrew, the sheep began to spread north again until they occupied the main range of the Rockies from Colorado into Canada, and the drier and more open mountains of western Washington and British Columbia. There are two main divisions of the brown bighorn: 1. The large, heavy-horned, small-eared sheep of the main Rockies, *Ovis canadensis canadensis.* 2. The various races of somewhat smaller sheep with longer ears and a tendency to somewhat lighter and less closely curled horns, *Ovis canadensis californiana.*

The sheep of western British Columbia are of this lighter-horned and larger-eared type, and so are all the desert varieties of sheep. Along the Colorado River somewhere, the two types merged, possibly in northern Arizona or southern Utah. Sheep are found in true deserts where the rainfall is 9 inches a year or less in Nevada, southern California, Sonora, Chihuahua, Lower California, and Arizona. They are divided into various subspecies, but in *Records of North American Big Game* they are all simply called desert sheep.

They are fairly recent immigrants to the Southwestern deserts. Caves inhabited by Indians for thousands of years and filled with animal bones and other refuse show that Indians had occupied the caves for many centuries before they began killing and eating sheep. During the Pleistocene era the Southwest had much heavier rainfall than it does now, and probably the sheep moved in after the forests that once clad the desert mountains had died out from lack of moisture, probably about twelve thousand years ago. The sheep go almost to the tip of Lower California and down the Sonora coast to the mountains opposite Tiburon Island. This is the point where the great, tri-continental chain of wild sheep ends. It has been my great good fortune to hunt sheep at both ends of this crescent. Both are in desert regions, and superficially the rocky sheep hills that rise out of the Sahara desert in Africa and those in southwestern Arizona and Sonora look much alike.

The late William T. Hornaday, a zoologist and director of the Bronx Zoo in New York City, hunted desert sheep in the Pinacates of Sonora in 1907. In his charming book, *Campfires on Desert and Lava,* he wrote about the desert sheep and was inclined to believe they were so little different from the Rocky Mountain bighorn he was familiar with in British Columbia and Alberta that they were the same species. The desert bighorn is a smaller, leaner, thinner, more muscular-looking animal than his northern relatives. Because he lives in a region of drought and heat, his hair is much shorter and his head and neck have a slender, deerlike look. Hornaday says the desert rams average 50 to 75 pounds lighter than the Rocky Mountain sheep. I have found that to be generally true.

As is the case with any variety of sheep, the desert bighorns vary from area to area. On his 1907 desert hunt, Hornaday weighed a ram and found that it went complete 192½ pounds. He says that a sheep he shot, but did not measure since his scales were not available, appeared to be much larger and at least 40 pounds heavier than the ram that was weighed. Incidentally, both the sheep were shot in November when the rams have not recovered from the rut, which begins in late August or early September.

I have been in on the weighing of two large Sonora rams. The heaviest was shot about the middle of April after a winter of excellent rains. He was an old-timer living all alone in an area of plentiful feed. He was hog-fat and weighed 225 pounds. The other, which had run off a mountain when wounded and died out on a flat where he could be reached by a car, weighed 175 pounds field dressed. Both of these were very large rams with heavy horns broomed back so far that the age had to be guessed, but they were probably twelve or thirteen years old.

By way of contrast, I know of a seven-year-old ram, shot in November, which was a much smaller animal without an ounce of fat on his body and, although I did not weigh him, I'd guess that he would have gone about 115 pounds field dressed, or about as much as a large, Arizona whitetail buck. This was a small ram to start out with. He was in poor condition, and he was not of an age to have attained his greatest weight. All rams continue to increase in weight as long as they stay healthy and their teeth remain good, but they generally go into a decline about their twelfth or thirteenth year. Rams taken during the legal hunting season in Arizona have not been anything like as heavy as the old Sonora rams weighed by Hornaday and by me. However, they have been killed in November when they are not in good condition, and they probably came from areas of poor feed and much competition with domestic stock. The few people I know who have hunted desert sheep in Lower California say they run larger than the Sonora sheep, and certainly the heads average larger.

The color pattern of desert sheep is the same as that of the Rocky Mountain bighorn. They are brown sheep with off-white rump patches, bellies, and noses. Old rams usually are darker than the young rams and ewes. In their fresh winter coats, old rams are what a hunting friend of mine years ago called "gun-metal brown," but the hot, bright sun fades the coat, and in the spring as it begins to shed it is sometimes faded to a sort of a khaki.

Some years ago in Nevada a hunter shot an albino ram that was snow white. One of the Nevada game commissioners sent me a picture of the head, and the hunter, alas, had chopped the head off right behind the ears and had, of course, ruined the scalp. In Sonora many years ago I was climbing up a cliff when a melanistic bighorn that had been bedded down on a point poked his head over. My Mexican friends had told me of a black ram in the San Franciscos and I had blundered onto him. He was far darker than any Stone sheep I have ever seen, so dark that his brown horns looked almost yellow in contrast to his black head and neck.

One difference I've noticed in the color of the desert sheep as compared with that of the Rocky Mountain rams is that the noses and the rump patches of the Canadian sheep are more nearly white, and the demarcation of the white of the nose and the brown of the face is more definite. Desert sheep often have a line of light-colored hairs bordering their hoofs. The tails of the Rocky Mountain sheep are shorter and more heavily haired than the long, thinly haired, black tail of the desert sheep. I have never been conscious of any of the northern sheep elevating their stubby tails when they run off, but the tail of a scared desert sheep sticks up in the air like a twig.

In spite of the fact that the desert bighorn is a smaller sheep than those in the Rocky Mountains, the heads are not much smaller. Indeed the head of the record desert sheep, which was shot by an Indian in Lower California, Mexico, in 1940, has bases of 16⅞ and 17 inches, curl measurements of 43⅝ and 43 6/8, and a total score of 205⅛—only slightly less than the number one bighorn with its score of 207 2/8. This desert ram is the only North American sheep in the record book that actually has a base of 17 inches.

The largest Sonora sheep I have ever heard of was taken by Herb Klein in 1952. Both horns are over 15 inches around the bases, and one horn is just a hair under 40 inches around the curve. The total score is 187⅜. A ram I shot in 1939 had a base measurement at the time of almost 17 inches, but when the head was measured for the record book many years later it had shrunk to 15 6/8—still a large base and the largest of any of the North American sheep heads I have taken. This was a middle-aged ram, only about nine years old; the head would have been much larger if he had lived to be twelve or thirteen.

The largest desert sheep head I have ever seen myself was one from a ram killed by a poacher who caught two fine rams crossing a road in the Eagle

Tail Mountains of southwestern Arizona. Johnny Russo of the Arizona game department and I measured it. Russo is the author of *The Desert Bighorn Sheep in Arizona.* It went 40⅝ and 41²⁄₈ around the curls, and both bases were 15⅛. The third quarters went 13⁶⁄₈ and 14, and the total score was 188⁴⁄₈. It would have been number five in the records. However, I understand it was given to a worthy citizen who boiled it in crankcase oil to "preserve" it, and that it shrank.

Heads of desert bighorns are usually of the close-curl type, and because the upcurving horn tips interfere with the vision they are generally badly broomed. I have seen rams rubbing the points of their horns against rocks, as had A. A. Nichol, who made the first survey of the Arizona bighorn for the then National Association of Audubon Societies back in the nineteen thirties. Because the sheep live in an exceedingly dry climate, their horns also flake off and crack when the rams fight and when the horns are accidentally bumped against rocks. It is common to find pieces of horn in ram beds, and I have found pieces of horn flaked off in areas where tracks told there had been a battle.

I have occasionally seen rams with fairly wide spreads, but one never sees the outspread horns occasionally encountered in the Stones and Dalls. Another type of head seen in Sonora is that with the long, easy curve, where the horn does not start to come up again until the bottom part is well below the point of the jaw. Because this type of horn does not interfere with the vision, the points are often perfect, even when the ram is old. I have a photograph taken in the Desert Game Range near Las Vegas, Nevada, of a wonderful ram with a head of this type. I'd bet my bottom dollar it would measure nearly 44 inches. The argali-type horns that pinch in and then flare out—fairly commonly seen among the Stone and Dall sheep but rarely among the bighorns—is, as far as I know, never seen among the desert sheep. This would seem logical, as the desert sheep is the farthest removed from the primitive ancestor of both the Asiatic argali and the North American sheep.

A North American trophy hunter has less chance of getting sheep of the desert variety than any other species. Sheep hunting has been closed in Mexico for many years, and the rams can be taken only on museum permits, which are very difficult, although not impossible, to obtain. Nevada has had two or three limited hunts for residents only—and these have been on drawings. New Mexico has allowed the taking of a very few rams in southwestern New Mexico in the area of the Dog and Hatchet mountains. Arizona now holds an annual hunt for desert sheep in certain areas. A nonresident who buys an Arizona hunting license and then applies for a permit has as good a chance to be drawn as anybody. California, which has a good many sheep in the mountains around Death Valley, has never had an open season. Neither has Utah.

When O'Connor finally got across the slanting shelf, his toes were an inch from a 200-foot drop.

Ever since Grancel Fitz wrote an article called *Grand Slam on Rams* over a decade ago and listed the hunters who had taken all varieties of North American sheep, many hunters have been filled with ambition to complete their grand slams. Anyone with time, patience, and enough money can get the other three varieties, but getting a desert ram is a problem. In Fitz's article I was, I believe, listed as the fourth person to collect the four varieties, but until I read the article I had no idea that this was true.

Because of the fantastic climate in which he lives, the desert bighorn has a different set of habits than his relatives who live in more favored areas. The best time of the year in the southwestern deserts is in the early spring after the winter rains of December and January. In order that the lambs be dropped at this favorable time, the sheep breed earlier than they do farther north. The rams in Sonora start getting interested in the ewes about the last week of August, and by the first week in September the rut is under way. It is at its height in September and extends into October.

The rams stay with the ewes until the lambing season begins around the first of February. Then the ewes go off alone into very rough country. After the lambs are old enough to be able to follow their mothers nicely, the ewes join up into small bands that often include immature rams. The mature rams go off by themselves and stay apart from the ewes until the rut begins again.

The gestation period is the same as that of domestic sheep—about five months. Indeed, all North American wild sheep will breed with the domestic variety. At one time in southwestern Arizona close to the Mexican border, a Mexican had a few domestic ewes, and the desert rams used to come down from the surrounding hills and impregnate them. Some of the sheep this old chap wound up with were about three-fourths bighorn. In areas where the wild sheep are very few, one of them will, on occasion, join up with a herd of domestic sheep for company.

It's not generally realized, but one hundred years or so ago, the desert Southwest was one of the great sheep countries of the world. In New Mexico, west Texas, Arizona, Nevada, southern California, Sonora, Lower California, and Chihuahua there are thousands of square miles of rough country suitable for sheep. The Spanish explorers of the Southwest saw many sheep, and so did the American pioneers. They were found in all the rugged hills and mountains, in canyons, on isolated buttes. My grandfather hunted sheep on Camelback Mountain in the suburbs of Phoenix, Arizona, back in the late eighteen eighties, and when I was a boy I found a weathered ram head near Hole-in-the-Rock a few miles from Phoenix.

The season on sheep was closed in Arizona and in most Southwestern states in the early nineteen hundreds, but little attempt was made to protect them. They were quickly shot out of country into which one could get on horseback, and out of the lower mountains close to settlements. At one time sheep were plentiful in the Grand Canyon, and it is said that the crew that built the Bright Angel trail down to the Colorado River lived on sheep meat. They were regularly hunted for the market, and an extraordinarily large ram shot near Tucson and displayed in a butcher shop was supposed to have weighed, according to a newspaper account, 235 pounds field dressed.

In areas where there's little dew and not many water-bearing cacti, the sheep have to find another source of water in the hot summer months. When a band of them found it and came to drink, it was no great trick to shoot every one of them. So common was this slaughter of sheep at waterholes that almost all springs and tanks in sheep country are surrounded by rock blinds where meat hunters used to lay in wait. At one of them, not far from Gila Bend, Arizona, the ground was littered with cartridge cases of every description—from .45/70s and .40/40s through .30/06s to .30/30s and .270s. In the course of the years hundreds of sheep had been killed at that one waterhole.

In many desert ranges the sheep were the only game animal, and prospectors who combed the mountains lived on them. This was particularly bad during the depression of the nineteen thirties when the hills were full of amateur prospectors. In Mexico there was no law enforcement, and anyone who had a chance to shoot a sheep did so. All the fishermen carried rifles with them and shot sheep off the rocky headlands from boats. In the days when the Navajo Indians had to hunt with bows and arrows, there were many sheep in the mesa and canyon country of northern Arizona, but they didn't last long once these hungry Indians got repeating rifles.

Plant growth is slow in this land of little rain and summer temperatures that go up to 130 degrees in the shade, but cattlemen moved in to overgraze the country. In many areas there is little vegetation on the mountains, and the sheep have to come down from the hills late in the afternoon and during the cool hours of the morning to feed. Cattle overgrazed the valleys between the hills, and the sheep did without. Some ranges were overgrazed by domestic goats, and in others wild burros descended from stock abandoned by prospectors also used the ranges and kept the sheep away from water. Fences, highways, railroad tracks, and irrigation ditches interfered with the natural and necessary sheep migrations from range to range. Rivers that the desert sheep depended on for drinking water during the hot dry months were dammed and diverted for irrigation, and many streams that ran cool and clear the year around are now hot and arid sand beds most of the time.

When I lived in Arizona I used to agitate for better protection of the sheep, for studies to determine limiting factors, and for occasional restricted hunts for mature rams under special permits to acquaint sportsmen with the wonderful sport of sheep

As O'Connor lined up his sights on the big ram, the young one bounded up the rocks toward him and passed within a dozen feet.

hunting and to get them interested in saving the unique animal. Mostly my agitation for the sheep simply gained me the reputation of being sort of a harmless nut, but since I have left the state the game department has followed the program I used to plead for.

The first study of the desert sheep in Arizona was made in 1936 or 1937 by A. A. Nichol, then of the University of Arizona, a good friend of mine and another sheep enthusiast. Since then, other studies have been made, and limited ram hunts have aroused much sportsman interest. The Kofa and Cabeza Prieta Game Refuges were established in Arizona in 1939 and also the big Desert Game Range near Las Vegas, Nevada. Sheep country adjacent to the Hoover dam is patrolled.

The desert sheep have been saved from extinction, and the population within the preserves is now probably up to the limit of the food supply. Much remains to be done, however—establishing herds in former sheep country and reducing the domestic stock in areas where they compete with sheep for food.

To me, hunting the desert sheep is one of the world's great sports. I love the isolation of the sheep mountains, the dry purity of the air, the fantastic vegetation, the sense of being completely alone. The deserts of the Southwest are harsh and hard. Just about everything wears thorns, and in the summer it is hot enough to fry a salamander. It's no place for weak men or weak animals.

I have never run across a smarter animal than an old Sonora ram that has been shot at by fishermen and prospectors and vaqueros and has survived ten or twelve years. He has eyes like an eagle and is as suspicious as a banker. Typically, he'll see the hunter before the hunter sees him, and suddenly the hunter is aware that a ram is on the skyline watching him—wild, free, lean, tough, and muscular.

I have been outwitted by old rams on so many occasions that I hold them in the deepest respect. Once I had glassed a ram and made a long stalk and was about to come up over a ridge behind and above him when my clumsy foot misplaced a rock. Suddenly I became aware that the ram had come up over the comb not 50 yards away and was looking at me. As I raised my rifle he dived out of sight, ran under a cliff into a canyon, and I never got a shot.

The black ram I mentioned earlier was on a point just above me. He heard me as I climbed up a little cliff with the rifle strapped across my back. I scrambled onto the point where he had been lying, but he was nowhere in sight. I had expected him to plunge down into the canyon and climb out on the opposite side. Instead he ran around the point behind me and climbed out of the canyon while I was looking the other way. I caught a glimpse of him just before he went over the comb. No dumbbell he.

I remember another very spooky ram. I had glassed him lying by himself on a point in the sunshine one rather chill, winter day. I worked around out of his sight and was sneaking down the ridge behind him. Suddenly a cruising crow saw me, let out a squawk, and started flapping for other parts. I heard rocks roll as the ram took off, and presently I saw him bounding up the other side of the canyon. But his luck ended right there.

If my space were not limited I've love to spin some yarns of hunts for desert rams back in the days when the Sonora coastal desert country was almost as unknown to Americans as Inner Mongolia; when one could pick up water at the last ranch well and never see another human being until he had to get some more. I could tell about the ram that crossed the old mine road in front of the car I was in, or the time I saw around thirty big rams in one wide arroyo in the Rosarios; of good luck and bad, and of the late Charlie Ren, one of the greatest desert sheep hunters who ever lived. But I'll wind this up with a simple tale of a very lucky hunt.

It was springtime in the desert, and the day before an amigo and I had crossed the border at the Mexican village of Sonoyta, Sonora, and had driven into the San Franciscos. The next morning we were up before dawn, and when we had eaten we parted —my pal to go in one direction, I in another. Not much over half a mile from camp, I came on the tracks of two rams—one young, the other an old-timer. They had been feeding slowly along the base of a steep, granite mountain, and so recently that some of the twigs they had bitten off were still damp with saliva.

The wind was right as I quietly followed the tracks. Every moment I expected to see them in front of me moving through the scant desert growth, but presently I saw that the tracks swung into a canyon. I turned up the mountain to my left and made my climb. About this time the sun came over the horizon, and instantly I could feel its warmth displacing the delicious coolness of the dawn. I was in my middle thirties then, tough and enduring, and it didn't take me over half an hour to get to the crest of the ridge. Before I went over, I glassed the basin below me in case there might be sheep in it, but nothing did I see.

In the saddle at the head of the canyon into which the rams had turned, there was a little sand from decomposed granite and some sheep beds. The droppings around them looked fairly fresh and so did the tracks. I hoped that this was the spot for which the rams were headed.

I fed a cartridge into the chamber of my .30/06, sat down behind a boulder large enough to conceal all except my head, and took out my binoculars. Below me I could see the ocher desert threaded with the wandering white lines of dry arroyos. The ocotillos were tipped with scarlet and the paloverdes were masses of yellow bloom. Behind me a white-wing dove was giving his deep-throated, melodious call.

I waited. It grew warmer, and on the desert plain below me the mirage began to dance and shimmer. I began to wonder if the rams had turned out of the canyon or had bedded below me.

Then, about 200 yards below in the canyon, a vague movement behind a bush—a movement almost as much sensed as seen—caught my attention. My good 8 x 30 glasses showed me it was a sheep. Then it moved again, and I made out the head and horns of a ram about five or six years old. Presently he moved out into the open and stood browsing interminably.

Once he stopped eating and gazed down into the plain below, and I finally made out a coyote slinking home from his night's hunting. One moment there was but one ram, and then there were two. The other had somehow approached from behind the brush and boulders across the narrow canyon from his partner. I could first only see his rump, but finally he moved and I got a look at his head. He was an old-timer, with heavy, close-curled horns broomed off wide and flat at the ends.

I reached down, picked up my old .30/06, laid it over the boulder, and snuggled down behind it. Much to my disgust I was shaking a little, but I waited for the ram fever to pass. The ram fed behind more bush and boulders and I thought he would never come out. But finally he did, and stood there broadside, lithe and taut and muscular, his slender neck looking too thin and delicate to hold up those heavy horns.

I put the intersection of the crosswires low behind his shoulder, and when I completed the trigger squeeze and the rifle roared in the silent desert air, he disappeared as if the earth had been jerked out from under him.

The younger ram stood still for one horrified moment and then came bounding up the canyon right toward me. I remained quiet behind my rock and he passed within a dozen feet. When he caught my scent he jumped sidewise about 10 feet, then ran down into the basin and up the other side. On the crest he stopped for one last look, but when I got to my feet he turned, and that was the last I saw of him.

I carried the head and the backstraps down out of the canyon to camp, then returned for the rest. With no rifle, canteen, or binoculars to bother me, I managed to get the heavy carcass the 1,200 feet or so down the canyon and then carried it to camp.

Eating sheep meat is one of the things I do best, and that night my amigo and I had fried backstraps. To go with them we had a pot of frijoles that we had put on to soak as soon as we got to camp and that had been simmering all day on ironwood coals. My pal made a Dutch ovenful of biscuits, and we washed all this wonderful provender down with a delicious Hermosillo beer. It was still cold from the rapidly melting ice in our little camp refrigerator.

And then we lay on our cots under stars that were very close and incredibly big and bright. A gentle evening breeze began to move the paloverde branches above us, and somewhere a coyote howled. My amigo went to sleep right in the midst of one of my best hunting stories, and began to snore. I became conscious that carrying the ram down off the mountain had left me with a few aches and twinges, and the next thing I knew it was gray dawn and the whitewings had started to talk.

# The Natural History of the Bighorn

[OVIS CANADENSIS]

## DESCRIPTION

The Rocky Mountain bighorn is a heavy-bodied sheep with massive, curling horns, thick at the base and tapering sharply toward the tip. It has comparatively small ears, large, far-seeing eyes, and pelage varying from grayish-brown in the northern Rocky Mountain subspecies to pale buff in the desert forms.

Most adult male bighorn sheep measure between 54 and 70 inches long, stand from 38 to 42 inches at the shoulder, and weigh about 185 pounds, with some going as high as 225 to 300 pounds. Ewes are much smaller than rams.

The bighorn's hair is not woolly like the domestic sheep's, but is long, coarse, and full, and extends straight outward from the hide. Each hair has a cellular pithy center with a hard outer surface, forming a sealed air pocket, as an insulation to conserve body heat. The bighorn has a characteristic white patch on its rump which surrounds the short, black tail. The nose and ears are a paler brown than the rest of the head, and a narrow band of white extends down the backs of the forelegs and inside the hind limbs.

All mountain sheep, including the bighorn, are digitigrade and walk on the tips of their toes. An even-toed ungulate with its third and fourth digits evenly and well developed, the bighorn has dewclaws on all four feet that serve as emergency brakes. Equipped

with high-tension muscles and rubber-like, shock-absorbing pads on each section of its hoofs, the bighorn can gallop up and down precipitous cliffs 1,000 feet high on which a Rocky Mountain goat would have to travel step by step. It is easier for a bighorn to go up a cliff than down, but there have been instances when a sheep has descended a chimney in the rocks at full speed, controlling the velocity of its fall by bouncing from side to side, while one false move would send it crashing to the bottom.

The bighorn is a ruminant, or cud-chewing, ungulate, lacking teeth at the front of the upper jaw, but equipped with lower front teeth and broad-crowned, sharp-edged molars for milling green vegetation. The bighorn consumes a large amount of fodder in a comparatively short time. The fodder is stored partly chewed in the first compartment of the stomach—the paunch. The sheep then retreats to a position where it has a wide view of the surrounding country to rest and chew the cud.

## HORNS

The animal's horns are thick at the base and taper sharply toward the tip. Each horn is made up of a hollow, horny sheath growing over a bony core. An adult ram's sheaths weigh about 21 pounds. One exceptionally large ram had horns measuring 49 inches along the outside curve, a spread of 24 inches, and a circumference at the base of 16 inches.

## ORIGIN

The bighorn is without known ancestors in America prior to the Tertiary period and represents one of the emigrating elements which reached the New World from Asia no earlier than the middle Pleistocene. There is well-substantiated evidence of the presence of man in America at that time.

The wild mountain sheep are far removed from the breeds of domestic sheep of today. Our barnyard sheep have a woolly fleece instead of a coat of stiff hairs, and a long tail. Both were derived from a common ancestor. There is ever increasing evidence that sheep were domesticated at a very early date in man's history. Quantities of domesticated sheep bones have been found in native village kitchen middens that date back to a considerable time before 3,000 B.C. There is sufficient reason to believe that the domestic sheep was derived from the fox-red mountain sheep (*Ovis orientalis*) native to Asia Minor. It has a short, woolly fleece beneath its longer and coarser hair that could have been developed by selective breeding.

## RANGE

The American bighorn, or Rocky Mountain sheep, is found on high, mountainous ridges, usually above timberline. Its general range is western North America from southeastern British Columbia and southwestern Alberta in Canada south through the Rocky Mountain regions in the United States and south in the mountains to Chihuahua and Lower California in Mexico.

The tracks of a bighorn walking in snow resemble those of a white-tail deer, except that the edges are straighter and less heart-shaped.

The massive horns of the bighorn ram, in contrast to those of the Dall, describe a tight spiral curl, often making more than one turn.

The home range of the bighorn is small; a flock may remain within a home range of from 1 to 4 miles if undisturbed and if conditions are right. They have their favorite pasture for feeding and return to a particular location to rest and sleep. Before lying down, a bighorn scoops out a shallow depression in the ground with its forefeet. There is some seasonal migration, for when the winter comes the bighorn sometimes has to move from localities where the snow lies too deep to windswept mountain sides or to the edge of timber to find cover and food.

Seven subspecies of bighorn sheep are now recognized: The Rocky Mountain bighorn has the widest range and is the largest of the bighorns. Its range extends from southern Alberta through the Rocky Mountain region to New Mexico.

The Lower California bighorn is the palest of the desert bighorns and is found in the isolated desert mountains of the northern half of Lower California, Mexico, and southern California.

The Mexican bighorn ranges in the high, arid mountains of Chihuahua and southern New Mexico. It is a large, pale-colored form with comparatively slender horns and large ears.

The Nelson bighorn inhabits the desert mountain ranges of southeastern California and southern Nevada. It is a small, pale-colored bighorn with slender horns and a white rump patch divided by a dark line.

The Weems desert bighorn is native to the Sierra de la Giganta of southern Lower California, Mexico. A large subspecies for a desert sheep, it has long, slender horns and short, dark pelage.

The Badlands bighorn, formerly found in the Badlands of western North and South Dakota, Nebraska, Montana, and Wyoming, is now believed to be extinct. It differed from the typical bighorn in having longer and narrower horns.

The Rimrock bighorn formerly occupied the lava bed

country of Oregon, northern California, western Nevada, and north into British Columbia. It is probably now extinct. It was a large sheep with loosely curled horns widely spaced at the base.

## HABITS

The bighorn is a dainty feeder and selects only the freshest and greenest food available. It is primarily a grazing, or grass-eating, animal and feeds on the meadows above timber line. On occasion its diet may be varied with sedges, clover, leaves, sprouts and twigs of bushes such as mountain mahogany, Mormon tea, buckbrush, aspen, spruce, fir, willow, currant, rose, and juniper. It may also eat the fruits and flowers of prickly pear, organ pipe, barrel cacti, and saguaro. The bighorn drinks water every three or four days. Like most other ungulates it regularly visits salt licks, especially in the spring.

The bighorn has regular feeding hours and is up at dawn for breakfast. It feeds steadily until ten or eleven o'clock, storing about a peck of food in its paunch. By noon it has eaten its fill and lies down to rest and chew the cud. In the early afternoon it is feeding again, followed by another siesta. Late afternoon is the main feeding time and this continues until dusk, when the animal goes to sleep.

Sight is the all-important factor in the daily life of the bighorn. It can recognize moving objects 5 miles away; thus it is practically impossible for a predator to surprise the bighorn on its summer range. It also has a keen sense of smell and of hearing. The bighorn has well-developed pocket glands in the face, groin, and flanks that are used to some extent as a means of intercommunication.

## LOCOMOTION

The tracks of the bighorn are not unlike those of a Virginia deer, but the sides of the hoofs are straighter and the tips are less pointed. The length of the hoof of an adult ram is about 3½ inches. The tracks are in an almost straight line and when walking the hind foot comes down in the impression left by the forefoot. The stride places the footprints at from 17 to 35 inches apart. When the bighorn gallops, all four feet come down together. It can maintain a speed of 35 miles per hour for a short distance and in one bound can cover a distance of 17 feet. It can also leap safely from a vertical cliff 50 feet high.

## ENEMIES

Wolves and coyotes hunt the bighorn, but they are only successful at the points where the sheep cross over from one mountain range to another. They are much too slow to catch up with the sheep on the open range. The wolverine and cougar may get a few sheep by ambushing them in the cliffs and along the rimrocks. In years when the population of snowshoe rabbits is at low ebb, the lynx and bobcat will attack and kill lambs, yearlings, and some ewes. Golden eagles, it is claimed, get a few lambs, but predators are not a serious menace to the mountain sheep population.

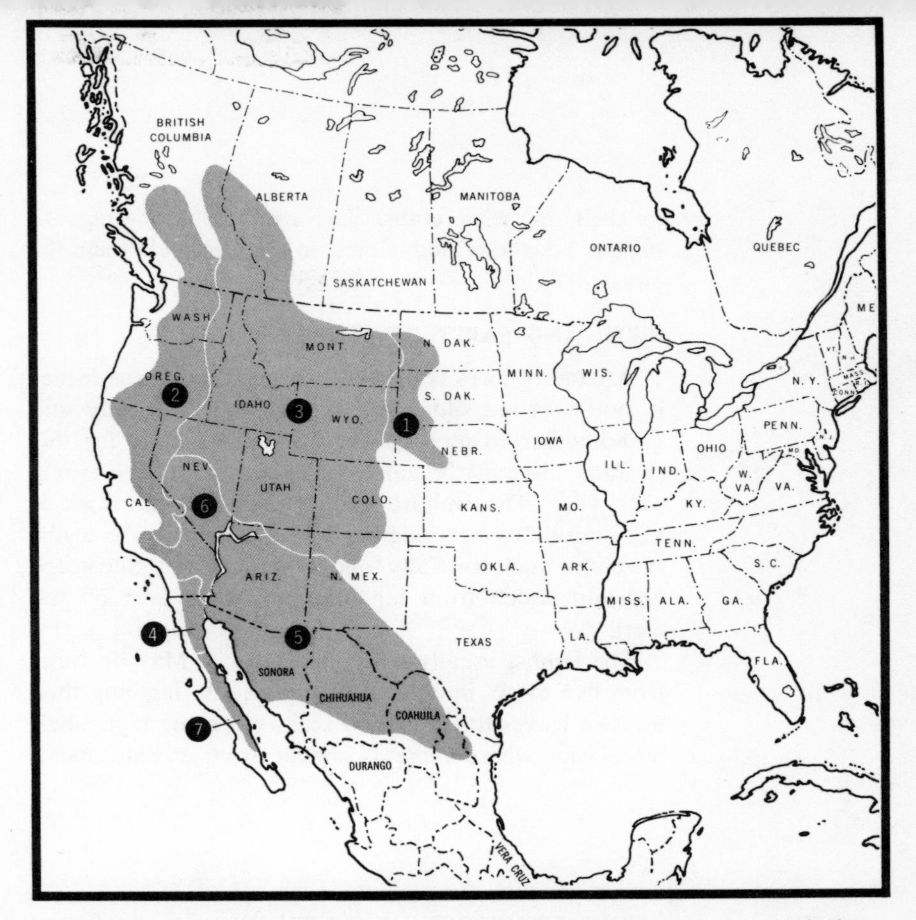


Distribution of the races of the bighorn *Ovis:* 1. Badlands bighorn, 2. Rimrock bighorn, 3. Rocky Mountain bighorn, 4. Lower California bighorn, 5. Mexican bighorn, 6. Nelson bighorn, 7. Weems desert bighorn.

## MATING

Mountain sheep are sociable and love the company of their kind. However, except for the short mating season, there is no mixing of the sexes. The rams keep together in bachelor groups of from three or four individuals up to twenty-five or more. Ewes are never tolerated or accepted in the bachelor bands. The ewes are more active than the rams and travel in larger herds or flocks along with the newborn and yearling lambs of both sexes. The mating season begins in December and is over early in January. In late autumn the rams get restless and at first playfully spar among themselves. By November the rams are beginning to round up little groups of ewes. Sometimes the competition becomes intense, the rams eye each other with hatred, and fierce, brutal battles are inevitable. In a typical rutting-season duel, two evenly matched rams face each other in silence, back off 20 feet or more, then charge with head lowered. Their 300 pounds of bone, muscle, and horn, empowered with a velocity of 20 miles per hour, meet with atom-smashing force, and the sound of the impact can be heard for 2 miles. How any creature can survive such punishment is a mystery, but the performance is repeated time and time again until weight plus endurance eventually decide the conflict. For this purpose and for this purpose alone were the ram's mighty horns developed.

With the first of January, peace is once more restored, the rams lose all interest in the ewes, and retreat to their bachelor clubs. The rams usually range at higher elevations and closer to the rimrock than the ewes.

**BIRTH AND EARLY DEVELOPMENT**

A band of ewes is usually a family affair. The leader is not a proud old ram, but a portly old lady and grandmother to most of the flock. To qualify for this position she must be still vital enough to raise a family each year. The welfare and guidance of the flock is left entirely to her judgment, and wherever she leads, the entire flock trustfully follows her as a unit. She keeps constant watch from high places and is ever on the alert.

The lambs, usually twins, are born in May or June, from five to six months after mating. At lambing time the ewe leaves the flock and seeks out some high, sheltered spot where there is shelter from storms and a view of all approaches to limit surprise attacks from predators. A ewe will remain here for some time without food or water. The newborn lamb is grayish-brown in color with a dark stripe down the back. A ewe licks her lamb from head to foot to clean and dry it; by this time it is ready to stagger to its feet and nurse For one week the ewe and her lambs stay in seclusion and then join the flock. By the time a lamb is a month old it is taking a substantial amount of green food, but it continues to nurse until the beginning of the winter. During resting periods, there are always at least two of the elders keeping constant watch. By the end of the fall, lambs are about three-quarters grown and weigh 80 pounds or more. The male lambs are not sexually mature until 3½ years of age; ewe lambs reach maturity at 2½ years. The average life span of a bighorn is ten or eleven years and a favored few may live to the grand old age of fourteen.

## Popular and Scientific Names of the Bighorn

**ORDER:** *Artiodactyla* **GENUS:** *Ovis*

**FAMILY:** *Bovidae* **SPECIES:** *canadensis*

**SUBSPECIES**

| | |
|---|---|
| Rocky Mountain bighorn | *Ovis canadensis canadensis* |
| Lower California bighorn | *Ovis canadensis cremnobates* |
| Mexican bighorn | *Ovis canadensis mexicana* |
| Nelson bighorn | *Ovis canadensis nelsoni* |
| Weems desert bighorn | *Ovis canadensis weemsi* |
| Badlands bighorn | *Ovis canadensis auduboni* |
| Rimrock bighorn | *Ovis canadensis californiana* |

CHAPTER 3

# THE ROCKY MOUNTAIN GOAT

I SAW my first Rocky Mountain goat in 1943 when Jack Holiday and I made a hunt along the backbone of the Canadian Rockies north of Jasper National Park in Alberta. We camped late one afternoon on the bank of the big Smoky River three days away from the railroad. As soon as we had stowed our duffel and rifles in our tent and had blown up our beds, Jack got out his big 10 x 50 Zeiss glasses, rested his back against a pack box, and started looking over the mountains across the river. Their gray and serrated ridges went above timberline, but their lower slopes were clad in thick dark spruce streaked by long, apple-green slides. In past springs, great masses of snow had broken loose and had swept down those steep slopes and cleared off the trees as if they had been matchsticks. In time, grass had come up on these smooth slopes, and these slides were excellent pastures for grizzlies in the early spring and for goats almost anytime.

"This," said Jack, "is goat country. I'll bet I'll show you a goat."

"Show me a goat then," I said.

"Here's one," he said presently. "It's right at the top of that middle slide and to the right just under the cliff."

I had noticed a fleck of white there, but it had been stationary and so very white that I'd thought it was a spot of snow. I swung my glass back to it and soon could see it move. Then we set up a 20X spotting scope, and there, sharp and clear in the cool, thin, evening air, was my first goat. Against the short grass he looked incredibly clean and white. I could see the shoulder hump, the head carried low, the short beard, the pantalet effect of the long hair on his legs, and the squarish, blocky-looking body.

A few minutes later we saw two more goats on another slide not far away, and others joined them until there were about fifteen, large and small. Then more put in their appearance until over thirty were scattered along the top of the slides under the rocky cliffs. Three or four were solitary old billies, but most were family groups of nannies and kids. Then, not far below one of the largest groups of goats, a great bull moose walked out of the heavy timber onto the slide. His black-brown body was as round and sleek and stuffed-looking as a sausage, and his recently cleaned horns looked almost as white as the goats.

As I watched the goats, my blood pressure went up by the minute. I knew it was the plan of Roy Hargreaves, our outfitter, to travel fast for two more days, then make camp and hunt bighorn sheep. At the time I had never shot a Rocky Mountain bighorn, but neither had I shot a goat. It struck me that a goat in the hand was worth two or three bighorn rams on some as-yet-unseen mountain.

"What do you say we stay here and hunt goats a couple of days?" I asked Roy.

"Nothing doing," Roy said shortly. "I want to get those rams behind us. Nothing to getting a goat. You'll see the things by the thousands. We'll knock one over when we don't have anything better to do."

When we hit the trail the next morning, the goats were back at their dinner table—big goats, medium-size goats, and little goats. I hated to leave them, and Roy apparently read my mind. "That mountain's no good," he told me. "There are a few moose and an odd grizzly there, but mostly nothing but those damned goats. You'll get so tired of seeing goats you won't pay any attention to them."

And we did see a lot of goats. If we didn't see them by the thousands, we at least saw them by the hundreds. At one camp, by the banks of the Muddywater River, I could always see somewhere between fifty and one hundred goats on a hill less than a mile away. Almost anywhere we hunted, a few minutes' work with binoculars would produce from two or three to a couple of dozen goats.

I didn't realize it at the time, but I was then in some of the finest white-goat country in the world. We were hunting along the British Columbia-Alberta border, and the goat is primarily a British Columbia animal. There are goats in the mountains along the mainland of the Alaska Panhandle, in the Kenai Peninsula of Alaska, a few in the Yukon, some in Washington, Montana, and Idaho, and, as we have seen, in the Alberta Rockies. I understand that a few have recently been planted in Colorado, and some that escaped over a score of years ago from a roadside zoo are doing well in the Black Hills of South Dakota.

It has been estimated that one quarter of the goat population is in the Rockies and 95 per cent of all goats range in Canada. However, there are goats in the Cascades, the Selkirks, the Coast Range, and the Bitterroots. I have seen goats a few hundred feet above tidewater in the Alaska Panhandle and at over 10,000 feet elevation in the rugged mountains above the Middle Fork of the Salmon River in Idaho, the southern tip of the goat range in North America. And as odd as it may sound, I saw the carcasses of winter-killed goats right on the beach up there in Alaska.

Mostly the goat occupies high and rugged country too rough and too far from civilization to be of economic use, and in the winter in many areas instead of coming low, as sheep often do, he stays up on the high ridges where the wind sweeps the snow off. As a consequence, goats are about as plentiful as they ever were.

They are found in huntable numbers in Idaho, Montana, and Washington, in Alaska, in the Alberta Rockies, and in a few places in the Yukon as well as in British Columbia. For whatever the reason, they cling to the coastal mountains as they go north. There are none in interior Alaska and very few on the west side of the Rockies in northern British Columbia, but there are many on the east side in the famous Cassiar district. I have made half a dozen long hunting trips in the Yukon, but I have never seen a goat in the territory, and on a forty-five-day trip into the Muskwa-Prophet River country of northern British Columbia I saw hundreds of Stone sheep but not over a dozen goats.

Except in areas close to roads, hunting has little if any effect on goat numbers, and goat populations are pretty well stabilized wherever the animals are found. In 1925 it was estimated that there were about 15,000 goats in the United States, and it is believed that there are about that many today. A study in Jasper National Park showed that goat numbers remained about the same in spite of the fact that there was no hunting and limited predation. Goats long ago filled up the suitable country, and from then on their numbers have remained about the same. A rough estimate puts somewhere between 3,000 and 4,000 goats in Idaho and something over 5,000 both in Montana and Washington.

It is often said that goats and sheep are never found on the same mountain, but that is not true. I have seen bighorn sheep and goats on the same mountains in Alberta and British Columbia, and one time I had an opportunity to shoot both a sheep and goat without moving out of my tracks. In 1951 my son Bradford shot a Stone ram and a goat on the same mountain in the northern Cassiar, and on several occasions I had sheep and goats in the field of my binoculars at the same time.

However, goats seem to like a wetter and rockier country than sheep. Because of their wonderfully warm, thick coats, heavy rain generally does not seem to bother them. Indeed, the Alaska Panhandle, where they are found in good numbers, is one of the wettest portions of the globe. Sheep as a rule like to feed in high alpine pastures with rocks and cliffs nearby for protection against wolves, but goats will stay in rough country where there is little of the grass that sheep love.

It is often said that the Rocky Mountain goat is not a goat at all but an antelope. It is true that he does not belong to the tribe of long-horned goats such as the ibex and the markhor. Instead he

Standing on the guide's shoulders, O'Connor aimed at the billy perched far up on the canyon's steep side.

belongs to the subfamily of short-horned goats—*Rupicaprinae*—and is related to the chamois of Europe and the serows, gorals, and takins of Asia. The little Indian serow, which can be seen now and then in zoos, looks just like a small and dingy edition of the North American white goat.

The mountain goat is one of the few large animals in the world that is pure white the year around. Others are the Dall sheep and the polar bear. His coat is long, soft, luxurious in the fall and winter, but he sheds in the spring, and a goat seen in the late spring or early summer has an oddly skinny look, like a bird dog that has just been clipped so he won't collect cockleburs.

His eyes are straw color, and his horns short, black, slightly curved, and as sharp as needles. Both sexes are horned, and often the nannies grow longer horns than the billies. Horns of the males are heavier, however. There is less variation in the horns of goats than there is in any other animal I know, and there is little difference between just an ordinary trophy billy and a record. I have never shot anything better than a fair-to-middling trophy goat. My best head is 9¾ inches around the curve. The world record is only 12. Goat heads are very difficult to judge, and it isn't even easy to tell a nannie from a billy. In the fall hunting season, if I see an adult goat with other goats I conclude it is a nannie. If it is alone I guess that it is a billy. Generally goats of either sex can be taken, with the result that many small goat heads are brought home by sportsmen. I have seen many goat heads pictured or proudly mounted that are from immature animals and wouldn't go over five or six inches. I'd say that any goat with a horn length under nine inches should not be shot. The best way I know of for the beginning goat hunter to guess about goats is to assume that any goats in a herd are females or immature males, and that the old billies are solitary.

Like the mountain sheep, the goat puts a ring on his horns every year, and consequently the age of an animal is easy to tell. A billy, like a ram, is old at eleven and seldom lives longer than thirteen. Apparently the nannies have, for some reason, a higher rate of survival than the billies, as under wilderness conditions there are usually a few more old nannies than billies in a stretch of country.

The goat is a solidly built animal. For his size, his bones are heavy. His hoofs are large and squarish, and his tracks can be told from sheep or deer tracks at a glance. Because he has to travel on narrow ledges, he is somewhat slab-sided, but he is deep through the chest. A big billy in his late fall coat will measure from the top of the hairline on the hump to the bottom of the hair on his brisket almost as much as a fair-size elk.

I have never weighed a goat, but I'd guess that the average big billy would field dress somewhere around 200 pounds, with some very large and fat ones dressing out at around 300. One shot in British Columbia weighed, as it fell, 276 pounds. Another field dressed at 225, and a very large one shot in southeast Alaska is supposed to have weighed 502.

What looked to me like the largest goat I ever saw was an old billy I got the glasses on in Idaho. I had gone with two friends into the Middle Fork of the Salmon River in central Idaho. They had sheep permits and were hunting bighorn rams, but I had not drawn one and was simply along for the ride. On our first day in camp I went out with only a pair of binoculars to see if I could locate some rams.

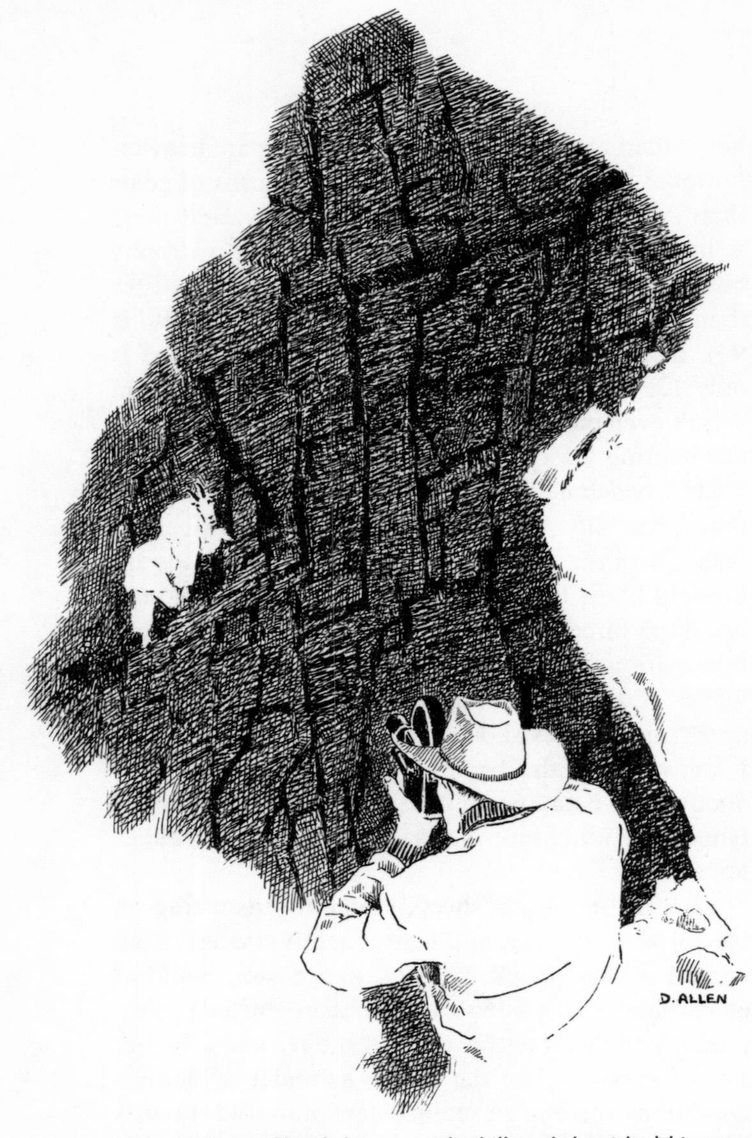


While O'Connor filmed the scene, the billy calmly picked his way up the almost vertical cliff.

I found some ewes and lambs, a couple of immature rams, and an enormous billy. The goat was so large that I sneaked up to within 250 yards of him, and the closer I got the bigger he looked. Compared with the 9½- and 9¾-inch goat heads with which I am familiar, the horns of this old billy seemed much longer, and I could estimate that they went over 11 inches. He was not only the largest goat I have ever seen but the dirtiest. He lay in a dusty wallow under a rimrock right at the head of a sharp, steep canyon. None of us had goat permits, and we didn't bother him. I saw him the next day, and I don't think he moved 100 yards from his bed. I suspect that there are many very large billies in Idaho as all the Idaho heads I have seen have been well above average.

No two animals could be much more different than the Rocky Mountain goat and the wild sheep. The sheep is a wary, nervous, high-strung animal, swift of foot and agile, a jumper and bounder. The goat is a slow, careful, phlegmatic animal that seldom travels faster than a sedate walk.

However, the goat can get over country in which a ram would break his neck. Many times I have seen goats on cliffs so sheer that they looked to me to be pasted against them. Even when a goat is being shot at, he takes his time, climbing slowly and deliberately, testing each foothold before he puts all his weight on it. He will stand up on his hind legs, put his front feet over a narrow ledge as high as he can reach, and then muscle himself up like a man. The only other animal I have seen that I thought was a better mountaineer than the white goat is the ibex of Asia—and the ibex can go anywhere a goat can go and get there ten times faster.

The goat is primarily a trophy animal. I have heard that the meat of the kids is not bad, but I can testify that the flesh of the old billies is so tough that it would break the jaws of a crocodile. When I shot my first billy I expressed a desire to eat some of the meat. My guide looked at me as if I had lost my mind. "Eat that damned old billy?" he asked. "I'd sooner eat skunk. If you want some of it, cut it off and take it back to camp. For my part, I want none of it."

So I cut out the backstraps and gave them to the cook. The meat was as tough as an inner tube, and I wound up giving what was left to Tango, the camp dog.

Except that he is apt to live in very tough and rugged country, the goat has never struck me as being difficult to hunt. When he lies down, he generally finds a spot that will give him a view of a wide piece of country, and there he stays, drowsing through the day and looking things over. He seems to expect enemies from below, and, unlike the sheep, he never seems to get up and look over the country behind him.

The fact that billies are generally solitary during the fall hunting season and that the hunter has only one pair of eyes to guard against, also makes him easy to hunt. Actually, an old billy probably does not have many natural enemies. He usually dwells far above the scourge of the north, the timber wolf —which is primarily a killer of moose and caribou— and I don't think that even a grizzly would care to tangle with a goat's sharp horns. In the southern part of the goat's range, mountain lions probably kill goats now and then, but there would be no particular reason for them to do so as they have access to the much more succulent sheep and more numerous deer. Eagles occasionally kill kids, and so do coyotes, but for the most part predation does not seem to be much of a goat problem.

The tough thing about goat hunting is the climbing, and in some areas the country can be so difficult that the goat hunter risks serious injury. This is not always true, however, as I have seen places where a hunter could ride a horse up to the edge of a cliff and shoot goats below him. I have also seen goats along the walls of dinky little canyons where they could be stalked by a leisurely stroll from below along the bank of a creek. The toughest goat country I have ever seen is in the Middle Fork country of Idaho's Salmon River, but there is a lot of goat country I haven't seen.

I shot my first goat in Alberta in 1943. On that trip I saw at least 1,000 goats, but until I had been out a couple of weeks I did not go after one. Roy Hargreaves and I glassed this big lone billy from the bottom of Copton Creek, 2,000 feet below. He was lying in the sun on a little patch of grass about 500 feet above a narrow, steep-walled, side canyon. We decided that we could work up the canyon out of sight, then climb until we were about on a level with the billy and let him have it.

But we had made our plans without taking into consideration a colony of hoary marmots on the opposite side of the canyon. No sooner had we started up than they began to whistle. We couldn't make much time, as the sides of the canyon were almost straight up and down, and we could climb only by holding onto tiny dwarf firs that grew out of the rocks and pulling ourselves up hand over hand. The more noise the whistlers made, the more nervous I got. Now and then I could put myself in a position where I could take a quick peek at the billy far above me. First his ears began to twitch. Then, still lying there, he began to look around. Finally he got apprehensive enough to get to his feet.

"The son of a gun is going to move off," Roy Hargreaves said. "Can you kill him from here?"

He was a long way off, mostly up, but I told Roy I thought I could.

"Well, kill him dead," he cautioned me. "If he ever starts rolling he'll wind up in the bottom of the canyon and he'll bust his horns off."

Then I found that every time I let go the shrubs by which I had been pulling myself up, I started to slide down. But Roy managed to get one foot on a ledge, another firm against a dwarf alpine fir, and I stood on his shoulders. The position wasn't very steady, but it was then or never.

My first shot was high and just creased the billy, sending a shower of long white hair 20 feet in the air. My second wobbly let-off put the bullet a bit far back, but my third was right through the heart, and the billy sank down in his tracks,

One of the major hazards of goat hunting is the danger the goat may fall and break his horns. Many goat hunters have shot their billies only to find that all they had to show for their efforts was a bloody and battered carcass with no horns whatsoever.

Once when I was hunting in British Columbia, my guide and I spotted a fine billy lying on a ledge far above us. The terrain was such that we could work around to our left out of sight and end up on what looked like a fairly wide ledge across a straight up-and-down canyon from the billy. It was a long and laborious climb, but we finally made it. I edged around a little point and there the billy lay, not over 60 yards away. The ledge on which he had been lying was not over a foot wide, and I saw that if I shot him he'd fall over 1,000 feet. My guide had my movie camera in his rucksack. So I passed him my rifle, took the movie camera, and started shooting. The goat looked me over for a few seconds, then began climbing straight up. The cliff looked to be almost perpendicular, but that didn't bother the billy. While the camera rolled, he worked his way calmly up that cliff and over the top. When he had finally made it, he turned around and looked at me calmly for a moment or two, his chin whiskers waving in the breeze. Then he turned and walked off as if he had all the time in the world.

Goats breed in late November and early December. After a gestation period of six months, the young are born in May. Singles are the rule, but some twins are born. The billies are polygamous, but not to the same extent as the ardent mountain sheep, and the males seldom battle the way mountain sheep do. That is fortunate, as the billies, with their sharp horns, have far more dangerous armament.

Apparently billies get restless as the mating season approaches. When I was hunting in the northern Cassiar section of British Columbia in 1951, all the old billies were traveling. We would see nannies and kids day after day in the same location, but the billies were constantly on the move. They might stop to feed and rest for an hour or so, but they never stayed in the same place long. Big, lone goats were constantly popping up in new and unexpected places. One day while I was sitting on a rocky mountainside, I saw an old billy come off a rocky hill, cross a wide willow-filled valley, and climb another hill. I have seen this same pre-rut restlessness in caribou and mountain sheep.

It was on that same trip that my son Bradford, then eighteen years old, intercepted and shot a traveling billy. A few days before he had killed a Stone ram on the same mountain. We had been all over it and had not even seen a goat track. Then late one afternoon, after we had put in a tough day hunting sheep on another mountain, we got back to our little jack camp to rest our weary bones and prepare a leisurely supper. Suddenly, about a mile away on a steep and boulder-strewn hillside, I made out a moving fleck of white. I grabbed my binoculars and saw it was a traveling billy.

Our Indian guide, Bradford, and I quickly threw our saddles on our weary and protesting horses and took off toward the mountain. When the going got tough, we tied them to some willows and began our climb on foot. The boulders on that steep hillside ranged from stones as big as baseballs to great chunks as large as small houses. Between them were little patches of soil where grass, moss, and lichens grew. We stole quietly along the mountainside at the level at which we had seen the goat, but we did not find him. But we found his tracks leading into the jungle of boulders in the saddle to the south. We went back to the saddle at the north to see if he had come out. No tracks did we find, so that goat had to be in that great pile of boulders somewhere, a hillside perhaps 1,500 feet high and half a mile wide.

This time we crossed the boulder field somewhat higher. We were about halfway over when the goat suddenly stood up, about 200 yards away and something like 300 feet above us. Brad sat down and went into action. His feet were almost as high as his head, and every time his .270 went off it would kick him so that he lay flat on his back for an instant. His first shots were around the edges, but he finally managed to get one just behind the shoulder and the billy was his—a fine, big, fat fellow with 9½-inch horns.

Among many mountain hunters, the goat has a reputation of being almost as hard to kill with one shot as a grizzly. His hide is thick and his hair long. Bullets have a tendency to open up prematurely on goats, and the phlegmatic nature of the animal makes him almost impervious to shock. The hunter either has to put that first bullet just right or keep shooting. If he isn't hit in a vital spot, a goat will walk on as if nothing has happened, and even with a perfectly placed shot right behind the shoulder—a shot that would kill a sheep or a mule deer in his tracks—a billy will have enough life left to stagger to the edge of a precipice and fall over to break his horns and make recovery of the carcass difficult.

The only animal I've ever wounded and lost in Canada was a billy. He was about 300 yards away and a bit above me. I had a fine shot from the prone position, but the bullet—a 160-grain in the .270—struck a bit too far back, just forward of the diaphragm. The goat flinched and began walking off, and I could see a spreading circle of red against the white fleece.

I worked the bolt of my rifle, but only the head of the case came out. The rest of the case was stuck in the chamber—an example of the danger of full-length resizing of cartridge cases too often. Because it is against the law for Alberta guides to carry rifles, we were helpless. When I told my guide what had happened he shook his head. "You're lucky it wasn't a grizzly," he told me. "If it had been, we'd both be dead men."

The goat walked slowly for about half a mile, and the last time we saw him he was standing on a ledge with his head down and very sick. When we came back the next day with my spare rifle to see what had happened to him, we found that he had fallen off the ledge and his crushed and battered body lay far below.

He's a great animal, this patriarch of the cliffs and canyons, a trophy unique in the world, and one that should be hunted more than he is. With his little dagger-sharp horns, he isn't as spectacular a trophy as the wild ram, but anyone who has collected a goat has generally put out some work to do so—and he has done it in some of the most beautiful and spectacular country on the globe.

# The Natural History of the Rocky Mountain Goat

[OREAMNOS AMERICANUS]

### DESCRIPTION

Except for its polished black horns and black hoofs, the Rocky Mountain goat is snow-white mixed with a slightly yellowish color. Larger than the average domestic goat, it has a short body humped at the shoulders, and a comparatively long, narrow head. Both sexes have a pair of small, slender, spiked horns placed well back on the head and curving slightly backward. The horns, which are more slender in females than in males, are horny sheaths which grow over a bony core attached to the skull and are never shed. Both sexes also have a tuft of long hair hanging from the chin.

Long legs terminate in evenly paired hoofs and well-developed dewclaws. The soles of the hoofs are cushioned with rubber-like pads which give the animal a suction grip for sure footing on rocks.

The mountain goat is clothed in a coat of shaggy, long, white hair and an under coat of soft wool that is as fine and delicate as cashmere and three to four inches long. During the warm summer days of June, the goat sheds its coat, which may be found draped on bushes and strewn over the ground.

A full-grown male mountain goat measures from 60 to 70 inches long, stands from 35 to 40 inches high at the shoulder, and weighs from 150 to 300 pounds. Females average about fifteen per cent smaller than males. The horns of an average male are about nine inches long, running up to twelve inches for large individuals, with a horn spread of about ten inches.

A member of the even-toed ungulates, order *Artiodactyla,* and included in the family *Bovidae,* or hollow-horned ungulates, the mountain goat is a typical ruminant, or cud-chewing, mammal. It has no teeth at the front of the upper jaw, but it has sharp-edged ones in the lower jaw and flat-crowned molar teeth in both jaws. Food, which is ripped off by running the tongue across the lower front teeth, is partly chewed and swallowed, and temporarily stored in the paunch, or first stomach, where it is mixed with gastric juices. Later, when the animal is resting, the contents of the paunch is returned to the mouth in the form of small pellets to be thoroughly milled. The cud now bypasses the first stomach and is passed on to the second and third stomachs for further processing and digestion.

### ORIGIN

Without known ancestors prior to the Pleistocene era, the Rocky Mountain goat somehow managed to survive the great flow of ice during the glacial age. Perhaps it sought refuge on the upper mountain ridges and peaks while the creeping glaciers spread out below some 600,000 years ago and covered a large part of the Northern Hemisphere. No trace of the Rocky Mountain goat has so far been found in all of Asia or Europe, yet there is a probability that it is of Asiatic stock and migrated across the land bridge joining Asia to America during the Mid-Pleistocene era.

The Rocky Mountain goat is not closely related to any other form of ungulate in America except perhaps the muskox. In fact, it is not even a goat but an offshoot of an ancestral stem of the antelopes. The closest living relatives to our mountain goat-antelope are the goral and serow of Asia and the better-known chamois of Europe. Living as it does on the highest peaks of the northern Rocky Mountain ranges, the mountain goat escaped the attention of the white man until 150 years ago. In 1811 Alexander Henry reported that large white goats were numerous on the Great Divide near the Natural Boundary. Henry's record was not accepted without some skepticism. However, it was not until sixty-eight years later, in 1879, that J. C. Merrill gave a full report on the animal as it existed in the mountains of Missoula, Montana, and thus definitely put the Rocky Mountain goat on the roster of modern big game of North America.

## RANGE

The Rocky Mountain goat is restricted to the high mountain ranges of northwestern North America. From Idaho and Montana and the Cascade Mountains of southern Washington, the range extends north to Alaska in the region of the Copper River. By choice it lives in the Arctic Zone where naked, jagged cliffs and desolate rocky mountain peaks tower above timberline. No stormy blasts or blustering snowstorms of winter can drive this rugged mountaineer down to the friendly shelter of the timber. This does not necessarily imply, however, that it never enters the upper reaches of the tree growth; when traveling from one mountain ridge to another the mountain goat often descends to the bottom of deep valleys and passes through forest growth, but it does not linger there for long.

There are four races of Rocky Mountain goats now recognized: The Cascade Mountain goat, found in the Cascade Mountains of Washington and formerly abundant in Oregon, is a medium-sized form, 41 inches high at the shoulder. The Columbian mountain goat, found in the mountains of British Columbia, is a large form with a narrow skull, standing 43 inches high at the shoulder. The Montana mountain goat, found in the mountains of Montana and Idaho, is the smallest of the known forms and has a relatively narrow skull. The Alaska mountain goat, found in the mountains near the mouth of the Copper River in Alaska, is similar to the Cascade, but its horns are more widespread at the base.

## HABITS

There is no doubt about the Rocky Mountain goat's love of company. Females with kids and yearling males associate in herds of twenty to thirty individuals; full-grown males usually associate in pairs or groups of three and four. The full-grown males have a home territory usually covering not more than 2 or 3 miles. They rest on the high, rocky ledges and move down to green slopes to feed. The larger herds of females must travel farther afield to find sufficient fodder.

The mountain goat can subsist on a minimum of food as indeed it must at times. During the winter months it depends on the twigs of a few frozen bushes and dried grasses exposed by shifting winds. The summer fare is much better—fresh green grasses, herbaceous plants and banks of flowers that flourish in little meadows between the rocky crags and broken cliffs.

The tracks of the mountain goat walking in snow resemble those of the bighorn sheep; the toes spread evenly on the solid ground and the lateral hoofs do not register.

The mountain goat's sharply pointed black horns curve backward, and the glands are located right behind the base of the horns.

Perhaps the most sure-footed of all the mountain climbers, the Rocky Mountain goat keeps a cool head and never hurries. It moves at a deliberate, confident pace, following narrow, treacherous trails, scaling the faces of almost sheer cliffs to dizzy heights. Occasionally a goat will follow a narrow ledge that peters out and is seemingly too narrow for any four-footed animal to make a turn. Calmly and without panic, the goat rears up on its hind legs and, facing the wall of the cliff, makes a complete turn. It complacently views the world beneath confident that no land-bound beast can follow. It can if necessary break into a rather slow, lumbering gallop and leap from ledge to ledge, covering a distance of 12 feet at a single bound. On level ground its speed has been checked at 20 miles per hour by an automobile speedometer. The soles of its hoofs are fashioned like rubber suction-cups which clamp on smooth rock surfaces so there is little or no chance of mishap. The mountain goat is a good swimmer and crosses large lakes when necessary. In the northern part of its range, especially in parts of Alaska, where the timber line edges downward to low elevations, the mountain goat may be found close to the coast.

## MATING

At a time when a man could scarcely survive in the bleak, cold mountains, the male goats meet in competition for possession of the females. No one has visited these broken crags and treacherous, mountain ledges in November to witness the challenging males, but as far as we know, the mountain goat is not especially aggressive during the rut. The males display some pugnacity, and rub their horns against rocks and shrubs, leaving an oily substance from a gland situated directly behind the horns. When contesting over females, they circle each other with a stiff-legged gait, sparring at intervals. A successful thrust of the dagger-like horns may find a vital spot and inflict a deep wound.

### BIRTH AND EARLY DEVELOPMENT

Some time between the end of April and the beginning of June, the female has a single kid. Occasionally twins occur, but they are unusual. The newborn kid comes into the world fully clothed in a beautiful, soft, snow-white robe which will keep it snug and warm despite the cold nights at high elevations. With eyes wide open from the very first, the kid is able to stand and take its first meal in a matter of minutes after birth. The mother follows the common ritual of the ungulates and licks her offspring from the tips of its toes to the crown of its head. A newborn kid measures about 12 inches high at the shoulder and weighs 6 or 7 pounds. Born in an isolated, sheltered spot some distance from the general herd, the kid spends its first few days in hiding. If danger threatens it will freeze flat on the ground, resembling a patch of snow. During these early days, the mother visits the nursery every two hours or so to nurse her kid, but never stays more than a few minutes. Later, the mother leads her offspring back to the herd, which includes other females and their kids, yearling males, and possibly an old billy or two. These herds may number up to twenty-five head or more.

### ENEMIES

Having sharp, far-seeing eyesight, a remarkably keen sense of smell, and well-developed hearing, the Rocky Mountain goat is not likely to be taken by surprise. Its four-footed foes are the grizzly and black bears, cougar, lynx, wolf, and wolverine. But given sufficient warning in its own domain on the narrow, precipitous trails of goatland, this sturdy hunchback can take care of itself. Normally, rather than fight, a goat prefers to seek safety in flight to the security of towering rocky pinnacles. However, when necessary it will not hesitate to meet an aggressor. Black bears and even grizzly bears have been mortally wounded by a goat's dagger-like horns. On a narrow trail one goat can guard a pass against an entire pack of hungry wolves. Fortunately, the predators know that the chances of catching a goat off guard are too slim to warrant the effort of climbing high mountain slopes. Only when the goat moves down to graze on the smooth, green pastures of mountain sides is it open to attack. A golden eagle will occasionally attack a small kid, but only when the mother is not close by. Even then, the kid's cries would bring such prompt action that the eagle would have difficulty escaping with its quarry.

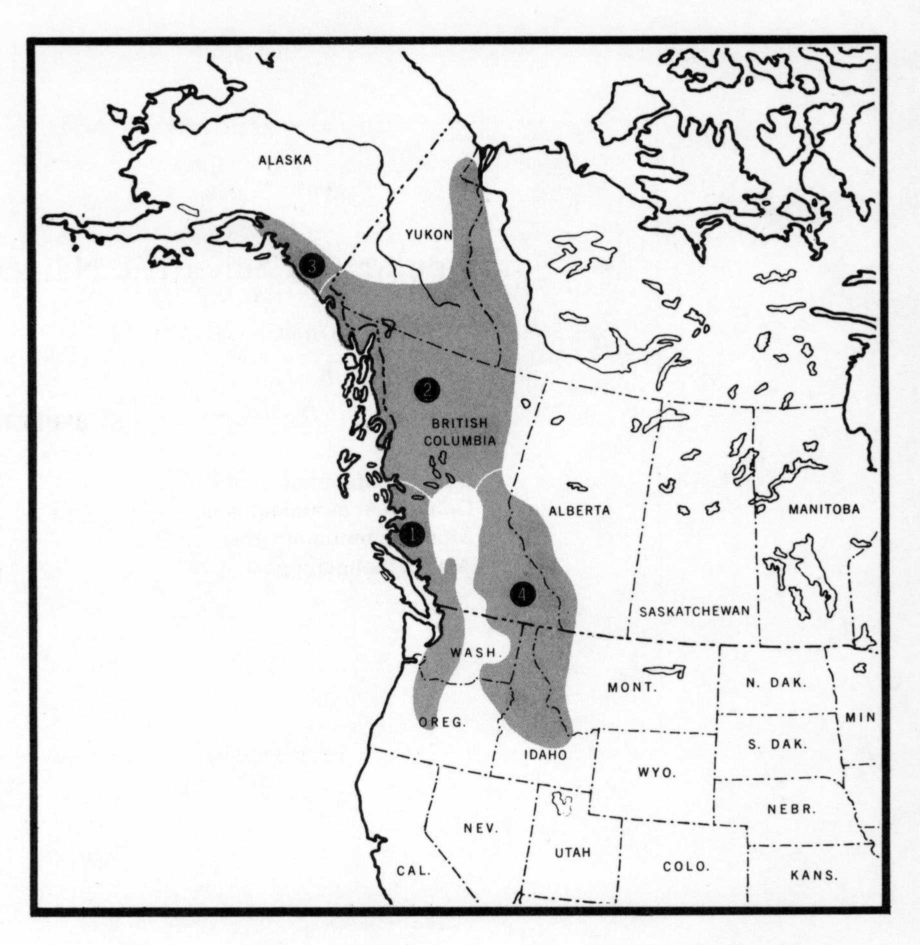


Distribution of the races of the Rocky Mountain goat *Oreamnos:* 1. Cascade Mountain goat, 2. Columbian mountain goat, 3. Alaska mountain goat, 4. Montana mountain goat.

The major enemy of the white goat is the avalanche, a constant danger in the spring and fall. Anything caught in the path of this irresistible force must perish. Winter snows, sometimes piled 20 feet deep at the mountain tops, may come roaring and crashing down to the valleys below; occasionally a whole forest of timber on a mountain side is flattened to the ground. The peaks of the avalanche seasons are in the fall, when an over-abundance of snow piles up in one spot and topples over, and again in the spring, when the sun's heat undermines the great masses of snow and starts a slide. To avoid these snowslides, the white goat lives among the high peaks in the spring and fall and shuns the ravines and canyons where it might get trapped. At the first sign of a rumble—the beginning of a crashing snowslide—the goat instantly begins to retreat upward and never pauses until it is well above the moving snow.

## Popular and Scientific Names of the Rocky Mountain Goat

**ORDER:** *Artiodactyla*

**FAMILY:** *Bovidae*

**GENUS:** *Oreamnos*

**SPECIES:** *americanus*

**SUBSPECIES**

| | |
|---|---|
| Cascade Mountain goat | *Oreamnos americanus americanus* |
| Columbian mountain goat | *Oreamnos americanus columbiae* |
| Montana mountain goat | *Oreamnos americanus missoulae* |
| Alaska mountain goat | *Oreamnos americanus kennedyi* |

CHAPTER 4

# THE PRONGHORN

OF ALL the odd and eccentric beasts that walk the face of this earth, the North American pronghorn antelope is one of the oddest. He has characteristics of many animals but is closely related to none, a creature unique in the animal kingdom.

His horns are branched like the antlers of the deer, and also like the deer he sheds them annually. But they are true horns, which are hair, and not antlers, which are bone. Like all horns, they grow over a core, but the antelope is the only animal in the world with branched horns and the only one that sheds the outer sheath. Like the females of the sheep and goat family, doe antelope are also horned, but their horns are small. Also like the sheep and goats, the pronghorn has a gall bladder, and like the giraffe he has no dewclaws. He is the only member of his family and is not even closely related to the antelope of the Old World.

Although popularly called the antelope in the United States, the name for this unique creature is not very well given, just as elk is not a particularly good name for the wapiti, lion for cougar, or moose for the animal which in Europe is called the elk.

An exceedingly adaptable creature, this antelope. As long as he has the food he likes, the snow doesn't lie too deep, and the country is open enough so he can spot his enemies and run away from them, climate doesn't seem to bother him. I have seen antelope above timberline at 11,000 feet in Wyoming, and within sight of the sea in northern Mexico. He can take temperatures from 130 above in the broiling summer desert of Sonora to 40 below in the Wyoming winters. And the more desolate and God-forsaken a country looks the better he seems to get along in it. He is a creature of the arid plains, the dry and empty coulees and arroyos, the waste places of the earth.

The early trappers and buffalo hunters of the West always referred to antelope as goats, and there is just about as much reason to call them goats as to call them antelope. A more distinctive name would be pronghorn, which is sometimes used, as well as pronghorn antelope. However, they are antelope in popular terminology, just as wapiti are elk, elk are moose, cougars are lions, and (in Mexico) jaguars are tigers.

Unlike the elk, the moose, the caribou, and the wild sheep—all of which originated in Asia and migrated to North America—the pronghorn is an American of ancient lineage. He is the last survivor of a group of animals to which he was related but which, for whatever the reasons, did not survive the climatic changes of the various geological eras. Bones of these other pronghorns have been dug up in many places in the West, and the animals varied considerably. Some were large, some small, some with one horn, some with four. Pronghorns of one sort or another have been around for millions of years.

The first glimpse most of us have of a herd of pronghorns is a series of white dots scattered at random on the slope of some hill a mile or so away. Because of this impression of white, I always think of an antelope as a white animal incidentally marked with brown, tan, and black. His rump patch is pure, glittering white, and so is his belly, his breast, and the inside of his legs. He has two white bars on his neck, and he is white at the base of his ears and on the inside of his neck. His saddle is a rich tan, but his horns, the bridge of his nose, and a patch under each ear are black. Yet, for an animal almost as conspicuously colored as a zebra, he is sometimes surprisingly hard to locate. The hair of his rump is erectile, and when he fluffs it out to warn other antelope of danger, he looks as if he had a white pillow tied to his behind.

The pronghorn is not a large animal. According to Arthur S. Einarsen in his book, *The Pronghorn Antelope,* the average bucks killed in Oregon over several seasons weighed 114 pounds, the heaviest going 138. Dressed weights, he says, went 20 per cent less. I have not hunted antelope in Oregon nor even seen an antelope in Oregon, but I have hunted them in Arizona, northern Mexico, and Wyoming. It is my distinct impression the antelope that inhabit a belt of high country running across central Arizona and New Mexico are a good deal larger than the Wyoming, and probably also the Oregon, pronghorn. It is not uncommon for an Arizona buck to weigh from 120 to 135 pounds field dressed. On the other hand, the antelope I have seen and shot in Sonora are even smaller than those in Wyoming.

The comeback of the pronghorn in the past thirty years or so has been one of the most encouraging and spectacular aspects of North American game conservation. When Americans first invaded the great plains they found antelope by the millions. In the early nineteen twenties a government survey showed fewer than 27,000 in the entire United States. Wyoming, with about 7,000, had the most antelope. Biologists found only 651 in Arizona and only 1,327 in the two Canadian provinces of Alberta and Saskatchewan.

There were many reasons for the decline of antelope. For one thing, much of their natural range on the great plains became farm country. For another, there was much meat hunting and little law enforcement. Many thousands of homesteaders took up 640-acre grazing homesteads in the antelope country, and before they starved out they tried to live off the pronghorn. When I lived in Flagstaff, Arizona, during the early nineteen thirties, old-timers told me that in spite of the fact there was no open season on antelope in the years between 1900 and 1917 they shot the pronghorns for meat at all seasons of the year.

But most important, in many areas, I believe, was the killing off of the buffalo herds. Before the great buffalo slaughter in the eighteen seventies, the millions of buffalo kept the grass down so the weeds and forbs on which antelope feed could grow. The antelope is a weed eater, a browser on sagebrush, bitter brush, and only incidentally a grass eater. In Einarsen's book, a graph shows that about 60 per cent of the Oregon antelope's food is composed of sagebrush, around 30 per cent of weeds and forbs, and less than 3 per cent of grass.

It is in such figures as these, I believe, that the answer to the spectacular decline of the pronghorn from the millions in the eighteen seventies to the thousands in the early nineteen twenties lies. As the herds of buffalo were killed off, the grasses grew unchecked, and the early cattlemen in Montana and Wyoming found seas of waving grass belly high to a horse, something that no one saw when the buffalo were present to graze it off. As the grasses grew, the plants on which the antelope fed were choked out and the antelope decreased in number. Not until cattle came in to eat down the grass so the antelope food could recover did the herds start to increase. Overstocking by cattle has turned the overgrazed and eroded range lands of Wyoming into an antelope paradise.

Some years ago, the Arizona game department acquired a portion of the wonderful Anderson Mesa antelope country south of Flagstaff. For years the country had been heavily grazed and browsed by both antelope and cattle. The sections that the game department owned were fenced off and cattle were excluded. For a time the antelope did well, but as the range recovered and grass grew thick and lush they did less well. Then they began to decline. In order to bring them back, the department was forced to bring in a herd of buffalo to keep the grass down.

The same thing happened to a Texan of my acquaintance. He put a small herd of antelope into a fenced pasture from which he had removed the cattle. In a few years he had a fine stand of grass, but his antelope were about gone. As curious as it may seem, the resurgence of the pronghorn in the West

Many an engineer will tell you that fleet-footed antelope can run a little faster than a freight train.

has gone hand in hand with overgrazing and abuse of the land by cattle. There is but little competition for food between pronghorns and cattle, as many studies have shown, but there is serious competition between antelope and domestic sheep. However, the numbers of sheep seem to be on the decline throughout the West.

Given good range conditions, the antelope is a tremendously prolific animal, as the does breed early and generally produce two fawns. In the Anderson Mesa area when the pronghorns were at their lowest ebb in 1923, biologists found only twenty-five antelope. Probably there weren't many more than one hundred. Yet when I moved to Flagstaff in 1931, there were estimated to be 4,500 antelope in the area, and they had become so plentiful that the junipers on their winter range, where they ranged when snow lay deep, were browsed off just about as high as an adult antelope could reach. In the trans-Pecos region of Texas there were only 692 antelope in 1924, over 7,000 in 1946. But Wyoming is the greatest of the antelope states. In the early nineteen twenties there were less than 7,000. By 1936 there were 33,500, by 1946 over 65,000, and today the herd is estimated to be around 100,000—this in spite of the fact that many thousands are taken annually by hunters.

In some of the better antelope areas of Wyoming, game is seen in numbers comparable to that of the plains of East Africa. In 1944 I hunted between Rawlins and Lander in what is known as the Red Desert, and I am quite sure I saw at least a thousand antelope a day. In 1950 when I hunted near Gillette in northeastern Wyoming, antelope were constantly in sight—a single here, a small herd there, a big herd in another direction. I do not see how I could have seen less than two thousand animals a day. In addition, I must have seen somewhere around a hundred deer a day, right out in the little coulees that cut through the antelope plains. To me, an old deer hunter, it was a surprising experience to see big, fat, buck mule deer burst out of a little patch of brush in a coulee and go trotting off through the low sagebrush of an open plain.

So famous has the antelope hunting of Wyoming become, and so sure is a hunter to get an antelope of some sort, that thousands of nonresident hunters come to the state each year from places as far apart as Pennsylvania and California. In many cases a Wyoming hunt for mule deer and antelope is the first shoot a man makes outside his own state. A Wyoming antelope license is only twenty-five dollars, and a deer license only twenty. No guides are required, and hunters can camp on a ranch or stay at tourist courts. It may cost more than a thousand dollars to shoot a grizzly bear or a mountain sheep, but antelope can be hunted for peanuts.

The antelope has two principal means of protection—his eyes and his legs. By preference he stays in open country where he can see his enemies a long way off and run away from them. It has often been said that the eyes of the mountain sheep are as good as human eyes aided by 8X binoculars. Those of antelope are just as good, if not better. I have spent much time hunting both wild sheep and antelope, and I think that, if anything, the pronghorn uses his eyes even better than the sheep.

This may be because, as a rule, antelope have more experience with hunters, or it may be that they have greater power to resolve stationary objects. A sheep is good at picking out moving objects, even at fantastic distances, but generally a stationary object doesn't mean much to him. I once sat on a big boulder about 15 feet from a feeding desert bighorn and it did not notice me at all for several minutes and did not run until I moved. But many times I have had antelope notice my head over a ridge half a mile away almost as soon as I stuck it over. An antelope may not know what a head is under those circumstances, but he knows it wasn't there the last time he looked.

And when the antelope sees something, he can really run away from it—and how! Antelope cannot only run fast, but they can run great distances. They love to run, and will run just fast enough to beat what they are racing. A cowboy will tell you that an antelope can run a little faster than a good horse, and a locomotive engineer will tell you that an antelope can run a little faster than a freight train. Many times drivers of automobiles have pulled alongside herds of running antelope and decided they were traveling just as fast as the antelope could go. Then the antelope have decided to put an end to the foolishness, have put on an extra burst of speed, and have passed in front of the car. It is also a common experience for someone to think an antelope is going flat out and then take a shot at him. Suddenly the antelope goes twice as fast.

Hundreds of observers will testify that whole herds will cruise for miles at 35 miles an hour with no show of fatigue, that whole herds can keep with a car traveling at 50, and that individual antelope have been clocked at 60 miles an hour or a little better.

In a herd of running antelope, the big old bucks are always at the tag end of the procession, yet they manage to keep up with a herd doing 50. I have often wondered just how fast a young, thoroughly frightened doe could travel on good ground. I'd like to bet that one could do 70. Explorers on the plains of central Asia have clocked gazelles at 60 or more, but I'd lay my money on the nose of an American pronghorn. I have chased African antelope in motor cars, but none of them have anything like the speed of the pronghorn. He's probably the world's fastest animal.

One approach is to walk at right angles to a buck until you are hidden by a tree, then run directly toward it for a closer shot.

The good head of a big, mature buck antelope is an excellent trophy, and I think anyone hunting pronghorns for the first time is justified in working hard for one. It is no trick to tell bucks from does, as the bucks are larger, appear generally darker, and their pronged, beetlelike black horns are unmistakable. The horns of the bucks vary enormously. Sometimes the hooks at the top of the horns curve in together. Sometimes they curve to the front or back. It is not uncommon to see heads with horns that project almost straight out to the sides, or even grow forward at an angle of about forty-five degrees. The best heads are massive, with well-developed prongs and well-curved tips. A good way to estimate the length of the horn is to compare it with the length of the head. If the horn appears to be as long as the head from the back of the skull to the nose, it is an exceedingly good one. If it looks longer, it is probably of the highest class.

The largest heads I've ever seen were on Anderson Mesa in Arizona back in the days before the season was opened. The country was full of wonderful bucks about to die of old age, and some of the heads I saw would make a trophy hunter drool. One old boy I glassed many times had horns about 1½ times the length of his head. They were well curved and had massive prongs. If that head didn't go 22 or 23 inches, then I am no judge of antelope heads. He was so old and stiff he couldn't run very fast, and he didn't survive the winter. I offered to take a game warden to him so that his head could be collected and preserved for posterity, but I had no luck.

If I were looking for an antelope head of the very highest class I would concentrate my efforts in Arizona. I have seen more big heads there than anywhere else, and as a matter of fact the first two heads in the world records are Arizona heads. The number five head is also an Arizona head. Three out of five of the great heads of all time are from Arizona, and not one antelope has been shot there in the past twenty years where one hundred have been shot in Wyoming. Why no truly great heads from New Mexico are recorded I cannot fathom, as the animals there are the same breed as those in Arizona, and I have seen some beauties.

For the man who wants a nice trophy but not

O'Connor likes to use a rest for long shots at eagle-eyed pronghorns; often uses his hat for the purpose.

necessarily anything in the record class, a head that goes 14 inches or a bit over around the curve does very well. Anything over 15 is good, and the head that is massive, has a well-developed prong, and goes much over 16 is in the record class. A massive head that measures 17 inches or over is the prize of a lifetime. The most beautiful antelope head I have ever seen was shot by my wife on Anderson Mesa. It was very massive and handsomely shaped. The horns were almost 17 inches around the curve and had beautiful prongs with tips that were as translucent as plastic.

Antelope are hunted in many ways and by all kinds and conditions of hunters. One of the least sporting and generally illegal methods is chasing the animals by automobile and pouring the lead into a fleeing herd from the moving vehicle. I have even heard of people who chase the animals in a small plane and shoot at them with buckshot. Not much better is the common practice of putting on a burst of speed in an automobile, getting as close to a herd as possible, and then jumping out to shoot promiscuously at running animals. It is perfectly legitimate to cruise around antelope country, to get out, and to take a good shot if it's offered, but chasing animals and shooting from a moving car is bad business.

The most sporting way is to locate a wanted animal, then to make a long stalk and a clean, quick kill. On perfectly flat plains this stalking takes a lot of doing, but in most antelope areas the country is cut with draws and coulees so an approach out of sight can be made, or it is rolling enough so that the hunter is able to approach behind a fold in the ground. In some areas antelope are found where there is scattered timber that will give the hunter some cover. One successful method of approach is for the hunter to walk at right angles to a buck until he is protected by a tall brush or tree and then cut directly toward the antelope and run like the devil. Generally the antelope will wait for him to come out from behind the tree, and the hunter thus gets close enough for a shot.

It is my experience that antelope are killed at the longest range of any North American big game. I have made a few long shots at sheep, but most of the rams I have taken have been shot at less than 200 yards. I would guess, though, that the average range at which I have taken antelope has been something over 300 yards. Before several witnesses I once shot an antelope at just under 500 yards, and without witnesses I killed another at about the same distance. Let's forget the antelope I have missed clean out there at a quarter of a mile or more because I didn't guess the range right.

Once the hunter gets it through his head that antelope move fast and have to be led a lot, the running animals are not too hard to hit. They have a smooth, level run, as compared with the bouncing gate of mule deer. As in any running shooting the secret is to swing the rifle, get well ahead, and let off the shot without slowing or stopping the swing. A running antelope is as hard to hit with a stationary rifle as a duck with a stationary shotgun. The best shot I believe I have ever made on a running antelope was in Wyoming several years ago when I was out with Fred Huntington, the loading-tool manufacturer. I killed the buck with my first shot at 285 paces. My rifle was moving, and if I remember correctly the intersection of the crosswires was 2½ lengths in front of the animal's chest. Luck was with me, and I nailed the buck right behind the shoulder with my first shot.

Most hunters with experience and good equipment will have their best luck and make more clean kills by getting into a good solid position with a rest, if possible, and then shooting at a standing antelope. Varmint hunters who knock off woodchucks at 300 yards won't find it difficult to hit antelope at 400.

Very often the bucks with the best heads are the old ones that have been run out of the herds. Because they only have one pair of eyes they are easier to stalk than a herd. Most solitary old bucks feel fairly safe if they have 400 yards or so between themselves and the hunter, and even if they see the hunter during the last stage of his stalk they often stand and watch him, ready to take off if he gets much closer.

This habit generally gives the hunter time to get into a good position and take a deliberate shot. If I can, I like to take a rest and shoot from prone. And often I have laid down jackets and 10-gallon hats over stones and over clumps of Wyoming's ever-present sagebrush.

It is easy to misjudge the range when shooting antelope. On overcast days, the colors of a buck show up less plainly, and the antelope looks farther away than he really is. On bright days, the buck glistens, stands out against the background, and seems closer. When the hunter has crawled up over flat country with his eyes close to the ground, range judgment is very difficult. Animals seen at a sharp angle from above or below always appear smaller and farther away.

For this reason, a range-finder reticule of some sort is a good idea—a four-minute dot or the Weaver range-finder reticule with the crosswires six minutes of angle apart.

The flattest-shooting load in the hunter's favorite rifle is the one to use—the 150-grain bullet in the .300 Savage, the .308, the .300 Magnum, the 130-grain bullet in the .270, the 125-grain in the .280, the 130- and 140-grain bullets in the 7 mm. With proper bullets and loads the various .24 and .25 calibers make excellent antelope medicine. Because shots are generally long, antelope shooting is the only type of American hunting that I think justifies a scope of more than 4X. Many antelope hunters use 6X and even 8X scopes.

Because antelope are fragile, thin-shelled creatures, best bullets to use are those which open up rapidly against light resistance. Tough, heavy bullets of the controlled-expanding type will often go right through an antelope's chest cavity without knocking him down, allowing him to run a considerable distance before he falls.

The antelope is a nervous, highstrung creature. If he is taken unawares with a well-placed shot, he's quite easy to kill. But if he is thoroughly scared and hit in a nonvital area he is difficult to bring down.

I once shot the bottom of a buck's heart off and he ran about a quarter of a mile before he fell. Another time I took a running shot at an antelope skimming over a ridge, and he ran at least 300 yards with his stomach and intestines shot away. The well-placed first shot is the answer.

There isn't too much meat on the average antelope, but it's good meat. A rutting buck has a strong, musty odor that persists even for months after a mounted head is received from the taxidermist. But if the animal is properly handled, skinned quickly, and cooled, even a rank, rutting buck has surprisingly little wild taste. Antelope are seldom fat, but fat or lean they are fine eating.

The pronghorn antelope should be with us as long as we want him badly enough to give him a little protection. There will always be vast, empty spaces of cattle country suitable for the antelope in the West. Bad storms like the great one of 1948-49 may thin them out now and then, but with their tremendous breeding potential they always bounce back. At one time coyotes were a serious predator on antelope, but that terrible poison 1080 has so thinned out the little prairie wolves that nowadays they seldom take the fawns in the spring and the cold-weakened adults in the winter. The only real antelope predator is man, and an antelope hunt is a poor man's safari, the only chance for real plains hunting there is in North America these days. And this poor man's safari is something that everyone who likes to hunt should plan on.

# The Natural History of the Pronghorn

[ANTILOCAPRA AMERICANA]

## DESCRIPTION

A graceful, slender phantom of the prairies and tablelands in western North America, the pronghorn is a little smaller than the average American deer and can be recognized by its pronged horns, erect posture, tawny color, and slender limbs.

When full grown, a pronghorn buck measures from 4 to 4½ feet in length and stands from 32 to 40 inches high at the shoulder. Mature bucks weigh from 100 to 125 pounds. Females average 10 per cent smaller.

Often referred to as the American antelope, the pronghorn is not a member of the antelope family, nor is it even closely related to any of the modern groups of ruminants or cud-chewing ungulates. A member of the order *Artiodactyla*, the pronghorn is a hollow-horned, even-toed ungulate separated in a family of its own, the *Antilocaporidae*.

As with all even-toed mammals, the third and fourth toes of the pronghorn's fore and hind feet are evenly paired, and the tips are encased in a horny sheath which is the hoof. The animal actually travels on the extreme tips of its toes. The small lateral hoofs, or dewclaws—the second and fifth toes—usually present in other even-toed ungulates, are entirely absent in the pronghorn, a development for high speed on firm ground.

As a protection against the sharp, cold winds of the western prairie, the pronghorn has a coat of long, thick, brittle cellular hair ranging in color from light tan to deep reddish-brown. A large patch of longer white hair is always present on the rump; the sides of the head are white, and two broad stripes of white cross the underside of the neck. The tip of the nose and a patch below the eye are blackish-brown, while the short tail, about 5 inches long, is white or pinkish-buff. As in most plains animals, the underparts of the body, which are usually in shadow, are white or yellowish-white, blending with the darker-colored upper parts for effective camouflage.

## HORNS

Perhaps the most outstanding characteristic of the pronghorn is its remarkable horns, usually present in both sexes but more slender or vestigial in the does. Hollow, deciduous sheaths growing over a blade-like bony core, the horns project upward and are placed directly above the eyes.

The hollow sheath of the horn is shed annually soon after the rutting season is over. This is the only instance where a hollow-horned ungulate ever sheds its horns during a life time. Even before the old horn is shed a furry growth—the new horn—begins to form at the tip of the bony core, growing upward from the base. The new growth eventually eases off the old casing. The bony core is now covered with a soft, thick, blackish membrane, coated with stiff hairs. The new horns continue to extend beyond the tip of the horn core and the spike, or prong, grows up from the base and from the side of the horn. When full growth is reached, the horns dry up and harden. About four months elapse between the time the old horns begin to loosen and the new ones are completely formed, sometime in July.

The horns of a mature five-year-old buck average about 10 inches in length. The record length is 20-5/16 inches, with a spread of 16 3/16 inches. In females the horns rarely exceed four or five inches. The shed horns never last very long; if they are not eaten by rodents they are soon disintegrated by exposure to the sun, rain, and winds of the plains.

## ORIGIN

The pronghorn of today is the sole survivor of a vast group of prehistoric hoofed animals that populated the North American continent between one and two million years ago. Its ancestry dates back ten to twenty million years. Of strictly American lineage, the pronghorn never migrated across the land bridge that once stretched across the Bering Sea to Asia, nor did it travel south into South America.

The early pronghorns ranged in a great variety of forms approaching that of the modern African and Asiatic antelope and were contemporaries of the great-giraffe camels, hornless deer, giant elk-moose, and the great saber-toothed cats. There were diminutive, graceful pronglets no bigger than a jack rabbit while others were as large or larger than forms living today. One of these early forms, the *Hayoceros*, had forked horns, while the *Tetrameryx* had long, slender vertical horns, the *Stockoceros* had four horns, and one very early form had spirally twisted horns.

## RANGE

At home on the rolling prairies, barren wastes, and great plains of western North America, the range of the pronghorn extends from southern Alberta and Saskatchewan in Canada south through the Rocky Mountains region to the plateau country of central Mexico. Early pioneers seldom attempted to estimate the numbers of pronghorns in the herds they saw, but referred to them as countless multitudes. One calculation put the total population at one hundred million, and there must have been at least 40 or 50 million head. By the early nineteen hundreds the antelope in western North America had shrunk to about 20,000; today there are about 160,000 in the United States.

There are two generally recognized forms of pronghorn in the United States and three in Mexico, but the boundaries of the ranges have not been worked out in detail. The typical American pronghorn is buff-colored and ranges across the western United States and southern Canada. The Oregon pronghorn is bright cinnamon-brown with longer horns and less black about the tail than the typical form and ranges in the upland regions of Oregon and Washington. The Mexican pronghorn occurs south of the Mexican border and is a pale buff-colored form. The Peninsula pronghorn occurs on the peninsula of Lower California and has sooty-black facial marking, dark tips on the ears, and the white rump patch is divided by a broad band about an inch wide connecting the reddish-yellow area of the tail to the back. In other species this dividing line is usually indistinct or nonexistent. The Sonora pronghorn, found in western Sonora, Mexico, and southern Arizona, is the smallest and is paler than the other forms.

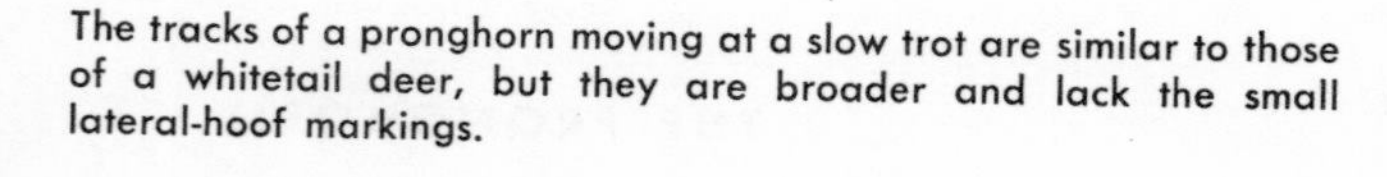

The tracks of a pronghorn moving at a slow trot are similar to those of a whitetail deer, but they are broader and lack the small lateral-hoof markings.

## HABITS

The pronghorn is a sociable animal and loves the company of its own kind. During the summer months the animal moves up to the high plateau country where it is free from annoying insect pests and may frequent rocky country or open park ranges, but it never strays far from the open plains. When food is adequate it may stay in a home territory of about three or four miles in diameter for a month or more before moving to new territory. As fall approaches, the pronghorn moves down to the plains and sheltered valleys to avoid the deep snow.

There are no fixed feeding or resting periods in the daily life of the pronghorn. Many kinds of grasses and a great variety of shrubs and bushes are included in its diet. The pronghorn browses on shoots of sagebrush, greasewood, rabbitbrush, juniper, bitterbrush, and many other shrubs. Range weeds such as chicory, onion, larkspur, and dandelion are also part of its diet, as is a wide variety of grasses. It is a dainty feeder and only plucks the tender, green shoots. During the winter months the pronghorn does not paw through the deep snow for food like other ungulates, but moves to wind-swept hillsides.

The pronghorn has sharp hearing, a keen sense of smell, and remarkable eyesight. Its eyes are as large as those of a horse, which is generally credited with having the largest eyes of any living mammal. The pronghorn's eyes are set wide apart and deep in bony sockets and have a diameter of 1½ inches. These far-seeing eyes have almost spherical vision and a range so great that on clear days a pronghorn can recognize moving objects three and four miles away.

The pronghorn's ability to send heliographic messages is really unique. The large, white patch on the rump consists of a pair of muscular disks supporting a mass of comparatively long, bristly hairs. When the animal is alarmed or disturbed, the muscles contract causing the mass of white hairs to rise abruptly and reflect a remarkable amount of light. The white flashes from the disk patches can be seen for a distance of two miles and in bright sunlight for an even greater distance. As the flaring disk patches of one animal flash their signals of danger they are instantly repeated by others until the whole plain is dotted with flashes of light. At the same time, the twin glands in the disks release a powerful scent that can be recognized by man more than a hundred yards away, and as much as a mile or more down wind by another pronghorn.

The pronghorn's summer coat is light and thin compared with its warm, winter robe, necessitating a complete change of pelage in spring and fall. The pelt is useless as an article of clothing or for a rug as the leather is of poor quality and the hair is so loose and brittle that it falls out or breaks off at the least pressure.

## LOCOMOTION

Built for speed, the pronghorn is the fleetest terrestrial animal on American soil. It can travel at a rate of

60 miles an hour for a short distance and maintain a speed of 40 miles an hour for 2 or 3 miles. Checked by a car speedometer, one barren doe was credited with a speed of 70 miles per hour. A pronghorn can walk, trot, run, or gallop and leaves tracks much like those of the whitetail deer. A band of pronghorns loves to compete in a test of speed and will often run alongside an automobile in an attempt to pass it and cross in front. A leap of 14 feet is not unusual for the pronghorn and individuals have cleared as much as twenty-seven feet. It is a good swimmer, but whenever possible will bypass bodies of water.

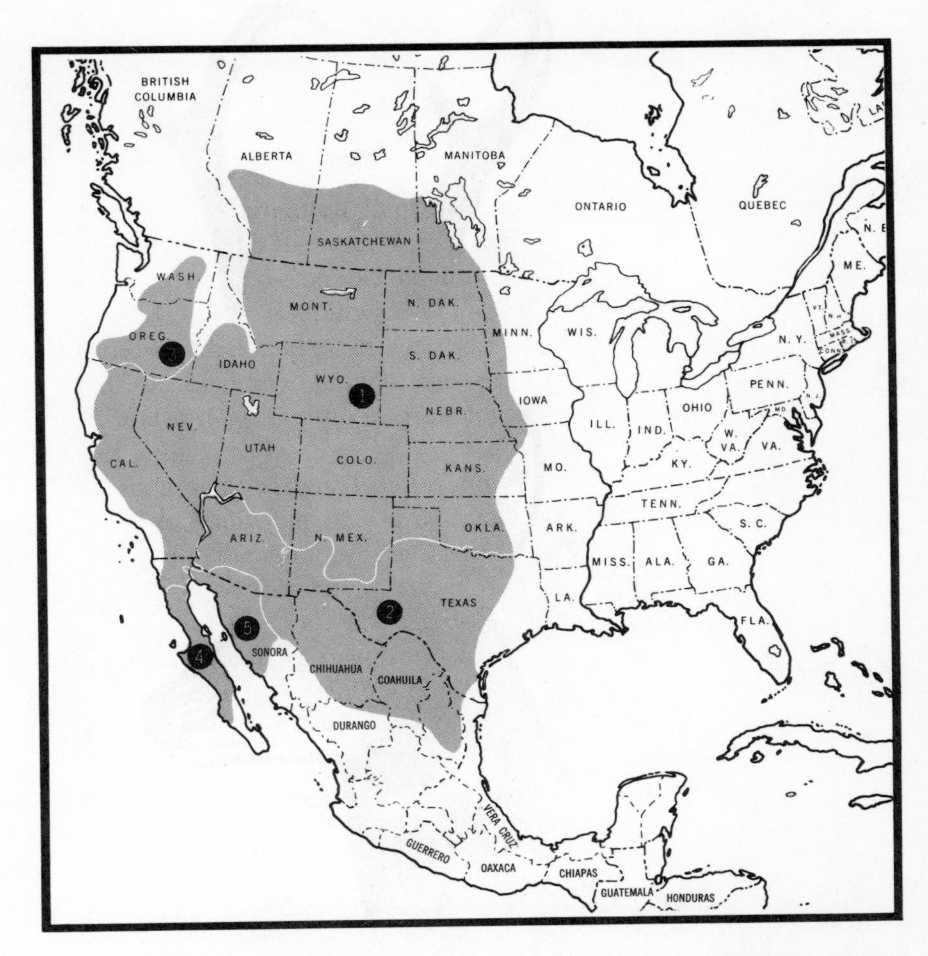

Distribution of the races of the pronghorn *Antilocapra:* 1. American pronghorn, 2. Mexican pronghorn, 3. Oregon pronghorn, 4. Peninsula pronghorn, 5. Sonora pronghorn.

## VOCAL

A snort or blow through the nose is the only sound made by the pronghorn. This sound caused the Indians to name the animal *Cha-oo*. When disturbed, a baby pronghorn will utter a quivering, high-pitched ventriloquial note lasting no longer than a second or two.

## MATING

Early in September the mature pronghorn bucks begin to segregate small groups of does for themselves. The beginning of the rut, or breeding season, may occur a little earlier in Mexico and extends well into October in western Canada. Each successful buck rounds up a harem of three or four does, rarely more. An especially ambitious buck may gather as many as eight does in his harem, but this is unusual. The slender female can run faster than the sturdy male, and she will lead him on a long chase that will carry them far afield before allowing herself to be caught and herded back to his fold. In the meantime, some aspiring young buck may cast covetous eyes over the unprotected does and try to lure them away from the harem.

At the beginning of the rut there is some competition between the bucks for possession of the does but the battles between the aspirants are rarely very serious. There are usually enough females to be divided among the fully mature bucks. A young buck may try to coax a female away from a harem, but usually retreats without a fight in the face of the charge of the infuriated master buck, who keeps up the chase for half a mile or more before returning to his submissive does. Occasionally, when evenly matched bucks meet in conflict and neither will accept defeat, a bloody battle may follow. The young bucks usually live in small bachelor groups during the summer and fall, but join the regular herds once the rutting season is over.

Scent glands are distributed over most parts of the body, including the rump patch, at the bases of the horns, in the hind leg near the hock, between the hoofs, and on the lower jaw.

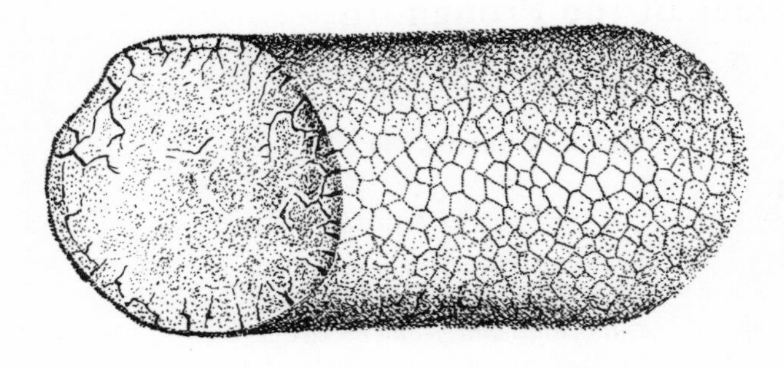

Each strand of a pronghorn's hair is composed of numerous pithy air cells as a protection from extremes of heat and cold. This is a section of hair magnified 250 times.

## BIRTH AND EARLY DEVELOPMENT

Fawning time for the pronghorn comes during the long, sunny days of May or June, when the western plains are green with fresh grass. The fawns are dropped a full eight months after the fall mating, ranging from the first day of May in Mexico to six weeks later in western Canada.

A doe about to deliver her young stays a short distance, but not more than a couple of hundred yards, away from the herd. A little knoll with a few scrubby pine trees or clumps of sagebrush is an ideal spot for fawning, but the fawns may be dropped almost anywhere. The first-born is usually a solitary individual but in the succeeding years there are frequently twins.

The new-born fawns appear to be all eyes, ears, and legs, stand about 16 inches high at the shoulder, and

The pronghorn sheds the outer shell of each horn every year, retaining the permanent bony core underneath.

weigh from 4 to 5½ pounds each. For the first week the fawns stay hidden, lying during most of this time flattened on the ground with their ears folded back. Twins are never less than 75 feet apart, and the doe never ranges far from her fawns, keeping a close watch over them while feeding from a distance. Should a stray coyote or other predator discover her treasures she will be there fighting in an instant. There are few individual foes that will not rapidly flee before the onslaught of her sharp, cutting hoofs.

The little pronghorn develops very fast and, when only a day old, can run for a short distance at a speed of twenty-five miles an hour. The young are marked like the parents but in a pale shade of tan. The little females do not show the slightest indication of horns, but the new-born bucks have a whirl of hair where the horns will eventually grow, and they are further distinguished from the baby does by a pair of dark lines along the lower jaws. During the first few days, the mother visits the fawns only at nursing time, which is accomplished in a few minutes. Before a week is out the fawns are up and following the mother to join the other fawns in the herd. Small spike horns begin to show when the little pronghorn is about ten months old, and the horns of males may reach a length of 2 or 3 inches by shedding time the following fall. Young does begin to breed when they are from fourteen to sixteen months old, may breed for five or six successive years, and reach old age when they are twelve. The young bucks, however, must wait until they have reached full maturity—usually in their fifth year—before they are strong enough to compete for the does.

## ENEMIES

There are few predators that can be classed as habitual enemies of the pronghorn. It can easily outrun a wolf or coyote and can rout either one with its cutting hoofs. Young pronghorns may be taken by surprise, and black bears may account for a few as do eagles at fawning time. Deep snow and parasites are the principal enemies of the pronghorn, especially ticks and lice externally and worms internally. The pronghorn is extremely nervous and high strung, and few ever survive long in captivity. They most frequently die of pneumonia or a disease called lumpy-jaw.

### Popular and Scientific Names of the Pronghorn

**ORDER:** *Artiodactyla*

**FAMILY:** *Antilocaporidae*

**GENUS:** *Antilocapra*

**SPECIES:** *americana*

**SUBSPECIES**

| | |
|---|---|
| American pronghorn | *Antilocapra americana americana* |
| Oregon pronghorn | *Antilocapra americana oregona* |
| Mexican pronghorn | *Antilocapra americana mexicana* |
| Peninsula pronghorn | *Antilocapra americana peninsularis* |
| Sonora pronghorn | *Antilocapra americana sonoriensis* |

CHAPTER 5

# THE AMERICAN BUFFALO

MOST of us think of the buffalo as a creature of the Western plains. The name conjures up pictures of thundering herds of the great hump-backed creatures, Indians chasing them on pinto ponies and driving arrows through their heavy bodies, the buffalo runners piling them up at long range with their powerful Sharps rifles, blood-maddened tourists blazing away at them from the windows of rickety railway trains drawn by wood-burning locomotives with funny smokestacks. All of these scenes are part of the romantic heritage of the American, a piece of nostalgia along with the slit-eyed Western sheriff, the dance-hall girl with the heart of gold, the sturdy pioneer in his covered wagon, Benjamin Franklin flying a kite to discover electricity, and young Abe Lincoln lying on his belly by the fireplace and doing his homework with a bit of charcoal on a shingle.

Our notion of the buffalo on the plains is more or less true so far as it goes, but it is only part of the picture. When white men first came to North America, buffaloes ranged from northern Nevada and western Oregon to the eastern Carolinas, and in Pennsylvania almost to tidewater. Buffalo, N. Y., got its name from the buffaloes that used to frequent a salt lick in the neighborhood, and one of the subspecies of the American buffalo is *Bos bison pennsylvanicus,* an extinct form formerly found in Pennsylvania. One of the attractions of Kentucky for the restless folk of Virginia and the Carolinas was that buffaloes were to be found there. My maternal grandmother, who was born in Kentucky about 1847, told me that one of her grandfathers, who moved to Kentucky from Virginia not long after the Revolutionary War, told her of chasing and shooting buffaloes on the grassy savannas of Kentucky. She also told me that her own family, and many others in Crittenden County where she was born, still had, during her girlhood, robes made from Kentucky-killed buffaloes.

It is true that the best buffalo range was the short-grass plains of the Dakotas, Montana, Nebraska, Kansas, and the Texas and Oklahoma panhandles, but buffaloes were adaptable enough to range in the wooded Eastern states, probably mostly in the occasional open places in the woods. Mountain buffaloes were found in the open parks throughout the Rockies and north as far as northern Alberta.

When I was hunting Stone sheep around the heads of the Muskwa and Prophet rivers in northern British Columbia in 1946, our outfit on the way back to the Alaska Highway passed through a thinly timbered country of hills and grass that showed evidence of very extensive grazing at one time. All the hills had been terraced by heavy animals grazing around them in the manner of country hard used by cattle and horses in the Southwest. I asked Frank Golata, my outfitter, if Indians had wintered horses there. He said they had not. The hills had been terraced by buffaloes, he told me, and occasionally old buffalo skulls and bones were still found.

The Eastern and the Far Western buffaloes were never as plentiful as they were on the high plains, and by 1800 they were all killed off east of the Alleghenys. There still were buffaloes on the prairies of Illinois, in Indiana, and in western Kentucky. By 1820 they had retreated to Iowa and central Missouri, and by 1850 their range was restricted to the Western plains and mountains of the United States and Canada. The great slaughter occurred in the late eighteen sixties and eighteen seventies when railroads made their last stronghold accessible, when there were thousands of footloose young men who were veterans of the Union and Confederate armies, and when it was the policy of the American army to kill off the buffalo so the Plains Indians could be tamed and pauperized and herded onto reservations.

As big and as formidable as he appeared, the buffalo was a natural patsy doomed for early slaughter, and in any country where he was found he was the first animal to become extinct. He is a huge animal with a lot of valuable hide wrapped around hundreds of pounds of useful and delicious meat. His chosen country is open, and since he has no instinct for concealing himself he is easily seen. In addition, he is an astoundingly dull and stupid beast no more adapted to the modern world than the dinosaur.

The buffalo is not a sporting animal and never has been one. I have seen buffaloes "hunted," and as an object of the chase by a rifleman, I would rate him even lower than such an African plains animal as the wildebeest. This creature has the superficial appearance of an American buffalo but is not quite so stupid. Incidentally, I have seen tens of thousands of wildebeests, but I have shot exactly one, and that for lion bait. There is more sport in one smart whitetail buck in the brush than in all the buffaloes that ever trod the prairies of North America. For his size, the buffalo is not difficult to kill, and he is not dangerous as the African Cape buffalo, the elephant, and the Asiatic gaur are dangerous. I have no desire whatsoever to shoot a buffalo and look with astonishment on those hunters who have.

The name buffalo for this big, shaggy, addlepated creature is firmly established, just as the other misbegotten American popular names for other game animals are—elk for the wapiti, moose for the elk, lion for the cougar or puma, and in Mexico *tigre* or tiger for the jaguar. Actually, the American buffalo is not a buffalo at all, but a bison. He has relatives in the Old World, and during the Pleistocene period, which ended with the retreat of the glaciers only about 15,000 years ago, North America was the home of another relative of this animal, an enormous bison that was half again as heavy and had wonderful spreading horns. For whatever the reason, this giant bison could not adapt himself to the climatic changes that followed the retreat of the ice. Along with the saber-toothed tiger, the great American lion, the horse, the camel, and various relatives of our pronghorn antelope, it died off. It lived, however, long after the first men from Asia had crossed the Bering Strait and worked their way south. Bones of these gigantic bison are found in connection with the flint implements and the fires of those primitive hunters. Possibly the hunting, in combination with climatic change, was a factor in their extinction.

The Old World cousin of the American bison was at one time found over much of northern Europe and probably northern Asia. At one time the northern European variety survived only in the forests of Lithuania. Whether the Communists have preserved the remnant or not I cannot say. The other remnant of the Old World bison was found in the Caucasus Mountains on the border of Europe and Asia. This subspecies was heavily shot off during the Russian Revolution, but I understand that a few remain. The so-called Indian bison or gaur is not a true bison, but another species known as *Bibos gaurus.* It has the hump but not the skull and the long hair.

The bison is distinguished from other members of the ox family by the high forequarters, the tall hump at the shoulder, the form of the horns and skull, and the great mass of hair that clothes the forward portion of the body.

The American and Old World bison are about the same size, but the American animals are lower at the hindquarters. A big bull bison is about the size of an African Cape buffalo, and a heavy, fat bull will weigh as much as 2,400 pounds. Cows weigh about one third less. The bison is by far the heaviest of the North American game animals, almost twice as heavy as an Alaska brown bear. To find a North American mammal as heavy one would have to go to sea and collect a big bull walrus.

In primitive times, the great plains of North

The railroads ran hunting excursions for sportsmen through the buffalo country. Even ordinary passengers took pot shots at the shaggy animals from the moving trains.

America formed one of the most productive game areas of the world. Unlike those of East Africa, the plains did not abound in a great number of species. The reason for this is that the glacial and interglacial eras of the Pleistocene in North America killed off many species, whereas Africa south of the Sahara did not go through the various ice ages and still retains its Pleistocene fauna.

But the North American plains made up in numbers what they lacked in variety. It is estimated that there were about sixty million buffaloes ranging on the plains. To those must be added elk that lived on the plains, the whitetail deer that lived in the river bottoms, the mule deer found in the foothills, and the bighorn sheep that had worked their way out from the mountains and made their homes on isolated little buttes far out on the open plain and in the badlands and the brakes of the rivers. Preying on all this game were the great plains grizzlies, which the early explorers called white bears, yellow bears, and red bears to distinguish them from the common black bears. Nor should we forget the packs of wolves that hung around the outskirts of the herds to pick off the stragglers, the calves, the old, the weak, and the sick.

The whole economy of the Plains Indians was based on the buffalo. The meat fed him, and probably no people who ever lived had finer, richer, more nourishing food. From the hides he made the robes that kept him warm in winter and the leather from which he constructed his tepee. The Plains Indians hunted the buffalo with arrows and lances before they acquired guns, and afoot before they got horses from the Spanish. The Indians ran buffaloes, chasing them on horses until they could pull alongside and drive an arrow into the heart or lungs. They thrust lances into the great shaggy bodies in the winter when the buffaloes were slowed down by deep snow and the hunters could overtake them on snowshoes. They stalked them through high grass, and they drove them over cliffs. Several hundred Indians would surround a herd and kill every buffalo they could. They drove them into corrals and then slaughtered them at their leisure.

The white man is always blamed for killing off the buffalo, and indeed the blame is mostly his. However, the Indians themselves were making noticeable inroads into the herds even before the hide hunters came into the picture. Horses and guns had increased their ability to slaughter buffaloes. This good and easy food supply meant an increase in the Indian population, and more Indians meant more dead buffaloes. More buffalo meat meant more Indians, and so on.

I have read at times that the Indian was a natural conservationist. As the French say, it is but to laugh. The Indian is no more a natural conservationist than the white man or the African native. If Indians are numerous and well enough armed, they will kill off the game, just as the Navajos killed off the mountain sheep, the deer, and the antelope in their vast reservation. They didn't just thin them down. They exterminated them to the last animal. The natives of Africa, who a hundred years ago had been decimated by slave raiders and by intertribal wars, have increased rapidly and have exterminated the game in many areas and are doing their best to wipe it out everywhere else.

To an unreflective primitive man, a wild animal is useful only when it is dead so it can fill his belly or clothe his body. Even today on this continent an Indian will kill a moose to get meat for a meal and will go off and leave the rest of the vast carcass. The notion of preserving game for the future is a product of civilization and is absolutely incomprehensible to the primitive man. Anthropologists now believe that hunting by primitive men exterminated the mammoth (a long-haired relative of the Indian elephant) in Europe and perhaps in Siberia. These hunters killed mostly the young and based their whole economy on the big, stupid pachyderms.

The vast amount of game on the great plains attracted foreign sportsmen. The first was probably George Ruxton, an adventurous Englishman, who lived with the mountain men who hunted buffaloes on the plains and trapped beaver. Ruxton wrote a wonderful book about life with the trappers in the plains and mountains. Titled *Life in the Far West,* it is the source book on habits, customs, clothes, and dialect of these mountain men. Ruxton was eventually killed by Indians.

Ruxton toughed it out, ate buffalo hump, and slept on buffalo robes. Others who followed outfitted elaborate expeditions into the buffalo country. A famous one was that of Sir St. George Gore, a wealthy Irish nobleman who is reputed to have spent 500,000 dollars on a three-year hunt. He had forty servants and a scientific staff. He slept in a brass bedstead set up in a handsome tent with costly rugs for ground cloths. His outfit was contained in twenty-seven carts and wagons. He devoured much game, and with him he took fine wines and exotic foods. By the time his shoot was over he had killed 2,000 buffaloes, 1,600 deer, 105 bears, and other animals such as mountain sheep, elk, and antelope.

The Grand Duke Alexis of Russia hunted buffaloes and other plains game after the Civil War with Gen. Phil Sheridan and Col. George Custer, who was later killed by the Sioux on the Little Bighorn. Although the grand duke's hunt was a minor production compared with that of Sir St. George, his highness went to the buffalo country on a private train, was served by a host of retainers, and lived in a tent furnished with stove and carpet. In the evenings, if time hung heavy on his hands, he was entertained by Indian dances and by a cavalry band.

As the railroads penetrated the plains, they ran excursions for sportsmen. Ordinary passengers took pot shots at buffaloes from the windows of railway cars, and sometimes the engineer would stop the train long enough for them to get off and carve out a few steaks.

My paternal grandfather, an Irishman and onetime officer in the British army, who landed in San Francisco on January 1, 1850, after going by ship around Cape Horn, rode east across the deserts, mountains, and plains in 1861 leading a packhorse and dodging Texans and Indians. He died not long after I was born, and I have no recollection of him. However, he told his sons that he and his companion, a New Englander and a Harvard graduate, were exhausted and starving when they reached the plains of northern Texas and ran into their first buffaloes. They killed some of the animals, devoured meat until they got their strength back, made jerky, and were able to push on to St. Joseph, Missouri, where they struck the railroad. Both became officers in the Union army. It is odd when one thinks of the turns of chance on which one's existence depends. If my grandfather had not run into those buffaloes, I would not be here.

When my maternal grandfather moved from Kentucky to the mountains of Colorado to establish a cattle ranch in the middle eighteen seventies, the great slaughter on the plains had already greatly reduced the vast herds, but there were still pockets of mountain buffaloes in the parks of the Rockies. He shot buffaloes, elk, deer, and mountain sheep and traded wild meat for supplies in Trinidad, Colorado. When he went across the plains in 1875, he said, big areas were whitened by the bleaching bones of slaughtered buffaloes.

The great slaughter of the buffalo herds began in the late eighteen sixties and reached a climax in the early seventies. By 1887 the herds that had once numbered uncounted millions had dwindled to about 1,000 animals. No slaughter like that of the great buffalo herds had ever before been seen in the history of the world.

The southern herd of buffaloes, the animals that ranged in Kansas, Oklahoma, and the panhandle of Texas, were just about wiped out by 1875, but a few fugitives were reported as late as 1889. The north herd was pretty well killed off ten years later. It is estimated that 4,500,000 buffaloes were slaughtered in 1871 alone, 4,000,000 in 1873, and 1,000,000 in 1874.

Originally the white men shot buffaloes for meat. The Indians killed them for meat and for robes for their own use as well as to sell to the white man. The hunters sold the meat for as low as three cents a pound, but transportation and preservation offered great problems, and the fresh meat could be shipped successfully only in cold weather. In those days buffalo meat was a feature of restaurant and hotel menus through the Midwest and East. Often

For his buffalo hunt, Sir St. George Gore had all the comforts, even a brass bed and costly rugs.

it was passed off for beef. Much of it was salted and dried—jerked, in the language of the Southwest.

For a long time there was no market for buffalo hides except in the form of Indian-tanned robes. These were standard equipment for winter use in those days of sleighs and open buggies, and many a lad and lassie became engaged snuggled up in a sleigh under a buffalo robe while the horse picked his way down some icy country lane.

Market for meat was limited. Professional hunters shot buffaloes for army posts, for frontier towns, and for construction crews driving railroads west as well as for drying and for shipment East in cold weather. But it was the discovery that buffalo hides could be made into good and useful leather which could be substituted for cowhides that doomed the buffalo.

In 1871 tanners, after a good deal of experimenting both in the United States and in Europe, discovered that the dried hides, or flints, of buffaloes could be made into good leather. It was then that buffalo hunting became a remunerative, year-round profession. Tanneries and hide dealers circularized the hunters, and the rush was on. In a short time an estimated 2,000 hunters were shooting buffaloes from the southern herd, and thousands of dry hides were stacked up around railroad stations for shipment. Easy money burning the pockets of the buffalo hunters attracted gamblers, light ladies, and con men, and some of the boom towns in the buffalo country were so wicked as to make Dawson during the Klondike gold rush in the Yukon seem a boy's summer camp. A granduncle of mine left Kentucky and went to the Texas panhandle with 25,000 dollars in gold coin to buy a ranch and to stock it with cattle. He was last heard from in one of those tough towns frequented by the hide hunters. It was later learned that he was murdered.

In the heyday of hide hunting, the outfits were organized as tightly as African safaris or Canadian pack trips. One large outfit, according to Wayne Gard's excellent book, *The Great Buffalo Hunt,* consisted of two hunters who shot the buffaloes, a cook, one man who reloaded the ammunition, one who pegged out the hides to dry, two who hauled them, and nine skinners. Wagons carried bedrolls, cooking utensils, and often tents. In the winter the hunters lived in dugouts.

The hunters quickly abandoned the exciting method of chasing the buffaloes and shooting them from horseback. This took too much time and scattered the dead animals too much. They wanted to kill as many buffaloes as possible and have them close together so the skinners could work efficiently.

The hunter would go out, locate a band of buffaloes, stalk to within range (200 to 300 yards), then lie down behind some cover and downwind. He would rest his heavy rifle on a forked stick, lay out his cartridges, and go to work. He avoided heart shots because, as all hunters know, a heart-shot

The hunter would get within range, prop his rifle on a stick, lay out his cartridges, and go to work.

animal will generally make a quick, frantic run of from 50 to 100 yards before it falls. Instead, the marksman would try to pick out the leader and shoot it through the lungs. Struck by the bullet, the animal would make a startled jump, then stand with the blood running out of its nose. Presently it would be down.

If any buffaloes showed signs of getting ready to run, the hunters would shoot them. Before long, at the smell of blood, the whole herd would be milling around the fallen. The hunters would shoot no more buffaloes than the skinners could take care of for the day.

The work was hard, dirty, dangerous, and not wildly remunerative. The hunters got from two to four dollars each for the hides delivered at the railhead. Let us suppose that the hunter had enough skinners to take care of fifty hides a day and that he averaged three dollars for a hide. He would then make 150 dollars a day. That sounds like a lot of money for the eighteen seventies, but it must be remembered that the hunters had to pay for their arms and equipment, for food and ammunition, that they had to hire men to skin and drive their wagons, and that they had considerable capital investment. And the hide hunters always ran a risk of getting their own hair lifted by indignant Indians who resented the invasion of their hunting grounds.

Few of the hide hunters had much money when the great slaughter was over. Gamblers and the dance-hall girls in the frontier towns usually managed to clean them out. Compared with the ivory hunters of Africa, the hide hunters of the American West were no better than a bunch of peons working for peanuts.

When ivory hunting was in full bloom, an average bull elephant that carried 100 pounds of ivory in both tusks was worth about 500 dollars, and sometimes a lucky and skillful ivory hunter would shoot 30 elephants in one day. That is 15,000 dollars' worth of ivory. Karamojo Bell, a Scotchman who died only recently and who was still a young man with most of his ivory hunting behind him when World War I broke out, shot about 1,200 elephants for a gross which must have been over 600,000 dollars. He traveled in luxury with a mile-long string of porters, lived in a fine tent, cheered himself up with brandy and champagne, became a British aviator during the 1914-18 war, and retired a wealthy man.

The elephant hunters of Africa shot mostly the old bulls, and now and then they would knock off an elephant carrying 250 pounds of ivory worth about 1,250 dollars—a pretty good return for a 10 cent cartridge. Over most of East Africa they left the elephant herds in good numbers, but with the big ivory shot off.

The hide hunters, on the other hand, exterminated the buffalo in a few short years for paltry returns and left most of the meat to rot on the plains. If they bothered with any meat at all it was the tongues and a few choice cuts.

The hide hunters used all sorts of weapons. Many were left over from the Civil War—muzzle-loading rifled muskets and Spencer and Henry repeaters. Some used old, muzzle-loading Kentucky and plains rifles. One of the favorites was the old .50/70 breech-loading Springfield, developed right after the Civil War. There were many on the plains in the hands of the military, and ammunition was not hard to come by at army posts.

Another favorite was the Remington-Rider rolling block in large calibers, but the most famous of all were the heavy Sharps buffalo rifles. These cost important money—often from 125 to 150 dollars—and were in many cases equipped with telescope sights. The buffalo hunters bought the best British Curtis & Harvey black powder and took kegs of it with them. They cast their own bullets, patched them with paper, reloaded their own ammunition. They used bullets of pure lead that expanded and were generally found under the hide on the far side. These were often recovered, recast, and used again.

One buffalo hunter said, after the slaughter was over, that he had killed 6,500 buffaloes with one of his Sharps rifles and 14,000 with another. The Winchester Model 1876 repeating rifle for heavy black-powder cartridges, although designed for buffalo hunting, got on the market too late to be widely used, although it was popular with ranchers and sport hunters for elk and grizzlies later.

Many are the tales told of the shooting skill of the buffalo hunters, and as the decades have passed these tales have grown no worse. The hide hunters were undoubtedly exceedingly skillful shots, and the heavy Sharps rifles were highly accurate. But the stories of the hunters' remarkable feats are on the incredible side.

I have read of buffalo hunters who thought nothing of killing buffaloes at 800 yards. They were no doubt very fine judges of range, but from all I can read they did their shooting at from 150 to 300 yards, and preferred to get as close as they could without disturbing the buffaloes. Within 300 or 400 yards they could probably judge range quite accurately. They were used to it, just as a golf pro who works within those distances becomes used to them. I don't believe, though, that they could always tell if an animal was 750, 800, or 850 yards away, and if they misjudged the range by as much as 50 yards at around a half a mile, the trajectories of the rifles they used would result in a miss.

The .40/70 Sharps drove a 330-grain bullet at a muzzle velocity of 1,258 feet per second and had a muzzle energy of 1,160 foot pounds. To get to 300 yards, the bullet had to rise almost 3 feet at 150 yards. The .40/90 Sharps used a 370-grain bullet at 1,218 and its midrange trajectory over 300 yards was about 30 inches. In comparison, the modern .375 Magnum drives a 300-grain bullet at a muzzle velocity of 2,550 at the muzzle, produces 4,330 foot pounds of energy, and the bullet rises only a bit over 9 inches in getting to 300 yards.

I have had letters from nostalgic readers of *Outdoor Life* wanting to know why no modern rifle has the killing power of the old Sharps buffalo rifles. The answer is, of course, that many modern rifles have far more killing power and much flatter trajectory than any Sharps that was ever made. The buffalo hunters were probably the best game shots that ever lived because they had vast experience, but compared with such rifles as the .375 Magnum the guns they used were pretty primitive. They killed well because the men behind them held them well. The big, heavy bullets penetrated well and opened deep wound channels in vital areas.

The last big herd of buffaloes was shot off around Miles City, Montana, in 1880-1882. By 1883 they were almost all gone, slaughtered by an estimated 5,000 whites and Indians. One hunter is said to have killed 5,000 in a season. One dealer shipped 250,000 hides.

And then it was all over. Only a few hundred buffaloes remained in the United States to become the ancestors of those that exist today. Presently, all that remained where tens of thousands of buffaloes had ranged were piles of whitened bones so thick that in some places they could be seen for miles. Like so many vultures, the bone gatherers then went to work, picking up the bones on the prairies and hauling them to the railroad. Some bones were used for whitening sugar. Others were ground into fertilizer. They brought two and a half to three dollars a ton. And so the melancholy tale ends.

There are still buffaloes in the United States and Canada. Some ranchers run small herds and allow anyone who wants to say that he has potted a buffalo to do so for 450 or 500 dollars. There are good herds at the National Bison Range in Montana, and at the Ft. Niobrara National Bison Refuge near Valentine, Nebraska. Arizona has a small, state-owned herd from which some animals are shot every year. Buffalo licenses are obtained by special drawings among hunters. In the fall of 1959 and 1960, hunts were held for woods buffaloes in the Woods Buffalo Park in the Northwest Territories of Canada. Buffaloes have also been hunted in the Big Delta country of Alaska, where a herd planted from remnants in the United States has done well. There are now something like twenty-five thousand buffaloes in North America.

For my part, I want no piece of a buffalo hunt. Once in Arizona I attended the annual buffalo hunt in the Houserock Valley north of the Grand Canyon of the Colorado. Cowboys had rounded up the herd. These animals were wild in that they were not confined by fences, but I have seen range cattle that were far wilder. Game wardens pointed out to the keen sportsmen the animals they were to shoot, and the lucky few who had drawn the permits blasted them. Several of the hunters shot so poorly they couldn't hit the enormous heart-lung area at a distance of 30 or 40 yards. Once a gutshot bull looked and acted resentful, and a game warden had to put it down. Another ran off and was chased and shot by a warden and several hunters.

But generally, buffaloes hit through the lungs just looked unhappy, bled at the nose and mouth, and presently lay down and died. Most of the hunters used .30/30s and .30/06s, and hit in the lungs with either of these two the buffaloes were dead in a few minutes.

One chap I knew paid five hundred dollars for the privilege of shooting a buffalo. The rancher penned it in a corral, and the hunter, brimming over with nostalgia, stood by the fence and plugged it with a Sharps rifle. Another rode around in a jeep, picked his buffalo out of the herd and shot it in the neck. I have never applied for a buffalo permit, and if I ever do I suspect my family will get me committed to the funny farm.

And how is buffalo meat? I have eaten some and I like it very much. In Arizona, hunters who pot buffaloes get to keep only the hide, the head, and one quarter of the meat. The rest of the meat is sold to sportsmen's clubs and various organizations.

Every year the Tucson Game Protective Association, of which I was president a couple of years, used to buy meat and throw a buffalo barbecue. Late one night, when members of the barbecue committee and I were laboring to prepare the feed for next day, we cut out some filets and broiled them over mesquite coals. I have never tasted better steaks than those from these grass-fed buffaloes. The old-time buffalo hunters always said that buffalo hump stuck to your ribs. I believe it. The hump meat is shot through with fine streaks of yellow fat. Apparently it takes a long time to digest. Once I ate a good meal of the stuff about two o'clock one afternoon and was not hungry again for over twenty-four hours. I might add that not only does hump stick with you but it is also delicious.

This sad story of greed and bloodlust is not entirely without its gains. The shooting off of the buffalo was inevitable to clear the prairies for farms and cattle. We lost the buffalo, but we gained the wheat farms and cattle ranges of Kansas, Nebraska, Montana, and the Dakotas. And this big, dumb, slow, and ponderous creature was never much of a game animal anyway.

# The Natural History of the American Buffalo, or Bison

[BISON BISON]

## DESCRIPTION

This somber mountain of a beast, best known as the American buffalo, is not a buffalo at all but actually a wisent, or bison. True buffalo are found only in Asia and Africa. However, the name buffalo for the American bison has been universally accepted and American buffalo it is and always will be. Though exceeded in height by the Alaska moose, the buffalo is the largest of American big game animals. A full-grown bull measures up to 12 feet long and stands 6 feet high at the shoulder. It is not unusual for bulls to weigh between 1,600 and 2,000 pounds each, with a maximum weight of about 3,000 pounds. Cow buffalo are smaller than bulls and do not stand more than 5 feet at the shoulder or weigh more than 900 pounds.

The buffalo has high, humped shoulders due to the great elongation of bony spurs on the backbone at this point. The massive head and deep muscular neck are slung low on the shoulders but the body is surprisingly narrow in cross-section, notably in the hindquarters. The forequarters, including the head and neck, are covered with a mantle of thick, shaggy hair that terminates abruptly below the knees on the forefeet and just behind the shoulders. The rest of the body, including the hind limbs, has a covering of close, short hair. The buffalo's staring, expressionless eyes are placed well down on the sides of the head. A member of the family *Bovidae,* the buffalo has short, stout horns which curve outward and upward from the sides of the head. The horns consist of hollow, horny sheaths growing over round, bony cores, which are never shed. Horns are present in both sexes but are larger in the bulls. Horns of large bulls may reach a length of 23 inches and have a circumference at the base of 17 inches. A long, black beard hangs from the chin, while the tail is short with a tassel of long hairs at the tip. In fresh pelage, the American buffalo is dark chocolate-brown, becoming almost black on the head and shoulders. By the time the spring moult comes around the buffalo's robe has faded to a pale yellowish-brown.

An even-toed ungulate, the buffalo belongs in the scientific order of *Artiodactyla,* terrestrial, herbivorous mammals whose third and fourth toes on the fore and hind feet are evenly and well developed, with the tips encased in horny sheaths supporting the animal's weight. Small lateral hoofs, or dewclaws, are present.

As it is a cud-chewer, the buffalo is in the class of *Ruminantia,* animals that have a compound stomach and temporarily store partly chewed food in the first compartment, or paunch. This food is regurgitated in small pellets to the mouth to be thoroughly milled, and is passed on to the second compartment to start digestion. As in other members of the *Ruminantia,* the buffalo has no teeth in the front of the upper jaw, but it has broad-crowned, sharp-edged molar teeth for grinding and milling food. If you watch one of the cud-chewers at work you will see the animal swallow and after a slight pause bring up a new pellet to chew. This is deposited in the cheek, causing a slight but perceptible swelling. The animal now chews with a rotary motion on this side of the mouth; presently the cud is shifted to the opposite side of the mouth where the upper and lower teeth take over the job of milling. The animal, therefore, chews only on one side of the mouth at a time. The more primitive cud-chewers, such as the camels, swing the lower jaw in a wide sweep from side to side, chewing on both sides of the jaws at the same time. This is a slow process compared with that of the modern cud-chewers, such as the buffaloes.

## ORIGIN

It is believed that the modern, short-horned American bison represents an immigrant of Euro-Asiatic stock that crossed the land bridge connecting Siberia with Alaska during the Pleistocene era. The swollen-nosed Saiga and the yak were among the immigrant contemporaries that reached America with the bison but neither survived to modern times. None of the true wild cattle, like the auroch, ever reached the Western Hemisphere. The magnificent superbison of the American Pleistocene ranged from Alaska to Kentucky and had a horn spread of up to 6 feet. None of the superbison continued until recent times. A wild bison very similar to the American species continued in Europe until the last few stragglers were exterminated when conservation laws were relaxed during World War II.

Why the buffalo populated the North American continent is easy to explain. The vast open plains and great open prairies of the Middle West raised a rich, luxuriant growth of grass. This wealth of forage had to be harvested and put to use. To let it die and rot on the ground was not part of the scheme of world progressive evolution. So the buffalo came from Asia, multiplied into the millions and spread from east to west and north to south.

Actually the historic highways laid out across the continent of North America were originally buffalo trails. The herds knew the best routes through the mountain passes, and now the great steel locomotives follow the trails once trod by the buffalo.

Not only were a large portion of the American Indians dependent on the buffalo for a livelihood but the frontiersmen and early settlers of the West would have starved without buffalo meat. On the open plains and prairies the great beast furnished food, material for clothing, shelter, and fuel. The Indian had many diverse ways of hunting the buffalo but the great round-up was at Buffalo Jump, a cliff in the valley of the Yellowstone in Montana. Periodically the Indians banded together and stampeded whole herds over the cliff. Squaws, children, and the braves took part in the dressing and skinning of the animals. The meat was then cut into strips, smoked, and sun-cured. Meat treated this way was known as "jerked meat" or "jerky." It was as hard as a rock and would keep indefinitely. Later the squaws would pound the dried meat into a powder, mix it with berries and fat, turning it into pemmican which was quite palatable.

## RANGE

Although buffaloes were once spread over a third of the North American continent, the great concentration of the herds was in the great plains of the Mississippi River valley. This was flat grass country, well watered and bare of large stands of timber. Here and here alone were the buffaloes found in herds numbering in the millions.

Today there are only two species of buffalo left in

The walking pattern of the buffalo's tracks may be grouped in pairs, as shown here, or individually and evenly spaced on either side of a center line.

The buffalo's horns, permanent sheaths growing over bony cores, are never shed. Its head is covered with shaggy hair and a long, black beard hangs from the chin.

America: One is the Plains bison that once ranged over suitable regions in the United States and the plains region of Canada. The second is the Wood bison, a larger species, still found over a large area in northern Alberta and Northwest Territory in the Great Slave Lake and Peace River districts. This species' head is higher on its shoulders and it doesn't show the whites of its eyes like the Plains bison.

Two other races, once recognized but now extinct, were the Eastern bison, an almost black form, grizzled about the nose and eyes, with the hump less developed than the Plains bison, which ranged in the forested regions of Maryland, Pennsylvania, and Virginia; the Mountain bison, a pale-colored form, restricted to the mountains of Colorado.

An extremely sociable animal, the bison is—or rather was—the most gregarious animal in America if not in the entire world. According to eyewitness records, one herd of bison was 25 miles wide, 50 miles deep and probably contained some four million head. It has been estimated that there were sixty million head of bison in North America when the white man arrived and by 1900 their numbers had been reduced to three hundred. Today the only truly wild bison are to found in the Slave River region of northern Alberta.

An Indian named Michelo Pablo deserves the credit for saving the Plains buffalo from complete annihilation. The basis for Pablo's herd consisted of calves captured by an Indian, Walking Coyote, in 1873. The Pablo herd continued to increase in number under the care of a Flathead Indian until there were 150 head in 1906 when the Canadian Government purchased the herd. It took three years to transfer the herd to Canada and by the time the last animal was shipped there were 709 buffalo. Derived from this herd were the Wainwright herd in Canada, the Yellowstone herd, the Montana herd, and practically all the other herds in existence. Today there are some five thousand buffaloes in the United States and another fifteen thousand in Canada.

### HABITS

The buffalo is a grazing animal and feeds almost exclusively on grasses. In winter when snow covers the ground it uses its large forefeet to dig and uncover the grass. As the buffalo visits water regularly to drink, buffalo trails always lead to water, a fact that the early pioneers of the West soon learned to their advantage.

Normally the buffalo herds have separate summer and winter ranges. The direction followed by the migrating herds when they were large was not always necessarily north and south and the distance travelled during the migration was 300 to 400 miles. It was during the migration that the buffaloes congregated into the immense herds. When the summer and winter ranges were reached, the herds broke up into smaller bands of from four or five individuals to small groups of thirty or forty.

The buffalo herds are continually harassed by mosquitoes, black flies, and bulldog flies. To get some relief the animals use regular dusting holes, or wallows, saucer-like depressions in the ground worn by constant use, 7 to 12 feet in diameter and a foot or more deep. Lying in the hole, the buffalo rolls first on one side, gets up, and then rolls on the other side. Sometimes a bull will roll completely over despite the tall spines supporting its hump. Magpies and cowbirds often perch on the buffalo's back to help rid the animal of the insect pests that swarm over its furry coat.

During winter storms and blizzards, a buffalo always heads into the wind and never turns its back to the storm like other ungulates. It has its warmest clothing in front.

The buffalo does not have especially sharp eyesight. It does have a good sense of hearing but depends more especially on the air currents to bring the scent of dangerous enemies to its nostrils.

### LOCOMOTION

A habitual nomad, the buffalo never lingers more than a few days in one place. Soon it gets the wanderlust and moves on 5 to 10 miles to new pastures. There is, therefore, never any danger of overgrazing by the buffalo in any one area. It travels with a steady, plodding gait at a speed of about 5 miles per hour, but it may swing into a steady trot or speed up to a fast, lumbering gallop with a speed of 32 miles per hour. It also has a most unusual stiff-legged, bouncing gait in which all four feet rise simultaneously off the ground and come down together. The buffalo is a good swimmer and swims with its nose, the top of its head, hump, and tail above water.

### TRACKS

Tracks left on soft ground by the buffalo are much like those of the domestic ox. Often only the outer rims of hoofs are clear, the cloven hoof effect being indistinct and presenting a slightly longer than round impression averaging about 5 inches in diameter, notched front and back. The forefeet are slightly larger than the hind feet. The tracks may be in a slightly staggered line spaced from 24 to 30 inches apart or in pairs one behind the other. The stride is about 2 feet long.

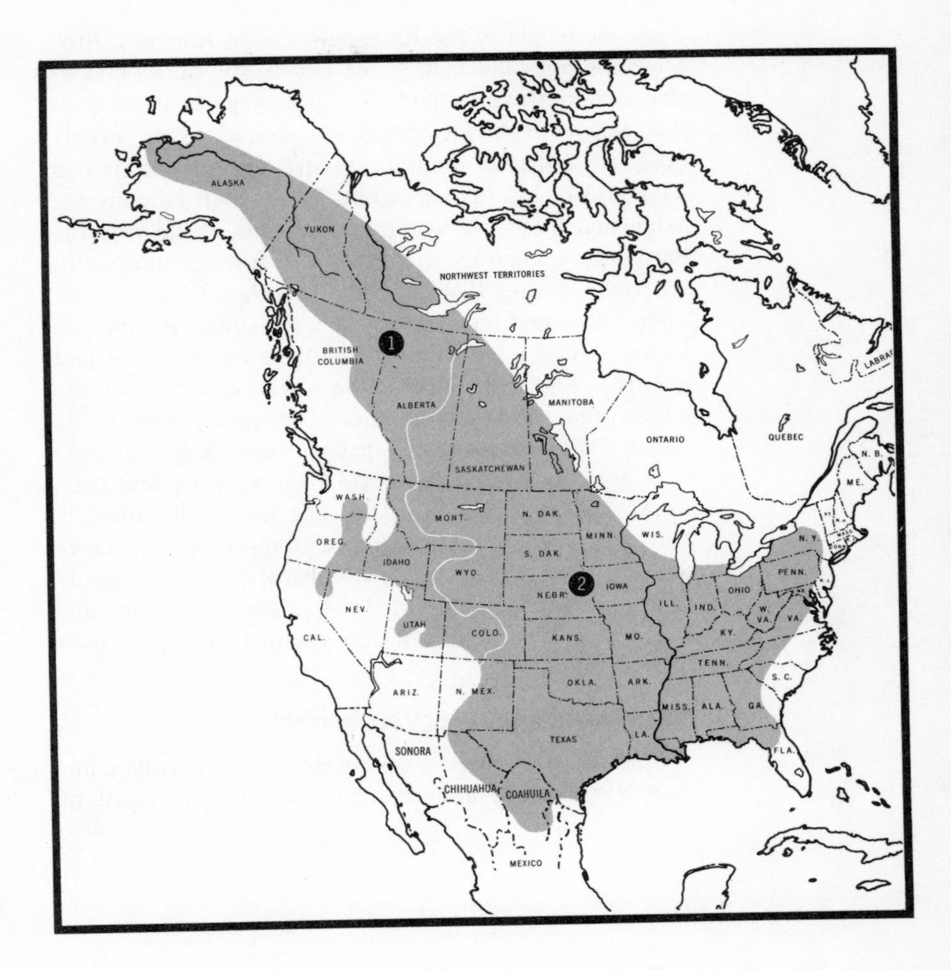


Distribution of the races of the bison *Bison*: 1. Wood bison, 2. Plains bison.

### VOCAL

When charging, a bull buffalo will emit a loud, shrill whistle that resembles the noise made by high-pressure steam suddenly released from a locomotive. During the rut, or mating season, bulls utter a deep, guttural roar. This terrifying sound, a challenge to any other bulls that may be in the neighborhood, can be heard intermittently day and night.

### ENEMIES

Indians, wolves, and bears were natural enemies of the buffalo but its greatest natural enemy was the melting ice of rivers and lakes each spring. The weight of the great herds sent them crashing through the thin ice and the surging mass behind forced wave after wave of struggling animals into the surging torrents, swollen by the melting ice and snow. Thousands perished.

## MATING

At the height of the rutting season, in June and July, the bulls not only fight fierce battles for possession of the cows but two individuals will engage in fierce conflict when there are no cows around. Two evenly matched bulls will continue to struggle for one or two days and nights in succession. When both animals are exhausted they sink to the ground, only to take up the battle again when sufficiently rested. It is not unusual to see bulls during the rut with their horns caked with dried blood and their curly foreheads smeared with red. In the case of a herd bull the battle is more violent and decisive. The issue settled, the victor is master of the harem and the vanquished departs, giving vent to its feelings with frequent dissatisfied roars. A harem consists of some twenty cows and their yearling and two-year-old calves of both sexes. The herd bull—there is only one during the rutting season—keeps its cows under careful watch. Outside the herd, 100 to 200 yards away, are small groups of three or four bachelor bulls that are either too old or too young to compete with the herd bull.

## BIRTH AND EARLY DEVELOPMENT

Mature cows breed every year, and the calves are born 9½ months after mating, from late in April to early in June. Usually a cow has a single calf; twins are rare. The newborn calf is a bright-tawny color with a dark-reddish band down the middle of its back. After the mother has gone through the ritual of licking and cleansing her offspring, the calf is strong enough to stand on its own wobbly legs and take its first meal. During the early days the cow stays close to her calf and makes no attempt to hide it in the bushes. The bulls as well as the cows are always ready to defend the calves from predators. In two or three days the calf is gamboling about with the other calves and can keep up with the herd. A calf is nursed for almost a year but has taken to grazing for itself long before this. The calf grows rapidly and soon loses its bright-colored coat. The bulls begin to get a shoulder hump when two or three months old and there is some indication of sprouting horns. Cow calves are ready to breed when three years old. The bull calves are sexually mature at the same age but are not big enough or strong enough to compete with the fully grown bulls. Bulls are not fully grown until the eighth year. Most buffalo have a life expectancy of about twenty years but records dating from the beginning of man's knowledge of the buffalo show that some lived all of forty years and were quite healthy and strong.

### Popular and Scientific Names of the American Buffalo, or Bison

**ORDER:** *Artiodactyla*
**FAMILY:** *Bovidae*
**GENUS:** *Bison*
**SPECIES:** *bison*

**SUBSPECIES**

| | |
|---|---|
| Plains bison | *Bison bison bison* |
| Wood bison | *Bison bison athabaseae* |
| Eastern bison | *Bison bison pennsylvanicus* |
| Mountain bison | *Bison bison haningtoni* |

CHAPTER 6

# THE WHITETAIL DEER

THE whitetail deer is the most widely distributed big game animal in the United States, the most plentiful, and the smartest. So crafty is the whitetail, and so much joy to hunt, that no one whose hunting is confined to the whitetail deer should feel very sorry for himself. He's got the best.

Whitetails are found, or have been found, in every state of the Union, in all the southern provinces of Canada, and throughout Mexico, with the exception of the peninsula of Lower California. Today he is still hunted over most of his original range, even in such prairie states as Illinois, Iowa, and Nebraska. Whitetails are shot even in tiny Delaware, and the ancient commonwealth of Pennsylvania, with an annual kill of over 100,000, is one of the best whitetail states in the Union. The middle-aged states of Michigan and Wisconsin have almost as large a whitetail kill each year as does Pennsylvania.

Give the whitetail a little cover, some food and water, and protection from year round hunting, and he'll take care of himself. He can get along with a minimum of even these essentials. In the deserts of Sonora, Mexico, whitetails live and die without ever tasting water; they get all their needed moisture from dew and the sap of plants. One of the best whitetail countries I have ever seen is a chain of low hills of decomposed granite near La Cienega, Sonora. Rain sinks into the ground the moment it strikes, and any open water in the country is found in deep wells that are fenced off and used for cattle and not available to deer. But this does not bother the whitetails at all.

And whitetails can get by with very little cover. Although they are traditionally animals of thick brush and forest, they'll often surprise you. I remember one time in Idaho when I was hunting pheasants in an enormous stubble field. There was not a tree in sight, but through the field ran a shallow draw which had been planted with grass about two feet high to check erosion. Mike, my Brittany spaniel, went on point at the edge of the grass. He had a sneaky, shifty-eyed look about him. I knew he wasn't on a pheasant because when he has one of the gaudy birds under his nose he wears the all-gone expression of a hepcat digging some sharp clarinet work. I suspected he was on a porcupine, something which surprised me because he hadn't paid any attention to porcupines since he'd got well stuck up by one when he was a pup. Anyway, I walked in on the point, and out from under my feet barreled the biggest, fattest, sleekest, most beautiful whitetail buck I have ever laid eyes on. The evidence showed he had been lying up in that grassy little draw for weeks. Adaptable? You're telling me.

Some of the whitetails in southern Arizona and northern Mexico are found in country rough enough for mountain sheep. Nowhere can they negotiate solid rock the way sheep can, but I have found these deer far up in sheep mountains wherever there was sufficient soil and broken talus to give them footing. Yet in the great plains, whitetails have been found in the brush and trees along the river bottoms. I have seen whitetails in wilderness country where man seldom comes, and in the outskirts of Westport, Connecticut, that haven of commuters. Many deer are killed annually in New Jersey within sight of the towers of Manhattan.

There are undoubtedly more whitetails in North America now than there were when Columbus discovered the New World. The reason is largely that the virgin forests have been cut down and light has been let in to bring up plants and brush suitable for deer fodder. Deer almost always multiply when forests are cut over or burned off.

For many years deer were hunted hard twelve months of the year, and their numbers in the older states decreased to the point where the sight of a wild deer was a rarity. Then, along about 1900, game laws began to have a few teeth in them, and with some protection and more forage the whitetails began to increase. In Pennsylvania, for example, only two hundred were killed in 1907. By 1923, 6,452 legal bucks were taken. At the turn of the century Maine was a land with great areas of wilderness and afforded the best deer hunting in the East. In 1899, 7,579 whitetails were killed there, compared with 38,413 in 1958.

O'Connor nailed the buck as it sneaked out ahead of another hunter, its tail down between its legs.

Most states passed buck laws around sixty years ago, and there is no doubt that protecting the does did much to speed the comeback of the whitetails. However, deer are prolific animals. The does breed young, and if they're in good condition they generally produce twins.

During the years of the buck law, the doe became a sacred animal to the American hunter, and his attitude toward the doe was about as rational as the attitude of a Hindu toward the sacred cow of India. The man who would shoot a doe (even legally) was in the same class as one who would rob widows and orphans or swindle his aged mother. I grew up in Arizona under the buck law and as a youngster was thoroughly indoctrinated. In my day I have shot a few fat does for meat, but in spite of the fact that they have all been perfectly legal, I have not enjoyed it and have always felt a nagging sense of guilt.

About 1920, game rangers and foresters began to see that in many areas deer were too plentiful for their own good. In places the second-growth forests that had furnished plentiful deer forage had grown up to the point where they no longer made good deer range. As the years went on the situation became acute, and in bad winters there was wholesale starvation among the deer.

Then the game managers began to tell license-buying sportsmen there were too many deer for their range and that does should be shot to hold the increase in check. A generation raised under the buck law reacted in shocked alarm. Too many deer? That was like saying a man had too much money, or that a woman could be too beautiful or too virtuous. Shooting does was like desecrating the American flag, casting doubt on the morals and motives of George Washington, or sneering at mother love. A violent controversy raged in Pennsylvania between those who opposed the shooting of does and wanted more and more deer and those who felt that to preserve the forage and the deer themselves does had to be shot and the herd reduced to the carrying capacity of the range.

The management of game is a difficult proposition because every man who has ever shot a deer becomes an authority on deer, and every man who has shot a duck knows all about ducks. In general, sportsmen have always opposed any reduction of deer numbers, and the rhubarb that had Pennsylvanians at each other's throats over the deer situation back in the nineteen twenties has been repeated elsewhere. When he becomes too plentiful, the whitetail is his own most serious enemy. Throughout the

East the situation has been complicated by the fact that all the natural predators of the whitetail have been killed off. The mountain lion and the wolf are extinct there, and bobcats and wild dogs are the only things, besides man, that prey on the deer.

However, today's sportsmen are better educated in the realities of game management than they were a generation ago, and game departments are better staffed, have more revenue, and more skilled and convincing technicians. Whitetail hunting in the United States should remain good for generations.

Not only has the adaptable whitetail increased in the East, but he has also come back in the Midwest and the South. A generation ago, deer were very rare in Missouri, but in 1950 the kill there was almost 14,000, and does are shot in some areas. In Kentucky and Tennessee the whitetail is coming back, and the annual Texas deer kill of around 100,000 is composed largely of whitetails.

The wide distribution of the whitetail, his vast numbers, and his nearness to civilization make him by far the most important game animal in the United States. Many hunters can only dream of a hunt for sheep and grizzly bears, for white goats or caribou, but they have whitetail hunting right next door. More rifles are purchased especially for whitetail hunting than for any other, and more man-hours are spent in the woods for whitetails than for any other game. The next most important animal is the mule deer, and after it would come the elk, the Pacific Coast blacktail, and the antelope.

Because whitetails are so widely distributed and range in so many different kinds of country—from chilly Maine to the semi-tropical everglades of Florida, and from the hills of Pennsylvania to the deserts of the Southwest—they are found in many subspecies. However, all have the same sort of a white tail, the same pattern of antlers, and the same general coloring. A New Yorker hunting for the first time in northern Idaho or Mexico would instantly recognize his old friend, the whitetail deer.

The antlers of a whitetail are different from those of the mule and blacktail deer in that all the points come off the main beam, and that the eye guard, or brow tine, is long and conspicuous. The antlers of the mule deer and the blacktail, in contrast, are evenly forked, and the brow point is smaller and sometimes absent altogether. Normally, the mature and well-fed whitetail buck of the East has four points and a brow point and would be what an Easterner would call a ten-pointer. In the West, where the brow tine is not counted, and where points are counted only on one side, the same buck would be called a four-pointer.

The whitetail found in Arizona and northern Mexico is the subspecies with which I am most familiar. He is a smaller deer on the average than those of the East, and the normal, mature Arizona whitetail head has an eye guard and three points, rather than four. Farther south in Mexico some bucks have only two points besides the brow tine.

As is the case with any deer, the antlers of old whitetail bucks often freak. They grow abnormal numbers of points. Often the antlers flatten, or palmate. Once in Arizona a hunter brought me a widely palmated, freak whitetail head and assured me it was a cross between a whitetail and a caribou. I tried to tell him there wasn't a caribou within 1,500 miles, but it made no difference. He knew a deer-caribou cross when he saw one. Freak heads are a sign of glandular imbalance and lagging sexual powers. If by accident or design a buck is emasculated, he never sheds the velvet from his antlers, and the antlers stay on until they are broken off or frozen. Glandular imbalance is responsible for the antlered doe that is shot now and then, and also for the antlerless bucks that one hears about occasionally.

Whitetails do not grow the tremendous antlers one finds on the best mule deer, but a big whitetail head is a handsome and impressive trophy. The new world record, entered in the Boone and Crockett Club's 1958-59 competition, is from Minnesota and was killed in 1918. It has a main beam of 31⅜ inches and eight points on each side. Of the other heads in the first ten, two are from Canada and one each from Minnesota, New York, South Dakota, Iowa, Texas, Montana, and Ohio. The number one and number two freak heads are from Texas. The record has twenty-three points on one side, twenty-six on the other.

I have always felt that the Black Hills of Wyoming should produce some excellent whitetail heads, because when I drove through there one time I saw excellent ones taken from local deer nailed up on the walls in every garage and filling station. Some excellent heads are also found on the northwestern whitetails of northern Idaho, Washington, and southeastern British Columbia.

In the summer, whitetails wear their "red" coats. Generally it is a soft, reddish-tan, but in the winter this is replaced by the "blue" coat, in most subspecies a salt-and-pepper, brownish-gray. In some areas the top of the whitetail's tail is body color, but in others the top of the tail is brick red. The inside of the front legs, belly, buttocks, and underside of the tail are pure white.

As anyone who has ever seen a whitetail knows, the animals throw up their tails when frightened, and to a jittery hunter the big, white "fan" sometimes looks as large as the deer. The tail is the most conspicuous thing about the animal and is, of course, responsible for the name. The mule deer, on the other hand, does not elevate his dinky, thinly haired little tail, and the Pacific Coast blacktail (which in many ways looks as if it might be an ancient cross between the mule deer and the whitetail) compromises and holds his medium-size tail horizontally.

It is commonly believed among hunters that when a whitetail is wounded he clamps his tail between his legs as he runs off. Often this happens, but on at least two occasions I have seen mortally wounded whitetail bucks run off with their flags flying gallantly in the air.

The mule deer has a black V on his forehead and a light muzzle, but the whitetail's face is dark almost to the nose. No one who knows the two species will ever mistake any whitetail scalp for that of a mule deer, and a freak set of mule deer antlers will resemble those of a whitetail.

The metatarsal glands of the whitetail are much smaller than those of the mule deer, and those of the Pacific Coast blacktail are about halfway in size between the two. In areas where mule and whitetail deer range in the same country, an animal occasionally is shot that is plainly a cross between the two species. Oddly enough, these hybrids look just about like Columbian blacktails. In the northwestern Sonora desert, where the mule deer range out on the flats and the Coues whitetail is found on all the little hills, these crosses are fairly common. When I lived in Tucson, Arizona, several specimens were brought to me by puzzled hunters who wanted to know what manner of animal they had shot.

In some places whitetails have degenerated because of poor range conditions until they are much smaller than their ancestors. In parts of Pennsylvania, where the range has long been overbrowsed and the deer are half starved a good part of the year, they are skinny, slab-sided, little animals that compare very poorly with the fine, sleek, and chunky bucks from the same state that come out of agricultural areas where they find plentiful food. Whitetails from the Texas hill country around Kerrville are scrawny little fellows, and from what I have seen of them it takes a big buck to weigh 85 pounds field dressed. Presumably the deer in the brush of south Texas along the Rio Grande are the same subspecies, but they are much larger deer that will weigh almost twice as much.

The Coues, or Arizona whitetail of southern Arizona, southwestern New Mexico, some mountains of west Texas, and northern Sonora and Chihuahua, is a small whitetail, but not as small as many of those who have written about him claim he is. The average buck will dress out at from 85 to 100 pounds. One weighing 110 is a large one, and the largest of several dozen that I have shot myself weighed 118½. The largest I have actually seen went 128½. I have heard of one that weighed 135, but I'm a bit skeptical of the report.

How heavy are the very largest whitetail bucks? About as heavy, from all I can find, as the largest mule deer. The average mature buck from Virginia will weigh about 150 pounds on the hoof and the average doe about 100. In the North the deer are heavier and in the South lighter, with the tiny Florida Keys deer the smallest of all.

I have heard of many whitetail bucks that were said to have weighed as much as a spike bull elk, well over 400 pounds field dressed. I wrote the State Conservation Commission for verification, but, like most stories of such deer, the tale blew up. No biologist saw the buck, I was informed, until it was cut up and partly eaten, and no one who would make an affidavit of the weight could be located. I was told that the largest Missouri whitetail the commission had any record of weighed 369 on the hoof. That's a walloping big whitetail, but it's a long way from 460 pounds field dressed.

As in the case with the mule deer, a whitetail buck that will weigh 200 pounds field dressed is a big buck. And also like the mule deer, an occasional, extraordinarily large whitetail will field dress over 300 pounds and weigh 400 pounds or so on the hoof. Maine and northern Michigan have produced many heavy bucks, and some very large ones have been shot in northern Idaho, Montana, Washington, and British Columbia. But even in the Northwest a buck that will dress out at 200 pounds is an exception. A buck from Michigan was recorded with a dressed weight of 354 pounds—a tremendous buck but within the realm of reason.

The owner of a locker plant in Lewiston, Idaho, reports that the heaviest deer ever brought into his place was a whitetail, not a mule deer, and that its field-dressed weight was about 325 pounds. I have never laid eyes on a buck of any sort that heavy.

As one goes south in Mexico deer are smaller, with those of Sinaloa running lighter than the Coues deer of the northern part of the state. I have shot several of these bucks, and I doubt if the largest would dress out to 60 pounds. Still farther south, around Acapulco, deer don't go much over 40, I have been told.

Whitetails are generally animals of small range, and as they increase they move into new country

A handsome buck barreled from the shallow draw when O'Connor, bird hunting, went in on the point.

slowly and experimentally. The average deer lives and dies in a few square miles of territory, and often deer will starve in an overpopulated area a few miles from good forage.

Even if hard hunting pushes a whitetail out of the little area which he regards as home, he'll come back as soon as he thinks the coast is clear. A frightened mountain sheep or an elk will travel for miles if he's had a good scare, but the whitetail buck will run a little way, sneak into some thick brush, and hide. In whitetail areas with which I am familiar, I find the same deer in the same canyons day after day, week after week.

I remember one very fine buck that lived all his life in an area not over two miles square. He grew an exceedingly fine head with, if I remember correctly, ten points on one side, nine on the other. His haunts were well known, and many hunted him. He was easy to see but almost impossible to get a good shot at. No matter which way hunters came at him, he had his escape routes all figured out. If he thought he had not been seen, he'd sneak off with his tail clamped between his legs. If, however, he was sure the hunter had glimpsed him, he'd tear out rapidly, giving his pursuer only a quick look at gray-brown body, flaunting white flag, and shining, many-pointed antlers. I finally learned his habits so well that a couple of friends and I ganged up on him and nailed him. He must have been twelve to fourteen years old at the time because he had been an exceptionally fine buck for six or seven years.

I remember another big buck with a very restricted range. A Mexican cowboy had seen a large, desert bighorn ram on a low and isolated but rough little chain of hills down on the Sonora desert about twenty-five miles from the Gulf of California. It looked like an easy sheep hunt, so every day for three days I would ride about five miles from the well where I was camped to the foot of the hill, tie my horse, and hunt.

Every day a big whitetail buck would get up from under a certain tree and trot off. I never did manage to see the ram. His tracks were all over the place, but there was a good deal of brush all over those hills and, because he would lie down where he was screened by brush, I could never get him in the glasses. One day I found where he'd come off the hill in the morning, fed for a time on cholla fruit on the flat, and had then left for the Sierra las Mochis. He had apparently been traveling from the Sierra Picu toward Las Mochis and had used the little chain of rugged hills as a rest house. There was a sheep migration route that passed right by the hills, and sheep commonly rested there.

When I learned that my ram had left, I decided to see if I could get the buck. Before that, I hadn't wanted to shoot because I was afraid I'd spook the ram. I rode over from camp and tied my horse about a half mile from where I usually saw the buck. There was a good cross wind from the sea, so I pussyfooted quietly along, approaching a little higher than I usually did so that when the buck came out I would be on the same level and not below him. The buck did not disappoint me. When he finally heard me I wasn't over 75 yards away. He looked at me as if wondering what in the world I had done with my horse. I nailed him.

The tales of the craft and cunning of the whitetail are legendary. He can sneak away more silently, lie quieter, and outwit the hunter better than any other game animal in North America. I remember one occasion when my wife and I were hunting in south-

As O'Connor got up from the fallen tree to continue hunting, a deer exploded from the branches.

ern Arizona. At noon we stopped, tied our horses at the edge of a brushy canyon, and prepared to eat lunch. Deer sign was everywhere, so, while the little woman was getting out the food, I picked up some rocks and tossed them into the brush below. Nothing moved. Finally I gave up. We ate our sandwiches, drank our coffee, and stretched out for a brief snooze in the warm and pleasant midday sun.

Eventually, it was time to move on. I still couldn't get the notion out of my head that there should have been deer in that particular canyon. Again I started half-heartedly tossing rocks. Finally one slipped from my hand and fell almost directly below us. The brush popped, and out came a handsome, whitetail buck. We almost dislocated our shoulders getting to our rifles. That darned buck had been lying within 50 feet of us for an hour.

Another time I was hunting the Chiricahuas in Arizona. I had walked 10 to 12 miles, hunting as I went, but about a mile from the ranch house where I was staying, I came across an oak that had been cut down, probably so it would dry for firewood. The leaves were still on it, but dry, and it was right out in the open with no tree or brush nearby. The night before it had been cold enough to freeze water, but it had warmed up during the day, and I was hot, thirsty, and leg weary. I sat down on one of the branches of the oak, took a drink of water from my little canteen, and smoked a cigarette. Finally I decided to move on. My rifle was leaning against a limb about six feet from where I had been sitting, and as I reached for it a buck exploded out of the branches and threw dry leaves all over me. I shot the buck as he scooted for cover. Then I went back to the place where he'd been lying. To save my life, I couldn't figure out why I hadn't seen him before.

And can a whitetail be sneaky. Once in Sonora a pal and I were hunting a brushy, star-shaped hill with seven or eight ravines that came together toward the top. Both of us had horses, and we were accompanied by a Mexican vaquero. One of us would stay at the head of a ravine and the other, with the Mexican lad, would go around and come up the bottom, riding through the brush and making plenty of noise to move deer. My pal had shot a buck in the morning and now it was my turn.

On this particular occasion I saw something gray about a half a mile away moving ahead of my pal. The glass showed it to be a good whitetail buck. It would sneak quietly off, stop, and listen. Then it would move on again. Because I was above, I could see both hunter and buck. Finally the buck edged around and went into some thick brush between the vaquero and my partner. Then, when they were about 50 yards past, he sneaked off until he got to the mouth of the ravine. He then tossed up that white tail and the last time I saw him he was making knots across the flat.

And here's a story with a better ending—at least for me, if not for the deer. Two pals and I decided to hunt a brushy hill. I was to go low on the left side, one companion was to be low on the right, and the third up on the top. We thought one of us would surely move a deer to one of the others. We hadn't gone far when I glimpsed a movement about 50 feet in front of my friend on top. It was a big whitetail buck, and he was sneaking along with his tail between his legs as if he were walking on eggshells. I sat down, held the crosswires on a little opening the buck would have to cross, and when he got there I put a .270 bullet right through his lungs. To make the story even better, the shot spooked a second buck that had been sneaking off and that I hadn't seen. Frightened into losing his caution, he exposed himself and my pal nailed him. If I hadn't been fairly bright eyed and caught a glimpse of that first buck, none of us would have known there were deer so close.

Incidentally, that whitetail buck I shot had two complete antlers on one side, each with three points. I gave it to the zoology collection at the University of Arizona, and presumably it is still there.

Because of the many different types of country that whitetails inhabit, there are many different ways of hunting them. In the wooded East, I have been told that the deer are usually driven, with the standers placed on runways and the drivers working through the brush to move the deer. I hunted deer that way once in Pennsylvania. In South Carolina I hunted deer driven by dogs and beaters. In some areas the deer feed low and then move up to the hardwood ridges to lie up during the day, and the smart hunter is out as soon as he can see to catch them while they are moving. I have a lazy friend who gets his buck every year simply by waiting in a saddle back where deer come through and letting other hunters move the bucks over him.

In country where a man can move quietly and where deer lie up for the day, I like to pussyfoot along upwind, going 50 yards at a time, and then stopping to look and listen. If a hunter barrels right along as if he were competing in a walking contest, the deer will let him walk right past them. It is this business of stopping that upsets them. They begin to wonder if they haven't been seen, and often they lose their nerve and take off.

In areas of thick brush in the southern Arizona mountains, I used to like hunting with a companion. One man would take one side of a canyon and one the other. Usually the hunter would not see the deer on the same side of the canyon that he was on, but would shoot the deer his companion jumped. Generally it is more successful for two to hunt together and have a plan. Like most animals, the whitetail deer has a one-track mind, and as he sneaks away from one hunter he's often been known to walk right over another.

In thinly brushed country, the queen of all ways of hunting is to work out the canyon on horseback, riding up the cattle trails that usually go along the sides and pausing occasionally to roll stones down into the brush. It makes for some pretty fast and fancy shooting.

Whitetails are shot with everything from single-barreled shot-guns taking buckshot and rifle slugs to .300 Weatherbys and .375 Magnums. They are shot at 20 yards and at 400, by dubs and by crack shots. Generally in the wooded East they are killed at ranges under 100 yards, but some crack shots shoot deer in openings across wide ravines, and in thin brush.

The .30/30 is the classic deer cartridge, and with bullets of proper construction it does very well to 150 yards or so. Other widely used cartridges for short and intermediate ranges are the .35 Remington and the .300 Savage. The .308 and the .358 are coming up in popularity. For short-range whitetail shooting the .30/06 is a lot of cartridge, but it is widely used, even in the East.

The average whitetail is a small animal, as big game animals go, with thin skin and fragile bones. Whatever the caliber used, the bullet should be one that will open quickly against light resistance. In rifles of the .30/30 class I am convinced that the best medicine is still the old-fashioned, soft point with soft lead core and thin jacket. Some bullets of the controlled-expanding class open up too slowly to do the job right.

In the Southwest, where I've done most of my whitetail hunting, I have got the quickest kills with relatively light bullets at high velocity—the old 139-grain open point in the 7 mm., the 150-grain in the .30/06, the 120- and 130-grain bullets in the .270, and even the 87-grain in the .250/3000. With these a shot in the chest cavity usually means an instantaneous kill, and even a gut shot will generally disable a deer so that it will not go far. I don't recommend gut shots with anything, but sometimes they cannot be avoided.

The whitetail is a grand animal, and the man who hunts him owes it to himself and to the deer to use good equipment, shoot carefully, and kill cleanly.

# The Natural History of the Whitetail Deer

[ODOCOILEUS VIRGINIANUS]

## DESCRIPTION

One of our most graceful big game animals, the whitetail deer has a long, slender neck, rather narrow face, large appealing eyes, large ears, long, slender legs with high-tension muscles, and small, sharp-pointed hoofs. The whitetail is a moderately large deer varying from 60 to 75 inches in head and body length and from 30 to 40 inches high at the shoulder, according to the species. The average full-grown buck weighs about 150 pounds; a doe, 100 pounds; a large buck may weigh up to 200 pounds. A northern whitetail buck (*O. v. borealis*) may have a maximum live weight of 400 pounds. Coues whitetail, the dwarf deer (*O. v. couesi*), scarcely ever exceed 100 pounds. A buck with a live weight of 170 pounds will weigh 110 pounds when dressed.

As its name implies, the whitetail has a long, bushy tail, long for a deer, snow-white on the underside and brown or reddish-brown above. When the animal is disturbed and bounds away, the tail is carried aloft swaying from side to side, an unmistakable signal to other deer close by that danger is not far away. Hence the name flagtail that is often applied to this deer. When the animal wishes to steal silently away unobserved in the underbrush, the tail is held tightly down concealing the white flag.

A member of the even-toed hoofed mammals, order *Artiodactyla,* the whitetail walks on the extreme tips of its toes in a manner known as digitigrade that has been adopted by some of the mammals for fast locomotion. The third and fourth toes of the fore and hind feet are large, evenly paired with the terminal joints encased in horny sheaths which make up the hoof.

During the summer the Virginia deer has a short coat of reddish-brown hair over most of its body, a distinct white band across the nose and a less noticeable white ring around the eye, a white bib on the throat and white underparts. The short "red" summer coat is replaced in the late fall by the "blue," a grayish-brown coat of longer and rather brittle hair. Lachrymal and pear-shaped metatarsal glands are well developed in the whitetail.

## ANTLERS

A member of the deer family *Cervidae,* the whitetail has solid antlers as opposed to some other ruminants (cud-chewers) which have hollow horns. Typically male attributes, antlers may appear on does suffering from glandular disturbance, although they are rare.

The antlers of the whitetail are low, compact, and well suited for a life in the dense, tangled undergrowth of deciduous woodland. The main beam of the antler rising from back of the head behind the eyes curves slightly upward, forward, outward, and then curves inward over the face. A series of short, unbranched tines, or points, project upward from the main beam and a small, short spike, or brow tine, projects upward from in front just above the base of the beam. The record length of the main beam is 31⅜ inches with eight points on each side. Abnormal or freak antlers may have as many as twenty-six points on a side.

Antlers are usually shed in January or February, but some are dropped early in December and some as late as early April. Discarded antlers are eaten by the gnawing rodents and in some regions where there is a scarcity of lime, by the deer themselves. The new antlers begin to show in April or May. About two weeks after the old antlers are shed a soft, spongy rounded ball covered with velvet-like fur begins to rise from the pedicels left by the former antlers. This is the beginning of the new ones. As time elapses the ball of fur becomes elongated and takes on a definite form or pattern peculiar to the species. During all the stages of growth until full size has been attained, the antlers are covered with velvet; they are soft, spongy, with a complete circulatory blood system. Up to this time the antlers are easily damaged and carefully guarded from injury. When the final form, size, and consistency of the antlers has been reached, some time about the middle of August, the blood stream is cut off, the antlers dry out and the velvet covering begins to crack, peel, and is scraped off by the buck. The antlers, now hardened, are finally rubbed and polished on branches and trunks of trees.

For the first year the spotted fawns of both sexes are without antlers. At the age of four months roughened outgrowths begin to form on the parietal bones of the skull in male fawns. These are not the beginning of the actual antlers but the bases or pedicels from which the antlers will eventually grow. A young buck gets its first set of antlers when sixteen months old, usually a simple pair of straight spikes 1½ to 5 inches long; in the subsequent year, two points and then perhaps three until the fourth or fifth year, when a typical pair of four-point antlers is normal, each main beam having four main points and for the first time a short brow tine. From this time on the size of the antlers and number of points is not an indication of the age of a buck but of its vigor. A whitetail is in its prime from the ninth to eleventh year and has a life expectancy, under favorable conditions, of sixteen years. During the last five years in the life of a buck there is a tendency to irregularity in the size and shape of its antlers. Few whitetails live out their full allotted time. A deer, if it escapes hunters, cougars, and wolves, lives as long as its teeth last, which are getting worn down close to the gums in its eleventh or twelfth year.

**ORIGIN**

Unlike the big-horn sheep, elk, moose, and caribou that emigrated to America during the early Pleistocene period over the land bridge that once extended across the Bering Sea from Asia to Alaska, the whitetail deer is of New World origin. It was derived from a primitive cervid stock that existed in North America during the Pliocene and Miocene periods, between ten and twenty million years ago. Modern whitetail deer, much the same as the animals we see today, populated this continent during the Pleistocene period a million years ago. The whitetail deer *Odocoileus* and its North American allies, the mule deer and the blacktail deer, represent a branch of the cervid stock that split off from the main stem at a very early date.

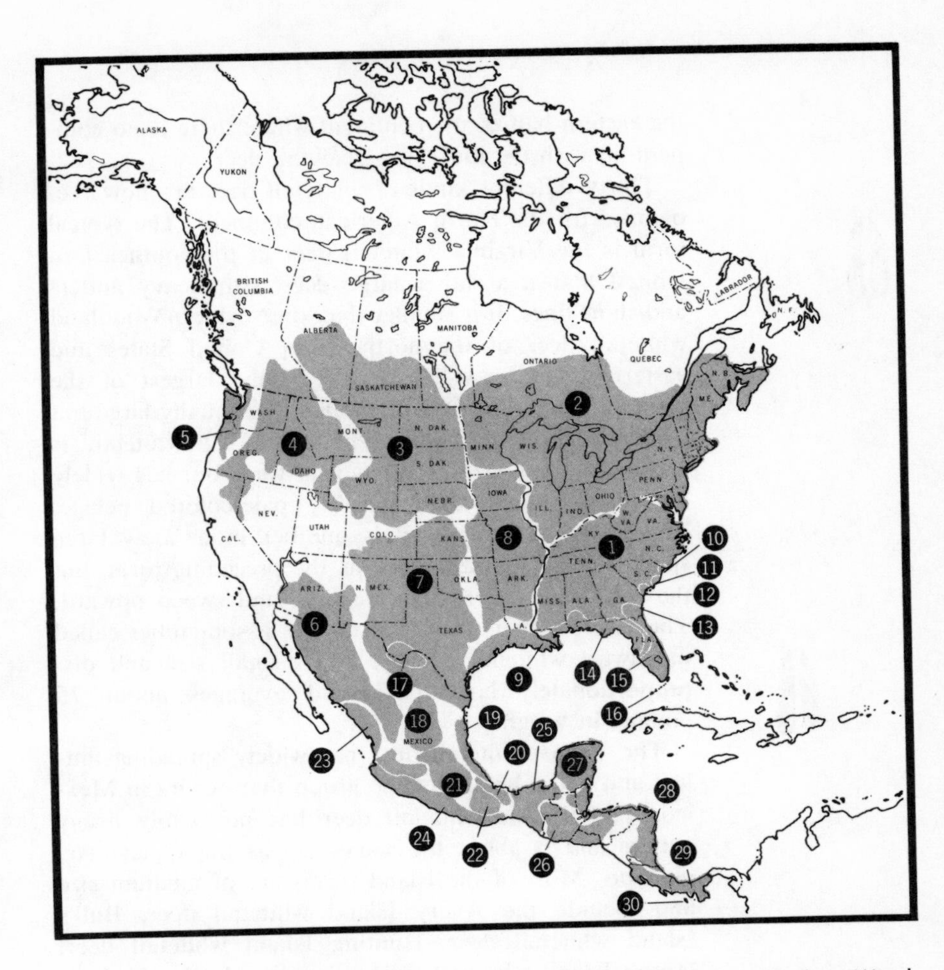


Distribution of races of whitetail deer *Odocoileus:* 1. Virginia whitetail, 2. Northern Woodland whitetail, 3. Dakota whitetail, 4. Northwest whitetail, 5. Columbian whitetail, 6. Coues, Fantail or Dwarf whitetail, 7. Texas whitetail, 8. Kansas whitetail, 9. Avery Island whitetail, 10. Bull's Island whitetail, 11. Hunting Island whitetail, 12. Hilton Island whitetail, 13. Blackbeard Island whitetail, 14. Florida Coast whitetail, 15. Florida whitetail, 16. Keys whitetail, 17. Carmen whitetail, 18. Miquihuana whitetail, 19. Northern Veracruz whitetail, 20. Rain Forest whitetail, 21. Mexican Tableland whitetail, 22. Oaxaca whitetail, 23. Sinaloa whitetail, 24. Acapulco whitetail, 25. Mexican Lowland whitetail, 26. Chiapas whitetail, 27. Yucatan whitetail, 28. Nicaragua whitetail, 29. Chiriqui whitetail, 30. Coiba Island whitetail.

Ever since the white man arrived in America the whitetail deer has been of great economic importance and recreational value and is perhaps the most important big game animal on the North American continent. It provided not only the early pioneers, but the Indians as well, with an important source of meat for food, skins for clothing, and sport for recreation. Deer hides served as a standard medium of exchange during colonial days and when money was scarce hunters nearly exterminated the whitetail in many parts of New England and other eastern states. The whitetail soon responded under the protection of modern conservation laws and there are now more deer in the East than in primitive times.

**RANGE**

The overall geographical range of the whitetail deer extends in suitable terrain from Nova Scotia and the southern tip of Hudson Bay across Canada to British Columbia, south through the United States, Mexico, Central America to Colombia in South America and some of the adjacent islands, but not Vancouver or Newfoundland. Whitetail deer are most abundant in the eastern half of the continent where there is no competition with the mule and blacktail deer.

Thirty different kinds of whitetail deer are now recognized for the North American continent. The typical form is the Virginia whitetail deer of the southeastern United States, a rather large deer with heavy antlers and short tines. It is smaller than the Northern Woodland whitetail deer of the northeastern United States and eastern Canada, which is one of the largest of the whitetail deer. The Dakota whitetail is equally large but usually darker in color. The Northwest whitetail is about the same size as the typical form but has widely spreading antlers and relatively pale-colored pelage. The Columbian whitetail is another moderately large species about the same size as the preceding form, but the antlers are narrowly spreading and sweep upward. The Coues whitetail deer, or fantail, is sometimes called the dwarf whitetail because of its small size and disproportionately large ears, and averages about 75 pounds in weight.

The Texas whitetail deer has widely spreading antlers and is the largest of the group that occurs in Mexico. The Kansas whitetail deer has noticeably heavy antlers and is about the same size as the typical *virginianus*. Most of the island forms are of medium size and include the Avery Island whitetail deer, Bull's Island whitetail deer, Hunting Island whitetail deer, Hilton Island whitetail deer, Blackbeard Island whitetail deer, and Florida Coastal whitetail deer. The Florida whitetail deer is a moderately large form with narrowly spreading antlers. The Florida Key deer, or Key's deer, is the smallest of the eastern species with very small antlers. The Carmen Mountain whitetail deer is another small form with spreading antlers that have very short tines. The Miquihuana whitetail deer is a small, grizzled form similar to Coues deer but with smaller ears. The various other forms that occupy Mexico include: Northern Veracruz whitetail, Rain Forest whitetail, Tableland whitetail, Oaxaca whitetail, Sinaloa whitetail, Acapulco whitetail, Lowland whitetail, Chiapas whitetail, Yucatan whitetail, Nicaragua whitetail, Chiriqui whitetail, and Coiba Island whitetail, smallest of the Mexican forms.

## HABITS

Pleasant, sunlit woodland glades and quiet, sheltered meadows are the choice habitat of the shy, elusive whitetail deer. It is a browsing animal and feeds on the fresh green leaves and twigs of shrubs and the lower branches of trees that flourish in the undergrowth, especially of deciduous woods. Its search for food leads the whitetail to where there is an abundance of green shoots and leaves of blackberry vines, raspberry canes, greenbriar, witch hazel, elderberry, maples, oaks, sassafras, dogwood, rose, water lilies, sedges and other kinds of aquatic plants, as well as many kinds of grasses. In the fall it feeds on nuts, fruits and seeds, especially acorns and apples. During the scarcity of food in winter it will eat the needles and sprouts of evergreens such as spruce, balsam, white pine and fir trees, along with dead and dried leaves and grasses, as well as some mosses.

A ruminant, or cud-chewing, mammal, the whitetail has no incisors or front teeth at the front of the upper jaw. The long, flexible, grayish-blue tongue draws twigs, leaves and grasses into the mouth and cuts them off across the sharp edges of the lower front teeth. Broad back or molar teeth with razor sharp tubercles on the surface and cutting edges mill and grind the food to pulp. A combination or multiple compound stomach is characteristic of the cud-chewing hoofed mammals. The advantage of being a ruminant is that it enables the animal to consume a large quantity of food in a comparatively short time in exposed areas and store it temporarily in the paunch or first stomach. Later, the animal can retire to a sheltered, secluded spot to rest in safety and chew the cud, when the partly shredded fodder mixed with stomach gastric juices is returned to the mouth in a succession of small balls to be thoroughly milled and then passed on to the other stomach for further processing. This time the food bypasses the paunch.

Social life of the whitetail deer is largely limited to the doe and her fawns. The whitetail, however, is not anti-social. Several individuals may occupy the same thicket during the summer but at a discrete distance and may yard together during the days of winter snow. With a natural homing instinct each whitetail has its own particular summer range which is smaller than might be supposed, considerably less than 1 mile in diameter. The winter range may be even less, especially when deep snow necessitates yarding or trampling down the snow to find fodder.

The sharp-pointed hoofs of a whitetail are its principal weapons of defense. Bucks may use their antlers but they are only servicable for a short time each year. For some unknown reason the whitetail has an inherited dislike of snakes and will fiercely attack and kill rattlers or any other kind of snake it meets. By repeatedly leaping into the air and coming down with all four feet together, it soon rips the surprised reptile to shreds with its hoofs.

## LOCOMOTION

Moving with remarkable grace and rhythm, the whitetail has a number of forms of locomotion. It may move at a slow, meditative walk or a leisurely trot; it may canter in a succession of three or four low leaps, followed by a long, broad jump, then break into a more uniform, steady canter. In a long chase it can build up a great speed with a steady, fast, low gallop cutting out the long leaps which cut down speed. The whitetail has been clocked at speeds of 20 and 35 miles per hour. At 25 miles per hour it can cover several miles without slowing down. A running long jump of 29 feet actually has been measured for the whitetail and it can make a succession of long jumps up to 20 feet. The measured high jump is 8½ feet but it probably can do

Walking on hard ground, the whitetail places its hind foot in the rear of the track left by its forefoot. The lateral hoofs do not register.

The tracks left by a galloping whitetail are spaced well apart, the hind feet falling in front of the forefeet, the lateral hoofs registering.

better than this. An excellent swimmer, the whitetail will cross a channel in the sea or a lake 5 miles wide and one was recorded swimming at a speed of 13 miles per hour for a quarter of a mile, then slowed to 11 miles for the next quarter mile.

## TRACKS

When walking on firm ground, the whitetail's traditional foot print or track is heart-shaped. The left and right fore and hind foot prints are slightly staggered, about 13 inches apart. The heart-shaped walking track is made when both sides of the cloven hoof are drawn close together. The walking track is always a double print; that is to say, there is an imprint of two sets of hoofs, one partly covering the other. As the whitetail leads with the right front foot the left hind foot comes forward; then the left front moves forward and the right hind foot is brought forward and comes down on the track left by the right forefoot. Galloping, all four feet come down together making four distinct separate foot prints in a staggered line or bunched in a triangle with a distance of about six feet between each set of four. The hoofs spread outward when galloping or jumping, leaving a broad V-shaped track with the dewclaws making two dots one behind each side of the paired hoofs. The dewclaws show just behind the hoof prints of the forefeet and are shown farther back on the hind foot track. On an average the length of the imprint left by the forefoot, including the dewclaws, is about 4 inches, the hoof itself being 3 inches. The overall length of the track left by the hind foot of a large northern buck would be 4¼ inches but the hoof alone, 2¾ inches. In a small Texas deer the hoof would be about 2 inches long.

## VOCAL

Although having well-developed vocal powers, a whitetail rarely utters a sound. It is curious about things it does not understand and will snort and stamp on the ground when a strange object fails to move and declare itself.

## MATING

The whitetail deer is prolific and the does begin to breed at an early age. Bucks begin to show an interest

The whitetail derives its name from the snow-white underside of its tail, which it carries aloft when disturbed.

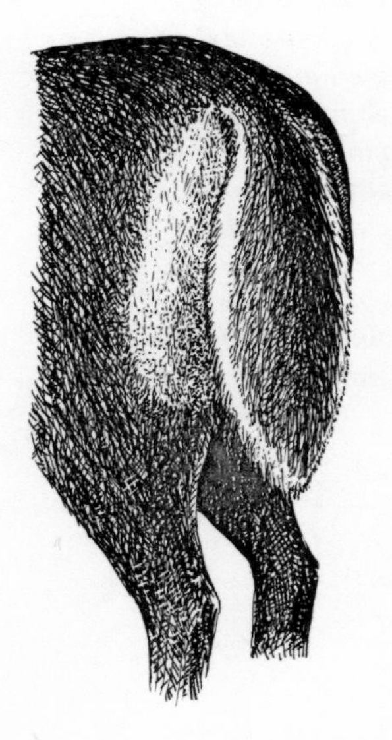

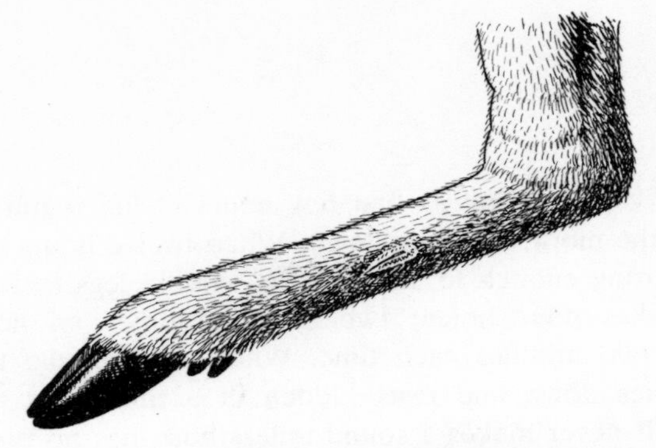

A small metatarsal gland, a narrow slit about one inch long, is located on the inner side of the whitetail's hind foot.

in the opposite sex in September soon after their antlers have hardened and been polished. At this time of the year, the bucks' necks swell due to the development of the neck muscles, signifying their combative disposition. The height of the rutting season comes in November but some does may not mate until February. Deer, especially bucks, are extremely dangerous during the rut. Pets that have been friendly, docile, and trustworthy even with children, suddenly become possessed with a maddening desire to attack and kill their most cherished friends. Normally young does are ready to breed in their eighteenth month but some mate when only eight months old. Young bucks are ready to breed when 1½ years of age but most of the breeding is done by the older and more vigorous bucks 2½ years and over. Fierce battles may be fought between contestants for possession of a doe. Battles are fought with the antlers, each keeping an armed front toward a foe to escape getting gored in the body. When two evenly matched fighting bucks meet head on, the impact is terrific and on occasion the blow may spread the antlers enough to inseparably interlock the two heads together, when both animals must die of exhaustion or starvation.

In general it is believed that most whitetails are polygamous but there is sufficient evidence to prove that in some instances a particular doe and buck will pair regularly for several years in succession. However, there is no attempt by whitetail bucks to round up a harem as is common practice with the elk.

## BIRTH AND EARLY DEVELOPMENT

In the sunny days of May when spring flowers begin to bloom, the fawn in its bright polka-dotted coat is born in a secluded spot or sheltered thicket. This is 201 days, give or take one or two days, after mating. The newborn fawn is fed within the hour. The first-born is always a solitary individual but in the succeeding years a doe may have a single, twins, triplets, or even quadruplets, but two fawns to a doe each year is near the average. Newborn bucks weigh about 7 pounds each; does 5 pounds. From the very first the fawn has its eyes wide open and is completely covered with warm hair. Its coat is a bright bay-red with numerous snow-white spots in marked contrast. The first duty of a mother is to lick the fawn thoroughly from tip of the nose to the end of the tail and tips of its tiny hoofs. This is not only to wash the fawn and eliminate the possibility of its getting fly blown, but the mother will now recognize it

Bunched sets of tracks distinguish a whitetail's bounding gait. Again, hind feet land in front of forefeet, and lateral hoofs register.

as her own. During its first few hours of life it nurses while the mother is lying down. When twelve hours old it is strong enough to stand on its wobbly legs to feed and takes nourishment two or three times an hour about two minutes each time. When not feeding, the fawn lies down and rests hidden in a thicket or tall grass. It never makes a sound unless hurt, has no body odor to betray its presence; a bear or dog may pass within a few feet of its hiding place without stopping to investigate. The doe never visits her fawn except at feeding time. Deer milk is about three times richer in solids, butter fat, and protein than dairy cow's milk. A fawn soon outgrows the awkward stage and gets control of its high-tension muscles. When less than a month old it can evade capture by the average man. For the first month the fawn stays closely hidden in the brush or thicket, but is out accompanying its mother when five weeks old. Its spots begin to fade in the third month and have all but disappeared by September, about the time the adults change from the "red" summer coat to their "blue" winter coat.

Fawns are weaned just before the start of the rut when three or four months old. Family ties are not completely broken until the following spring but bucks do not normally associate with the does at any time except during the rut.

There is reason to believe that the whitetail deer will survive all other big game in North America. During the past century moose, elk, grizzly bear, cougar, pronghorn, and caribou all have rapidly diminished in numbers, while the whitetail deer has increased and in some regions more than doubled its original numbers.

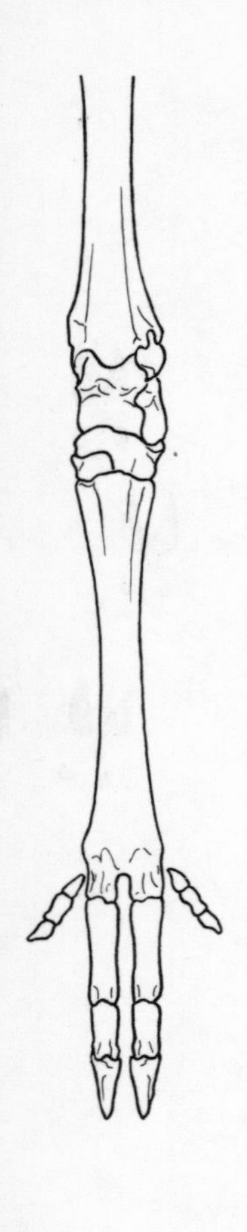

The front view of the whitetail's hind-foot bone structure reveals the formation of the large, well-developed third and fourth toes of the hoof, with the second and fifth toes—the lateral hoofs—above.

The side view of the whitetail's hind-foot bone structure shows the deer's manner of walking on the tips of its toes. The small lateral hoofs are visible above the main hoof.

## Popular and Scientific Names of the Whitetail Deer

**ORDER:** *Artiodactyla*

**FAMILY:** *Cervidae*

**GENUS:** *Odocoileus*

**SPECIES:** *virginianus*

**SUBSPECIES**

| | |
|---|---|
| Virginia whitetail deer | *Odocoileus virginianus virginianus* |
| Northern Woodland whitetail deer | *Odocoileus virginianus borealis* |
| Dakota whitetail deer | *Odocoileus virginianus dacotensis* |
| Northwest whitetail deer | *Odocoileus virginianus ochrourus* |
| Columbian whitetail deer | *Odocoileus virginianus leucurus* |
| Coues, Fantail, of Dwarf whitetail deer | *Odocoileus virginianus couesi* |
| Texas whitetail deer | *Odocoileus virginianus texanus* |
| Kansas whitetail deer | *Odocoileus virginianus macrourus* |
| Avery Island whitetail deer | *Odocoileus virginianus mcilhennyi* |
| Bull's Island whitetail deer | *Odocoileus virginianus taurinsulae* |
| Hunting Island whitetail deer | *Odocoileus virginianus venatorius* |
| Hilton Island whitetail deer | *Odocoileus virginianus hiltonensis* |
| Blackbeard Island whitetail deer | *Odocoileus virginianus nigrabarbis* |
| Florida Coast whitetail deer | *Odocoileus virginianus osceola* |
| Florida whitetail deer | *Odocoileus virginianus seminolus* |
| Keys whitetail deer | *Odocoileus virginianus clavium* |
| Carmen whitetail deer | *Odocoileus virginianus carminis* |
| Miquihuanna whitetail deer | *Odocoileus virginianus miquihuanensis* |
| Northern Veracruz whitetail deer | *Odocoileus virginianus veracrucis* |
| Rain Forest whitetail deer | *Odocoileus virginianus toltecus* |
| Mexican Tableland whitetail deer | *Odocoileus virginianus mexicanus* |
| Oaxaca whitetail deer | *Odocoileus virginianus oaxacensis* |
| Sinaloa whitetail deer | *Odocoileus virginianus sinaloae* |
| Acapulco whitetail deer | *Odocoileus virginianus acapulcensis* |
| Mexican Lowland whitetail deer | *Odocoileus virginianus thomasi* |
| Chiapas whitetail deer | *Odocoileus virginianus nelsoni* |
| Yucatan whitetail deer | *Odocoileus virginianus yucatanensis* |
| Nicaragua whitetail deer | *Odocoileus virginianus truei* |
| Chiriqui whitetail deer | *Odocoileus virginianus chiriquensis* |
| Coiba Island whitetail deer | *Odocoileus virginianus rothschildi* |

CHAPTER 7

# THE MULE DEER

WHENEVER anyone assures me that all mule deer are morons, I think of the first really big buck I ever shot. I knew of a chain of hills where early in the season I had always seen a good many does, fawns, and young bucks. One year I turned down easy shots at two or three perfectly legal males, knowing that late in the season a big fellow would probably show up to boot out the small bucks and take over the harem.

So it came about that one afternoon when the Arizona season had only a couple of days to go, and when every morning white frost glinted on the grass and the brooks up in the mountains were frozen at the edges, I hit my little chain of hills again. By taking a game trail up the side of a wide canyon I had an easy walk to the top. When I got there I planned to work along the ridge and hunt the points and the heads of the draws.

I hardly started up the trail when I saw a movement in the buckbrush and junipers about 400 yards ahead of me and toward the top of the ridge. It was a doe. Then I saw more shadowy gray forms, and I could tell that about a dozen deer were going over the top. Then a larger form detached itself from the group and sneaked off to the left. Even at a quarter of a mile or so I could see a big gray body and heavy, many-pointed antlers. Here was the buck I had been looking for, the old boy himself. He had collected his harem and chased the young bucks out, but now that danger threatened he was abandoning the ladies and looking after his own sleek hide.

I felt that he'd cut over the ridge into the head of the next draw. So the moment he was out of sight, I ran over the ridge that separated the two canyons and stopped in a spot that gave me a good look at the far side. I hadn't got my wind back when I heard a stone roll, and in a moment I saw him slipping through the scrubby junipers and piñons with his head up and his great antlers laid back so they would get through the brush easier. If he kept on coming he would go by me on the opposite side of the draw, so I switched off the safety of my Springfield and waited.

It was the first time I'd ever been close to a really big trophy buck, and I'll never forget the sight he presented—the blocky, dark-gray body, the heavy brown antlers with the many points polished sharp and bright, the massive neck swelled from the rut, the maniacal look of lust and excitement in his eyes. I had the wind on him and I could smell the oily rancid odor of the rutting mule deer, a smell at once fascinating and repellent, heavy, musky, greasy. He saw the movement when I lifted the rifle to my shoulder, and stopped less than 50 yards away. Winded, and shaking with excitement though I was, I couldn't very well miss him. There was nothing wrong with that buck's brains. In the grip of the strongest of instincts, he was yet smart enough and cool-headed enough to leave his does as decoys and try to slip out to one side and around the danger.

The mule deer is no boob, but I must admit that he generally isn't as smart as his cousin the whitetail, or as hard to get. Part of this comes from the fact that he is more of an open-country animal and hence is easier to see and hunt. But part of it also comes from the fact that he does not lie as close, that he takes longer to make up his mind, and that he often is addicted to the fatal habit of stopping for one last look before he gets out of sight.

A whitetail will conceal himself in a patch of brush hardly big enough to hide a pheasant. If he thinks he can't sneak off unseen, he'll sit tight with hunters all around him. When he thinks he has to move, he's off like a rocketing grouse and he doesn't stop for a backward look. The mule deer, on the other hand, has a tendency to move off and reveal himself in the face of danger, to jitter around, unable to decide which way to run, and to stop for one good look. But old trophy bucks get cautious. They select their beds with care, and get almost as good as the whitetail is at slipping away from the hunter.

A very smart and close-lying buck mule deer I'll never forget was one I shot in northern Arizona in 1934. I had made a long trip to hunt an area I knew well, and I was after a trophy head. I turned down several small bucks and a couple of good average ones with four points to a side. About two p.m. of my last day I stopped on the brink of a canyon to eat a sandwich. I was still without a deer and was kicking myself for passing up the two four-pointers. Below me I could see the trail that led to about camp five miles away. I was going to have to start back, pack up, and leave empty-handed.

After I finished my sandwich, I drank from my canteen, smoked a cigarette, and started to lead my horse down the side of the canyon which was too steep and rocky to ride down safely. I hadn't gone more than 30 yards when a tremendous buck got up from beneath a juniper below me about 300 yards away and took off. On my second or third shot he fell head over heels and lay in the scrubby sage. When I got to him I found he needed another shot. The bullet that dumped him had passed through the knee joint of his left front leg. He must have had most of his weight on this leg when it was struck, and the fall must have stunned him. He had seven points on one side, six on the other, and a spread of 34½ inches. A right fair buck. All the time he'd been lying there getting more and more nervous, and when I started toward him he must have thought he'd been seen. If I'd gone the other way, I'm sure I would never have known he was there. All mule deer aren't dumb.

The fact that they have adapted themselves to great varieties of climate and terrain also shows they have their share of brains. They are found from the Dakotas to the crest of the Coast Ranges, from the hot subtropical deserts of Sonora, Mexico, to the subarctic tundras of northern British Columbia. I have seen mule deer in country rough enough for mountain sheep and have, in fact, seen bighorns and deer feeding on the same hillside. I have likewise seen them in the cactus and brush on the level deserts of northern Mexico. When I was hunting antelope some years ago around Gillette, Wyoming, there were many mule deer in the brushy coulees where little streams wandered through the antelope plains. When they were frightened they'd take right off across the sagebrush flats with the antelope.

In most areas mule deer have increased enormously in the past twenty or thirty years, so much so that they have starved on their winter range. They have invaded the suburbs in many Western cities, particularly in the winter when feed is scarce. In the north they have followed the Alaska Highway up into southern Yukon, where they have never been known before. So plentiful have the mule deer become in some states that in certain areas hunters can legally take two, and even three, deer.

The mule deer got his Latin name of *hemionus* from his large ears, *hemionus* being the Latin word for mule. In general, the muley is a different breed of cat from his whitetail cousin. Instead of having the whitetail's large, floppy tail—generally body-colored on top and snow-white beneath—the mule deer has a small, thinly haired tail of dingy white with a black tip. He does not throw it up when frightened, as the whitetail does. He always keeps it hanging down. The tail of the muley's near relative, the Columbian blacktail, is about halfway in size between the small one of the mule deer and the large one flaunted by the whitetail. It is black on top, and instead of tossing it up when frightened, as the whitetail does, he carries it horizontal. In many ways the blacktail looks like a compromise between the mule deer and the whitetail. It's an odd fact that in areas where both mule deer and whitetails range, one occasionally comes across bucks that look like Pacific Coast blacktails. They are crosses between

The mountain lion is the greatest natural predator of the mule deer and helps control its population.

whitetails and mule deer. I have never shot one, but I have seen several that were taken in southern Arizona and northern Sonora.

The mule deer has a strongly marked face with a dark V on the forehead and a light muzzle, as compared with the whitetail's fairly uniformly dark face. All the points of the whitetail's antlers come off of one main beam, but the antlers of the mule deer are evenly branched. The brow tine of the whitetail's antlers is always conspicuous and large, but that of the mule deer is smaller and sometimes absent altogether. Pacific Coast blacktail antlers look like those of mule deer, and both differ so much from those of the whitetail that it is almost impossible to confuse them. In the West the brow tine is not counted, and only the points on one antler are referred to. A four-pointer by Western count would be a ten-pointer in the East.

An odd thing about the facial markings of mule deer that I have never seen referred to in print is that the latitude from which the deer comes can pretty well be told by the black line around the lower jaw. In the northern portion of the range in Alberta and British Columbia, the black line goes completely around. Somewhat farther south the line is divided in the middle, and at the lower end of the range—in the deserts of southern Arizona and northern Mexico—the line has degenerated into two dark spots on either side of the lower jaw.

In favored localities mule deer grow tremendous antlers, and a fine muley head is one of the most beautiful of all North American trophies. These big heads are found wherever there is plenty of lime in the food and water. Colorado has produced many great heads, and so have the limestone ranges of Alberta. Many spectacular ones have come out of Arizona's Kaibab National Forest north of the Grand Canyon. I have not hunted there for many years, but I believe I have seen a higher proportion of exceptional heads there than anywhere else. I once measured a Kaibab head with a spread of 47½ inches and about 20 points to the side. Another region of fine heads that is little known is in Sonora south of the town of Altar, and I have seen some beauties from southern Idaho. In the latest edition of *Records of North American Big Game*, the world record typical mule deer head came from Arizona's Kaibab.

On average the mule deer is the largest of American deer, but many tales told of their size are on the giddy side. For the past forty years I have been following up rumors of bucks that are supposed to have field dressed at 400 pounds and more, but I have yet to find an authentic instance of one. Apparently the very largest mule deer and the heaviest northern whitetail from Maine and Michigan are about the same size, with dressed weight running something over 300 pounds and live weight at close to 400.

For many years all deer brought into the hunting camps of Arizona's Kaibab were weighed, and in years of good forage the heaviest bucks would weigh something over 300 pounds hog dressed. The largest bucks I have authentic weights on all go about like that, with records running from 300 to 335 pounds. I have heard of many bucks that weighed more, but when I investigated I found the weight was estimated. I have shot two bucks that went 175 and 176 pounds in the quarters (the four quarters weighed without skin, head, or entrails).

One was shot northwest of Flagstaff, Arizona, and the other down in the Sonora desert. The Arizona buck had been hit in the ham as he ran away from me and I had cut away 10 or 12 pounds of bloodshot meat. How much would they have weighed field dressed? I don't know. They might have gone 250 pounds or so and well over 300 on the hoof.

I have only seen one buck I thought would weigh 300 pounds field dressed, and it was shot in exactly the same area, Slate Mountain northwest of Flagstaff, where I killed my heaviest Arizona buck. He was distinctly larger than any other buck I've ever seen. But anyone who gets a buck that weighs 175 pounds field dressed has a large one, and anyone who gets one that weighs 200 has a very large one. A Western game warden I know has weighed hundreds of mule deer and says he has never seen one that weighed more than 225 pounds dressed. I have yet to see a buck mule deer as large as a spike bull elk.

In most areas with which I'm familiar, the mule deer begin to show signs of the rut by the end of the first week in November, and by the middle of November most of the bucks have swelled necks and are starting to get interested in the does. The height of the rut for most Rocky Mountain mule deer is probably about the last week of November and the first week of December. Then each big buck collects as large a harem as he can and defends it from other bucks.

The desert mule deer of southern Arizona and northern Sonora are not well into the rut until about the middle of January, apparently a provision of nature for the does to be in milk during the summer rains. The old bucks have a grim time. Each will have from four to twelve does, and the bunch will move endlessly, restlessly. Hanging around the outskirts will be from two to four smaller bucks. Now and then when one of these approaches too closely, the big herd buck will chase it away. Occasionally one of the hangers-on will do battle, but generally they turn tail and run. On many occasions I have seen a small buck slip in and cover a doe while the lord of the harem was chasing off another one, but I have yet to see the big, heavy-horned bucks in the act of mating. I have a notion that most of the breeding is actually done by the young bucks, and that big fellows have all the responsibility and little else.

At the height of the rut the old buck is a sight awesome yet piteous, and at that time he's easily killed. He has a wild and desperate look in his eyes —as anyone would who had twelve wives ready to two-time him—and he looks gaunt and ragged. Generally he has a point or two broken off his antlers and skinned and bleeding places on his neck. The ones I've seen have always been running around with their mouths open as if they had difficulty in breathing, and I have had them go by me within 20 feet and pay no attention to me.

A Mexican cowboy I once knew was sitting on a hillside one January day brewing a can of coffee and heating up some tortillas when he saw a desert mule deer doe trot by about 50 yards away. A minute or so later a big buck, following her trail with his nose to the ground, came into sight. The vaquero had a little Winchester Model 92 .25/20 carbine on his saddle. He unlimbered it and shot the buck in the neck. Before he could get to it a smaller buck came along on the trail. He shot that one and a moment later yet another—this an ardent little forkhorn. I went by his place a week afterward and he had jerky strung up everywhere.

Once the rut is over, the bucks leave the does and start putting some fat on their ribs. Sometimes one sees solitary bucks, but generally a couple will travel together, often a large buck and a small one. Occasionally before the rut I have seen several together, and one time near Slate Mountain I saw a herd of about thirty fine big bucks. But that was exceptional.

The gestation period of the mule deer is seven months, and in the Rocky Mountains the young are born in late May and early June. In the deserts, of course, they are born later. Young does generally give birth to single fawns, but mature does almost always have twins. In areas where food is plentiful and predators are not numerous, around 40 per cent of the deer should be taken annually if the herd is to be kept within the limits of its food supply.

Coyotes and bobcats take fawns, and some are even killed by golden eagles. But the greatest natural predator of the mule deer is the mountain lion. Every one of these big cats, the most skillful deer hunters in the world, will kill from 100 to 150 deer a year—a lot of deer. Compared with the incredibly stealthy mountain lion, man isn't a very good hunter.

One factor in the astonishing increase of mule deer throughout the West has been the thinning out of the lion population in certain areas. In Arizona's Kaibab, which for years was open to lion hunting but closed for deer, the explosion of the deer population came about because there were too few lions. The result was that tens of thousands of them starved to death and the range was permanently damaged. In the West today there are many problem deer areas because there is not only a shortage of lions but because the coyotes have been poisoned off.

As is the case with most other game meat, mule deer venison varies enormously with the time the deer was taken, his condition, the manner in which he was killed, and what he'd been eating. No deer taken during and right after the rut is much good to eat, and no deer is good if he's been wounded and chased all over the country before being dispatched. The deer of some localities produce fine venison and of others they do not. I think the answer lies in their food.

The desert mule deer of southern Arizona and northern Mexico (like the bighorn sheep and white-tails that occupy the same country) are almost always fine eating. The answer probably lies in what they eat—mild and nourishing plants like jojoba, mesquite beans, leaves of the ironwood, and cactus fruit. Some mule deer in the Southwest spend the entire year on the winter range, and without exception these are poor eating because of the bitter plants, such as juniper and quinine brush, they devour. Deer that have fattened on mild morsels such as aspen leaves, mushrooms, and piñon nuts are as good as the best beef. I have shot several deer on the Salmon River upstream from Riggins, Idaho, and I have yet to find one that furnished first-class venison. On the other hand, all the deer I have taken off the Snake River upstream from Lewiston, Idaho, would melt in your mouth.

One of the worst bucks I ever ate was a fine, fat three-year-old I took in the piñon-juniper belt in northern Arizona, and one of the most delicious was an old-timer I shot in the Kaibab. He was hog fat with 4 inches of lard on his rump, and I think I must have taken him right after he came down from the summer range where he'd been feasting on mushrooms and aspen leaves. He was blind in one eye, and so old I think he'd lost his interest in the gals. Although I shot him on Armistice Day—a time when the necks of most of the bucks were swelled and some of them were showing interest in the does —he gave no sign at all of the rut. His meat was so tender you could cut it with a fork. But once the rut has begun, the venison is strong and musty.

Some of my most pleasant memories are of hunting mule deer. I have hunted them right at timberline in the Rockies, where they can be glassed and

Hunting from horseback can be wild when you see a buck slip from cover or rip over the flats.

stalked like sheep. On those lofty ridges right at the limit of trees it has been my experience that the deer are almost always bucks—generally big ones—as the does and young bucks like to summer lower where there is more cover. And I have still-hunted them down in the flat deserts of Sonora so close to salt water that I could see the blue Gulf of California by climbing a little hill. It's a great joy to sneak quietly along upwind in the fresh, chilly hours of early morning watching through the cholla and palo verde for the glimpse of gray that means a deer. It is easy tracking country, and often I have taken up the fresh track of a buck as he fed along.

But some of the most interesting hunts I have ever had have been on horseback for the great bucks of Arizona's north Kaibab. I used to like to hit it late in the season after a snow on the summer range had pushed the big bucks down onto the semi-open winter range. It is easy riding country for the most part—wide, shallow draws and long ridges clothed with a scattering of junipers. A couple of horsemen riding down a ridge will usually push deer off the points. The action can be fast and furious when a big buck comes tearing across an open flat or trotting along a hillside flashing in and out of the junipers. That used to be a great deer country, and I presume it still is. Many times I've seen from ten to twenty big bucks in a day, and well over one hundred deer, and the man who could pass up the ordinary heads had a good chance of finding a trophy to be proud of.

Once a friend and I were hunting there on horseback when we saw a tremendous buck just going over a ridge. The footing was good for horses, so we dug in the spurs and went after it. We chased it over about three ridges, never having it in sight long enough to jump off and shoot. Then the buck (no dumbbell he) cut to the left up a draw and turned left again about 300 yards away in an effort to get into heavy timber. I jumped off my horse, grabbed my .30/06 out of the scabbard, swung ahead of him, and let drive. I saw him go down at the front quarters, and then he was out of sight.

We jumped on our horses again, took after him, and found him down. He looked not long for this world, but he was still breathing. Foolishly I decided to cut his throat. At the prick of the knife he came frantically alive. I dropped the knife and threw myself on his head, with a hand on each antler. The buck dragged me in a 50-yard circle, bumping me against every bush and tree around. When he finally collapsed I was skinned, dusty, and covered with blood. From that time on I have never tried to dispatch another animal by attempting to cut its throat.

Because mule deer are usually found in open, hilly country, and because they tend to move out ahead of danger, they are generally shot at longer ranges than are whitetails. As I look back on forty years of hunting them, I'd guess the average range at which I've shot muleys has been well over 200 yards—maybe 250. I have shot a good many at 300 or a little over, but doubt very much if I've ever shot more than one or two at 400. Those I have taken in the brushy desert have been much closer.

I believe I've taken more mule deer with a .30/06 than with anything else, and because they usually open up quicker I like the 150-grain bullets better than the 180s. Compared with a moose or an elk, even a large mule deer is lightly constructed, offering no great amount of resistance to a bullet, and
country, and because they tend to move out ahead
the heavily constructed bullets don't open quickly enough to nail deer in their tracks. The .30/30 with the old soft-point bullet with plenty of lead exposed is good deer medicine up to about 150 yards, but beyond that distance it won't anchor a deer unless the shot is placed just right. With the 150-grain bullet in the .30/06 or .300 Magnum, or the 130-grain bullet in the .270, quick and spectacular kills are the rule.

Oddly enough I have killed more deer with fewer shots with the 7 x 57 Mauser than with anything else—all with 140-grain bullets. I believe I have killed twelve deer with twelve hits. In Mexico, over a score of years ago, I once had to shoot a desert mule deer twice with a 7 mm., but a few years ago I let fly at a fat doe at about 300 yards and the bullet went through her and killed a spike buck on the far side. Both came rolling down the hillside at the same time.

Once I literally killed a big buck in his tracks with the 7 mm. I was out with my wife, who had shot a buck earlier, when we saw this beautiful buck standing by a tree about 200 yards away across the canyon. I dropped into a sitting position and let one go. He collapsed like a paper deer in a puff of wind. When we went over we could see that his feet were still in his last tracks. I have a lot of respect for that little 7 mm.

Much as I like old *Odocoileus hemionus,* I have to admit that he doesn't have as much in the way of gray matter under the antlers as an elk or a whitetail, and that he won't give the hunter quite as much of a run for his money. We all can't be geniuses, though, and the mule-deer hunter who confines himself to the hunting of big bucks will get all the action he could want. And when he gets a real trophy head he has something—the finest antlers worn by any American deer.

# The Natural History of the Mule Deer

[ODOCOILEUS HEMIONUS]

### DESCRIPTION

Rather heavily built for a deer, the mule deer has a thick-set body, stocky legs, rather large feet, and ears that are 25 per cent larger than those of the white-tail deer. Largest of the American deer, the mule deer has a total length of from 55 to 70 inches, stands from 35 to 43 inches at the shoulder, and weighs from 140 to 200 pounds, with about 475 pounds the limit.

During the summer, the mule deer's close, light coat varies from yellowish-brown to light-tawny. The throat, inside of the ears, and legs are dull-white, while the abdomen is a dull-brown or black. There is a dark, chocolate-brown patch on the forehead; the rest of the face from below the eyes to nostrils is white. There is a large white patch on the rump and the tail is short and white except for the rounded tip which is broadly black. When the mule deer is disturbed it flashes the black tip of its tail back and forth across its white rump patch, producing a very effective signal that can be recognized by other deer several miles away. Late in August, when the nights are getting cold on the high mountain slopes, the mule deer begins to shed its thin, yellowish summer coat and puts on its thick, grayish winter pelage.

The mule deer is a typical artiodactyl, or even-toed ungulate. The animal walks on the tips of its toes, digitigrade fashion. The third and fourth toes are the longest and the tips are encased in a horny sheath. Small lateral hoofs, or dewclaws, are present.

### ANTLERS

High, branched antlers project upward and forward from the top of the mule deer's head. Antlers are normally present only in the male. The main beam of each antler is evenly divided at the first fork and each of the tines is again evenly subdivided into two smaller tines making a normal complement for an adult buck of four points, evenly spaced, on each antler.

The mule deer's antlers are composed of a solid bone-like structure. Soon after the rut the antlers begin to loosen just above the crown of the head and are shed between the middle of December and the middle of January.

### ORIGIN

The mule deer is a descendant of American ancestors that included the three-horned deer *Cranioceras* and other strange forms. There are approximately two million mule deer in western North America at the present time and two hundred thousand are killed by hunters every year. For some unknown reason the mule deer, like the magpies, plentiful in the west, never moved into eastern North America. Conditions, apparently, are not just to its liking. Perhaps the Mississippi valley is an impassable barrier for the mule deer.

### RANGE

The range of the mule deer is the western United States and southwestern Canada from central Alberta and eastern British Columbia, and western Minnesota south as far as northern Mexico.

There are nine named forms of mule deer *Odocoileus hemionus:* The Rocky Mountain mule deer is the best known, has the widest range, and is the largest of the subspecies. Large bucks may weigh as much as 475

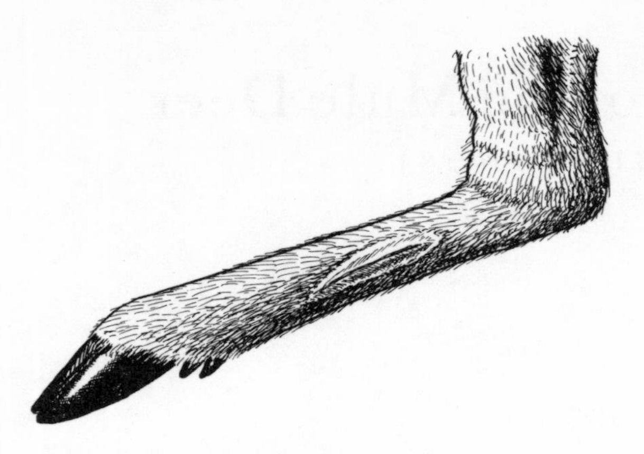

The metatarsal gland, situated on the inner side of the mule deer's hind foot, has a slit-like opening about 4 inches long.

pounds; large does average about 144. Its range extends from British Columbia and Alberta south to New Mexico, except the Pacific coastal region, and east to Minnesota.

The California mule deer is similar in color pattern to the Rocky Mountain form, but the winter pelage is paler in color. Bucks average about 145 pounds and weigh up to 218 pounds. This form is found in California where the mule deer population has been estimated at 263,000.

The Southern mule deer, a very dark-colored form with a dark line down the back and the upper surface of the tail almost all black, is found in the northern half of Lower California.

The Peninsula mule deer, a pale-colored race with a dark dorsal line and with less black on the tip of the tail than the southern mule deer, ranges only in the southern half of Lower California.

The Inyo mule deer, a medium-sized form with scarcely any black on the tail except at the tip and the underparts marked with a white stripe along each side, occupies the southern Sierra Nevada and eastward into the Inyo and White Mountains.

The Burro mule deer is similar to the Rocky Mountain race but is lighter and more grayish-yellow in color. It is known only in the Colorado River desert.

The Tiburon Island mule deer, a small, brownish form, is found only on Tiburon Island in the Gulf of California.

The Desert mule deer is a small, pale-colored form with a comparatively small white rump patch which is usually divided down the middle by a dark line, and the dark patch on the brow is greatly reduced in size. This race has a rather wide range that extends in the desert regions from Texas to New Mexico and south into Mexico.

The Cedros Island mule deer differs from all the other races of mule deer in the extremely light color of its coat, the absence of a white rump patch, a well-defined, dark dorsal stripe that extends down the tail, and white areas on the body that are tinged with buff. It is found only on Cedros Island off the western coast of Lower California.

## HABITS

The mule deer has no fixed home range, although when food is plentiful a group of animals may stay within a radius of a few miles. Usually the mule deer rests at night and during the heat of the day, and feeds in the early morning and evening.

Social gatherings are based on family relations. A group of mule deer consists of a buck, which is the leader, a full-grown female, fawns of the year, yearlings, and subadult but sexually mature does with fawns. The unit does not keep in close association but may be spread over a hillside a hundred yards or so apart.

Although the mule deer feeds on a wide variety of young, green herbs and grasses, it is primarily a browsing animal. Its food consists of sprouts, twigs, and leaves of most of the trees and bushes found in the Rocky Mountain region. Included in its diet are leaves and twigs of willows, aspens, oaks, ash, mahogany, juniper, sagebrush, dogwood, elderberry, buffalo berry, fir, chokeberry, currant, raspberry, grape and many others, as well as mistletoe and mushrooms. During the winter months, the mule deer feeds on the windswept slopes and reaches into the trees for low-hanging branches; unlike the moose and elk, it rarely digs into deep snow for food.

The mule deer spends the summer in the mountains at elevations of up to 8,000 feet. Unable to survive there during the deep winter snows, it retreats to the lower levels and sheltered valleys. The migration begins with the slow drifting of small bands downward. With the first snowfall, the migration speeds up and the small bands come together forming large herds. The summer and winter ranges are usually about 50 miles apart, but in some instances may be as much as 150 miles.

Like most other ungulates, the mule deer frequently licks itself and in so doing manages to swallow some of its hairs. This foreign matter occasionally lodges in the stomach and becomes a small, round ball that is hard and smooth. As times goes on, more calcium and other salts are deposited on the surface of the ball, gradually

The tail of the mule deer is short and white except for the black tip.

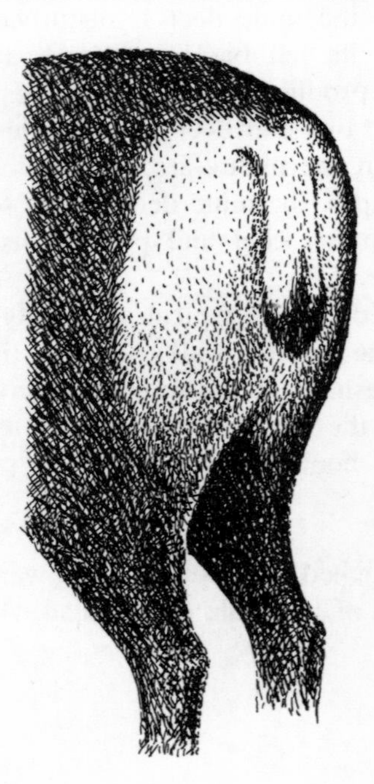

enlarging it until it may reach the size of a golf ball. This ball is called a "bezour stone" or "madstone." According to early tradition, a madstone applied to the bite of a rabid dog would draw out the poison and neutralize the disease. In the Old World, especially in Persia, it was used as an antidote for poison and is still regarded by the Persians as a remedy for most diseases.

## LOCOMOTION

A mule deer can travel as fast as 35 miles per hour and cover a distance of 25 feet in one leap. It cannot, however, keep up a fast speed for more than a mile. Fawns a month old can travel 28 miles per hour when pursued. When disturbed, the mule deer bounces boldly away in a series of high leaps that has earned it the name of "jumping" deer in some localities. It is also known as the "waiking" deer, because it is very seldom taken by surprise.

The mule deer is a strong swimmer and will take to the water when pursued by dogs or wolves. It frequently swims across mile-wide expanses of fresh and salt water merely to feed on the other side, and one instance is on record of a mule deer seen 3 miles from shore crossing a channel 12 miles wide.

## TRACKS

Tracks of the mule deer are much like those of the Virginia deer except that they are larger—about 3¼ inches long. The mule deer's walking tracks are in a slightly staggered line, with the hind foot falling partly in the impression left by the forefoot. The stride is wide—between 12½ and 24 inches. When galloping, the hind feet land well behind the forefeet and all four feet are off the ground at the same time.

## VOCAL

The mule deer is not very noisy—even during the rut. Bucks utter a deep, low-pitched, guttural growl, but also have a rather pleasant, low vocal note. When alarmed, mule deer utter a shrill whistling snort and fighting bucks utter short, coughing grunts.

The mule deer's face is white, except for the blackish crown, and the main beam of antlers is divided into two prongs, each with two equal points.

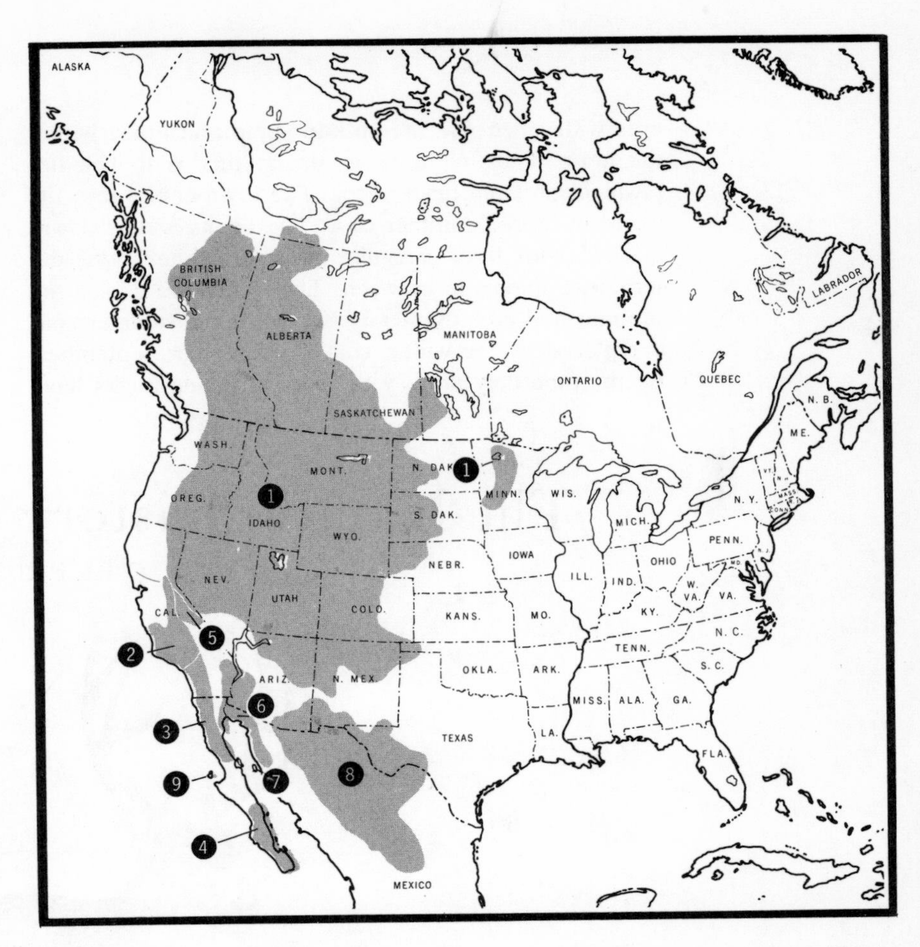


Distribution of races of mule deer *Odocoileus*: 1. Rocky Mountain mule deer, 2. California mule deer, 3. Southern mule deer, 4. Peninsula mule deer, 5. Inyo mule deer, 6. Burro mule deer, 7. Tiburon Island mule deer, 8. Desert mule deer, 9. Cedros Island mule deer.

## ENEMIES

Both black and grizzly bears take a considerable number of mule deer fawns each year but the older animals are too alert to get caught by bears. The cougar, however, is the mule deer's number one enemy, and coyotes, wolves, bobcats, lynx, and wolverine may get a few deer during the deep snows.

## MATING

Mating season starts in October and lasts for about two months. The bucks are not always as aggressive as other kinds of deer at this season and there is comparatively less competitive fighting for possession of the does. A buck may gather a harem of three or four does but if a mightier buck comes along he may relinquish the harem with only a few bluffing passes. There are usually enough does, however, to go around.

The mule deer is well provided with scent glands that play an important part in intercommunication between the sexes. The principal skin glands are the preorbital glands, tarsal glands, metatarsal glands, and interdigital glands.

## BIRTH AND EARLY DEVELOPMENT

Most fawns are born in June or July, seven months after the doe has mated. There are usually twins and not infrequently triplets. The newborn fawns will weigh about 6 to 7 pounds each. They are born with their eyes wide open and are able to stand and nurse within the hour. The first duty of the mother is to lick her fawns clean from head to toe. The fawn comes into the world in its red summer coat. The flanks and back are marked with three irregular rows of white spots and some extra spots in between. The spots fade during the summer and are completely lost when the summer coat is replaced by the winter coat in August or September. By the time they are a year old, the young bucks have antlers that are either spiked or forked. Twins are never hidden together; they may be secreted as much as 100 feet apart. When about a month old they are ready to follow the mother and begin to take some solid food. They are ready to be weaned in October. Mule deer are sexually mature when two years old but full growth is not attained until the third or fourth year. Most mule deer have a life expectancy of from eight to twelve years with a potential longevity of twenty-three years.

# The Natural History of the Blacktail Deer

[ODOCOILEUS HEMIONUS]

## DESCRIPTION

Scientists contend that the little blacktail deer is a relative of the mule deer, but concede that it has a sufficient number of peculiarities in its own right to be recognized as distinct. The resemblance of the blacktail to its larger cousin with the big ears is evident in the shape of its high, branched antlers. The main beam is evenly divided at the first fork and each prong of the fork is evenly subdivided into two prongs, making a total of four points on each antler. The blacktail's antlers are small and unimposing as might be expected of a forest-loving animal, and few heads have a spread of more than 30 inches. Its comparatively large ears are not to be compared in size with those of the mule deer. It has a characteristic tail which is broad at the base, evenly tapered to the tip, black on the entire upper side and white underneath. During the summer, the blacktail's coat varies from reddish-brown to yellowish-brown. The winter coat is rich grayish-brown, darker down the middle of the back, and the nose, forehead, and chest are black or blackish. The rest of the underparts, and the inside of the ears, are white.

The blacktail is a sturdy little deer: it measures as much as 60 inches long, stands 38 inches high at the shoulder, and weighs up to 150 pounds, with exceptionally large individuals weighing as much as 300.

A member of the deer family *Cervidae,* the blacktail sheds its antlers annually. It also belongs to the great order *Artiodactyla,* the even-toed ungulates that walk on the tip of their toes (digitigrade), and whose third and fourth digits are evenly and well developed, the tips encased in a horny covering which is the hoof. Small lateral hoofs, or dewclaws, are present in the blacktail. It is a ruminant, or cud-chewer, having the compound stomach associated with this function, and no teeth at the front of the upper jaw.

Skin glands are well developed in the blacktail and enable the animals to locate each other. The preorbital gland is a simple sac located just in front of the corner of the eye. The sac contains a waxy substance and can be opened or closed at will. The tarsal gland is marked by a tuft of coarse hair at the inside of the heel joint; it secretes an oily substance that gives off a strong ammonia-like smell. It is present in both sexes. The metatarsal gland, present in both sexes, is an elongated area of glandular tissue on the hind leg near the middle of the shank and is marked by a tuft of elongated hairs over an area 3 inches long.

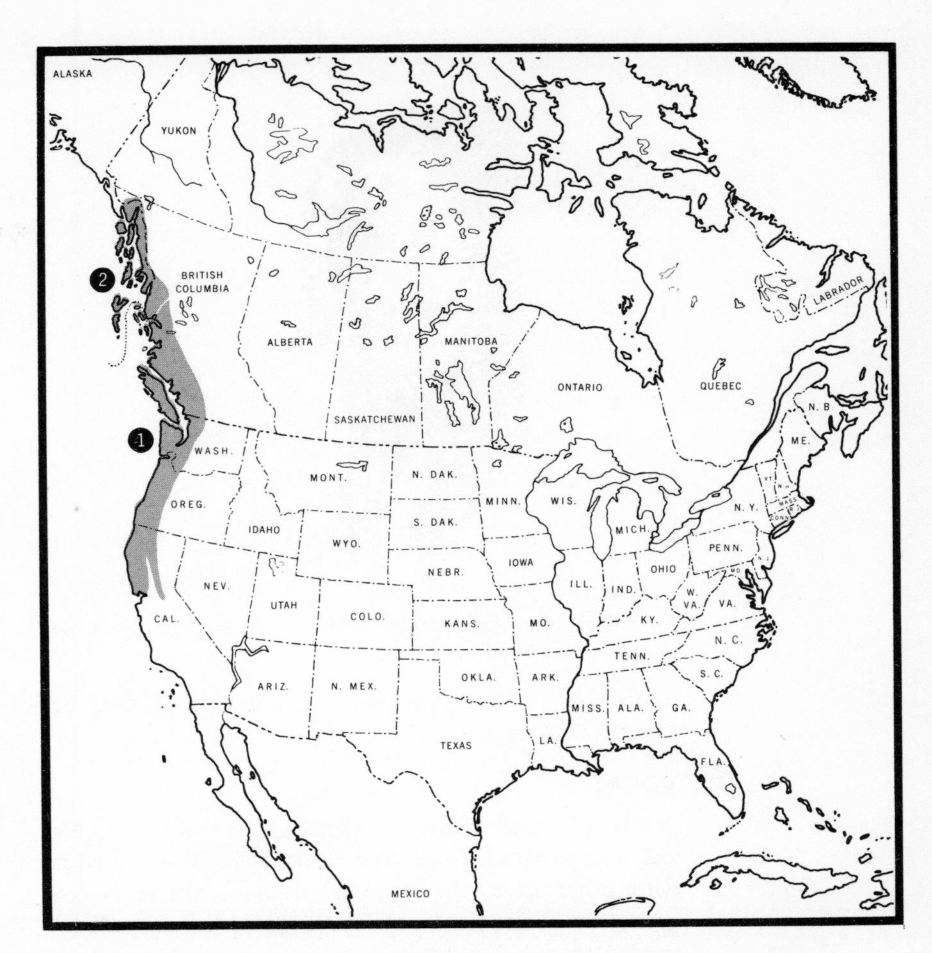

Distribution of races of blacktail deer *Odocoileus:* 1. Columbia blacktail, 2. Sitka deer.

## RANGE

The home of the blacktail deer is in the stands of great redwood trees and spruce-fir forests along the Pacific Coast of North America. In the low-lying humid forests the deer will remain in one small area the year round, but in the foothills and mountain regions it follows a set migratory route, spending the summer at high elevation in the broken alpine meadows and the winter months in the sheltered valleys. The mountain-dwelling blacktail may mingle during the summer months with the mule deer in the northern part of the range, but when fall arrives the mule deer descend the eastern slopes, and the blacktail deer move down the western slopes. Only in the southern part of the range do both deer winter in the same general area. The overall range of the blacktail is the forested regions along the Pacific Coast and the western slopes of the Sierra Nevada and Cascade Mountains from the region of Glacier Bay, Alaska, south to about central California.

There are two recognized kinds of blacktail deer: the Columbia blacktail deer, or Coast deer, is also known as Sound deer, Pacific buck, Columbian deer, and Coast blacktail. The deer is known to interbreed with races of mule deer in the southern part of its range. Its range includes a narrow strip of forested territory on the Pacific slopes of extreme western North America and the coastal islands from Point Conception in central California north to Bella Bella on the central British Columbia coast.

The Sitka deer differs from the typical blacktail in its darker, less reddish summer coat, the smaller, dark brow patch and the presence of a prominent dark line down the nose. The Sitka deer is confined to the deep forested regions on the Canadian and Hudsonian zones of the coastal strip in southern Alaska and northwestern British Columbia and the adjacent coastal islands.

## HABITS

The blacktail deer is a browsing animal and feeds on leaves, twigs of shrubs, bushes, and trees, but eats very little grass. Fortunately, it lives in a region where the snow is rarely deep. Among the choice foods of this deer are mistletoe, which grows profusely in the humid forests, twigs and leaves of raspberry, elderberry, dogwood, mountain ash, sedges, huckleberry, maple, acorns, and hazelnuts in season. Year-round items in the diet are twigs and leaves of cedar, hemlock, and oak trees.

Though endowed with an excellent sense of hearing and sharp eyesight, the blacktail deer depends on its sense of smell to determine the presence of its enemies.

## ENEMIES

The cougar takes the largest toll of blacktails, bears kill a number of fawns each year, and coyotes, bobcats, and wolverines kill the crippled, weak, and diseased. Golden eagles get a few of the very young fawns.

## LOCOMOTION

When disturbed in the forest, the blacktail steals secretively away through the thick brush, rather than bounding away in great leaps like the mule deer. Its walking tracks are in a staggered line with toes together and a stride of between 20 and 23 inches. When it is bounding, all four feet leave the ground at the same time and come down in a group covering about 30 inches. The toes are spread and the dewclaws leave an

The metatarsal gland is situated on the inner side of the blacktail's lower leg near the heel and has a slit-like opening three inches long.

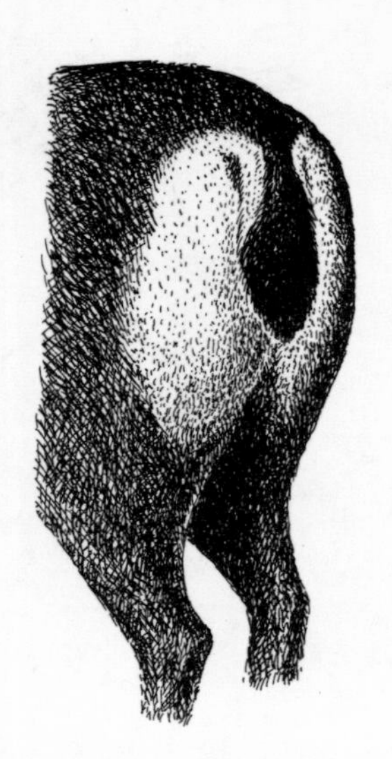

The tail of the typical blacktail is white underneath, black on top.

impression. There is a space of about 80 inches between the bounds.

## VOCAL

The blacktail snorts or whistles when alarmed, and will stamp with a front foot in defiance. When feeding with other deer, the blacktail utters a series of low grunts and soft vocal expressions as if the animals are talking among themselves.

## MATING

The deer begin to get restless with the arrival of the crisp, sunny days and cool nights of Indian Summer, and the mating season, or rut, begins in October and lasts for two months. Mating bucks with swollen necks are fewer in number than the available does, which travel in small groups of eight or nine individuals. For that reason there is rarely, if ever, any serious competition among the bucks for possession of the females. Mating usually takes place under cover of darkness.

## BIRTH AND EARLY DEVELOPMENT

The fawns, usually twins, are born some time between April and July, 210 days after mating. At birth they are reddish-brown and marked with numerous conspicuous white spots. Does about to fawn drift off by themselves for concealment near the margins of open meadows. After the mother has licked and dried her newborn fawn, she moves away and does not return to her young except to nurse. Feeding times are few and wide apart, and are determined solely by the doe.

The fawns weigh 5 or 6 pounds each at birth and are able to stand and nurse within the hour. When a month old they are strong enough to run along with the mother, and are beginning to feed on green vegetation. During the fawns' early development, the doe and her fawns have a home range of about one square mile. The fawns' white spots begin to fade toward the end of August and disappear completely when the summer coat changes to the warmer winter pelage in September. Weaned completely in October, the fawns will run with the doe for about two years. Young bucks have their first antlers when one year old.

## Popular and Scientific Names of the Mule and Blacktail Deer

**ORDER:** *Artiodactyla*

**FAMILY:** *Cervidae*

**GENUS:** *Odocoileus*

**SPECIES:** *hemionus*

### SUBSPECIES OF THE MULE DEER

| | |
|---|---|
| Rocky Mountain mule deer | *Odocoileus hemionus hemionus* |
| California mule deer | *Odocoileus hemionus californicus* |
| Southern mule deer | *Odocoileus hemionus fulginatus* |
| Peninsula mule deer | *Odocoileus hemionus peninsulae* |
| Inyo mule deer | *Odocoileus hemionus inyoensis* |
| Burro mule deer | *Odocoileus hemionus eremicus* |
| Tiburon Island mule deer | *Odocoileus hemionus sheldoni* |
| Desert mule deer | *Odocoileus hemionus crooki* |
| Cedros Island mule deer | *Odocoileus hemionus cerrosensis* |

### SUBSPECIES OF THE BLACKTAIL DEER

| | |
|---|---|
| Columbia blacktail deer | *Odocoileus hemionus columbianus* |
| Sitka deer | *Odocoileus hemionus sitkensis* |

DOUGLAS ALLEN

CHAPTER 8

# THE ELK

BACK in the early nineteen thirties, I camped late one September afternoon on the Mogollon Rim, that gigantic fault across half of Arizona and into New Mexico where the earth cracked and slipped a half mile or so. Romantically, I had made a dry camp out on a point overlooking the Tonto Basin at an altitude of around 8,000 feet above sea level. Any water I used would have to come from a little spring about a mile away.

But the view was worth it. As the sun began to slant down in the west, the whole great basin below me became hazy purple, and I could see the Sierra Anchas, the Four Peaks, the Mazatzals—all rugged and beautiful mountains with lovely names, all part of the romantic heritage of the native Arizonan. It grew chilly up there on that high point, and the wind that sighed through the great yellow pines around me gave a hint of the hard frosts of the coming winter.

I planned to cook a simple meal, climb into my blankets, and go to sleep. The next morning I'd be up before dawn to scout the country for the season on deer and turkey that was to open in a bit over a month. As I cooked, I kept hearing a shrill, thin cry that at first I thought was being made by a bird. Then, after a time, a great braying and shrieking broke out below me. The noise reminded me a little of the serenade of a Southwestern burro that was feeling lonely. The "braying" was mixed with grunts.

While making camp, I'd seen the droppings and the round, cowlike tracks of elk. It finally dawned on me that what I was hearing was the famous bugling of a bull elk. I got out my binoculars and walked quietly north to where a canyon headed, then sat down and watched. Presently a big six-point bull elk came walking out of the timber into a little clearing. He viciously attacked a little pine with his antlers until the bark flew. Then he lifted his head, and I heard him "bugle."

Bugling, this famous accomplishment of the North American elk, is an oddly selected name for the noise a lovesick bull makes. To me, the noise sounds nothing like that of a bugle. Nor would I call it "melodious," as I have heard it described. It is wild and exciting, but hardly melodious. The shrill cry of the young bull elk is called "whistling," and that is about what it sounds like. The habit of making a racket during the mating season is also shared by the cousins of the elk, the European and Asiatic red deer. But in Europe the red stags are said to "roar"—not bugle.

In the western United States, the elk start bugling early in September, and by about the middle of that month the rut is in full swing. As the rut plays out, the bugling is heard less often, but I've heard young bulls whistling as late as November. I'll never forget one cold and starry night in the Wyoming Rockies when I lay in my down sleeping bag in a deep canyon that was full of bugling elk—hoarse old-timers, middle-aged bulls with tenor voices, and adolescents with shrill, high-pitched whistles. Until I dropped off to sleep, I heard the whole canyon ringing with their challenges. There must have been at least twenty bulls there.

During the rut, the bugling of the bulls makes them much easier to hunt. The sportsman can locate a bull by his bugle, and then sneak up on him, going quietly and watching the wind. More exciting is to call up a bull. Elk calls are manufactured and used for this purpose, but some hunters simply use a child's tin whistle—or nothing at all. The notion of a young bull trying to horn in on his preserve seems to enrage an old bull.

One time in Idaho a friend and I were riding along a trail when we heard the challenge of an old bull about half a mile away. Apparently he'd heard the hoofs of our horses on the rocky trail, thought it might be a herd of elk, and was warning all competition away from his harem.

We led our horses back into the timber and tied them. Then we sat down fairly well hidden, and my friend broke out a tin whistle and sent a shrill challenge back at the bull. Immediately there was an answering bugle. My pal waited for a couple of minutes and then whistled again. This time the roar of the indignant bull was closer.

He was working himself up into a rage, and between challenges we could hear him threshing his antlers against the jackpines. Finally he challenged —not over 100 yards away. My friend answered, and we both got ready to shoot.

Presently he burst out of a jackpine thicket, neck hair on end, red eyes glaring. He was urinating all over himself, and the gentle breeze brought us his scent, rank and strong. When the .300 Magnum crashed, he turned dazedly, lurched back into the timber, and fell.

The American elk, or wapiti, is the largest round-horned deer in the world, and one of the grandest and most beautiful of the deer tribe. Like many other North American game animals, he is a migrant from the Old World and has relatives all over Europe and Asia, and even some in the Atlas Mountains of North Africa. He belongs to the genus *Cervus,* or true deer, which includes the red deer of Europe, North Africa, Asia Minor, and northern Iran, the Indian sambar and baraṣingha, the Japanese sika deer, the spotted axis deer, and even the little hog-deer or para of the Asiatic jungle. All are characterized by round antlers which are set on the skull at an oblique angle and which have a brow tine.

So closely related is the North American elk to some of his Asiatic cousins that the British classify him in the same species as the Tien-Shan, Baikal, and Bactrian wapiti from China, Siberia, and Turkestan. The Tien-Shan wapiti are so closely related to their North American cousins that they would appear just about identical to the average sportsman. As geological time goes, the elk is apparently a fairly late migrant to the New World.

Actually he is not properly called an "elk" at all, but the correct term—wapiti—is generally used only by Europeans and to some extent by Canadians. The European elk is closely related to the North American moose.

The elk, by deer hunters' standards, is a lot of animal. An average bull will probably stand about five feet at the withers and weigh about 650 to 700 pounds. Undoubtedly some very large bulls in good condition will weigh 1,000 pounds on the hoof, and perhaps a bit more. In meat-hunting Idaho, where I live, the commonest practice is to say a bull "quarters" out so much, and then give the weight of one quarter. Quarters which weigh 125 pounds are very large, and if you assume that about half the live weight is lost with head, hide, neck, legs below the knees, lungs, and viscera, this would again indicate a live weight of around 1,000 pounds for the largest bulls.

I shot my first elk in Arizona in 1934 or 1935. And though I was used to deer-size animals, I was astounded at the bulk of the creature. To a hunter used to seeing deer hanging up, an elk carcass in a tree looks like that of a horse. The elk hunter must always provide for some means of getting his meat to a road. One does not carry an elk out as if it were a deer. Two large elk quarters are about all that can possibly be put on a husky pack mule.

In the fall, the elk is a tan animal with a yellowish rump patch and a dark-brown neck and head. The summer coat is deeper in color than the winter coat, and the hair is shorter. With the cows, the contrast between the tan of the body and the brown of the neck and head is generally less marked than with the bulls.

To sportsmen, elk are elk, but various subspecies have been recognized: the large—presumably pale —form that was killed off in the White Mountains of Arizona along in the last part of the nineteenth century, the small Tule elk of California, and the dark Roosevelt elk of the Olympic Peninsula of Washington. The commonest elk is the animal of the

Rockies, *Cervus canadensis canadensis.* In fact, many people think the elk is found only in the Rockies.

Actually elk were found in primitive times over a great part of North America, from Arizona to northern British Columbia and from the Atlantic to the Pacific. They were plentiful in New York and Pennsylvania, and were found as far south as Tennessee and Georgia. Only one hundred years ago, elk were plentiful on the Great Plains that now form the states of Nebraska, Iowa, and the Dakotas.

Since the elk is a large animal, he's a generous dividend for one properly directed bullet. His hide and even his antlers are useful. The elk was relentlessly hunted by the pioneers. His sheltering forests were cut down in the East, and on the plains his range was turned into farms and cattle ranches. Not only was he shot for meat and for his hide, but thousands were slaughtered and left to rot because some lodge members liked to wear his "tusks" for watch charms.

Eventually the elk found refuge only in the mountains. In the summer they ranged high, but in the winter, when snow lay deep, they had to find forage in the valleys and on sidehills. Then these were preempted for farms and ranches. Now there is a drive to dam all the tributaries of the Columbia River near their source. If this is done, the resulting pools will cover the critical winter range of vast numbers of elk. Right now elk are plentiful in the West and have been increasing since their low point brought on by unrestricted tusk and meat hunting. That occurred about 1915. The greed and shortsightedness of man being what they are, the outlook for huntable elk herds fifty years from now in many parts of the West is not too good.

Today most Western states, including the Southwestern states of Arizona and New Mexico, have open seasons on elk. Native Arizona elk had become extinct because of market hunting during the late eighties or early nineties, but elk imported from the Yellowstone herd of Wyoming increased to the extent that an open season was warranted in 1934. I took part in that first elk hunt and shot a bull on the Mogollon Rim not far from where I had first heard an elk bugle a couple of years before.

Colorado's elk have come back spectacularly, and that state is now one of the most productive elk areas in the nation. Colorado's annual elk kill is about 15,000, and in Idaho the elk harvest has increased from a bit over 6,000 in 1937 to around 16,000 in 1958. In the famous elk state of Wyoming, the annual kill runs around 10,000; in Montana, over 12,000. Kills in Washington and Oregon are also substantial. There are fair numbers of elk in New Mexico, and in California there is a remnant of the tule elk.

About fifty years ago, the late Dr. W. T. Hornaday, former director of the Bronx Zoo in New York City, made a hunting trip in southeastern British Columbia near the Alberta boundary. At that time, the elk were about gone there, and in a thirty-day trip, he and his companions saw only one elk, a bull. Today this area and that across on the Alberta side is one of the finest elk ranges in North America. Until the Alaska Highway was built, it wasn't generally known that there was an isolated herd of elk in far-northern British Columbia. But they are there, and have apparently been there for centuries; some of the country shows signs of long use by elk. When I was hunting Stone sheep and caribou in that country in 1946, I saw no elk, but I did see their sign. Elk have been stocked in the Yukon, and seem to be increasing. I heard bulls bugling off the Klaza River when I was on a sheep hunt in 1956.

So far as elk hunting goes, the sportsmen of North America have never had it so good. But if elk hunting is to remain, a continual fight is going to have to be waged to protect elk range against encroachments of the dam builders and the grazing interests.

An elk hunt is generally the first hunt the average American sportsman takes for game larger than deer. The elk is generally a wilderness animal, and more often than not he is found in high, rough mountains. Going after elk is far more of an expedition than going after deer or antelope.

There are some areas in the West where the elk hunter can drive in along some narrow road in a national forest, park right in elk country, and then make camp, and hunt. In most such areas there are packers who will follow the hunter back to his kill and bring it out for him on a packhorse. Generally, though, such easily accessible elk country is very crowded, and sometimes everybody decides to go to the same place at the same time.

A few years ago some friends and I drove to a high narrow ridge overlooking Idaho's Selway River and made camp a couple of days before the elk season began. Ours was the second camp there, and from the lofty ridge we could look over hundreds of square miles of good elk country. About noon the day before the season opened, other cars and trucks started coming in. All that night we could hear the snort and roar of automobile motors, the braying of mules, the moans and bellows of hunters as they fell over tent ropes.

We were up before dawn to hunt a canyon where we had seen some elk and found plenty of elk sign the day before. But when we got to the canyon, I became aware of voices below me, of the flare of matches as cigarettes were lighted, of the occasional wavering beam of a flashlight, of resounding curses as hunters ran into stumps or stumbled over stones. Awed and shaken, we decided to hold off a while and see what we were getting into.

When it grew light enough to see, we discovered that our canyon held about fifty hunters. Then, far across the great canyon, a couple of cows and a calf showed up, and at least twenty of the hunters started shooting. It sounded like the invasion of Iwo Jima. My amigo and I looked at each other, shrugged, and went back to camp. As we drove out that day to find a less congested spot, we discovered that for four miles the ridge was covered with tents and automobiles, horses and mules, men, women, and children.

It's better to pack in for elk, and get away from the crowd. But there are pack trips and pack trips. Most dedicated Idaho elk hunters have accumulated an outfit—tent, stove, sleeping bag, ax, saw, cooking utensils, and grub boxes. They drive to a packer's camp, and the packer takes them 10 to 25 miles back into the elk country. He puts them down in a campsite and then arranges to come and pick them up at some specified time. When he arrives, he goes back to where the hunters have hung up the elk quarters, and packs them into camp. Then he takes the outfit back to the road. This service usually costs around one hundred dollars for each man, and is well worth it. To me, camping in wilderness country is half the joy of hunting.

If the hunter doesn't want to bother with buying his grub, cooking his meals, and pitching his tent, he can ride on horseback into an elk camp, where the outfitter has tents in which he can roll out his sleeping bag, and a cooktent where he can eat his meals. A deal like that is naturally somewhat more expensive.

If the hunter wants a guide, that can be arranged, and if he wants to take the wear and tear off his legs and hire a saddle horse, that can be arranged also. On such hunts in Idaho, one guide will generally take care of two or three hunters. In that case—with horse, guide, grub, and tent furnished—the charge will be somewhere between twenty-five and thirty-five dollars a day per man.

There are elk hunts and elk hunts. I know of one place where a hunter can fly to a luxurious lodge in wilderness elk country, have a shower every night if he wishes, sleep on inner-spring mattresses, and devour well-cooked food off a white tablecloth. This is not a cheap hunt, because every bale of hay, every sack of oats, every box of groceries must be flown in.

To me, the queen of the elk hunts is to leave with a packstring and a complete pack outfit with cook, guides, and a horse wrangler. Such an outfit can move where the hunting is good and can try different areas. In most parts of the West, such a hunt will cost each hunter from fifty to one hundred dollars a day, depending on the outfitter and on how many hunters there are to split the cost.

My own first elk hunt was on the Mogollon Rim (it sounds like mo-goy-YON) in Arizona. I hired a couple of men who ran a few cattle in the elk country. They brought in horses and put up a couple of tents, and my wife and I brought in the grub. We all took turns cooking. It was in late November and bitterly cold. We had no stoves for the tents and were otherwise poorly prepared for cold-weather camping. When I think of the clothes I wore, I marvel that I didn't freeze to death—light underwear, a pair of cotton pants, a wool shirt, and a leather wind-breaker. My wife and I shivered from the time we got out of bed in the morning until we got back in and thawed out at night. But we got elk, slept soundly, and ate hugely. I'll never forget how astonishingly tall those bull elk looked, and I also learned that a thoroughly frightened bull elk can carry a good bit of well-placed lead before he goes down. The simple trips are sometimes the most memorable.

If given any chance, elk reproduce well. In Arizona, 150 Wyoming elk were planted in the Mogollon Rim country about 1915, and in 20 years they

When their antler growth is complete, bulls rub their horns on trees and bushes to get rid of the velvet.

had increased to around 5,000. In 10 years, a herd of 11 elk put on an island in Lake Superior increased to 250. The substantial elk herd in western Washington is, I believe, descended from a plant of elk from Wyoming.

When Lewis and Clark went through the Bitterroot Mountains of Idaho and Montana over one hundred years ago, elk and other game was so scarce that members of the expedition almost starved. In those days it was virgin forest that afforded little game feed. Today this is the home of one of North America's largest elk herds, and about 4,500 elk a year are taken from it. As late as 1900, elk were rare there. But about the time of World War I, a series of great fires swept the area, and the brush that came up later made good elk feed.

Among elk, single births are the rule, but twins are seen occasionally. Survival is high, and the elk —once it is an adult—is too large to be bothered by the smaller predators. Even the cougar would rather prey on deer. In the old days, the great gray wolf was a serious predator of the elk, just as in the far north he is today of the caribou and moose. Grizzly and black bears have probably never been serious predators of elk, yet neither will turn down an elk calf if he has a chance to kill one.

The greatest enemy of elk is man—as a predator with a rifle in his hands, but far more important in an indirect way as a user of land. Unlike deer, the elk eats considerable grass at certain times of the year, and there is much conflict in various areas between cattle interests and the elk herds. In Arizona, almost all the elk country is on national-forest lands where cattlemen have permits to run herds. The cattle interests begrudge the elk every bite of grass and browse they take, and have forced a great reduction in the elk numbers there. Cattle interests in the Northwest have taken over the lowland valleys where the elk have wintered since time immemorial, and consequently the elk are forced to winter on less desirable land and in some cases, as in the Jackson Hole area, they are fed.

In areas where there is much human use, the elk is in many ways an irritating and undesirable neighbor. He is a large, powerful, and perpetually hungry animal. In the winter, he'll knock down a rancher's fences, drive off his cattle, and devour his hay. In the summer he'll invade an alfalfa field and kill the farmer's dog that tries to drive him away.

In cases where the elk has increased to the point where he's destroying his winter range, he is his own worst enemy. Most of the winter range in the Jackson Hole country is in bad shape from overuse, and grows worse every year. In Idaho's famous Selway and Lochsa country, much of the low creek bottoms that the elk must use in tough winters are so badly overbrowsed that the best forage plants have been killed off and the elk have eaten twigs an inch in diameter.

In many cases the elk is also a poor neighbor for lesser game animals. In Yellowstone National Park and other parts of the Rockies, elk have overgrazed the winter range of the bighorns, and when the sheep get down from the high ranges, they die of malnutrition and disease. Generally, an increase in elk means a decrease in deer, for in tough winters the elk can browse higher than deer can reach. They eat off the browse and chase the deer out of desirable areas. Competition with elk is believed to have caused the great decrease if not extinction of the whitetail deer in Yellowstone Park.

In Idaho's Selway country, there were many deer before elk became so plentiful, but as the elk increased, deer numbers went down. In the nineteen thirties the increase of elk on Arizona's Mogollon Rim meant fewer deer. One elk will eat as much as three or four deer, so in many areas it would seem that the planting of elk in good deer country would be of doubtful wisdom.

Throughout the West today, elk numbers are limited by the extent of the winter range. Most elk go through a tough period each winter, and in years of great cold and heavy snow, there's a heavy winter kill. The two largest elk herds in the United States—the Jackson Hole herd in Wyoming and the Clearwater herd in Idaho—are seriously threatened by the proposed construction of dams. The Wyoming herd will be seriously depleted, in the words of A. F. C. Greene, former Wyoming Game and Fish Commissioner, "if only a small part of the total dams being studied on the upper Snake River are ever constructed. Their overall effects would so alter the natural conditions of the area as to cause the Jackson Hole elk herd, as we know it today, to be a thing of the past . . . Impoundments of the Snake River and its tributaries would inundate irreplaceable big game wintering range and feed grounds as well as obstruct vital elk migration routes."

A similar situation exists in Idaho, where U. S. Army Corps of Engineers want to build a dam at Bruce's Eddy on the North Fork of the Clearwater River and one at Penny Cliffs on the Middle Fork of the Clearwater. It looks as if the Bruce's Eddy dam will be built; Congress has appropriated a great deal of money for detailed surveys and plans. This dam would obstruct migration routes for elk, flood vital winter elk and deer range, exterminate a large herd of whitetail deer, and destroy one of the most pro-

Always hungry, elk foraging for food often flatten ranch fences in winter, drive off cattle, and eat hay.

ductive steelhead spawning grounds in the Northwest. The proposed dam at Penny Cliffs would be even more destructive to elk range and likewise to steelheads.

The great Clearwater elk herd produces a kill of around 4,500 elk annually, in spite of the fact that the terrain is so wild and rough that only about 30 percent of it is hunted. If the two dams are built, this herd would—in the opinion of the Idaho Department of Fish and Game—be a thing of the past. After a survey of the two areas, the Idaho commission recommended that, because of their adverse effect on wildlife, the dams not be built. Their construction is opposed by the National Wildlife Federation, the Idaho Wildlife Federation, and state sportsmen's groups throughout the Northwest. However, the Army Corps of Engineers, chambers of commerce, and powerful lumber interests are lobbying for the dams. If the projected dams are built on the upper Snake and on the Clearwater, the two largest elk herds in the United States will cease to exist as we know them.

It is this winter-range problem that has had a great effect on the wonderful antlers of the great wapiti bulls that are of primary interest to the trophy hunter. Because most elk go through a starvation time in the winter and begin growing their new antlers at a period of low vitality, the antlers don't average so large as they did in primitive times. Wealthy Englishmen were the first to hunt elk for trophies, and today some of the world's finest elk heads decorate baronial halls in England. Most of these heads came from the Jackson Hole country of Wyoming, but today the elk there don't grow antlers as large as they once did.

The world-record head is an old one shot in the Big Horn Mountains of Wyoming in 1890. The number two head was taken in the Ruby River country of southwestern Montana too recently—in October, 1958—to be included in the Boone and Crockett Club's *Records of North American Big Game*. But it replaces the trophy presently in the number two spot on the list—an Idaho head which, incidentally, I discovered and measured.

In the current record book, there isn't a single Jackson Hole head in the first ten, only one in the first fifteen. This isn't to say that the country around Yellowstone Park doesn't produce some fine heads, because it does. The largest head I have ever taken was one I shot out of Cody some years ago. The antlers of any big, mature, six-point bull elk make a magnificent trophy, and a hunter doesn't need to get a top record-class head to be proud of it. I believe the largest antlers I have ever seen on a freshly killed bull were in Arizona. About 1946 or 1947 I heard of a gigantic Arizona bull elk that, according to those who saw it, might have been a new world record. It was never officially measured.

In his second year, a bull elk grows spikes. But the next year he generally grows a small five-point head or a small six-point head. Until the bull is in his seventh or eighth year, the antlers grow larger and finer, but the normal elk head always has six points to a side. After about the eighth year, the horns begin to freak, to palmate, to grow extra points. Elk with as many as twenty points (instead of the normal twelve altogether) have been shot. Then, as the bull grows older, the size of his antlers diminishes; very old bulls have been known to grow spikes.

Bull elk shed their antlers about the middle of March. In a month the bull is wearing a fuzzy bulbous arrangement a foot or so high that will eventually become a big six-point set of antlers. By August, the antlers are complete under their velvet, and late that month the bulls are horning the trees and bushes to get rid of the velvet. When the horns are clean and polished, they are brown with beautiful ivory-colored tips. During the summer, herds of bulls dwell apart from the cows and calves in perfect friendship, but once those antlers are polished and hard, the bulls seek out the cows, begin to bugle, and battle for their harems.

The bull elk is one of the most polygamous of animals. A big bull will often collect thirty cows, fight for their possession, and herd them around. One of the largest bulls I have ever shot was taken in Wyoming in 1943. The late Ernie Miller and I saw him late one afternoon across a tremendous canyon right at timberline. He was all alone, alternately wallowing in the mud around a spring, bugling, and horning the little timberline trees. It was too late to go after him, but we got a 20X spotting scope on him, and we knew we would recognize the head if we saw it again.

The next day we couldn't forget the picture of that magnificent head, and we passed up some lesser bulls hoping to see him once more. We finally found him in another basin two or three miles from where we'd first seen him. He had either rounded up a herd of about twenty-five cows or had chased another bull away from them. He lay in a great basin surrounded by his cows and was keeping a wary eye out for about a dozen smaller bulls that were hanging out in a narrow tongue of timber nearby, waiting to move in on him. Now and then some of them would venture toward his harem, but as soon as the big fellow made a threatening gesture, they had a change of heart.

Ernie and I watched the bull for a good fifteen minutes before I finally shot. He was the lord of the harem, the king of the basin, the biggest and proudest bull on the mountain, a fine six-pointer with a long and massive head with every point like polished ivory.

There was no way to get closer, so I decided to take him at long range. I sat on a small boulder and rested my rifle on my rolled-up down jacket over a larger boulder. I held about the width of the elk's chest over the top of his back, fired two shots, both hits, and the great bull's legs turned to rubber and he collapsed. As the crack of the .270 echoed and re-echoed through the lonely basin, the younger and weaker bulls came boiling out of that tongue of timber and fled with the cows in every direction. The next day, when we were packing out the meat, we saw what must have been the same herd of cows in yet another basin. This time they had a new bull, and as far as I could tell, none of them had shed a tear for the old one.

I have never seen a real elk battle, a knockdown and drag-out between two lordly and evenly matched bulls. Most of the fighting I have seen has been decided by a couple of brief clashes or even by the big bull unceremoniously chasing the smaller one away. However, the bulls evidently throw some hellbenders, as elk are often seen with scarred bodies and broken antlers, and now and then a pair of bulls get their antlers locked together and can't get them apart. Generally they both perish.

I have heard some hunters say that elk are dumb creatures and not difficult to hunt. To me, elk have always seemed very smart, keen of ear, eye, and nose, and—for an animal so large—able to hide in surprising little cover. Once in Arizona, a companion and I were riding through the beautiful open country of yellow pines, gamble oaks, and alligator-bark juniper through which the elk there move on the way from their summer range in the fir and spruce at around 8,000 feet above sea level to the junipers at around 5,000 to 6,000 feet.

We had ridden past a clump of oaks about 20 feet in diameter, a clump so thin that no one would have suspected it would hide a deer much less a big bull elk. When we were about 75 yards past the clump, something made me look around; I saw a big bull sneaking out. No dumbbell he!

Like all of the deer family, elk have wonderful noses, and I'm convinced that their eyes are better than those of deer. In September, 1944, I was hunting bighorn sheep on a lofty plateau above timberline near Yellowstone Park. As we rode across it with a little pack outfit toward the ram country, we saw herd after herd of bull elk. Often we picked them up with binoculars a mile or two away. In almost every instance the elk had seen us first. A mountain sheep could not have done better.

And elk have ears like bats. In Idaho it is pretty warm in many areas during the early part of the season, and the elk lie up for the day in heavy green timber. It takes the sneakiest kind of still-hunting, as well as constant watching of the wind, to get up on them.

Most of the Idaho elk country is mountainous and so steep that if Idaho were ironed out flat, the resulting state would make Texas look like Rhode Island. Because of this up-and-down quality of the country, the Idaho elk hunter either shoots his elk at less than 100 yards, or at from 300 to 500 across a canyon. One time I shot a fat cow across a canyon. She rolled about 100 yards and then got hung up in some heavy brush. To get to her, I had to climb hand over hand through the brush like Tarzan. When I chopped down the brush that was holding her, she crashed into the bottom of the creek 300 feet below, and I don't think the carcass bounced more than twice. My packer managed to get a couple of mules in to carry the quarters out, but it was quite an operation. Rugged stuff, this Idaho elk hunting.

Most meat hunters try to pick dry cows, calves, or spike bulls, but I believe the finest piece of elk meat I ever had was from a big six-point bull shot just at the beginning of the rut, before the animal got strong and lean. If meat is the objective, the time to shoot elk, particularly old bulls, is as early in September as possible. When the rut is well along, even the cows can get pretty strong, although a cow never gets as lean as a bull. Actually I don't find much difference between the properly handled meat of a good elk, and beef. Most bad elk meat comes from poor handling in the field, from shooting an animal too late in the season, or from wounding an elk and having to chase and frighten it.

An elk is a big animal, and unless it is skinned, quartered and hung up to cool immediately, it is very likely to sour even in cool weather. Simply gutting an elk out and letting it lie on the ground is a good way to lose meat; the part of the animal toward the ground will not cool. Expert elk hunters always carry a hatchet, as an elk cannot be quartered with a knife.

A great game animal this elk—with everything that it takes. He is an adversary worthy of any hunter's skill, a magnificent trophy, and if properly handled and shot at the right time, several hundred pounds of valuable meat.

# The Natural History of the Elk, or Wapiti

[CERVUS CANADENSIS]

## DESCRIPTION

A typical representative of the deer family *Cervidae,* the wapiti is the largest and most handsome of the round-antlered cervids. Better known in the New World as the elk, the wapiti is pale fawn color over most of its body, but the head and thickly maned neck are a dark shade ranging from chestnut to tawny-brown. A large patch on the rump, surrounding and including the tail, is whitish in the younger elk and becomes straw-colored as the animal gets older. The pelage is darkest and richest-colored in the summer after the spring molt, but fades during the year to a color ranging from yellowish to almost white before the following spring. The legs and underparts are dark chocolate brown or even black.

A full-grown bull elk has a total length of from 8½ to 10 feet, stands 5 feet high at the shoulder, and weighs between 700 and 1,000 pounds. Females are considerably smaller and weigh about 25 per cent less than the bulls.

Characteristic of the great order *Artiodactyla* or even-toed, hoofed mammals, the elk's long, powerful legs terminate in evenly paired toes, with the tips encased in horny hoofs which support the animal's weight. Immediately behind and raised off the ground are a pair of small, lateral hoofs—the dewclaws—which aid the elk in traveling through soft mud or snow.

A ruminant, browsing animal, the elk has no teeth in the front, upper jaw, but it does have upper canine teeth, broad-crowned, sharp-edged molar, or back teeth, and incisors at the front of the lower jaw.

## ANTLERS

The elk's large, slender head has moderately large ears, each terminating in a pointed tip, and a superstructure of massive antlers. The antlers, which are present only in bulls, are solid, bone-like structures, each consisting of a main beam with long, branching tines, or prongs. The main beams sweep outward, upward, and backward for most of their length, curving evenly inward toward the tip. The sharp-pointed tines are directed forward so as to inflict the most damage in battle. In its prime a bull elk carries six tines on each antler. The first tine (the lowest one) projects forward over the face and is called the brow-tine; the second tine, which is about as long as the first and projects a short distance above it, is known as the bay or bestine. These two tines are variously known as dog-killers, wartines, and lifters. The third prong, a little shorter than the first two and projecting forward from about the middle of the main beam, is called the tray, or treztine. The fourth tine, the most dominant, is usually the longest, strongest, and deadliest, and is called the royal, or dagger-point. The two points forming the divided tip of the main beam (the fifth and sixth) are the sur royals. The last tine is bent downward. A bull with a full complement of twelve points, six on each antler, is called a Royal Stag, while a stag with a total of fourteen points is called a Wilson, or an Imperial. Antlers on large bulls may reach a length of 6 feet, with an inside spread of 47 inches and a circumference of the main beam between the first and second tines of 10¼ inches.

Bull elk begin to lose their antlers some time in late winter. The entire antler is shed at a point close to the top of the head, and it is a clean separation. The antlers would fall off automatically, but they are usually dislodged by a bump against a tree branch or trunk.

Early in May a rounded swelling begins to rise from the base of the previous year's antlers. The swellings become knobs and, gradually elongating, take on the form and shape of antlers. Throughout their growth the antlers are composed of a soft, spongy mass encased in a covering of soft, hairy skin, which has a complete system of blood circulation. When full growth has been attained, the antlers begin to harden, and the supply of blood and nourishment conveyed by the velvet and the arteries dries up. The skin covering, no longer of any use, begins to peel and itch, and the elk soon rubs it off against tree branches and trunks. During this period, the antlers are usually covered with blood.

## ORIGIN

Wapiti is the Shawnee Indians' name for this animal and it has been generally retained. Since the name elk is the most popular and better-known alternative vernacular for the animal, it must be recognized. Elk is the name used in Europe for the moose that is native to Eurasia as well as America. When the early English settlers arrived in Virginia and saw the wapiti for the first time, they thought it was the big Scandinavian elk they had heard about but never seen. They did not realize that it was a big cousin of the European red deer.

A comparatively recent addition to the fauna of North America, the wapiti is of Euro-Asiatic stock and apparently arrived in the New World over the Asiatic-Alaskan land bridge. During the glaciation of the Pleistocene era, waters of the ocean were transferred to the polar ice cap, lowering the sea level 300 feet or more and exposing the shallow straits of the Bering Sea. This land bridge provided an emigration route between Asia and Alaska. How long this thoroughfare remained open is not known, but eastward and westward migrations eventually must have been prevented by the ice fields which moved south from the polar cap.

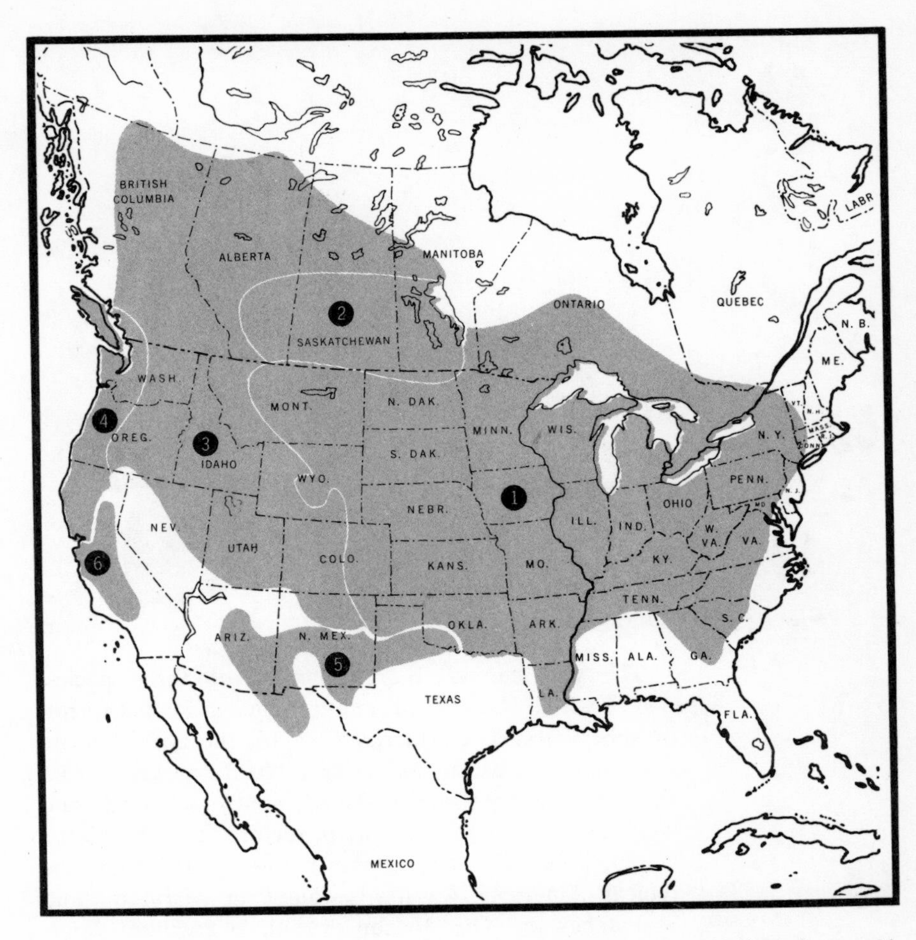


Distribution of the races of the wapiti *Cervus:* 1. American wapiti, 2. Manitoba wapiti, 3. Nelson wapiti, 4. Roosevelt wapiti, 5. Arizona wapiti, 6. Tule wapiti.

## RANGE

The elk's habitat is the tall timber in the high mountain regions of the evergreen forest belt. It once ranged from coast to coast over most of the upland country in the United States and southern Canada, but is now restricted chiefly to the forested Rocky Mountain region from New Mexico to northern British Columbia and Alberta.

The American wapiti are separated into three species, one of which has several additional geographical forms, or subspecies. The American wapiti, the typical form, once ranged eastern and middle North America from the St. Lawrence River in Canada south to Georgia and west to the Rocky Mountain region. The Manitoba wapiti, a smaller and darker-colored form than the typical American wapiti, is found in Manitoba and Saskatchewan. The Nelson wapiti, a medium light-colored form with comparatively small antlers, is found in most of the Rocky Mountains from California to northern British Columbia. The Roosevelt wapiti or olympic elk, a large, dark-colored wapiti with heavy, short antlers, ranges along the dense forests of the Pacific Coast region from Vancouver Island to northern California. The Arizona wapiti, a well-marked species with a blackish nose, reddish head and legs, originally occurred in the White Mountains of Arizona and the Mogollon Mountains of New Mexico, and is now probably extinct. The Tule wapiti, also called the Dwarf or California elk, is the smallest of the American wapiti, with shorter legs and paler color than any other species. Once on the verge of extinction, there are now well over 500 head, but it is found in the wild state only in Kern and Inyo Counties of California.

## HABITS

Having a strong social instinct, the American elk always travels in the company of its kind. A herd containing cows, calves, yearlings, two-year-olds, and a few grown bulls may number up to a hundred or more head during the migrations. Bachelor bulls carrying magnificent antlers associate in small bands of up to twenty-five or more and, except during the rut, live complacently together.

Shunning the deep snow of the mountains, the elk spends the winter months in the sheltered valleys and windswept meadows where food is available. In the spring, it moves up the mountain slopes to higher levels, escaping the hordes of blood-sucking insects that hatch with the coming of the warm weather. All summer long the elk remains in a comparatively small home territory, rarely straying beyond a limit of 5 or 6 square miles, providing the food supply holds out.

A ruminant, or cud-chewer, the elk has a multiple or compound stomach, a modern development present in most of the progressive ungulates which feed on green vegetation. Feeding largely in the very early morning before daylight and again about dusk, the elk consumes large quantities of food in a very short time. This fodder is only roughly chopped, then it is swallowed and stored in the paunch, a very large compartment of the stomach, where it is mixed with stomach juices and held until the animal has finished feeding and is ready to rest. The food is then returned to the mouth in the form of small pellets to be thoroughly milled to a fine pulp and passed on to the other compartments of the stomach for digestion, this time bypassing the paunch, or first stomach. During the summer months various kinds of grasses form the elk's staple diet, but it varies its diet with leaves and twigs of underbrush as well as evergreen and deciduous trees. In winter, when the snow is deep, it browses largely on twigs and shoots of trees, stripping the branches in the forest up to what is known as "the elk line."

## ENEMIES

The wolf, cougar, bear, and coyote are potential enemies of the elk, but a bull in possession of its faculties and antlers is beyond the danger of attack by any one of them. Not likely to be taken by surprise, the elk has excellent eyesight, a well-developed sense of smell, and a keen sense of hearing. One observer tells of a battle between a bull elk and a bear. The elk reduced the carnivore to a lifeless mass of pulp, ripping it through and through with its deadly, long-tined antlers.

Deep winter snow with a frozen crust is actually the elk's worst enemy. When the snow is soft and fluffy the animal can easily plough its way through, raising a cloud of white dust, and dig for grass and foliage with its strong hoofs. But a weak, hungry elk will get trapped in deep, crusted snow. Many die from starvation or become easy prey of wolves, cougars, and coyotes. Fortunately, the bears are denned up for the winter.

The tracks of a galloping elk are similar to those of a whitetail deer, but are larger and broader. The tracks of the hind feet are in front.

The development of an elk's antlers over a period of about six months: 1. In March both antlers are shed, exposing the naked pedicles which are part of the bony structure of the skull. 2. By late April new antlers appear as buds of velvety fur. 3. By mid-May the antlers show considerable growth. Although still covered with velvety fur, they begin to assume the pattern of the final form. 4. By early June the antlers are a dominating feature of the animal's appearance, but they are still soft, spongy, and easily damaged. 5. By early July the antlers are reaching the final stages of development. The animal is still docile and careful not to damage them. 6. After the antlers attain full growth in August, they harden, the blood stream dries up, the velvety covering—now dead tissue—is stripped off in shreds, and the bull elk becomes aggressive.

Woodticks, botfly larvae, round worms, tapeworms, and other parasites help reduce the elk's resistance to the hardships of the long northern winters.

### LOCOMOTION

The elk is not especially fleet-footed. Over long distances it can maintain a running speed of only 28 or 29 miles per hour, although in a short burst of speed it can travel at 35 to 45 miles per hour. It can jump a wooden fence 7 feet high, but always seems to gauge its jump so that its hoofs either graze or break the top rail. Its tracks are spaced much like those of the deer but the hoof-prints are wider and less pointed—more like those of domestic cattle. The elk is an excellent swimmer and even calves have been seen crossing lakes a mile wide.

### VOCAL

For ten or eleven months of the year a bull elk rarely utters a sound, but he makes up for it during the rut. Early in September the bulls become restless and suddenly start to utter their loud, challenging bugle calls. Bulls that have lived peaceably all summer now eye each other with hatred and suspicion, and move with a stiff, stilt-like gait. The bugle call begins with a low, stirring, clear note, gradually rises to a high pitch, and ends in a shrill scream, followed by a series of short grunts. The cows occasionally bugle at this time, but in a lower key and softer tone. When alarmed at any season of the year, the animals utter a brief call.

### MATING

The sultan of the animal kingdom, a powerful bull elk collects for himself by sheer might the largest harem of females of any land-bound mammal. With such a harem in tow, a bull must be on guard day and night. Small bands of unmated bulls skirt the fringes of large harems trying to provoke a major conflict with the herd bull. A cautious and experienced male will make one mighty charge at the offender and then return. If he should get entangled in an open brawl, the other lurking bulls will close in during the battle, split up the harem between them, and disappear in different directions. The old warrior may win the battle but lose his harem, and then he is usually too weak to recover any part of it.

The mating season, or rut, begins in September and lasts into October. The necks of the bulls swell with bulging muscles, the nasals become extended and the whites of the protruding eyes give the animal a vicious appearance. The antlers, now fully developed and hardened, the tips sharpened and polished for action, are soon rattling like swords as the bulls begin their annual contests for possession of the females. It was for this purpose and this alone that the mighty antlers were grown and carefully guarded. Soon they will have served their purpose and be discarded once more.

Fortunately, the antlers are so constructed that two fighting bulls seldom get them inseparably locked, as so often happens when two moose or whitetail deer meet. The rights of a master bull are rarely disputed and, after a brief test of his power, the weaker ones flee. Occasionally there will be a broken neck or a thrust of sharp-tined antlers in a vital spot. During the combat the cows stand by disinterestedly, with no more than a curious glance when a bull gains supremacy over a harem.

### BIRTH AND EARLY DEVELOPMENT

Baby elk are born in May or June, about 8½ months after mating, when the cows are moving from the winter feeding grounds on the low flats and valleys to the high summer range. The calving takes place in open park or grass land which affords shelter from predators.

The newborn calf—twins are rare—is a light tawny-brown color marked with numerous large, white spots, and weighs from 30 to 35 pounds. It is born with its eyes wide open and is able to stand and nurse within the hour. The mother's first duty is to lick her calf from the tip of its little black nose to the end of its tail, down to the soles of its baby feet, cleansing it of any odor. For the first few days the calf remains in seclusion and freezes flat on the ground at the first sign of danger, its spotted coat a perfect camouflage in

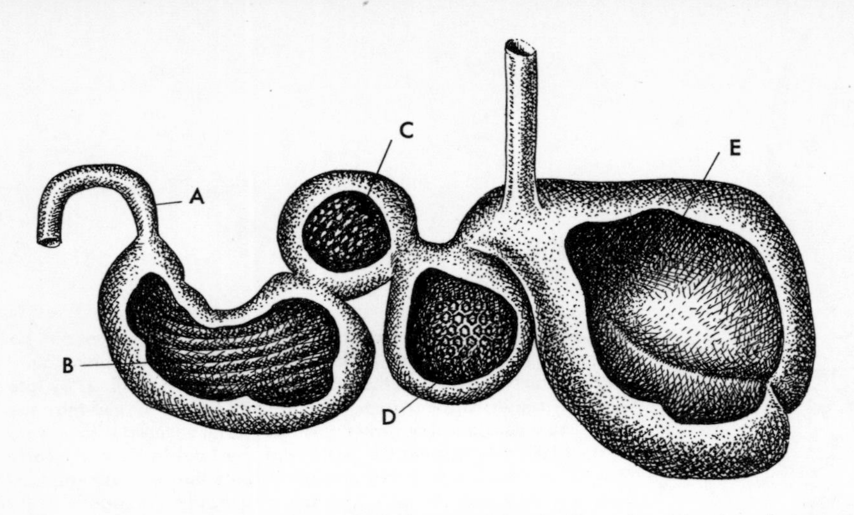


The elk, like all cud-chewing mammals, has a four-chambered stomach. The food is swallowed roughly chopped and passes through the oesophagus (a) and into the rumen, or paunch (b), where it is stored until the animal can find a resting place. Then the food is returned to the mouth and thoroughly chewed. Swallowed once again, the food this time by-passes the paunch and moves through the honeycomb bag (c), the manyplies (d), and enters the duodenum (e), where digestion is completed.

broken patches of sunlight, its body practically devoid of smell. A bear or coyote may pass within a few feet and never detect its presence. In a week the calf is strong enough to follow its mother and continue with the herd to higher land. Although it nurses on its mother's milk for the first six weeks, the calf also begins to forage for itself when it is a month old. It begins to lose its white spots in August and by fall they have completely faded away.

A calf grows so rapidly that at two months it generally weighs 130 pounds; at 9 months, 280 pounds; at 21 months, 475 pounds. A young bull's first set of antlers begins to grow in May, just about a year after birth, and by fall they are simple spikes from 10 to 20 inches long, occasionally with a forked tip. By the second year the antlers have four or five points each, but they are small and slender. In the third year the antlers are stronger but still usually have no more than five points each. At this age the young elk has its permanent teeth, having shed all its milk teeth. A full complement of six points on each antler usually occurs in the fourth year. Cows are sexually mature and breed for the first time during the rut of the third year. Bull calves are mature at about the same time but are not strong enough to compete with the older bulls until the fourth or fifth year. A few cows have been known to breed at the age of seventeen years, to live for twenty-five years, but most bulls, and many cows, are in their decline after the sixteenth year.

## Popular and Scientific Names of the Elk, or Wapiti

**ORDER:** *Artiodactyla*

**FAMILY:** *Cervidae*

**GENUS:** *Cervus*

**SPECIES:** *canadensis*

**SUBSPECIES**

| | |
|---|---|
| American wapiti | *Cervus canadensis canadensis* |
| Manitoba wapiti | *Cervus canadensis manitobensis* |
| Nelson wapiti | *Cervus canadensis nelsoni* |
| Roosevelt wapiti | *Cervus canadensis roosevelti* |
| Arizona wapiti | *Cervus merriami* |
| Tule wapiti | *Cervus nannodes* |

DOUG ALLEN

CHAPTER 9

# THE MOOSE

THE MOOSE of North America is the largest deer that has ever walked the face of the earth, larger even than the extinct Irish elk. It is difficult for the man who is used to hunting deer or even elk to conceive of the enormous bulk of a big bull moose. It takes a large mule deer, northern white-tail, or bighorn sheep to weigh 300 pounds on the hoof, but the largest moose of northern British Columbia, Alaska, and the Yukon will probably weigh as much as 1,800 pounds. A big northern moose is a much larger animal than the East African eland, the heaviest antelope. The only herbivorous creatures in the world other than the elephant, rhino, and hippo, that are larger are the wild cattle such as the American bison, the Asiatic gaur and wild water buffalo, and the African Cape buffalo.

The moose is not only very heavy, but with his long legs is also tremendously tall. The largest moose I have ever seen dead was one shot by my companion Myles Brown of Cleveland, Ohio, in the White River country of the Yukon in 1945. From the bottom of the hoofs to the top of his hump, he measured about 7½ feet. I have heard of moose that measured 8 feet and a bit over from hoof to hump, but the late Jean Jacquot, who lived in the Yukon for over fifty years and outfitted hunting parties, told me he didn't think a Yukon moose that tall had ever lived. However, moose that go 7 feet are not uncommon even in eastern and southern Canada, where they run a good deal smaller than they do in the far north.

I saw my first bull moose in 1943 when I was traveling by pack-train across a corner of Jasper National Park in Alberta on the way to the Sheep Creek-Muddy-water River country to hunt bighorns. The bull had just finished cleaning the velvet off his antlers, and they hadn't yet been stained by contact with brush. They were snow-white. His black-brown body was as round and fat as a stuffed sausage, and in the brilliant sunlight his hide shone as sleek as the hide of a wet seal.

The typical moose is black on breast, shoulders, and flanks, and fades to a reddish-brown on the withers, back, head, and neck. The net effect of the moose, however, particularly if seen in the shade of timber, is of an enormous black animal. The neck is short and the head is carried low. The ears are very large, the nose pendulous, and both sexes wear a "bell"—a growth of skin and hair which hangs from the neck. In young moose the bell is long, but in old ones it is generally much shorter. The story in the north country has it that the lower part of the bell, where circulation is not so good, freezes off in bitter weather. Tracks of the elk are round and cowlike, but those of the moose are pointed like those of an enormous deer, which, of course, is exactly what the moose is. The droppings look like those of a deer except that they are very much larger.

Like a great many other North American big game animals, the moose is a migrant from Asia and crossed Bering Strait over a land bridge that existed off and on for over a million years. He has relatives all the way across northern Asia and Europe as far west as Scandinavia, but the Old World form is a smaller animal whose antlers are less well developed.

Our "moose" is actually an elk, and he is so known in the Old World. When settlers in North America encountered the wapiti, they named him the elk, as they probably had never seen an elk but knew of it only as a large deer. Then when they found the true elk, they had run out of names, so it had to be given the Ojibway name, moose.

New World settlers managed to mix up the names of North American big game pretty badly. Used to the British red deer, which is related to the animal we call elk (but which is properly called wapiti), they gave the name deer to the very different whitetail and mule deer. Among other things, they called the cougar or puma a lion, and in Mexico and South America, the jaguar is a tiger. Our "antelope" is a unique creature only very distantly related to the antelope of the Old World. However, they did manage to recognize that wild sheep were actually sheep and that our bears were bears.

In North America the moose is found from arctic Alaska far north of the limit of trees, across Canada from west to east, and as far south as eastern Idaho and northwestern Wyoming around Yellowstone National Park. Moose are found close to the sea in the Kenai Peninsula in Alaska, and in the Northwest Territories and the northern Yukon they range not far from the Arctic Ocean. However, in Canada they are not found along the coast west of the mountains, and they are not present on the islands off the Alaska and Canadian coast. There are still moose in Maine and Nova Scotia, and there are likewise some moose in Minnesota. In historic times they ranged in New York state and even in Pennsylvania, but generally they are northern animals.

The only states where moose are regularly hunted today are Alaska, Idaho, Wyoming, and Montana, but Maine used to be famous for its moose hunting. Generally moose are increasing because of good protection and also because of changes in habitat. Logged and burned-off country supports more moose than virgin timber. In parts of southern British Columbia, where fifty years ago moose were very scarce, they are today so abundant that they threaten their food supply. In western Wyoming and eastern Idaho, moose were once so rare that there was some doubt as to their existence. Today they are common. Part of this upsurge of moose numbers can no doubt be laid to the scarcity of wolves, as it is the great, gaunt timber wolf that is the principal enemy of the moose.

The range of the moose in North America is continuous, but the moose grow smaller as they go east and south and, for purposes of record keeping, they are divided into four subspecies. The American moose and the Northwestern moose are found clear across Canada. The Shiras moose, or Wyoming moose, was first classified in the Jackson Hole country of Wyoming, but the moose of extreme southern British Columbia and Alberta and in that tongue of Rocky Mountain moose country that terminates around Yellowstone Park are presumed to belong to Shirasi and are so classified in *Records of North American Big Game*. Although the Shiras moose are much smaller and have less massive and less well-developed heads than their larger relatives, they are still big animals; a good Shiras bull will stand 6 feet or a bit over at the shoulder.

The Alaska or giant moose was first classified on the Kenai Peninsula of Alaska, but all the moose of Alaska, northern British Columbia, and the Yukon are the same breed—terrific creatures with spectacular antler development. I have never hunted moose on the Kenai, but I have hunted them in Wyoming, British Columbia, Alberta, and the Yukon, and presumably I have shot all four subspecies in those areas.

Certainly it has been my experience that the Shiras moose is the smallest, and the animals of northern British Columbia and the Yukon the largest. The largest moose I have ever laid eyes on, and the largest bull I have ever shot, were both in northern British Columbia around the head of the Prophet and Muskwa rivers in the some towering limestone mountains that produce the world's largest Stone sheep heads.

For whatever the reason, hunters most often speak of moose "horns," but they are antlers, not horns, and are shed annually like any antlers. The young bull grows his first antlers—two snags—in his second summer. The next year he grows prongs, which are often called "bootjacks." The third pair begin to palmate, and henceforth the antlers begin to grow larger until the seventh or eighth year when the bull is at the peak of his mature vigor. Then, after three or four years, they slowly go downhill

Huge antlers adorned the head of that bull, yet neither O'Connor nor his partner could fire a shot.

and tend to freak, just as with deer and elk. Moose antlers are usually shed in January or February.

The antlers of a mature bull are two wide, many-pointed palms. At one time, spread was the sole criterion of the excellence of a moose head, but now the head is judged not only by spread, but also by width and length of palm, number of points, and symmetry. This is as it should be, because some moose heads with very wide spreads and a high standing in the old records were actually quite narrow of palm, and spindly. The impressiveness of a moose head is in its great mass.

In the latest edition of *Records of North American Big Game,* the first three heads in the records are all from Alaska's Kenai Peninsula, and of the first ten, all are from Alaska except for one from the Yukon. More big moose have been taken from the Kenai than from any other area. There are two reasons for this. In the first place, of course, the moose there are very large. In the second, they are very plentiful; the trophy hunter there has a chance to look over a great number of heads before he shoots. At one time moose were very scarce or absent altogether on the Kenai, but a great forest fire about seventy-five years ago burned it over and turned it into ideal moose country. The moose then flourished, and trophy hunters came from all over the world for big moose heads.

I have heard of hunters looking over from fifty to one hundred Kenai bulls before firing a shot. That is a lot of moose—more than I have ever had a chance to see on one hunt. I believe time will prove that the moose heads run just as large in arctic Alaska, in the Wind River country of the Yukon, and in the Muskwa-Prophet country of northern British Columbia.

When I was hunting Stone sheep around the heads of the Prophet and Muskwa rivers in northern British Columbia in 1946, I saw a good many very large bull moose. One day on Lapp Creek, a tributary of the Prophet and not very far from where L. S. Chadwick killed the world-record Stone sheep, I saw seven big, mature bulls in one morning. I stalked and shot one. It was very massive and had a wide-palmed, many-pointed head with a spread of 62½ inches. It should score high in the records for the Canadian moose, and should show up very respectably in the list of Alaska-Yukon moose. It was never recorded, and the last I heard, it was on display in an Arizona sporting-goods store. The best Yukon moose I have ever shot had a spread of 57½ inches, but this head was massive and deeply cupped. As a rule, the moose antlers with the largest spread are those that do not cup but instead go out flat with only slight cupping.

The largest moose head I have ever seen on the hoof was not far from a little lake in northern British Columbia which was named by Frank Golata for an old packhorse by the name of Puss. Colin McGuire and I had spent a long and unsuccessful day hunting grizzlies. We had seen five and had stalked three, but in every case something managed to thwart us. A couple of times the wind shifted at the wrong moment and the grizzly took off. In another case the grizzly was below the brow of a hill and we had to complete our stalk through dry, noisy arctic birch. The bear heard us and was long gone.

We had covered at least 15 miles that day and were very tired as we headed back to camp. The sun was almost down and the chill wind of the mountain autumn was blowing in our faces as we plodded wearily down a hill. Suddenly we saw a bull moose lying down and not over 50 yards away. And what a moose! A big bull is such an enormous animal in the body that even a large head as a rule does not look really big. But even on that gigantic animal, this head looked tremendous. The spread was fantastically wide, the palms unbelievably broad.

"Great Scott!" McGuire whispered in my ear. "Shoot that moose. You'll never see another like it!"

But then he remembered that I'd already killed a moose on that trip and I had no desire to wind up in a British Columbia jail.

"You shoot him, Mac," I propositioned.

"Not I," Mac said. "I don't shoot heads. I shoot meat and I'm not going to shoot my meat until I get back to my trapline."

So that tremendous bull was destined to go uncollected. In order to see him in action, I whistled. He got up and trotted off down a game trail beside a creek, and I saw his antlers hit two willow branches. I went down immediately and found I could not cover in two long paces the distance between the points where the antlers had struck.

When Mac and I got back to camp after dark, I told our cook, Johnnie Cooper, an old guide and moose hunter, about the great bull I had just seen.

"I know just where you saw him," Johnnie told me. "I've been watching him all day. That's by far the largest bull moose I've ever seen. He looked like he was carrying around two table tops."

So that is the story of the great bull moose of Puss Lake. I don't see how that head could possibly have had a spread of less than 80 inches. It was enormously larger than the head of the great bull that Myles Brown shot in the Yukon when I was with him in 1945 and which, for a time, was the Yukon record. It was also much larger than the 75-inch head in the National Collection in New York, a head that I have seen many times.

The world-record Canada moose has a spread of 65⅝ inches and a score of 238⅝. It is from Quebec. The widest spread I can find recorded is 71⅝, an old head from Maine.

The largest head of an Alaska-Yukon moose is 77⅝; this head is from the Kenai and is mounted on an animal in the habitat group in the American Museum of Natural History.

The record Shiras moose has a score of 205⁴⁄₈, a spread of 53 inches, and was shot in Wyoming. The largest Shiras spread is from a bull shot in 1957 near Elk City, Idaho—62⅜. That is a most excellent spread, and many a trophy hunter has gone to the famous Kenai and has done no better.

In the eastern part of their range, moose inhabit very heavily wooded country where still-hunting, although not impossible, is very difficult. A famous and picturesque way of hunting them is to call them. I have never hunted moose in eastern Canada, and I have never seen a moose called, but I understand that the guide with his birch-bark horn makes like an amorous cow. The bull, equally amorous, hears what he thinks is a cow and comes toward the call, grunting now and then. It is undoubtedly a very exciting way to hunt, full of thrills and suspense.

It is generally believed that moose are semipolygamous, and that a bull will stay with a cow a week or so, as long as she is in heat, and then abandon her to find another. Be that as it may, one of the oddest sights I have ever seen was up in the Sheep Creek country of Alberta. Roy Hargreaves and I were hunting moose one day when, about a mile away, we glassed a whole line of moose. In the lead was a cow. Behind her was an enormous bull that looked as if he had a spread of around 60 inches. Behind him was a smaller bull, then a still smaller one. At the end of the parade was a hopeful little two-year-old. Wherever the cow went, the bulls were right behind, and each one knew his place in the line. As the lead bull looked very good, Roy and I tried to stalk it, but we had no luck. When we were no more than 100 yards from where we had last seen them, a treacherous breeze betrayed us. We found the cow, but the bulls had faded away.

Another famous method of hunting moose in the East is to do so from a canoe, slipping silently around the headlands to watch for a bull feeding along the shore. In Scandinavia the preferred way to hunt the "elk" is to follow them with hounds trained to trail silently.

In the mountains of western Canada, where I have done most of my moose hunting, the big bulls are generally found in fairly open timber and often above timberline. They are most often hunted by glassing them at long range and then stalking. The hunter will go to the top of a hill where he can look down into the timber, locate a suitable bull, and then try stalking quietly upwind. This is easier said than done because the moose has a wonderful nose, and ears like a bat. In spite of his great weight and enormous antlers, he can steal away as quietly as a shadow. It is an old saying among moose hunters that if a moose is shot at and makes any noise when he runs, he has been wounded.

In the Rockies, the moose love willows and are generally found near them. A big bull is so tall that often when he is seen in a willow patch tilted up on a mountainside toward the hunter, it will appear as if he were standing in a grassy meadow. But when the hunter is making his stalk, he will often find that the willows are as high as his head and so thick that the only way he can move is to travel along the moose trails. I remember shooting one moose in willows so high that the only way I could see enough moose to shoot at was to stand on a wobbly hummock and shoot offhand through willow leaves and twigs at the top six inches of the moose's back. Another time a friend and I made a stalk through a willow patch so high that we could

Heading the parade was the cow moose, followed by four bulls that all knew their places in the line.

hear the moose feeding and moving around not over 30 yards off. We couldn't see him, and my pal never would have got a shot if the moose hadn't heard us. He ran out of the willows, and my pal nailed him as he went over a rocky ridge above timberline.

I killed my first moose without a guide and all alone by still-hunting, using exactly the same methods I had used on mule and whitetail deer in the brush. I was hunting in Alberta, and my guide and I had seen a good many moose. The bulls had only recently cleaned the velvet off their antlers, and they shone snow-white in the dark timber. We would climb up the side of a mountain, locate a good bull in the timber below, and then make the stalk. But always when we got there, the moose would be gone; it was almost impossible to move without making some noise, and two men have more feet than one. To complicate matters, the wind was treacherous, and light eddies would swirl this way and that. We were getting nowhere.

So one afternoon I decided to try to still-hunt a moose along a creek where the timber was very thick and the moss underfoot very soft. We had seen a lot of moose sign there, and occasionally we had seen moose.

So I set out, walking quietly upwind, trying to avoid stepping on a twig, stopping often to look and listen. The result was that I almost walked up on a bedded bull. He got up in some thick jackpines not over 30 yards from me, and I'll never forget how enormously tall and massive he looked. My first shot with a 130-grain .270 bullet brought down a shower of twigs and small branches, and I counted it a miss. But it turned him to one side, and he came out into a little opening not over 50 yards away. He was quartering, and I held against his paunch, hoping to drive the bullet up into his lungs. I shot, and the moose was gone.

I stood in my tracks and listened. For a moment I could hear him run, and then all was quiet. Now that the excitement was over, I discovered that I was having a bit of moose fever. I then took up the trail. I could see his tracks in the soft earth, but not a bit of blood did I find. I wondered if, with a scope-sighted rifle, I could possibly have missed an animal so close that I should have been able to hit him with a rock.

That trail led out of the heavy timber onto a little muskeg meadow where the arctic willow grew about 4 feet high. I had hardly entered it when I saw where he had fallen and his knees had left holes a foot deep in the mucky ground. I was still following his trail 50 or 75 yards farther on, when suddenly he arose out of the willows in front of me like a genie from a bottle. He trotted off broadside, and I held for his lungs right behind the shoulder. But he didn't even flinch as he ran out of the meadow into the timber. Again I took up his trail, and in about 150 yards I found him lying dead—this huge animal as big as a large horse and with a 52-inch spread. He was, I was told later, a young moose about four years old. Both of my shots had gone exactly where I'd called them, and my first bullet would have done the business in a few minutes. It had penetrated up into the right lung, and I found it under the hide.

My best Yukon moose came as a pure accident. Myles Brown and I were moving with a jack-camp outfit, from our base camp where Harris Creek runs into the Generc River, to Moose Horn Creek at the foot of Mount Nazahat. We were strung along, crossing a big caribou barren above timberline, when suddenly I saw something brown move in a willow patch about a quarter of a mile away. I pulled up my horse, grabbed my binoculars, and took a hasty look. I thought I'd seen the back of a grizzly bear, but the glass showed me the velvet-covered antlers of two big bull moose.

We stopped the pack outfit, and Myles and I sneaked quietly forward. When we got to about 75 yards from the moose, we perched on a little rise so we could shoot from a sitting position. The bulls were still there.

We switched off the safeties of our rifles and I shouted, *"Cuidado!"* which is Spanish for beware.

Both bulls jumped to their feet and took off broadside with their long, space-eating trot. Shooting rapidly, I laid three 130-grain Remington Bronze Point .270 bullets right behind my bull's

Lured by O'Connor's bull-like grunt, the lovesick cow grunted back and trotted toward him. He fled to his horse.

shoulder. Myles, however, did not lead quite enough, and his 220-grain .30/60 bullets were a bit far back. For a mile, we could see his big bull legging it across the rolling barren until it finally entered the tall willows that bordered a little lake. Myles and his guide went over there and finished off the moose. A month later in Whitehorse, we learned that the head had a spread of 69¾ inches. Quite a moose!

Many myths are in circulation about the ferocity of bull moose and the danger of following up one that is wounded. During the past fifty years, American magazines have from time to time published a grisly photo showing the skeleton of a bull moose, the skeleton of a man, and the rusty remains of a rifle, all laid out neatly together. It is generally captioned "Will Moose Charge?" or "Proof that Moose will Charge," or something of the sort.

I first saw that photo published in the early nineteen twenties, if not earlier. The picture adorns the walls of bars and bistros all over the Rocky Mountain states, and the bloody encounter is supposed to have happened in Idaho, Montana, Wyoming, Alberta, and British Columbia. A negative must exist somewhere because every now and then an excited reader sends me a print. I think it is a phony. The whole thing is too neat, too stagy. The information about it is too vague.

I can well imagine that if a wounded moose were cornered he might get tough. The pint-size javelina will fight, and so will a cornered deer—and maybe even a mouse. But if there is a clear avenue of escape, I am sure a moose would take it. I have walked up on wounded moose and I have yet to see one show fight. In the midst of the rut it might be a different story, but I have never heard of a moose attacking a man—and I have known people who have shot many dozens of moose.

Any animal as large and powerful as a moose is potentially dangerous, of course, and a moose that feels cornered will certainly defend himself. A Canadian trapper once told me of finding the scattered bones of a bull moose mixed with those of three wolves. From the evidence, the trapper figured a pack of wolves had backed the bull up against a rock wall where he had defended himself to the death. Another trapper told me of snowshoeing after a bull through deep snowdrifts. Finally, said the trapper, the bull—every hair on end, and grinding his teeth—came plunging through the drifts toward him, and he had to flee.

One winter near Yellowstone Park, a bull moose was boxed in between the high snow walls of a plowed-out road and a school bus full of children. The driver did not push the bull, but stayed discreetly behind him. However, the bull apparently felt himself trapped, because presently he whirled around, attacked the bus, and put it out of commission.

I have read many tales of charges by wounded bulls in my day, tales in which the heroic hunter drops the raging monster at his feet. One yarn even described how a woman hunter dropped the charging bull while he was still 200 yards away. Anyone who is careless with a cornered, wounded, or rutting bull is foolish, and moose have undoubtedly scared many a hunter. However, when compared with really dangerous animals, the moose is not very formidable.

I once had an amusing run-in with a moose, but with a cow, not a bull. It was during the rut and in Wyoming. It was raining, and I was wearing a long black slicker. Off the trail about 100 yards away, I saw a cow moose standing under a tree. I tied my horse and walked toward the cow with the notion of taking a picture. When I was about 50 yards from her, I did my best to grunt like a bull moose so she'd move out into the open. Much to my amazement she grunted back and came trotting up to me, her eyes full of love. I gave an astonished yell and fled for my horse.

Incidentally, the tamest moose I have ever seen are those in the Jackson Hole country of Wyoming. The reason for this, I believe, is that there are no wolves there, and with the exception of an odd grizzly bear the only enemy these moose have is man. In the North the hungry wolves harry the moose constantly and keep them spooky.

I hunted moose in Wyoming in 1944, and at one

of our camps three big bulls used to come into a mountain meadow and feed with our pack mules. Morning and evening I could have shot any one of them from the door of the tent. My guide said it would save him a lot of time and trouble if I'd kill my moose where it was handy, but I refused, and instead of using a rifle I used a camera. When I took my moose, I did so in a meadow about five miles away. This bull was equally tame, but at least he wasn't an old friend.

According to the Indians of the Yukon, the moose begin to rut with the first full moon in September. Whether it is the moon or perhaps the first hard frosts that bring on the rut, I cannot say. By the middle of August the great antlers of the bulls are full grown under the velvet; by early September, the velvet is cleaned off, and the horns are white until they become stained brown by contact with brush. Then the bulls quit eating and begin to wander widely in search of receptive cows.

Before the rut, the bulls are hog-fat, and their meat is mild, tender, and delicious. The backstrap of a big northern bull is larger than of a beef steer, and the fillets cut from it are an epicure's delight. But when the bull stops eating and starts wandering, the meat quickly becomes curiously metallic in taste. In a few weeks the bull has lost all his fat, and the meat is foul. When I was hunting white sheep in the Yukon in 1956, a companion shot a bull in late September; the meat was so putrid that when the cook tried to prepare it, we were all driven from the tent.

At the end of the rut, the meat loses this evil smell, but November-killed moose is as dry, tough, and tasteless as an old shoe. From the Idaho city where I live, hunters go into southern British Columbia in November and bring back moose meat. Now and then they give me a chunk, and I have yet to see any fit for human consumption. I am told, however, by Yukon Indians who live on moose the year round that they fatten up after the rut and that bulls killed in January and February are often almost as fat as those killed in August.

Wolves, Indians, and trappers are the most serious enemies of the moose. And to the list might be added grizzly bears, particularly in the spring when the calves are young. Apparently in true wilderness areas predation is heavy, because by fall about 50 per cent of the cows seen have lost their calves.

There is a lot of meat on a moose. I have been told that big, fat bulls have been shot that dressed out 250 pounds to the quarter—or 1,000 pounds to the carcass. If true, that is a lot of calories. A few moose quarters put up in the meat cache at the cabin of a trapper or an Indian affords a lot of eating—and a lot of food for the dog team.

In spite of their size, moose do not seem very hard to kill. Many thousands have been shot with .30/30s, and even with .25/35s. I have shot more with a .270 than with any other caliber, and I have never even come close to losing one. One pioneer I knew in the Peace River country of British Columbia fed his large family on moose meat for 25 years and used a Remington .30 caliber pump action.

I have shot moose or seen them shot with the .270, the .30/06, the .300 Magnum, and the .375. I have never seen one killed stone-dead in his tracks with one shot, and it is rare that one is killed that fast unless he is hit in the neck, brain, or spine. However, the moose seems to be a "soft" animal, and when he is hit almost anywhere he goes off a little way and lies down. Then he can be stalked and shot. The famous Frank Golata, who homesteaded in the Peace River country and who has shot many moose and seen many more shot, says they won't carry off as much lead as the smaller, more high-strung deer. He tells of a time when he took a hasty shot at a bull, tracked it down, and killed it. His first shot, Golata discovered, had only injured a foot. With a wound like that, a deer or an elk would keep going all day.

A great animal, the moose—a tremendous pile of good meat if he is shot before the rut, a sporting animal with the keenest nose and ears in the woods, and an impressive trophy if you have a trophy room with a 14-foot ceiling.

# The Natural History of the Moose

[ALCES ALCES]

## DESCRIPTION

The moose is a huge, ungainly animal with a large, humped body raised 4½ feet from the ground on long, stilt-like legs. Its massive head, surmounted with huge antlers, terminates in a broad, pendulous muzzle. Its thick, bulging neck is so short that the animal cannot reach the ground to feed without considerable difficulty, nor can it drink without wading into the water. Adding to this strange appearance, the moose has a growth of skin and hair which hangs from the throat and is known as a "bell." It is present in both sexes, but is largest on a two- or three-year-old bull moose, on which it may reach a length of 36 inches. Twelve inches is about average, however, and in older animals the growth is reduced to a flap of hairy skin only a few inches long.

The moose has a short, inconspicuous tail and large donkey-like ears placed well back on its head. The tips of its fore and hind feet are encased in evenly paired horny sheaths, or hoofs. Despite its tremendous size and weight, the moose travels daintily on the tips of its toes and is a charter member of the order *Artiodactyla,* or even-toed, hoofed animals. Situated directly behind and slightly above the regular hoofs are the lateral hoofs, or dewclaws, which are utilized when the animal travels on wet, swampy land.

The moose's coat is composed of coarse, brittle hairs, each with a pithy center of air cells, which bristle straight out from the hide. The hairs provide an effective insulation to conserve body heat during the cold northern winters. The blackish-brown to almost black color of the moose's coat serves as a perfect camouflage against the dark shadows of the evergreen forests, and the brownish-gray legs and underparts are offset by the darker shades of the shadow of its own body.

Not only is the moose the largest antlered ungulate in the world, but it is also the tallest mammal in the Americas. It competes closely with the bison for the title of heaviest terrestrial animal in the New World. A bull moose may have a head and body length of from 100 to 125 inches, stand 60 to 94 inches at the shoulder, and weigh as much as 900 pounds. Some have been known to weigh as much as 1,800 pounds.

## ANTLERS

The crowning glory of the bull moose is its massive antlers which extend outward from the sides of the head, just above and in front of the ears. The main beam divides into two principal branches: the smaller reaches forward and outward, while the larger, a continuance of the main beam itself, extends backward, spreading into a large, flattened palm with numerous points around the edges. The forward branch is also flattened and has larger points extending from the forward edges. The actual shape of the antlers may assume many varieties but the basic pattern is always about the same. The average Alaska moose antlers measure 47½ inches from tip to tip and weigh 60 to 85 pounds.

Characteristic of the family *Cervidae,* the moose sheds its antlers between late fall and January, when it also sheds its coat of hair.

## ORIGIN

The moose (*Alces*) is a comparatively recent addition to the list of North American big game animals. Of Euro-Asiatic stock, it immigrated to North America along with the bison, bighorn sheep, and wapiti over the Asiatic-Alaskan land bridge which existed during the Pleistocene era. The moose is also native to Europe, where it is known as the elk, a name the early settlers applied to the American wapiti. Both wapiti and moose are Indian names.

## RANGE

Circumpolar in distribution, the moose is at home in the coniferous forests of the Northern Hemisphere. Its range in North America covers the evergreen forest belt north to the limit of tree growth, south to Maine on the east coast and west to Wyoming, Idaho, and northern Washington.

Although equipped to cover long distances in a relatively short time, the moose is not an avid traveler and may spend the better part of its lifetime in a home territory five miles square. It favors broken hilly forest lands with open sunlit glades bordering lakes and rivers and shuns the gloom of the dark, unbroken forest.

The American moose is separated into four distinct groups, or subspecies. The American, or Eastern moose, also known as the black moose, is found from Maine and Nova Scotia west to central Ontario and north to Hudson Bay. The Northwestern moose ranges from northern Michigan and Minnesota to western Ontario, westward to British Columbia, and north to the Yukon and Mackenzie Delta. The Yellowstone, or Shiras moose, which differs from the blackish, eastern forms in its rusty, yellow-brown color, is found in western Wyoming, eastern and northern Idaho, western Montana north to Alberta and west to southeast British Columbia. The Alaska moose, by far the largest of all the forms, ranges in the forested regions of Alaska including the Kenai Peninsula, west to the Yukon and south to northwestern British Columbia.

## HABITS

In place of teeth at the front of the upper jaw, the moose has a plate of tough, grisly skin. It draws food into its mouth with its long tongue. The moose's neck is too short for it to reach the ground and graze like an ox so of necessity it is a browsing animal. It feeds on a large variety of the twigs, leaves, and bark of deciduous and evergreen trees. It will strip the leaves from branches growing 20 feet from the ground by standing on its hind legs and may push over saplings 3 inches in diameter to get at the top leaves. The moose cherishes water lilies and the roots of most aquatic plants. It will swim out to the deep water of a lake and dive to the bottom in search of these roots, submerging for three or four minutes before coming up for air.

A ruminant, or cud-chewing mammal, the moose swallows its food roughly chopped and stores it in a special stomach, or paunch, where it is mixed with stomach juices. Later, when the animal is resting, the food in the paunch is returned to the mouth in the form of small, rounded pellets to be thoroughly chewed and is passed into the second stomach for digestion.

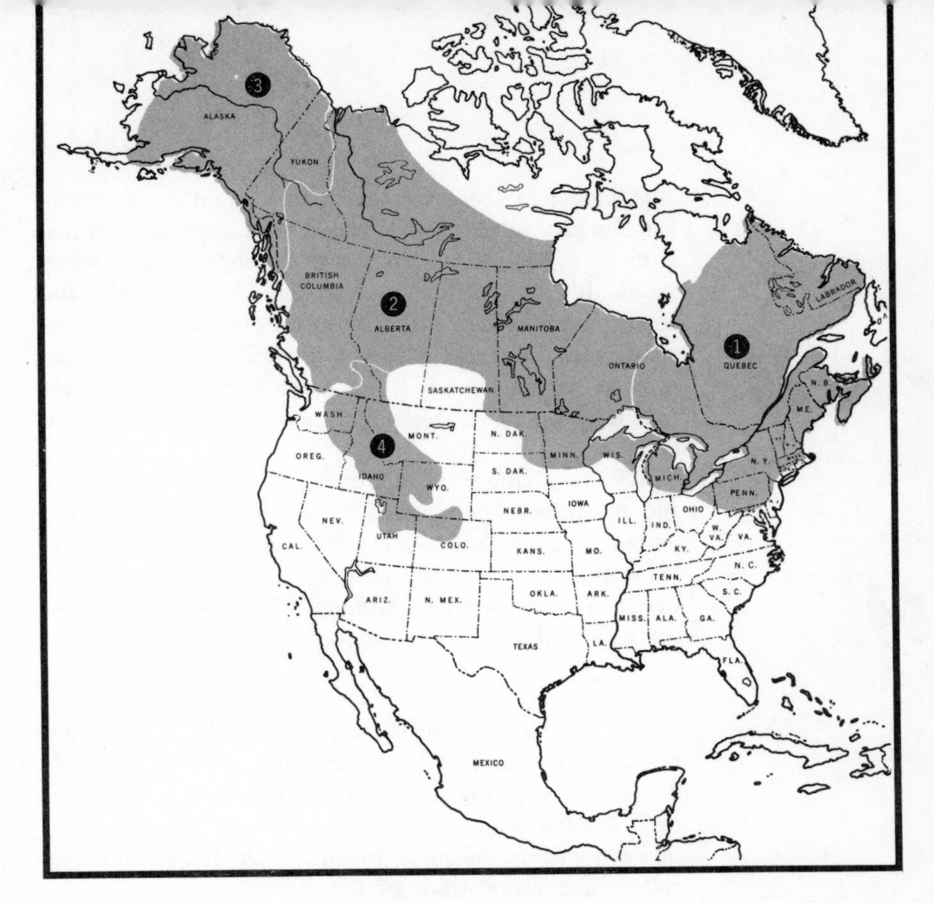


Distribution of the races of the moose *Alces:* 1. American moose, 2. Northwestern moose, 3. Alaska moose, 4. Shiras moose.

Throughout the summer the moose has a plentiful food supply. The cow needs adequate nourishment for milk for her growing calves, and the bull needs it for its growing antlers. As winter comes and the snow deepens on the ground, the moose keeps open a small network of trails known as a "moose yard," which he gradually extends as the food gets scarce. When the fresh spring grass arrives, the moose will go down on its knees for this much needed laxative, and will eat the bark of oak trees for its tannic acid content.

## ENEMIES

The moose has rather poor eyesight, compensated by a keen sense of smell and an excellent sense of hearing. It can catch the faintest sound with its constantly moving ears. A full-grown, healthy bull, and even a cow, can take care of itself against most of its natural enemies. Even a grizzly bear would balk at attacking an aroused bull, and a whole pack of wolves would have to be starving to attempt to bring down this northland giant. However, calves and aging, sickly moose are occasionally downed by predators, and others are caught in the snares of Indians and trappers.

## LOCOMOTION

As it spends much of its life in and around the water, the moose is an excellent swimmer. It can paddle along at 6 miles per hour, and will swim a lake 16 miles wide. Even a young calf takes readily to the water, sometimes attaching itself to its mother's back as she swims along. Water offers a safe retreat from the hordes of bloodsucking insects which infest the northern forest all summer.

A moose can somehow cross deep swamps and quicksands where other animals would flounder and go down, without getting mired. Its power of endurance is enormous. It can lope up a mountain side and over the top without a pause, travel miles through deep snow, or stride over the great stretches of down timber so common in the northland. In a charge a moose can maintain a speed of 35 miles per hour for a considerable distance.

When walking on firm ground, the moose leaves only the imprints of its paired hoofs. When trotting, the animal presses its dewclaws into the ground and they leave tracks. A walking moose leaves 15 to 20 inches between tracks; when trotting, 43 to 48 inches. Its tracks are always in a staggered line.

The antlers of a typical adult bull moose, spread like a huge fan with numerous points around their edges, weigh up to 60 pounds or more and are shed annually.

### VOCAL

For the greater part of the year a moose never utters a sound and, despite its huge size, can move through the forest as quietly as a shadow. During the rut, however, the bull stalks through the woods uttering a series of deep grunts, listening for the long, hoarse inviting call or quavering whine of the cow.

### MATING

Although not completely anti-social, the moose is definitely not a herd animal. Even during the rut a bull does not appropriate a harem. A bull and cow will pair off for about ten days, after which the bull deserts his partner and goes off in search of another female.

The rutting season begins in September and lasts from four to eight weeks. During this time the bulls fight violent battles for possession of the cows. Evidence of these deadly duels are visible on the surrounding trees and shrubs; sometimes a quarter of an acre is torn and battle-scarred.

During the rutting season a bull is dangerous, vicious, and suspicious. At the least sound he will charge through the forest savagely swinging his huge antlers. The only safety for an unarmed man is a quick retreat up the nearest tree, trusting to luck that it is thick enough to withstand the impact of 900 pounds of bone and muscle. When two evenly matched bulls collide the impact is terrific. Sometimes their antlers lock together inseparably, and both animals eventually die of starvation.

### BIRTH AND EARLY DEVELOPMENT

In May or June, eight months after mating, the cow moose gives birth to her calves. The first is usually a single, but a mature cow will frequently have twins and on occasion triplets. At birth the calf is not striped or spotted like most baby deer but is colored like the mother. It even has a little bell hanging from its throat. The calf is born with its eyes open and is able to stand and nurse within the hour, remaining in seclusion for two weeks or more. When it is a month old the calf is following the mother around the countryside and will stay in her company for nearly a year. The cow moose is solicitous for the welfare of her calves and will rout any black bear endangering their safety. Even a grizzly is no match for an infuriated cow protecting her young. A cow may be accompanied in the summer by her new calf as well as her yearling calves, which now have spiked antlers 6 to 8 inches long.

By the time it is two years old, a calf's antlers have become forked and in its third year it has a small palmed antler with a few points. Each succeeding year the antlers get bigger and heavier until the animal is twelve years old and past its prime. In its declining years the antlers are reduced in size.

## Popular and Scientific Names of the Moose

**ORDER:** *Artiodactyla*

**FAMILY:** *Cervidae*

**GENUS:** *Alces*

**SPECIES:** *alces*

**SUBSPECIES**

| | |
|---|---|
| American moose | *Alces alces americana* |
| Northwestern moose | *Alces alces andersoni* |
| Shiras moose | *Alces alces shirasi* |
| Alaska moose | *Alces alces gigas* |

The tracks of the moose trotting are similar to those of the whitetail deer but are much larger.

CHAPTER 10

# THE CARIBOU

NO MORE beautiful big game animal than a bull caribou walks the face of the earth. With his towering, heavily palmated antlers with their many points, his snowy neck, his flaring nostrils, his sleek, seal-brown body, he is a gorgeous sight, the very epitome of the wild and uninhabited northland of mountain and glacier and tundra. He is a handsomer animal than even the African kudu or sable, more regal than the wild sheep or the elk. For looks alone, the only creature that might shade him is the great gold and black tiger.

If he were as smart as he is beautiful, the caribou would be one of the world's great trophies, but he is, alas, a comparatively dumb and rattle-brained creature. At least he has been in the fall months when I have hunted him. During the rut, a bull caribou is the goofiest, most self-destructive large animal I have ever seen—even worse than a love-crazed mule deer, and that is saying a lot. To an amorous bull caribou everything looks like a cow caribou, even a packhorse with a white pack cover on top of a pile of bedrolls and panniers.

One afternoon in September, 1951, when my son Bradford and I were packing over a big rounded hill above timberline in northern British Columbia, we were in typical caribou country and had seen some of the animals at a distance. Then two big bulls showed up, one with a perfectly tremendous head with the largest shovel I have ever seen. They were convinced that the weary horses in our pack-string were a herd of cow caribou. They'd come trotting up to investigate, catch the man smell, and go prancing off. Then they'd look back, see the horses, think they were cows once more, forget what had frightened them, and come bouncing back. They did this several times, and I busily took still pictures and movies of them. But the horses were getting nervous, and finally one of our guides chased the bulls off. Caribou season did not open until the next day, but Bradford was dying to knock over that gorgeous bull. I refused to let him shoot. He later got a bull that was as good if not better—and it was entirely legal.

Our caribou are simply North American reindeer. Like many of our other large game animals, they crossed over from Asia by the land bridge, which existed across the Bering Strait for hundreds of thousands of years and was finally covered by the sea only about fifteen thousand years ago. They are found all over the Arctic and subarctic from northern Norway to Greenland, and they are likewise found far south along the high Rockies wherever altitude creates large portions of arctic climate and vegetation above timberline. I have seen many hundreds along the British Columbia-Alberta border in the timberline country on the crest of the Rockies, and I have seen equal numbers near the snow peaks and glaciers of the western Yukon.

In the southern part of their range, caribou often live in heavy forest in country below timberline. There are some of this breed in southern British Columbia, a few in northern Idaho, and possibly some in Washington and Montana. However, typical caribou ground is the tundra country of the arctic prairies and the similar country above and near timberline in the high mountains—a country of arctic willow, dwarf birch, and caribou moss, of glacier and snowfields, of muskeg and little meandering streams full of grayling.

Caribou are cold-country animals, and they seldom are found far from perpetual snow. Their coats are so warm that even on a nippy fall day, when the hunter is shivering in wool pants and down jacket, the caribou will be lying on glaciers and snow patches to keep cool.

During the ice age, caribou ranged much farther south than they do now. Their bones and horns are found in Pleistocene deposits far down in the United States, and in Europe our gifted Cro-Magnon ancestors not only hunted them but also drew beautiful pictures of them on the walls of their caves.

I have done all of my caribou hunting in the mountains of western and northern Canada, and to me caribou country means rolling hills above timberline—country so high and cold that there are snow patches in the hollows and on the north side of the hills, and where there are glaciers in the higher mountains.

Caribou generally range in lower, more rounded mountains than sheep, but many times I have found caribou on the same hill with Stone and Dall sheep. The first bull caribou I ever saw was alone in a basin with a large herd of bighorns. However, the caribou is not nearly so adaptable an animal as the wild sheep. The bighorn, whose ancestors also crossed the ice-sheathed land bridge across the Bering Strait, gradually moved south and established himself in subtropical Arizona and Sonora, but caribou must have their ice and their tundra.

The British believe that all the caribou of the world are of the same species, and that the various forms of caribou are simply subspecies. Americans generally divide the caribou of North America into four species—the Woodland caribou of eastern Canada and Maine, the Mountain caribou of the Rockies, the Barren Ground caribou of the arctic prairies, and the Greenland caribou of the island of Greenland.

Barren Ground caribou of the far north average smaller than either the Woodland or the Mountain caribou. However, some of the Barren Ground animals have wonderful heads. The best heads I have ever seen were in the Cassiar district of northwest British Columbia, and possibly the heaviest animals I have run into were in the Smoky River country of Alberta. To the layman's eyes, anyway, a caribou is a caribou, from the glaciers of Norway to the Barren Grounds of Canada.

The caribou is unique in the deer family in that the cows have antlers, but there is little difficulty in telling bulls from cows because the antlers of the cows are spindly little things whereas those of the bulls are enormous. In addition, mature bulls have white necks and are much larger than the cows. A big bull Mountain caribou is almost as large as a young bull elk, but a cow is about the size of a mule deer.

In late August and in September, when they are generally hunted, the caribou are getting their new winter coat. The hair is a dark, grayish-brown, with the coarse and springy outer hairs overlaying a coat of fine, warm wool. The necks of the bulls range from creamy white to a light gray, which looks white at a distance. Often this white neck hair extends clear back on the shoulders. It is my impression that the neck hair of the Barren Ground bulls is lighter than that of the Osborn caribou of the British Columbia Cassiars and much lighter than that of the caribou in the Smoky River country of Alberta. The hairs of a caribou's coat are hollow, and as a consequence caribou are great swimmers and float as if they were wearing life preservers. This coat is one of the warmest in nature, and before down sleeping bags became common in the far north, the trappers and Indians used caribou hides for winter sleeping robes. Even today in their winter camps they use caribou hides to floor their tents.

The ears of the caribou are small and heavily haired, and the gray of the head turns brown at the hairy muzzle. The legs are brown in front and on the sides, white in back. The tail is white, and a frightened caribou throws it up when it starts off, just as the whitetail deer does.

The caribou is built for the deep snow and the mucky ground of the Arctic. His legs are long and his hoofs large and circular. When the caribou is in a soft bog or in snow, the bearing surface of his hoof is increased by his bringing more of the foot against the ground. The tracks show as two wide-

Old Baldy, loaded to the hilt with gear, let go with his powerful hind legs and caught the amorous bull on the jaw with a crack that sounded like a rifle shot.

spread half-moons with the imprint of the patterns behind. The whole footprint of the caribou will be around 4 inches wide and 7 or 8 inches long. It is as if he were walking on snowshoes, and he can cross without difficulty boggy country where a heavy, small-footed animal like a horse or an elk would have difficulty. Oddly enough, the addax, a beautiful antelope that dwells in the sands of North Africa's Sahara Desert, has, through thousands of years of dwelling in soft sands, developed a foot much like that of the caribou.

A curious thing about the hoof of the caribou is that it clicks as the animal walks, and authorities say the click takes place within the ankle bone as the weight is taken off but before the hoof is lifted from the ground. I have never seen a big migration of caribou, but I first heard this clicking one time in the Yukon when I was high in a pass above the St. Claire River hunting white sheep. A little herd of cow and calf caribou traveling from one drainage to another came trotting by me not over 50 feet away, and I could hear this clicking.

Bud Helmericks, the arctic guide and explorer, tells me that caribou have very good ears, and that in the winter when snowshoes squeak on dry snow they are exceedingly hard to stalk. But in the fall when I have hunted them, they have always struck me as being very easy to stalk, just as long as the hunter watched the wind. Their eyes are very poor, certainly no better than those of a grizzly bear and maybe not as good. Many times I have got close to caribou simply by walking slowly upwind in plain sight but taking care to make no sudden movements.

It does not pay to take undue chances in stalking any animal, but if the caribou hunter doesn't have much cover, he shouldn't worry unduly about it. One time I was hunting exactly on the Alberta-British Columbia boundary, in what was then wonderful mountain caribou country, around a mountain that is perfectly flat on top. In the Southwest it would be called a mesa, but up there it had been given the names Coffin Top and Casket Mountain. A Cree guide named Isaac Plante and I came over a ridge one day to see a whole great basin filled with caribou—cows, calves, and big bulls.

The rut was just beginning, and the animals were restless. Several large bulls were in sight, and the best one was a big fellow with heavy antlers and double shovels. The wind was right in our faces as Isaac and I started moving slowly down the hill toward the bull. We were within 400 yards of him when suddenly he threw his head up and took off at right angles with his long, springy trot. We saw the last of him as he disappeared over a ridge about a mile away.

I knew the bull couldn't have smelled us because we had the wind right, and as far as I could tell there was no way he could have seen us. "What made that bull run?" I asked Isaac, disappointed.

"Nothing made him run," he told me. "He's just crazy. All caribou do crazy things."

The next best bull in sight had very long antlers with little shovel development and not much more palmation than an elk's—a type of antler, incidentally, which is quite common among the mountain caribou of the Smoky River country. The bull was lying on a little snow patch gazing off into space. There was no cover anywhere near, so Isaac and I simply walked slowly and quietly toward him.

When we were about 200 or 250 yards away, we sat on the hillside, looked him over with glasses, and decided to take him at our leisure. Then a couple of cows came prancing up to pay a social call on the bull. He got to his feet politely, but it looked as though he seemed a bit puzzled about the whole business.

Bored and disappointed at the bull's indifference, the cows started looking around. Presently they spied us and apparently decided we had an odd look. But, like all caribou, they wanted to check with their noses what their eyes had told them. They made a circle until they caught our wind. Then they jumped into the air, hoisted their tails, and took off at a high trot. The big bull had been watching them, and when he saw those tails go up he also started off. But I'd been anticipating the move. I swung the crosswires in my scope along ahead of him, squeezed the trigger, and the 130-grain, .270 bullet struck right behind his shoulder, passing through his lungs. He was instantly down, and I don't think he kicked more than twice.

Isaac and I went down to take some pictures of the bull, skin out the head, and quarter the carcass so we could come back for it with a packhorse. We forgot all about the big bull with the double shovels and were hard at work. Suddenly, there he was, running directly toward us, great antlers laid back almost to his rump, lifting his knees in that beautiful, springy trot typical of caribou. I was on the British Columbia side then, and at the time that province allowed two caribou to the license. I could have shot him without moving from my tracks, but somehow I preferred seeing him run.

During the madness of the love-making moon, caribou do some very odd things indeed. The bulls particularly are subject to aimless runs, and often in glassing for game, the hunter will see a big bull all alone traveling from nowhere to someplace else.

When the rut really gets under way, the hopeful and myopic eyes of the amorous bulls turn everything into cow caribou, and a couple of times I have been put afoot when lovelorn caribou ran my horse off. One time up on the St. Claire in the western Yukon, I saddled a horse and took off alone to ride as far as I could up the side of a mountain. I then tied my horse to some willows and started on foot toward the crest in order to glass the basins on the far side.

I had hardly got going when I noticed a small bunch of caribou about half a mile away—a young bull, a couple of cows, and two calves. Paying no further attention to them, I completed my climb and lay down to use my binoculars. I was engrossed in my task when I heard hoofs pounding behind me, and I looked up to find that the whole bunch of caribou had followed me so they could get a good whiff and decide what I was. They would smell me, flee in panic, then forget what they had smelled, come back for another good sniff, then flee once more. They simply couldn't figure out what I was doing lying there on the ground. Finally I lost patience with them, jumped up and let out a yell, and chased them off the mountain.

I found some ewes, lambs, and small rams in basins, but no big rams, so I decided to go back to my horse and ride to camp. But when I got to the spot where I'd tied him, he was gone. The reason? You've guessed it. That bunch of half-witted caribou had decided to investigate him. Their fresh tracks were all around. When I finally made my way laboriously back to camp through the muskegs and bug brush, the horse was there. The cook said that when he'd come in he had been running as if the devil were after him.

A couple of weeks later Field Johnson and I, taking a jack camp with two saddle horses and one packhorse, went clear to the glaciers at the head of the St. Claire. I shot two rams there. We packed our riding saddles with heads and sheep meat and started back for the main camp on Harris Creek, leading our horses. The packhorse followed.

Our poor old packhorse was pretty weary. He was heavily loaded, and for over a week he had been above timberline, deprived of his favorite pea vine and living on willow leaves. He dragged along, getting farther and farther behind, slogging along with his head down and wanting nothing except to get rid of his heavy pack and have a square meal.

The rut was in full swing then, and caribou were constantly in sight all around us. None of us paid any attention to them. Suddenly I heard the pounding of hoofs, and a big bull caribou dashed up to investigate Old Baldy, the packhorse. Baldy had never been so insulted in his life. His hind feet lashed out, and he caught that big bull right in the jaw with a crack that sounded like a rifle shot. Then he fled in one direction and the bull in the other. For the rest of our trek Baldy kept right behind us, and every time he'd see or smell a caribou he'd snort and roll his eyes.

The crowning glory of the caribou, and of most interest to the sportsman, is his wonderful rack, the largest antlers in proportion to body weight of any of the world's game animals.

All caribou antlers are built on the same pattern, and yet no two are just alike. The unique feature of all these antlers is the brow point, or snow shovel, which projects outward from the face. On the average caribou head, there is a shovel on one side and a spike on the other. Sometimes the shovel is only a few inches wide, but in the Yukon one time I shot a bull with a 17-inch shovel, and I've heard of some even wider. Those first seeing a caribou head always ask what the shovel is used for. It looks as if it would be useful for pushing snow away from the lichens on which caribou feed. But they shed their antlers in midwinter when, if they used their shovels to push away snow, they would be the most useful.

Occasionally one sees a head with a double shovel, and these heads are greatly prized. I have already told how I was about to stalk one double-shovel bull in British Columbia only to have him get up and trot aimlessly off. The only other bull I have seen with a double shovel was in the Yukon. I was riding along a river bar and he got up out of some big brush in which he had been lying. When I piled off my horse and grabbed my rifle, he faded back into some scrubby black spruce and I did not see him again. He was then in the process of cleaning the velvet from his antlers. The job was about half done, and long streamers of velvet waved from his magnificent antlers like moss from a live oak.

In the Yukon the big bulls leave the country above timberline and go down into the first scrubby trees when the time comes to clean off the velvet. One day there will be no big bulls up on the barrens at all, and the next day they are all over, their horns bright and freshly cleaned.

Curving forward above the shovel on caribou antlers is the formation known as the "bez," and about halfway up the antlers a spike projects to the rear. The top portion of the antlers is generally palmated, and it is this wide palm, combined with the shovel, that makes the caribou head so handsome. Occasionally, though, this palmation is absent, and instead the top portion consists of a number of points.

Even a fair caribou head is quite a handsome trophy. A really big one is a grand sight indeed. I have seen the famous Pop head in Vancouver, B. C., the head that has for years been the number one mountain caribou. The handsomest I have ever run into, though, is one from an animal shot by Elgin Gates, an old hunting companion of mine. It appears as number five in the 1958 edition of *Records of North American Big Game*. The finest freshly taken head I have ever seen was the one my son Bradford got in the Cassiars in 1951. He won the Boone and Crockett Club award with it, and it was number five in the 1952 record book, number twelve in that of 1958.

Of all the places I have hunted caribou, I be-

The bull with an excellent set of double shovels ran toward them in a beautiful, springy trot. O'Connor could have shot him, but preferred to watch.

The caribou disappeared into some black spruce as O'Connor piled off his horse for a shot.

lieve I have seen a higher percentage of outstanding heads among the great Osborn caribou in the Cassiar district of northwestern British Columbia. They average a good deal larger than the heads of the mountain caribou to the east and south, and in the record book almost all the big heads are from the Cassiar. The heads of the Barren Ground caribou shown in the record book average a bit larger, but I believe this is because more Barren Ground caribou are taken. Very few bulls of this type are killed in the Cassiar as compared with areas in Alaska and the Yukon where the bulk of Barren Ground caribou are found.

Caribou are restless wanderers. Some areas of suitable country always have caribou, but many sections of what looks like ideal caribou country have no caribou at all. Some of the wandering is from the winter to the summer range. Some of it may be drifting in front of storms, but much of this migration seems to be without reason. In 1956, when I was hunting white sheep around Prospector Mountain in the Yukon, we packed through great areas of fine-looking caribou country. The herds had been there once, as we saw many old bleached heads, but all the time we were there we saw not a single animal, not even a single fresh track. We had to move into an entirely different area for caribou trophies. Indians tell me that a certain piece of country may be full of caribou for a few years and then suddenly the animals move away. No one knows why.

In many areas the caribou move from open country in the summer and early fall to the subarctic forests in the winter, as the trees break the blasts of the bitter boreal winds. Often in the summer, I am told, caribou run long distances upwind to get away from the torture of northern mosquitoes. Before the frosts kill the mosquitoes in early fall, the caribou can be seen standing on high ridges in the wind. With their dark bodies and light necks, they are colored much the same as Stone sheep, and are often found right in sheep country. But even at a range of several miles it's not difficult to tell a ram from a caribou, as the caribou always stand with their heads down.

Eskimos and Indians in caribou country kill great numbers of the animals, eat the flesh, make clothes and sleeping robes from the hides, and tools from the horns. I have been told that the Eskimos even eat the acid-soaked caribou moss in the stomachs as a salad. The natives are not very numerous, but each family will kill great numbers of caribou annually. So will trappers and prospectors. It is no great trick to pile up ten or fifteen animals out of a herd.

The principal enemy of the caribou, however, is the big northern wolf. Probably the wolf is as necessary to the health and well-being of caribou herds as the cougar is to the well-being of the mule deer. Overgrazing is a far more serious enemy of any herbivorous animal than is predation. In Alaska there has been considerable wolf control by shooting from light airplanes and also by poisoning, and I understand that the caribou herds of Alaska are on the increase—so much so that some biologists are fearful that in some sections they are too plentiful for their food supply.

For my part, I have never seen an area where caribou were too plentiful. Even on a thirty-day trip around the head of the White River in the western Yukon, I seriously doubt if I saw a thousand caribou—and I was in excellent caribou country all the time. When I was in the Pelly Mountains of the eastern Yukon in 1949, I found them very scarce, by no means plentiful in the Cassiar or Muskwa-Prophet River country of British Columbia, and only in good huntable numbers in the high mountains along the Alberta-British Columbia border.

As near as I can remember, I have shot 14 bull caribou in British Columbia, Alberta, and the Yukon. Unless my memory plays me false, I have shot two of these with the 180-grain bullet in the .30/06 and the rest with the 130-grain bullet in the .270. My impression is that the big, offbeat deer are quite easy to kill. One of the reasons, of course, is that they are generally found in open country and the hunter has plenty of time to make his shots count. The only caribou I have ever had any difficulty killing was the very first bull I shot up in Alberta. He was something over 200 yards away and was trotting uphill broadside. I shot him three times through the lungs with the 130-grain Silvertip bullet from the .270 before he went down. He did not move out of his tracks after the first shot, but he took two others before he fell. This one experience made me believe for a few days that a bull caribou must be an animal of considerable vitality, but since that time no caribou I have hit has run over 30 paces, and most of them have gone down in their tracks with the first shot. In the far north the Eskimos who live on caribou prefer light cartridges like the .218 Bee, the .222, and the .22 Hornet for their caribou shooting, as they can carry a great deal of the light ammunition. Farther south the trappers and Indians use more .30/30's than anything else.

The best caribou I ever shot was taken in 1945 not far from Tepee Lake near the Alaska-Yukon border. I discovered a small bunch of caribou high on a ridge above camp and about three miles away. My guide, the late Johnny Johnson, and I decided to try for them in the morning.

When we got up it was a cold, dreary, overcast day. A little light, dry snow fell now and then, and all in all it looked like a fine day to sit in the cook tent by the stove drinking tea and telling stories.

But I couldn't get over those bulls on the skyline. A couple of them looked as if they had very good heads. So Johnny and I left camp, riding our horses to the base of the mountain and then climbing and leading. When we got on top, the place was all tracked up, but no caribou did we see.

There were high, snow-covered peaks in every direction, and big empty basins. Below us we could see the little white tents of our camp and faintly hear the tinkle of the horse bells.

Clouds hung low, filling some of the basins with the gray, dirty-looking mist and clinging to the peaks in ragged streamers. We glassed in every direction, moved on, glassed again. We saw nothing. Below us a big basin was filled with fog so thick that it looked as though you could walk on it. We decided if the caribou were anywhere, they were in that basin. And so it proved. Little by little the fog below us began to break up and drift off, and finally, right in the middle of the basin and about a mile away, our binoculars showed us four fine bulls.

We got behind a fold in the ground and kept out of sight of the caribou as we dropped into the basin. Then, carefully watching the wind, we made a long circle. We finally came out about 400 yards from the bulls. Johnny wanted to get closer, but I told him I'd rather shoot at a standing caribou at 400 yards than a running caribou at 300. I had plenty of time, so I lay down on a low ridge and got into a tight sling. Holding high to allow for the two-foot drop, I squeezed my first shot off at what looked like the best bull. He ran in a little circle and fell. The others slowly trotted off. Holding high and swinging well ahead, I shot again, and the second one I had picked went down in his tracks.

The best bull of the two is in the record book for the Barren Ground caribou, and the antlers of the second have massive top portions and one of the widest shovels I have ever seen on a caribou head.

I don't suppose a story on the caribou would be complete without something about the meat. Like that of almost any other animal, it is excellent in late summer and very early fall just before the rut—tender, juicy, and full of flavor. Once the rut starts, though, it quickly takes on a taste which to me seems like that of the strongest domestic mutton. I do not particularly care for it then, but it never gets foul, in my experience, as does the flesh of a rutting bull moose.

Near-sighted, jittery, not very bright, the caribou is nevertheless perfectly adapted to his environment, and a handsome addition to anyone's trophy room.

# The Natural History of the Caribou

[RANGIFER ARCTICUS]

## DESCRIPTION

A moderately large, deer-like animal, the caribou has a broad, hairy muzzle and rather long, loose body hair. Each hair has a pithy center containing air cells and is quite brittle. The caribou has a mane which covers its neck and a short tail. The main part of its body is dark brown during the summer and grayish-brown in winter. The neck, belly, feet, a patch on the rump, and the tail range from gray to yellowish-white. The caribou measures from 50 to 90 inches long, stands 40 to 60 inches high at the shoulder, and weighs from 200 to 700 pounds. Females are about 25 per cent smaller.

A typical member of the order *Artiodactyla,* or even-toed ungulates, the third and fourth toes of the caribou's fore and hind feet are evenly developed, the first joint or tip encased in a horny covering which is the hoof. Lateral hoofs, or dewclaws, are larger in the caribou than in other members of the deer family and, along with its wide-spreading hoofs, enable the animal to plough through deep snow and travel over soft ground.

An herbivorous, ruminant animal, the caribou has no teeth in the front of its upper jaw, but it has broad-crowned molars for grinding, and a compound, four-chambered stomach. When feeding, the caribou consumes a large quantity of green, partly chewed food that is stored in the first compartment of the stomach (the paunch), and mixed with stomach juices. Later, when the animal is resting, the contents of the paunch are returned to the mouth in the form of small pellets. After being thoroughly milled to pulp, the food by-passes the first compartment and goes to the second for digestion. Caribou moss, one of the lichens that grows profusely in the far north, may be indigestible to man in its natural state, but stored for a while in the caribou's paunch it becomes a delicacy relished by the Eskimos. When a caribou is killed, the natives empty its paunch of the *nerrock,* or *nerrokat*—the name given to the partly digested lichens—and carry it home for a feast.

## ANTLERS

The caribou is the only member of the deer family in America in which both sexes have antlers. The shape of the antlers varies among the different species, but generally it conforms to a basic pattern: the main beam sweeps backward, outward, and upward, spreads widely as it rises, and terminates forward in a flattened palm. The first, or brow, tine—usually present on only one antler—extends forward over the face in a vertical palm, or "shovel." It is supposed that this tine is used as a shovel to dig through snow when the caribou feeds, but this is only very rarely the case. The second tine, or bestine, is also more or less palmated, rising just above the brow tine and pointing upward. Like all deer, the caribou sheds its antlers—the bucks during the winter, the cows after the first calves are born in May.

## ORIGIN

A Mid-Pleistocene immigrant of Euro-Asiatic stock, the caribou is a comparatively recent addition to the big game animals of North America. It is an important source of food to the Indians, the Eskimos, and many white traders and frontiersmen of the northland. The Indians of the Tinne tribe are called the "caribou eaters," and the Eskimos of the Barren Grounds are known as the "caribou Eskimos."

Neither the Indians nor the Eskimos have made any attempt to domesticate the caribou. However, the

Tungus and Chukchi tribes of Siberia and the Lapps of Scandinavia utilized the animal as a beast of burden, and for its milk and meat.

## RANGE

In general the caribou is circumpolar in distribution. In the New World it ranges over Greenland, the islands of the Arctic Ocean and Alaska, and most of Canada.

There are four species of caribou: the Barren Ground caribou ranges over the arctic tundra from Labrador to Alaska; the Mountain caribou, the largest species, and the Woodland caribou live in the evergreen forest belt of western Canada and to some extent in the eastern part; the small Greenland caribou inhabits the island of Greenland. All the caribou in the United States are now gone except for a few in northern Minnesota. There are somewhere between two and three million Barren Ground caribou still alive today, but the Woodland and Mountain caribou have been greatly reduced except in the mountains of western Canada. The four species of caribou, including subspecies of each, are as follows:

The Barren Ground caribou is a small, pale-colored species with long, simple antlers, ranging over the Barren Ground from Hudson Bay westward to the Mackenzie River and some of the arctic islands. The subspecies of the Barren Ground caribou are: the Labrador caribou, a small subspecies resembling the typical form but with large brow and bestines, which ranges from Labrador west to Hudson Bay; the Peary caribou, a small, nearly all-white caribou, found in Ellsemere Land and some of the neighboring islands; the Stone caribou, one of the largest and darkest-colored of the Barren Ground caribou, which ranges the interior and northern areas of Alaska; the Grant caribou, a large, dark-colored caribou, not as large or as dark as the Stone caribou, with the beams of the antlers widely spread and recurving sharply forward, which is found on the Alaskan Peninsula and Unimak Island; the Osborn caribou, the largest and darkest-colored of Barren Ground caribou, which is native to the Cassiar Mountains of British Columbia and north to the border of the Yukon; the Dwarf caribou, a small member of the Barren Ground caribou, uniformly colored, with small antlers, now probably extinct, originally found in the Queen Charlotte Island group.

The Woodland caribou is much darker and heavier than any of the other Barren Ground caribou and has heavier and less rangy antlers. It ranges from southeastern Canada and originally northeastern United States west to the southern tip of Hudson Bay. The subspecies of of the Woodland caribou are: the Richardson caribou, similar to the typical Woodland caribou but darker in color, especially about the head and neck, whose range extends westward from southwest of Hudson Bay west and north to Great Slave Lake; the Newfoundland caribou, native to Newfoundland and paler in color than the typical Woodland caribou, with widely divergent antlers having many points.

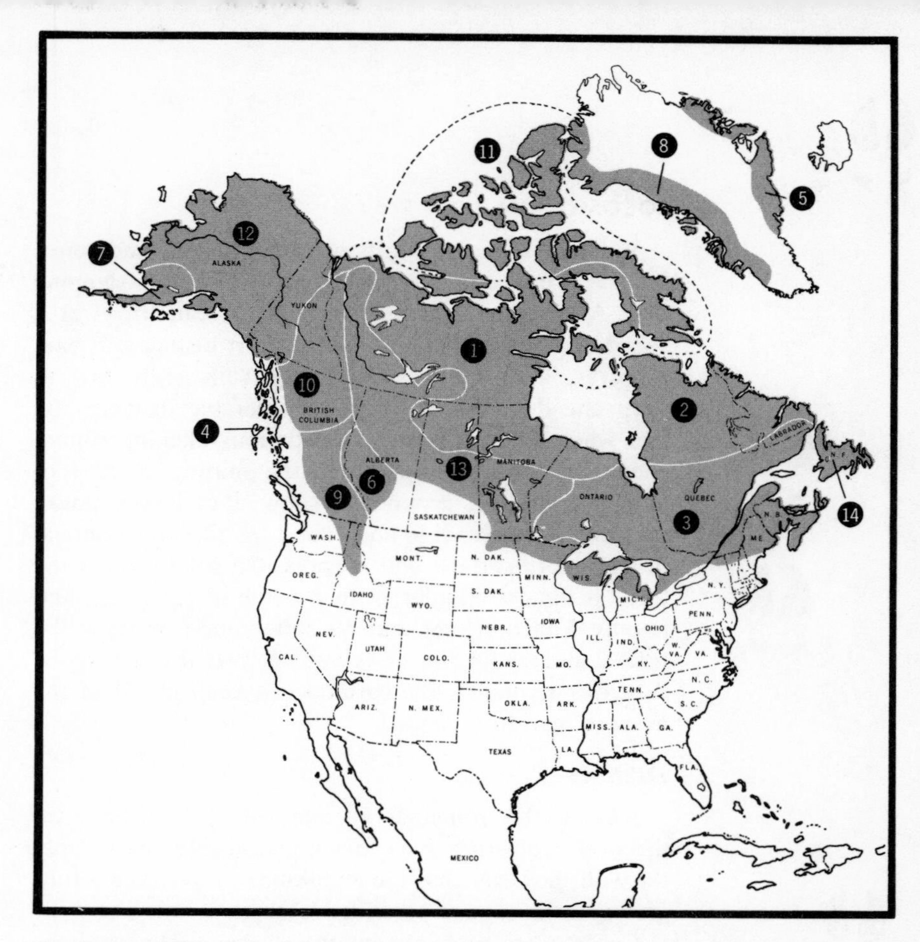


Distribution of the races of the caribou *Rangifer:* 1. Barren Ground caribou, 2. Labrador caribou, 3. Woodland caribou, 4. Dwarf caribou, 5. East Greenland caribou, 6. Rocky Mountain caribou, 7. Grant caribou, 8. West Greenland caribou, 9. Mountain caribou, 10. Osborn caribou, 11. Peary caribou, 12. Stone caribou, 13. Richardson caribou, 14. Newfoundland caribou.

The Mountain caribou is the largest and darkest colored of all the caribou. Its antlers, though heavy, do not attain great size. It is found in the Selkirk Range of British Columbia and formerly occurred in the Rocky Mountain regions of Washington, Montana, and Idaho. A subspecies of the Mountain caribou is the Rocky Mountain caribou, found in the Smoky Mountains and the Mount Robson region of British Columbia, which is a large, dark form with the Woodland type of flattened, palmated antlers.

The Greenland caribou includes two subspecies: The West Greenland caribou, a small, pale-colored form with slender, simple antlers, which is native to the coast region of western Greenland; the East Greenland caribou, similar to the West Greenland form but smaller and paler, found on the east coast of Greenland.

## HABITS

The Woodland caribou migrates short distances in small groups, from a summer to a winter feeding ground. On the other hand, the seasonal migration of the Barren Ground caribou from the open tundra to the shelter of timberlands is an inspiring sight, with thousands of animals often covering a distance of several hundred miles. In the far north the animals begin to collect in August for the trek southward.

During the summer months, the Barren Ground caribou grows fat on the twigs and leaves of blueberry, cranberry, woodrush, horsetail, crowberry, willow, dwarf birch, aspen, and other shrubs.

## LOCOMOTION

When disturbed, a caribou usually stands and stares for a few moments, then takes off with a high-stepping trot. Although not particularly fast, it can travel at a speed of 32 miles per hour for a short distance. It can, however, keep up a steady pace sufficiently fast to keep ahead of wolves for a considerable distance. Its feet when walking make a continuous clicking sound, caused by the ankle bones and the shifting of the foot tendons. On soft ground or snow a caribou's tracks are nearly always wide and round, as the hoofs spread to give more surface and support. On solid ground the track is almost circular, with a notch at the front, and is only 3 inches long, but on soft ground or snow the tracks also show the dewclaws as two distinct spots. A strong swimmer, the caribou can keep ahead of the average man in a canoe.

## ENEMIES

Among the principal enemies of the caribou are the wolf, wolverine, lynx, black and grizzly bears. Only the wolf, however, has the endurance to overtake a full-grown caribou on a sustained chase.

Caribou are molested by the swarms of mosquitoes which infest the north country, but even more troublesome are bot-flies or warble-flies, which lay their eggs in the hide. When hatched, the larvae of the warble-flies bore into the animal's skin and spread under the surface, eventually migrating back through the skin and falling to the ground to continue their life cycle. One caribou may be infested with two or three hundred warble-fly grubs, which are a great drain on its vitality. Other parasites lay their eggs on the caribou's nose and cause congestion, irritation, and loss of blood. Fortunately there are cold lakes in the Arctic and insect-free regions above the timber line, which provide escape for the caribou from these tiny enemies.

## MATING

By September the bull caribou have stripped the velvet from their antlers and polished them, and their necks are swollen, indications of the approaching rut. Before the end of the month, the bulls are sparring among themselves for possession of the cows. Occasionally two fighting caribou will lock antlers and, unable to free themselves, eventually starve to death. Each bull claims about twelve cows, and is kept busy night and day protecting his harem from rival bulls. Yearlings of both sexes and weaned calves usually remain with the cows at this time.

## BIRTH AND EARLY DEVELOPMENT

An average doe raises about six fawns during a lifetime. Most of the calves are born during the endless days of June, when every bank on the arctic tundra is a mass of spring flowers and the sun never sinks below the horizon. The earliest calves may come in May between eight and nine months after mating. They are born in a sunny, dry spot with some thicket for protection. At birth the calf's eyes are wide open and it is clothed in a uniform, buff-brown coat. It weighs about 8 or 9 pounds. The mother licks the newborn calf from head to foot and it is able to stand and nurse in a remarkably short time. A little wobbly on its legs at first, the calf is soon agile enough to follow its mother along with the herd. Usually the Barren Ground caribou have a single young, but the Woodland caribou often have twins. The calves are weaned by September but remain in the mother's company for another year.

## Popular and Scientific Names of the Caribou

**ORDER:** *Artiodactyla*

**FAMILY:** *Cervidae*

**GENUS:** *Rangifer*

**SPECIES:** *arcticus, caribou, montanus, terandus*

**SUBSPECIES**

| | |
|---|---|
| Barren Ground caribou | *Rangifer arcticus arcticus* |
| Labrador caribou | *Rangifer arcticus caboti* |
| Peary caribou | *Rangifer arcticus pearyi* |
| Stone caribou | *Rangifer arcticus stonei* |
| Grant caribou | *Rangifer arcticus granti* |
| Osborn caribou | *Rangifer arcticus osborni* |
| Dwarf caribou | *Rangifer arcticus dawsoni* |
| Woodland caribou | *Rangifer caribou caribou* |
| Richardson caribou | *Rangifer caribou sylvestris* |
| Newfoundland caribou | *Rangifer caribou terraenovae* |
| Mountain caribou | *Rangifer montanus montanus* |
| Rocky Mountain caribou | *Rangifer montanus fortidens* |
| West Greenland caribou | *Rangifer tarandus groenlandicus* |
| East Greenland caribou | *Rangifer tarandus eogroenlandicus* |

The caribou's trotting tracks are usually widely spread, and the relatively large lateral hoofs always register on soft ground. Walking, the caribou places its hind foot over the rear half of the track left by the forefoot.

Douglas Allen

CHAPTER 11

# THE JAVELINA

THE MOST maligned game animal in the United States is a bad-smelling, hoglike little creature known as the javelina or peccary. More wild and woolly tales are told and written about this poor little fellow than about any other animal—even the black bear and the mountain lion. And that is saying plenty.

Since World War II, many people have moved into the Southwest where the javelina is found. Javelina hunting has greatly increased, and fanciful tales about javelinas have kept pace. The new interest in javelinas has also resulted in the publication of many stories and articles about the little creatures. Some of these have really been lulus, so much so that in comparison they make *Peyton Place* look as factual as the annual report of U. S. Steel.

The animal that emerges from these yarns is an entirely different creature from the one I grew up with in Arizona and Sonora. He is two or three times as large, ten times as cunning, and about five thousand times more dangerous. One such article was called "This Little Pig Wants to Kill You!" Another said the javelina is more dangerous than the grizzly bear. Yet another told of a peccary having been shot that weighed 85 pounds dressed.

Actually, it takes a very large javelina to dress out at 40 pounds. The largest one I have ever seen weighed went only 38½ pounds, if I remember correctly. I have probably seen javelinas that would have weighed 45 pounds or so, but I doubt if one has ever lived in Arizona that would dress out at over 50.

A javelina is about as dangerous as a jackrabbit, and when he is shot at he runs as fast as he can. He may run toward the hunter, but if he does so it is because he is confused and not because he is charging. I have had deer and mountain sheep run toward me. A wounded and cornered javelina will try to protect himself, and he can look pretty tough while he is doing it, but for that matter so will a deer. I have known of several horses being seriously injured by the antlers of deer when hunters rode up too close to wounded bucks. I have also known of several hunters who were pushed about a bit by wounded bucks when they got too familiar with them. One of those careless hombres was me.

The origin of all these mad and fanciful tales about the ferocity of javelinas has always puzzled me. I presume that some of it comes through comparison with the javelina's distant relatives, the European and Asiatic wild boars. These enormously larger animals can get pretty tough sometimes, and those who have speared them on foot and on horseback have sometimes run into trouble. Domestic hogs, which, I understand, are descended from Asiatic rather than European swine, have been known to kill and eat small children. In addition, the sportsman who has a javelina head almost always gets it mounted with the mouth open and the dentures on display. Since the little pig is about one third head and has very good dental equipment, such a piece of taxidermy looks as if it had come from an animal about three times as large as a javelina actually is. The mounts likewise give an impression of ferocity.

In my trophy room I have the mounted head of a javelina shot in Sonora so long ago that my wife and I are both pretty vague about who actually shot it and precisely when. She thinks it's one I killed in 1934, and I think it is one she got about 1936. But whoever killed it, the mount gives the impression that the creature would probably tear your leg off if given half a chance.

Visitors usually do a double-take the first time they see it.

"Cripes!" they say. "What is that—a wolf?"

"No, a javelina."

"What is that?"

"It's a little hoglike creature found in the Southwest and Mexico."

"Yeah, I remember reading about them now. I'd sure hate to tangle with one. This one give you a bad time?"

When I say the javelina is about as dangerous as a chipmunk, I am only half believed.

A score of years ago when I was a professor at the University of Arizona, a group of savants among my colleagues used to spend their Sundays climbing around in the nearby mountains and picking up arrowheads and bits of pottery left there by ancient Indians. It was an innocent hobby which gave them some exercise and got them out in the fresh air after a week of sitting before their desks and boring the young with lectures on irregular German verbs and the Treaty of Tilsit.

One Sunday they spied a cave that looked as if it would bear exploring, so they all scrambled up a dim trail to its mouth. Just as they broke out their flashlights and were about to enter, a score of evil-smelling, hoglike little animals came pouring out right at them. Their academic dignity forgotten, my scholarly friends scrambled up on boulders or shinnied into trees. For a few seconds the javelinas jittered around, and then they faded away.

All of these amateur archeologists were convinced they had been charged and that their lives had hung by a thread. Two of them bought handguns and never budged into the hills without them. Another always armed himself with a stout stick before he approached a cave, and yet another was so unhinged by the experience that he gave up these healthful walks entirely.

The explanation is, of course, simple. Javelinas like caves. They go into them in cold and rainy weather, and also to escape the rays of the burning Southwestern summer sun. For some reason they like to eat charcoal and often root around for it in caves where fires have been built. That particular cave was shallow, and when the animals found themselves cut off and cornered they fled to safety. They were probably even more frightened than the Ph.D.'s. Anyway, the professors all told their classes about their narrow escape, and one more javelina myth was born.

At about the same time, a lady dude and a cowboy went for a horseback ride one afternoon and didn't come back to the dude ranch until about sunrise the next morning. Since the lady dude had a husband somewhere in the wilds of the East, and the cowboy had a wife who was running a small spread for him while he picked up some cash wrangling dudes, an explanation was in order. The reason they stayed out all night, they said, was that they had been kept in a tree from three o'clock in the afternoon until five o'clock in the morning by a raging herd of javelinas. And so came into being another item in the javelina saga.

The name javelina derives from the Spanish word for javelin, given to the little pigs because of their sharp tushes. Mexicans call a single hog a *jabali*. The word peccary derives from a name used by Indians in Brazil. His Latin name is *Tayassu tajacu*, and he has also been called the musk hog.

It would be more correct to call the javelina a hoglike creature than it would be to call him a hog. He is only distantly related to the true hogs, the Old World swine of Asia and Africa—about as closely related as you are to a chimpanzee. The teeth of the javelina are quite different from those of the Old World swine, and there are likewise important skeletal differences.

A sportsman would quickly see that the javelina is hoglike in appearance, having the typical snout of the swine. He would also notice that the javelina is much smaller than the imported "Russian" boars of Tennessee and North Carolina, and even smaller than the wart hog of Africa. He would also notice that the javelina has a musk sack in the small of its back and that, in general, it smells like a skunk.

In historic times, the javelina has always been confined to the Southwestern United States. At the present time, the only states in which it is found are Arizona, New Mexico, and Texas, but at one time it was also found in Arkansas. Javelinas today range from the Southwestern United States throughout Mexico, Central and South America, clear to Patagonia. In Arizona and Sonora, the javelina country with which I am most familiar, the habitat of the little pigs is pretty much limited to the Lower and Upper Sonoran climatic zones. That means from the hot and arid cactus country to the somewhat cooler and better watered areas from 4,500 to 6,000 feet in elevation where gambel oaks, pinones, and manzanita grow.

It is believed by some biologists that during the Pleistocene period another species of javelina was found in the Southwest, but that the animals died out when the country dried up at the end of the ice age. The present species is believed to have come in from the south in comparatively recent times, along with those other semitropical citizens, the Arizona whitetail deer, the coatimundi, and the jaguar. It seems to me that if the javelinas were long-time residents of Arizona, they would have spread to the southern part of California and to Lower California, but they have not.

Javelinas are not equipped to handle snow and cold weather. Their bristly hair would give little protection against cold, and their short legs and tiny feet would render them helpless in deep snow. Sometimes they are found on the edge of the yellow pine country at 7,000 and 8,000 feet in the Mogollon Rim country of Arizona and the Sierra Madres of Mexico. I have seen their sign in canyons breaking off the Mogollon Rim and they are present there only during the summer and early fall. When the snow flies and the boreal blasts blow, they surely head for lower, warmer country.

There are several subspecies of javelina in Mexico and the Southwest, but in the United States there are only two—the Texas peccary and the Sonora peccary of Sonora and southern Arizona. The Texas javelina is darker than the light gray of the Arizona and Sonora animals, and it is my impression that they are a little smaller. Both subspecies have dark-gray collars.

Both sexes are about the same size. The males may average a little heavier and may have longer tusks, but that would be open to argument. They look so much alike that it is just about impossible for the hunter to tell a male from a female.

Javelinas are very gregarious and run in herds of six or eight to sixty or more. If one encounters a single animal, it either comes from a scattered herd and is looking for his pals or is sick or wounded. I remember one time when I had been hunting deer in the Tortolita Mountains near Tucson. I found a lone javelina by a waterhole. It had some sort of an eye infection, was as blind as a bat, and was a very sick animal.

The javelina has been reported to eat carrion and kill sheep and calves. Ted Knipe, biologist with Arizona's game department and author of *The Javelina in Arizona,* says the animal does none of these things, and a javelina seen around the dead cow is after the bugs, not the carrion.

In reality, the little pig is a clean feeder. He eats the leaves and fruit of prickly-pear cactus, mesquite beans, roots and bulbs, piñon nuts, acorns, manzanita berries. He seldom browses, and he eats even less grass than do deer.

In arid, misused, and overgrazed Arizona—where almost every acre is overstocked with cattle—many ranchers are distinctly hostile to javelinas. They say the pigs root up the grass and foul the drinking water. Knipe's investigations showed that the shallow rooting by javelinas actually benefits the soil and the grass, and he was never able to find a javelina wallowing in a waterhole. Any defiling of the water, he discovered, was done by the cattle themselves or by wild burros or horses.

Javelinas seldom eat the grasses that are natural food for cattle, but on the worst eroded and overgrazed land, where all the perennial grasses have been killed off by too heavy stocking, cattle must eat cactus and other javelina foods to survive. On well-managed range lands, javelinas and cattle do not compete. However, there is little well-managed range land in the Southwest. State land, Taylor Grazing Act land, and privately owned land have all been overstocked and overgrazed by cattle for seventy-five years. Land which supported good grass and produced fat cattle when I was a child is now almost completely devoid of grass of any sort. Cattle stay alive on it only by browsing. Such land does not produce many cattle—nor many javelinas. On most Arizona grazing land there is no control over cattle numbers but the conscience of the rancher leasing it.

One of the most interesting features of the javelina is the musk sack in the small of the back 7 or 8 inches above the tail. The vent of this sack was mistaken for a navel by early explorers. The musk of the javelina smells to me about like the scent of a skunk, and a cave used by javelinas always has this characteristic odor. There are various explanations as to the purpose of the musk. Some think it keeps flies away. Others think it enables these highly gregarious little animals to keep track of each other.

It is my feeling that the little pigs use it for communication and warning. I know that often when I have jumped a bunch of javelinas I have smelled a wave of scent the moment the animals took off. I would hear their warning grunts, and then that smell would come followed by the patter of their feet—and they'd be gone.

It is the practice of those who plan to eat javelinas to remove the musk sack as soon as the animal is killed. It is generally believed that unless this is done the meat will not be good. I have noticed that if a javelina is killed cleanly and quickly, and the scent gland then removed, the meat is fairly palatable. If, on the other hand, the javelina is wounded, chased, and frightened before it is killed, it doesn't make much difference whether the scent gland is removed or not. The meat is terrible.

A piece of meat from a frightened javelina that is put into a frying pan will smell up a house like a battalion of skunks. Even an ideally cared-for piece of javelina is to me insipid and tasteless. Javelinas never get fat, and the meat at best is dry. It is as white as that of a rabbit, and I think it has about as much taste as cotton. The only good piece of javelina meat I have ever eaten was from an animal barbecued along with a buffalo by members of the Tucson Game Protective Association. But maybe what I liked was the barbecue sauce. I have eaten the flesh of wild boars of Asia and found it delicious, but it tastes no more like javelina than snapping turtle tastes like beef.

The facts that the flesh of the javelina is no epicure's delight, and that one javelina head looks about like another, have kept me from being a very avid javelina hunter. I simply do not care to shoot anything unless I am going to mount the head, eat it, or use it for bait. When I was a kid prowling the desert around Florence, Arizona, I killed two javelinas—one with a .25/20 and the other with an old .30/40 Krag that had a 30-inch barrel and cost me all of $1.50. Since that time I have knocked over a few in Arizona and a few in Sonora. I have been along with others when they hunted javelina, and occasionally when I was living in Arizona I acted as an unpaid guide for friends from other states.

In Arizona, javelinas are hunted in the spring when there is no open season on any other game animal, and hunters go out in the desert after the little pigs by the thousands. Bob Housholder, Arizona writer and guide, thinks the hunting pressure has seriously depleted the herds and he estimates that there are only about 15,000 left in Arizona. New Mexico has only a few of the animals. Texas for many years afforded them no protection at all, and even now the protection is pretty much up to the individual landowner as there is almost no public land in Texas.

Coyotes and bobcats kill many javelinas, and I have been told that golden eagles sometimes take the young. Once I saw a couple of sows chase a coyote down an arroyo and then go back to their young when he was well out of the area. I concluded that the javelina was no pushover for a coyote, but Ted Knipe thinks that a couple of coyotes have no trouble in killing one. In Mexico the jaguar is reputed to kill many javelinas, and in Arizona the mountain lion occasionally takes one.

The major enemy of the javelina is the human being with a rifle. Some ranchers, convinced that they damage the range, shoot them down at every opportunity. Trigger-happy hunters often exceed their limit of one when they jump a bunch, and bored deer hunters pot them and let them lie just to break the monotony.

At one time the hunting of javelinas for their hides was almost a major industry—first in the Southwest and later in Mexico. The hides are thin, strong, marked with bristle holes. They make excellent gloves and jackets. In 1934 I was told by customs officials at Nogales, Arizona, that 25,000 javelina hides had come through that one port of entry in a year. In the early nineteen thirties, almost every Mexican who lived in javelina country knocked off the little pigs for their hides at every opportunity.

I once hunted deer on a ranch where the manager supplemented his salary of about twenty dollars a month by hunting javelinas. He got only a peso a hide, if I remember correctly, but in those days a peso was worth about twenty cents, and a man would work hard all day for that much. He maintained a pack of mongrel dogs which he had trained, not to chase the plentiful deer on the range, but to go after javelinas, bobcats, and an occasional mountain lion. When the dogs jumped a herd of pigs they would take after it with a great yammering, and eventually the javelinas would come to bay in thick brush or against boulders. Then the *ranchero* would unlimber a stout, ironwood club he always carried, wade in, and knock the brains out of javelinas whose attention was distracted by the dogs.

He killed a great many javelinas, but there were casualties on both sides. All of the dogs bore scars, and now and then the pigs would injure one so badly it would die. The *ranchero* himself had not escaped unscathed. He had some scars on his legs,

Coyotes kill javelinas, but once O'Connor saw a couple of sows run off one of the predators.

and at the time I was hunting with him he had one fresh wound on a calf. Oddly enough this wasn't a slash. Instead it looked more as if a solid hunk of meat had been bitten out.

Javelinas will go right after dogs, and in Arizona most of the people who have got in trouble with the little pigs have been defending dogs. About twenty-five years ago, someone in Tucson had a pet javelina that escaped and went roaming the streets one night. Anything that smells as fruity as a javelina is bound to be investigated by dogs, and before long there were wounded and howling mutts all over that section of the city. The switchboard at the police station was swamped with calls from householders who said that some sort of an animal was on the prowl trying to kill every dog in Tucson.

But generally speaking, a javelina is about as much menace to a human being as a jackrabbit, and probably less of a menace than a wounded buck. One time my wife and I were hunting deer in the foothills of the Cubabai Mountains southeast of Sonoyta, Sonora, when we saw a bunch of javelinas about 300 yards away moving slowly along a hillside. It was too far away for sure shooting with iron sights on anything as small as javelinas, but we were bored and craved action. We sat down and opened up. Before the herd got out of sight we had knocked two down. When we rode up, however, we found only two blood trails. I took one, my wife the other.

I found one of the pigs in bad shape about 100 yards away, picked it up, and started off in the direction my wife had taken. I heard her scream, and then I heard a shot. She had found her pig backed up against a rock chattering his teeth threateningly, and when she walked up to within a few yards to finish it off, it came after her. I have seen deer do the same thing.

I am exceedingly skeptical about a javelina ever attacking unprovoked. Knipe tells of a couple of javelinas in the Tucson Mountain Park making threatening gestures toward him. He says he chucked a rock at them and they fled. But these animals had grown familiar with human beings, just as park bears do.

On many occasions I have found myself right in the midst of a herd of javelinas, and never has one given the slightest indication of wanting to do anything except get away. Apparently I smell as bad to a javelina as a javelina smells to me.

Once I was hunting javelinas in a mesquite thicket along a stream. The country was all tracked up with their little round, tiptoe tracks, so I got down on all fours and crawled into the thicket. Presently I saw a couple of javelinas bedded down near the trunk of a big mesquite about 40 yards away. I lay down and plugged one. Instantly the whole thicket erupted with javelinas. There must have been fifty there, and a couple of them ran within arm's length of me. If ever javelinas had a chance to cut a hunter to pieces that was it.

Spring hunts for javelinas come at a wonderfully pleasant time of year in the desert. It is usually neither too hot nor too cold. If the winter rains have been good, the grass is coming up and the desert plants are in leaf. The quail are in big coveys.

Now and then the hunter will see desert mule deer out on the flats, or whitetails in the little hills, or glimpse the long gray body of a coyote sneaking away.

Generally, when I saw a herd of javelinas I'd find a good excuse for not shooting. Nevertheless javelina season was a good excuse to get out in the hills and arroyos. Once a friend from California asked me, right at the end of the season, if I could show him some javelinas. I allowed as how I might, but I told him the pigs had been hard hunted and were pretty thoroughly scattered. I must have led him into a refuge area, because we saw at least a hundred in a morning. He thinks to this day that I am a red-hot javelina guide—something I'm not.

The last javelina I shot, and the last I'll probably ever shoot, was one of those things. My son Bradford, now a newspaperman and a father, was then thirteen. He had shot a couple of whitetail bucks and was filled with ambition to get a javelina.

I found an arroyo full of very fresh javelina tracks and told him to take one side while I went down the other. Presently I saw a herd of about fifteen or twenty of the little pigs just below Bradford. He was walking quietly along, looking everywhere except where he should have looked. For a minute or two I hoped he would look my way so I could signal him that the herd was just below him on the other side of the brush, but no luck. Finally I decided to shoot a javelina, thinking that the shot would at once warn him and send the pigs his way.

I knocked one over and the whole herd went boiling past him. He nailed one as it went by and was about the happiest thirteen-year-old in Arizona. I hung my kill in a tree, but he was afraid that if he did likewise someone would steal his precious trophy. He carried it all the way to camp.

I hope the day never comes when those who wander the deserts of Arizona and Sonora won't see the little round tracks of the javelinas along the arroyos, see the signs of their rooting, and smell their wild, skunklike odor in the caves and clefts in the rocks. I also hope the time never comes when a sportsman won't have an opportunity to add this interesting trophy to his collection. The javelina is a poor, friendless little creature, as harmless as a bumblebee. He has been slaughtered for the paltry sum his hide brings, and he has been shot and left to rot. His only sin is that sometimes he will defend himself instead of cringing before impending death like a rabbit. In the future I hope he gets some of the sympathy and understanding he needs, as well as protection from too much hunting. I am all for generous protection of javelinas and an unlimited open season on those who invent fanciful tales about them.

He is a part of the romantic and wonderful Southwestern desert, along with the desert bighorn and mule deer, the rattlesnake, the Gila monster, the cholla, and the saguaro. May his tribe increase.

# The Natural History of the Javelina, or Peccary

[TAYASSU TAJACU]

### DESCRIPTION

The peccary *Tayassu,* also known as the javelina or musk hog, is a pig-like animal with a sturdy, compact body that is arched along the back, a short, thick neck, short, slender legs, sharp-pointed hoofs, and a short, thin tail. Its head is large and wedge-shaped, with small eyes. It tapers sharply forward from the small ears to a most remarkable snout. No other animal except the pig has one like it. The nose terminates in a round, flat, dish-like plate of cartilaginous tissue reinforced by a bony structure; the nostrils open where they are the most useful, near the middle of this mobile plate. The peccary's snout is an all-purpose "hand" and is used to pry up rocks, turn over logs, dig in the ground, and for many other purposes where a hand would be useful.

Suited for life in the thick, thorny jungle of tropical regions, the peccary has a thick hide and coarse, rather long, bristly hair that is longer on the neck, shoulders and back than on the sides, forming a mane that can be raised at will. The hairs of a peccary are always arranged in evenly spaced little groups of three. The roots of the hairs have the characteristic markings always found on genuine peccary leather gloves. The trade can artificially duplicate the markings on other kinds of leather, but it is illegal to pass off an imitation as peccary leather. A peccary may be grizzle-colored with a lighter grayish collar, or black with a white lip or chin. The peccary is quite small when compared with a domestic hog. It has a total length of from 35 to 45 inches, stands about 20 to 25 inches high at the shoulder, and weighs from 36 to 65 pounds.

Though resembling a pig in many ways, the peccary is not a true pig and has been separated into a family of its own, the *Tayassuidae.* One of the even-toed ungulates, it is included in the great order *Artiodactyla.* The peccary walks on the tips of its toes and has small lateral hoofs, or dewclaws, that are raised off the ground similar to those of the deer. Unlike the ruminants, the peccary does not chew its cud and has teeth at the front of the upper jaw as well as at the front of the lower jaw. The back teeth are broad-crowned with raised tubercles adapted for crushing. The tusks, or canine teeth, are long, straight, dagger-like shafts with sharp points and keen cutting edges. The upper-jaw tusks are directed straight downward; those in the lower jaw project upward. The reverse is true of the Old World pigs, which have tusks in the upper jaw directed outward and upward while those in the lower jaw are directed outward and backward. Another obvious characteristic separating the peccaries from the pigs is that the peccary has only one small, lateral hoof on each hind foot. The pigs have relatively large lateral hoofs on the front and hind feet and they reach the ground when the animal walks. The peccary's lateral hoofs are small, raised off the ground, and are practically functionless.

The name musk hog comes from the large gland in the peccary's back, about 8 inches above the tail. The gland, buried in the long, bristly hair, has a large opening and contains a thick, pasty liquid with a strong musky odor which is quite objectionable at times. When disturbed or attacked, the mane on the peccary's back stands erect, giving the animal a larger and more formidable aspect, and the gland opens to exude a strong, powerful odor that can be recognized for a considerable distance. The musk from the gland is also used as an identification to others of its kind. The peccary leaves a tell-tale secretion on the undersides of branches and on shrubs which can be recognized by other peccaries.

### ORIGIN

Much has been written about the peccary but very little has actually been told about its habits and life

history. Many authors dwell on the fantastic tales of ferocious packs of peccaries attacking human beings. The stories tell of the animals treeing people for many hours and even attacking men on horseback. Though no doubt greatly exaggerated, the reports are too numerous to be entirely discredited and probably apply more directly to the larger white-lipped species from Central and South America than to the little collared peccary that occurs within the confines of the southern United States.

Peccaries, including several genera and a large number of species, were present in the warmer parts of North and South America during the Pleistocene times. Some were larger and others smaller than the modern forms. Primitive peccaries occurred as early as the Lower Oligocene in the New World and migrated to Europe and Asia during the Miocene or Pliocene times, but apparently died out in the Old World. The entelodonts, or so-called giant pigs, ranged over most of North America in vast numbers during the Eocene period—the dawn of the Age of Mammals—some sixty million years ago. They looked something like the wild pigs of today and had a long snout which was not suited for digging in the earth.

### RANGE

The peccary is found in various kinds of country. It occupies dense forests in the tropics, usually following along water courses, low plains, and valleys, In the arid desert regions, the peccary favors dense thickets of mesquite, scrub oak, tall grassland, and cactus growth, but avoids open plains where there is little or no cover. Though favoring low-lying country, bands of peccaries have been seen at elevations of 6,000 to 8,000 feet.

The present range of the peccaries extends from southern Texas, Arizona, and New Mexico, south through Mexico, Central America, and south to Patagonia in South America. A hundred years ago it was found as far north as Arkansas. Today there are not more than about 50,000 peccaries in the United States. There are two distinct species and twelve geographical races, or subspecies. The commonest and best known is the collared peccary, readily recognized by its small size, grizzled coat, and a light shoulder band which forms a collar. It also has the widest range, which extends from the southern United States to Patagonia in southern South America and from sea level to 8,000 feet.

There are ten named geographical forms of collared peccary found north of the Isthmus of Panama: The Texas collared peccary, found in Texas and northeastern Mexico; the Panama collared peccary, native to Panama; the Veracruz collared peccary, native to eastern Mexico; the Costa Rican collared peccary, a small form with a tawny instead of a white collar, found in the highlands of western Panama and over most of Costa Rica. There is also the Colima collared peccary, found along the west coast of Mexico; the Cozumel collared peccary, restricted to Cozumel Island off the coast of Yucatan; the Nelson's collared peccary, found in the province of La Vega, Yucatan Peninsula; the Honduran collared peccary, a dark-colored form found in the low, forested regions of Honduras; the Sonora collared peccary, a pale desert form found in northwestern Mexico; and the Yucatan collared peccary, found in northern Yucatan.

The tracks of a peccary walking in mud register in pairs, the hind foot falling immediately behind the forefoot. These tracks differ from those of other animals in that the lateral hoof of only one hind foot registers. On firm ground the lateral hoofs do not register at all.

The white-lipped peccary is larger than the collared peccary. It is covered with coarse bristles and is all black except for a white area on the lower side of the head. The range of the white-lipped peccary extends from southern Mexico south to Paraguay in South America. It frequents low-lying, heavily forested country.

The Mexican white-lipped peccary has the white area on the lip restricted to the lower part of the face and ranges from Veracruz in eastern Mexico south to southern Honduras. The Central American white-lipped peccary is about the same size as the Mexican form but the white on the chin extends to the muzzle and below the eyes and ears. This form ranges from Costa Rica to Panama.

### HABITS

The habits of the collared peccary are somewhat different from those of the white-lipped peccary. Both are sociable and travel in herds. The collared peccary is timid and inoffensive and travels in small bands, while the larger, white-lipped peccary congregates in large herds and is apt to take the offensive if its life is endangered. Furthermore, the white-lipped peccary is more roving and favors more heavily forested country than the collared peccary. Both species quarrel very little among themselves.

Anything edible is food for the peccary. Feeding time is mostly in the early morning and evening with some snacks taken in between. With its long, mobile snout the peccary digs up roots, tubers, insects, larvae, lizards, toads, mice, turtle eggs. It also devours birds' eggs and nestlings, acorns, berries, pine nuts, and fruits, is especially fond of prickly pears, and drinks water regularly. It never misses an opportunity to kill and eat

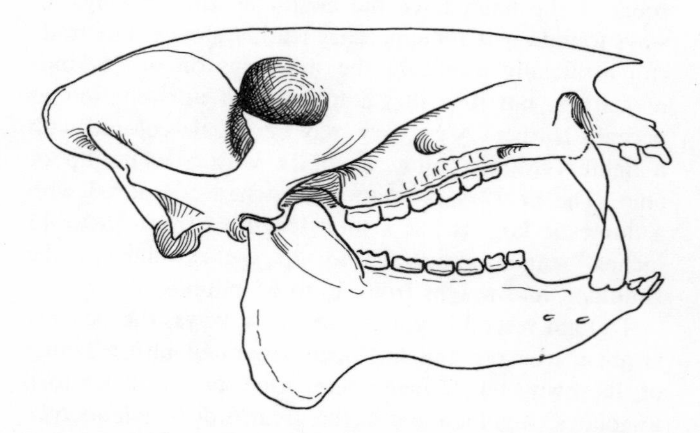

The peccary has low-crowned molars for crushing and sharp-edged canine teeth for piercing and cutting.

snakes of all sizes. Attacking a rattler, the peccary provokes the reptile to strike from a safe distance, then, before it can recoil, leaps in with all four sharp hoofs and cuts the snake to ribbons. It then devours the entire snake; the venom is quite harmless in the stomach, being dangerous only when injected into the blood stream. A troop of peccaries can clear a piece of land of fruit insects and other pests and vermin in a remarkably short time and must then move on to more fertile areas for food.

The peccary has an extremely acute sense of smell. By its sense of smell, the peccary knows exactly where to dig for tubers, roots, and burrowing animal life without exerting a useless amount of labor. The peccary's eyesight may not be of the best, but it has an acute sense of hearing and its little ears are always alertly twitching around to catch the faintest sound of approaching predators.

## ENEMIES

The jaguar is the peccary's number one enemy, but it is also preyed upon by the cougar, ocelot, coyote, and bobcat, as well as big snakes like the python. When frightened or attacked, the peccary emits a strong odor from the gland on its back.

## VOCAL

Far from being the silent type, a herd of peccaries keeps up a steady chatter of short grunts and soft yappings or barks. So long as the herd is not molested, their conversation is in a low, rumbling monotone. Disturbed, a few will utter shrill, protesting grunts at every jump as they speed away. A captured peccary squeals like a pig.

## TRACKS

The peccary moves along at an ambling gait. The tracks are staggered, and the hind foot usually comes down slightly behind and to the inner side of the track left by the forefoot on the same side. The distance of the stride is between 6 and 10 inches. When feeding, the left and right tracks will be separated but closer together. The hoof of the forefoot leaves a print 1½ inches long and that of the hind foot 1¼ inches. A peccary can easily cover a distance of 6 feet in a single jump and up to 10 feet in a running jump.

## MATING AND BIRTH

Surprisingly little is to be found in literature on the breeding habits of the peccary. It has no fixed mating

The peccary has only one dewclaw on the inside of the hind foot.

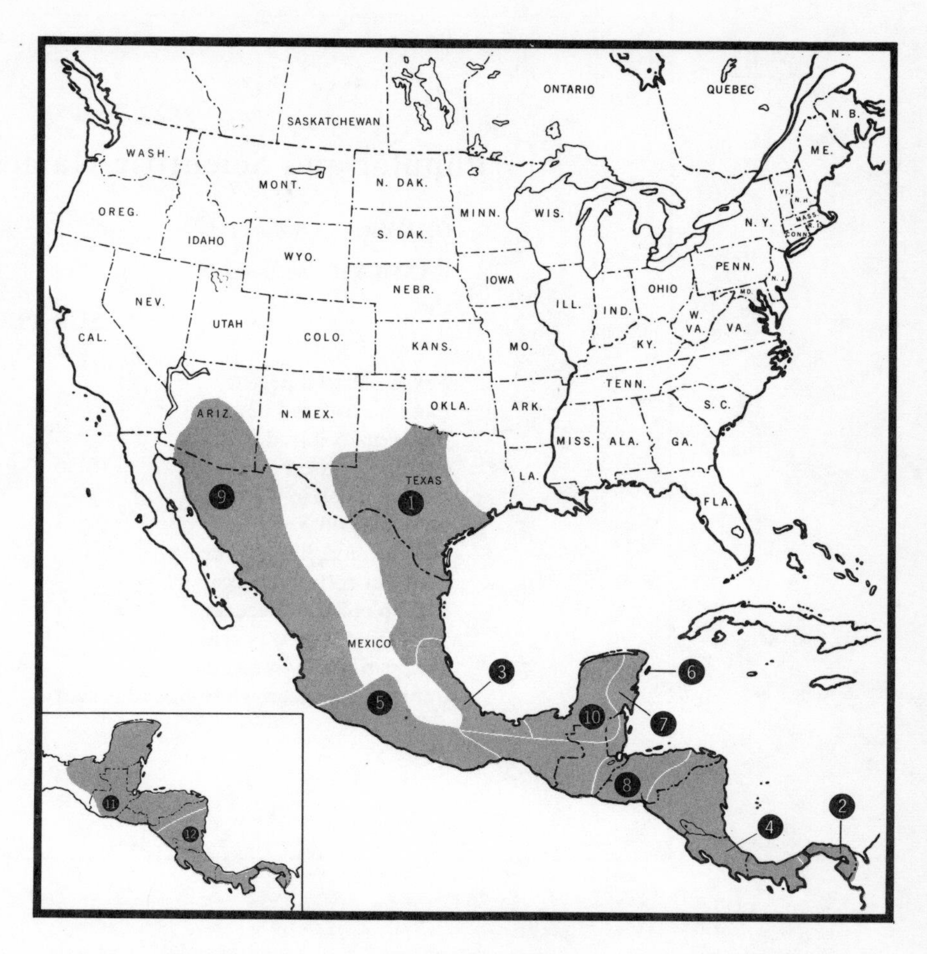


Distribution of the races of the collared peccary *Tayassu:* 1. Texas collared peccary, 2. Panama collared peccary, 3. Veracruz collared peccary, 4. Chiriqui collared peccary, 5. Colima collared peccary, 6. Cozumel collared peccary, 7. Nelson's collared peccary, 8. Honduran collared peccary, 9. Sonora collared peccary, 10. Yucatan collared peccary. White-lipped peccary (insert showing part of Mexico and Central America): 11. Mexican white-lipped peccary, 12. Central American white-lipped peccary.

time, and the young, at least in the tropics, are born at all seasons of the year. Unlike the domestic and wild pigs of the Old World, a litter of peccary rarely exceeds two young. The nursery may be a hollow tree trunk, a hole in the ground, or a thicket of tall grasses and underbrush on the forest floor. The peccary always backs into its den, tail first. At birth the little peccaries are about the size of a small rabbit, and are reddish-brown in color with a black stripe extending down the middle of the back. The baby peccaries are able to stand and nurse within a few hours after birth and when two days old are following the mother on her way to join the main herd.

The gestation period of the peccary is about sixteen weeks, the young begin to breed in the second year, are full grown in the fourth or fifth year, and have a life-span of from fifteen to twenty years.

## Popular and Scientific Names of the Javelina, or Peccary

**ORDER:** *Artiodactyla*

**FAMILY:** *Tayassuidae*

**GENUS:** *Tayassu*

**SPECIES:** *tajacu, pecari*

**SUBSPECIES**

| | |
|---|---|
| Texas collared peccary | *Tayassu tajacu angulatus* |
| Panama collared peccary | *Tayassu tajacu bangsi* |
| Veracruz collared peccary | *Tayassu tajacu crassus* |
| Colima collared peccary | *Tayassu tajacu humeralis* |
| Cozumel collared peccary | *Tayassu tajacu nanus* |
| Nelson's collared peccary | *Tayassu tajacu nelsoni* |
| Honduran collared peccary | *Tayassu tajacu nigrescens* |
| Chiriqui collared peccary | *Tayassu tajacu crusniger* |
| Sonora collared peccary | *Tayassu tajacu sonoriensis* |
| Yucatan collared peccary | *Tayassu tajacu yucatanensis* |
| Mexican white-lipped peccary | *Tayassu pecari ringens* |
| Central American white-lipped peccary | *Tayassu pecari spiradens* |

DOUG ALLEN

CHAPTER 12

# THE MOUNTAIN LION

WHEN I was about seven years old, I was wandering very early one morning out in the hills near the Arizona summer-resort village of Ironsprings. I was carrying a Daisy air rifle, and I was engaged in the worthy project of stalking and scaring the wits out of innocent cottontail rabbits. I never did kill one, but I hit a good many, and when the little pellets stung them they took off so fast you could almost hear them whiz.

There were deer in the area, and several times on my dawn excursions I had startled the graceful gray creatures and had sent them bounding off—generally does and fawns, but once a big four-point buck with swollen antlers in velvet. Then one morning I walked around a big boulder to within a few feet of a mountain lion.

I must have made remarkable time back to our summer cottage, for I burst in with my hair standing on end, and I was still pale from fright. But, alas, I was known as a moppet of some imagination, and my tale was greeted with considerable skepticism. I was so earnest, however, that finally one of my mother's brothers, who was up in the mountains cooling off from the fearful summer heat of the Salt River Valley, consented to go with me to the spot where I insisted that I'd encountered the big cat. He was a hunter and knew lion tracks. The evidence showed that the surprise had been mutual; the lion had taken off in one direction as fast as I had in the other.

Even in country where the mountain lion is common, it is very rare that one is seen unless it's put up a tree or otherwise bayed by dogs. I have spent most of my life in and around lion country, but on only one other occasion have I seen a lion without the aid of dogs. Back in the early thirties in northern Arizona, my wife and I went on a picnic with several other families, and some of the men worked up a game of one-eyed cat with a bat and a softball. After a while I wearied of it, found myself a comfortable seat on a rock, and started glassing the country for deer. I didn't locate any deer, but I did find a mountain lion sitting on a rock about 400 yards away and partially concealed by brush. He was watching the softball game with all the evidence of intense interest. I called out to my pals and showed some of them the cat, but apparently it decided it had been seen. It jumped off the rock and disappeared.

Of all the large American mammals, the mountain lion is the shyest, most furtive, and most difficult to encounter. Many people have spent their entire lives in lion country without ever having seen one. His eyes are excellent, his hearing phenomenal, and on his big soft feet he can steal away as quietly as a shadow. Catching a glimpse of him is made all the more difficult because he is almost entirely nocturnal. Generally he does not begin to hunt until dusk, and shortly after dawn he lies up in some secluded spot. He is one of the most silent of animals, and for a century there has been a controversy about whether he ever makes any noise except to snarl or spit.

A vast amount of testimony suggests that the lion occasionally makes some sort of cry. My mother grew up on a pioneer ranch in the mountains along the Colorado-New Mexico border, and she tells how several times one night she and her family heard what they thought was the screaming of a woman in mortal terror. The next day, she says, her father found mountain-lion tracks in the area from which the screams had come. As good an observer as Grizzly Adams, the famous California hunter of the middle nineteenth century, who caught grizzly bears and tamed them to the extent that he could march them down Broadway in New York City, claimed to have heard the screams of lions. However, Grizzly's book was ghostwritten, and in several instances I don't think the ghost made a good story any poorer in the telling.

The most reliable mountain men and lion hunters I have ever known claim that this story of screaming and caterwauling is a myth. The late Ernest Lee, famous Arizona lion hunter and a good friend of mine, told me he had never in his years in the mountain wilderness heard a noise that he could identify as the cry of a mountain lion. Ernest, his famous brothers, and their equally famous dogs have taken hundreds of mountain lions. Jay Bruce, for many years a predatory-animal hunter for the California game department, wrote that although he had seen lions under all sorts of circumstances—trying to protect their young, battling with dogs for their lives, searching for mates—he had never heard one scream. He thinks that those who claim they have heard lions scream have actually heard owls or coyotes. Government hunter T. J. (Shorty) Lyon of Mogollon, New Mexico, an occasional contributor to *Outdoor Life,* does not believe that lions scream. He further says that none of the lion hunters he is acquainted with believe it.

All big cats other than the mountain lion are fairly noisy. The African lion, with his grunts and roars, is a familiar feature of the African night, and the calling of tigers is one of my most thrilling memories of the Indian jungle. The jaguar roars, and the sawing, grunting cry of the leopard is often heard in both Africa and Asia. But the mountain lion wants not only to keep out of sight but also out of hearing. His quietness, his furtiveness have helped to make the mountain lion a subject of myth and folklore. The lion, like most other cats, is exceedingly curious. Once many years ago in the White Mountains of Arizona I had shot a turkey gobbler, and darkness had come on before I reached camp. I could see fairly well in the starlight, but I got a little mixed up, mistook one hill for another, and did considerable wandering around before I found my bearings and made it to the hot venison stew and mashed potatoes my companion had waiting. The ground was covered by a light, fresh snow that had made tracking easy, and the next morning when I went out I discovered that a lion's tracks paralleled mine for a good mile of my wanderings. He'd had no designs on me, of course, but had simply taken advantage of a good opportunity to observe a rather odd creature. It's a common and often unnerving experience in the mountains to discover that you've been watched by one of the big cats.

Another time I came within a split second of seeing a lion not put up by dogs. I was hunting above the Purgatorio River in Sonora, Mexico. I had tied my horse and was pussyfooting along a ridge on rubber-soled shoes. Suddenly about 50 yards ahead of me on the far side of a great pile of boulders I heard a scuffle. I ran toward the sound. A dead whitetail buck lay just beyond the rocks, and I could see (or thought I saw) the low brush moving as the lion ran off. It was a cold, raw, heavily overcast day, and apparently the lion hadn't made a kill the night before and had continued to hunt. As I look back on the incident, I can almost make myself believe that I actually saw the tawny hide of the lion as it moved off, but that detail was probably furnished by my imagination. At any rate, I heard the lion make the kill.

The odds are overwhelming against anyone's seeing and killing a lion by stillhunting, yet every year in the West a few lucky deer hunters do knock over lions. A couple of months after I came on that fresh kill, a friend of mine jumped an old lioness and two large cubs in the same area. He bombarded them, but didn't connect. One fall when I was living in Tucson, the fifteen-year-old lad who delivered our morning newspaper shot a big tom lion in the Rincon Mountains while he was hunting deer. He came up on top of a rock to look over some country, and saw the lion feeding on a deer carcass just below him. He was probably the proudest kid in Arizona.

This big cat goes by a good many names. In the Southwest he is generally called the mountain lion or simply lion, possibly because the Mexicans call him *leon,* or lion, just as they call the jaguar the *tigre,* or tiger. In the Northwest, he is universally known as the cougar, and in the days when he was found in the Eastern United States he was generally called the panther, or sometimes the catamount or painter. He is also called the puma, and his scientific name is *Felis concolor*.

He is an animal of enormous range. In primitive times he was found in every state in what is now the United States, wherever he found deer, water, and sufficient cover. Today he is found from central British Columbia down through all the Western States, in Florida, throughout Mexico and Central America, and in suitable country clear to the tip of South America.

In the Eastern and Southern states, with the exception of Florida, he is generally believed to be extinct. Endless hunting with packs of dogs is usually given the credit for killing off the Eastern panther, but probably the thinning out of his food supply—deer—and the conversion of great areas of forest into farmland were even more responsible. In the West there are vast areas of wild mountain country where the pursuit of lions by dogs is difficult and where deer were never shot down to the level that they were in the East. Here the lion is making his last stand, and in this fortress of cliff and canyon he should be able to hold out forever. Over most of the West he has been hunted and harried whenever the ground is damp enough to leave a scent. He has not been protected by a closed season; in most Western states a bounty has been put on his head, and professional hunters are hired to destroy him. Sportsmen hate him because he devours deer. Cattlemen cry for his scalp and offer rewards for his destruction because he has been known to kill sheep and sometimes a colt. Yet so sly is he that he gets by. From talking to a good many lion hunters, I am doubtful that the number of big cats has decreased much in my lifetime.

The lion will also kill wild turkeys, mountain sheep—even full-grown elk, horses, and cattle. But primarily he is a hunter of deer, the most skillful and efficient deer hunter in the world. He is part of nature's scheme to keep the deer within the limits of their food supply, something that's difficult for us heavy-footed, hamhanded human hunters. Almost always the destruction of an area's mountain lions is followed by rapid increase in deer numbers, depletion of forage, and wholesale starvation.

A classic example is Arizona's Kaibab National Forest north of the Grand Canyon. It was made into a game preserve by Theodore Roosevelt in the early years of this century. Deer hunting was not allowed, but the hunting of lions continued. As the number of lions went down, the number of deer went up. By the early nineteen twenties, there were probably at least 100,000 deer in an area that could support about 25,000. When the season opened, hunters were unable to thin them down sufficiently. Tens of thousands starved to death. The Forest Service had other thousands shot in an attempt to save the range—and the rest of the deer herd. Then for a time, the forest was open to deer hunting, but all predators, coyotes as well as lions, were protected. Because of poor management in the past, the Kaibab is still a problem area.

Back in the nineteen twenties the Lee brothers lived in the Chiricahua Mountains of southern Arizona. With their wonderful dogs, they pretty well cleaned out the local lions and they also got the wandering lions that came in from Mexico about as fast as they showed up. As a result, the whitetails became so plentiful that they overbrowsed their range and suffered a die-off. This story could be repeated endlessly. When the lions are thinned out, the deer increase, become so plentiful that they destroy their range, then die off.

A lion kills a lot of deer. Estimates run from one to three a week, and Ernest Lee, who followed many lions for days on end, told me that very often an old traveling tom lion will kill every day. Even in the

A Mexican cowboy was riding back to the ranch where he worked when a lion jumped him, knocking him from his horse.

most heavily populated deer areas, hunter success is only about 50 per cent, so one lion will take annually about as many deer as two hundred hunters. In heavily hunted areas of limited deer population, there is reason to control lions, but in rough country and wilderness areas, the lion is the deer's best friend.

I am convinced that the lion is a necessity for a healthy deer herd, and that the take of lions should be regulated with this in mind. One species complements the other; the best lion country is the best deer country.

This wonderful machine for hunting deer, this pair of hungry jaws on four big, soft feet, this gray shadow of the mountains is one of the smallest of the world's great cats. Much pure fiction is written about his size. I constantly hear about mountain lions as large as female African lions, and one lion hunter gave me dimensions of a lion he had taken that would make it as large as a respectable male Indian tiger. A lion weighing 300 pounds is supposed to have been killed in Arizona. I simply do not believe it—any more than I believe stories about mule deer that dress out at 450 pounds.

I have seen some dead and some live mountain lions, and likewise some leopards. My impression is that the average mountain lion is a little larger than the average leopard. One leopard a friend of mine shot was larger in every measurement than any we could find recorded, and I'm sure it weighed no more than 150 pounds. The largest mountain lion I have ever seen was only a little larger. Ernest Lee told me that of the hundreds of lions he and his brothers had taken, they'd never killed one that weighed 175 pounds. The average male lion taken probably weighs 125 to 140 pounds. In 1923 E. W. Nelson, then chief of the U. S. Bureau of Biological Survey, wrote that the lions of the Southwest averaged larger than those of the Northwest. However, a lion taken in the Clearwater region of Idaho looked from a photograph to be the largest and heaviest I have ever seen. It looked as if it might actually weigh around 200 pounds. Theodore Roosevelt is supposed to have killed a mountain lion weighing 227 pounds. If he did, it was some lion. From what I've seen, I believe the average big mature lion measures about 7 feet over the curves from tip of nose to the last joint in the tail. I have heard of lions measuring 9 and even 9½ feet, but I think they're in the same class with 11-foot tigers and Alaska brown bears that square out 13 feet. I have before me the skull of a mountain lion that is so large that I'm sending it to Grancel Fitz of the Boone and Crockett Club to measure for the record book. It will go right among the top listings, but compared with the skull of an African lion it is tiny.

Just as some African lions are grayish with black manes and some are tan with blond manes, there seem to be two color phases among mountain lions, some being more gray than tan and some more tan than gray. Lion hunters speak of "blue" lions and "red" lions. For their size, mountain lions have very long tails and very large feet. Their heads are small for their length, and their necks seem long compared with those of the other big cats. They are "snaky" looking creatures.

The mountain lion is an American of ancient lineage, but he is no doubt descended from some ancient Asiatic cat, probably spotted, as lion cubs wear spots and do not get rid of them until they are about six months old. Little is known about the breeding habits of lions, but probably the male is with the female only during the mating season. One reads many romantic stories about daddy lions defending the mamma and baby lions, but it is very rare for lion hunters to jump a mature male and a mature female together. Generally the males are alone, and if two or three lions are together it is almost always a female with her young. Two kittens seem to be the usual number in a litter, but litters of one to five have been reported. They are generally born in the winter or early spring. Probably the females breed only every other year, because it is common to find cubs well over a year old still traveling with their mother.

In spite of its relatively small size, the mountain lion is a formidable beast capable of killing even a full-grown horse or a bull elk. There are stories (whether true or not) of lions running the enormously larger grizzly bears off kills. One would think that like the tiger, the African lion, or the leopard, this big cat would become a killer of men. Human beings have been killed by mountain lions, but there are very few authenticated instances. About twenty-five years ago, a starving lion killed and ate a young boy in Oregon, and in California a lion with rabies attacked and mauled three children but did not kill any of them outright. Once on Vancouver Island, an ancient female lion, blind and starving, attacked two children. A Sonora Mexican cowboy I once hunted with told me that one night when he was riding back to the ranch where he worked, a lion jumped his horse, knocked him off it, and then realized his mistake before he did anything to either him or the horse, and that lion, horse, and cowboy all fled in different directions. In the forty-five years I lived in Arizona, I did not hear of a single case of an attack by a lion on a human being in that state.

Surrounded by dogs and hunters, the lion sprang from the tree, and bowled over one man.

The big cats are not only curious about human beings, but also deathly afraid of them. Hunters commonly climb trees after lions that have been cornered by dogs, take pictures of them, and toss ropes over their heads and around their legs. One hunter I know was actually knocked down when a lion, surrounded by dogs and hunters, jumped out of a tree. Apparently the lion simply made a miscue as it made no attempt to claw or bite the hunter. Nevertheless the experience scared the hunter half out of his wits. Another chap I know was sitting on the same limb with a treed lion, taking its picture with a miniature camera. Suddenly the lion decided it didn't like what was going on. It took one swat at the photographer, tore off part of the brim of his ten-gallon hat, and knocked his four-hundred-dollar camera to the rocks below.

Because such liberties can be taken with treed or cornered lions, and because lions are afraid of dogs, the big cats have a reputation of being cowards. Hundreds have been treed, roped, muzzled, and tied up, and I have yet to hear of a hunter getting hurt when so engaged.

About twenty-five years ago, a lawyer I know went trout fishing in northern Arizona and took along a worthless little white mongrel dog that weighed about 15 pounds. After he had fished for half an hour or so, he heard the dog barking about a quarter of a mile away, and when the barking continued he went to investigate. The little mutt had a lion up a tree. The lawyer went back to get a .22 revolver he had in the glove compartment of his car, and killed the lion. The dog was quite a hero; fisherman, dog, and dead lion all got their pictures in the paper.

On another occasion a friend of mine was hunting desert mule deer in Sonora, and when he left the ranch was followed by a nondescript cur with some vague hound ancestry. The dog stayed close, seemed friendly, and my pal didn't mind its company. The two of them were sneaking along when suddenly the dog let out a bellow and shot forward. An instant later my amigo saw a lion streak up a large saguaro (giant cactus) and roost on top while the dog yammered below him. My amigo carefully shot the lion off the saguaro, and that was that.

Not only is the mountain lion just about a necessity for maintaining healthy deer herds in wilderness areas, but he is also one of the great sporting animals of America. To anyone who likes dogs and dog work, there is nothing quite like it. Lion dogs are generally some breed of foxhound, sometimes crossed with bloodhound, and often by no means of pure type. Lion hunters breed for performance and not bloodlines, and a favorite hound may be part bluetick, part redbone, and part bloodhound. Now and then a beagle will be part of a pack, and a beagle will take to lion hunting just like his larger relatives.

Few types of hunting excel lion hunting in anticipation. The hunter who knows his dogs can, by their actions, tell pretty well how old the scent is and what the lion was doing, and he'll have a pretty fair notion about where the lion is heading. From the distant sounds he can tell when it is treed, if it makes a stand against a cliff and is fighting the dogs off, and when it jumps and runs. He can tell the voice of one dog from another, and he has fairly accurate ideas about the noses and intelligence of his various dogs. Every lion hunter has his tales of super-canine feats his dogs have pulled off.

And lion hunting is by no means easy. In the rugged mountains of the Southwest, even the dude hunter who is paying for the show usually has to do some desperate horseback riding over country so rough it's incredible. In the steep mountains and heavy forests of the Northwest, the dogs are usually followed on foot, and if anyone wants a job of work, that is it.

When the Lee brothers took paying guests out lion hunting, one of the older Lees used to stay with the dude and try to keep him within sound of the pack, but the youngest Lee, Dale, stayed right with the dogs, running up hill and down, through some of the roughest country on the continent.

I have done in only one lion with my own fair hands, and that was in the early twenties. I had a friend then whose business was the production of high-class moonshine whisky for the parched citizens of northern Arizona, but whose hobby was running cats with dogs—preferably lions, but bobcats if he couldn't find the big fellows. His ancestors had been pioneers ever since they'd come to North Carolina from England and Scotland long before the Revolutionary War. Gradually they had worked west, breeding their hounds, shooting deer, making whisky, raising a few cattle, and doing a little farming when there weren't any big cats to chase. Now and then my pal took out a dude and chased down a lion for a flat one-hundred-dollar fee, and also collected bounty from the state and from cattlemen's associations.

On this occasion he didn't have any dude in sight, he was pretty well caught up on whisky making, and he wanted to investigate some lion sign he'd run across while looking for a lost horse. I was handy, so we went together. The scent was apparently old, and the country was very dry. The dogs spent the morning losing the scent on the dry, wind-swept, and sun-baked ridges there at about 7,000 feet elevation, circling, then picking it up again in spots where it was shadier and moister. Now and then my keen-eyed pal would point out a track so dim or fragmentary that I wouldn't have noticed it.

Then along about two o'clock, the dogs, which had been letting out only an occasional bugle, all tuned up at once.

"Ai, Chihuahua!" my friend shouted. "Let's get out of here. They're on hot scent!"

He rammed his heels into his horse's flank and went tearing off toward the dogs as though his life depended on it. I was hard put to keep up with him, and he was out of sight when the dogs barked treed. However, I found my way to the pack. When I got there he was off his horse and had his lion rifle, a little Remington pump chambered for the .22 Special cartridge. The lion was sitting on the limb of a rather mangy alligator-bark juniper looking a bit annoyed but not particularly disturbed. As I got off my horse, the lion looked at me for a moment with a mildly contemptuous eye, then went back to its business of snarling at the dogs.

"Now kill him dead, for Pete's sake," my pal said. "Shoot him in the brain or behind the ear. I don't want no wounded lion a-fallin' on them dogs."

One of the dogs was making some high but ineffectual leaps, trying to get into the crotch of the tree, and the lion was watching it with its head turned away from me. I had a little Model 92 Winchester carbine in .25/20 caliber. I sat down at about 25 yards, aimed carefully, and squeezed off the shot. The bullet hit the lion right behind the ear, and it pitched out stone dead right in the midst of the dogs.

Incidentally, the hides of mountain lions are apparently very tough and rubbery. The pack chewed on the cat enthusiastically for some minutes, but later when we skinned it we found no breaks in the hide.

When my pal thought the dogs had mauled the dead lion sufficiently, he kicked them away, tossed the carcass out of their reach across one of the lower limbs, and we made coffee, ate our sandwiches and apples. The lion had made a kill the night before, a very large handsome buck, and had been sleeping it off in some rocks. It was a tom that measured a bit under seven feet, and I guessed it to weigh about what a large Arizona whitetail buck would weigh—around 115 pounds. Some months later I went along for the ride with my same amigo. This time he had a paying guest armed with a .30/06. Using the old Remington umbrella-point 150-grain bullet, he blew a 6-inch hole in the far side of the lion.

Shots at lions treed by dogs are usually very easy, and something like the .25/20 or .22 Hornet is generally about all the lion hunter needs. Many hunters carry revolvers, and Jay Bruce, the famous California lion hunter, made all his kills with a Colt Woodsman in .22 Long Rifle.

But hunting lions with dogs is by no means a setup. If the scent is fresh, the dogs good, and the country suitable, a lion often comes very easy. A friend of mine from the East came out to hunt lions with the Lee brothers some years ago. In the late afternoon they arrived at a ranch with the dogs. They were out at dawn the next morning, and had a fine tom lion by nine o'clock.

Sometimes the lions get into country so rough they simply cannot be followed. Sometimes the dogs get so far away they cannot be located; though they have the cat treed, conditions of wind and terrain may be such that they can't be heard.

There are lions in most of the rough, mountainous country of the Western states. Famous areas are southern Utah, northern Arizona around the Grand Canyon, the Salmon River country of Idaho, Vancouver Island, and southern British Columbia generally. There are many in the Sierra Madre Mountains of northern Mexico.

There are generally local lion hunters with dogs who are willing to take out a tenderfoot for a fee. The great sport in lion hunting is following the wonderful dogs through wild and beautiful country. The actual shooting is generally very easy.

A grand animal, old *Felis concolor,* and one that I'd hate to see extinct. If he ever is, it will be a sad day for all of us who love wild country and wild creatures, and it will be a sadder day for the deer.

# The Natural History of the Mountain Lion, or Cougar

[FELIS CONCOLOR]

## DESCRIPTION

The lithe, tawny cat *Felis concolor* of North America is known by a number of names—cougar, mountain lion, puma, painter, and catamount. In Spanish-speaking countries it is called *el leon,* or lion. The name panther is often used for melanistic (black) specimens.

A large, slender cat with a long, rounded tail, the cougar is without spots and is uniform in color, varying from reddish-brown and golden yellowish-brown to dull gray. Occasionally one will see a black cougar, most of which are found in Florida. The cougar's long cylindrical tail is covered with thick, soft fur, almost uniform in thickness throughout, becoming slightly bushier toward the dark-brown or blackish tip. The soft fur on the flanks and shoulders is paler in color than the back and merges into the white of the under parts.

The cougar has a remarkably small, bullet-like head for such a large cat, small rounded ears, and a comparatively long, muscular neck. The face is short and rounded with the eyes placed well in front of the head; the body is long, lithe and somewhat narrow, supported on long muscular limbs.

The cougar measures from 6 to 9 feet long, and has a tail ranging from 28 to 36 inches. It stands from 26 to 30 inches high at the shoulder and weighs from 100 to 150 pounds with rare specimens weighing as much as 200 pounds. The females are much smaller than the males and weigh about 40 per cent less.

The cougar's front paws contain five toes but the hind feet contain only four. The bones of the toes and fingers are lengthened, raising the cat off the ground so that it walks digitigrade fashion on the tips of its toes. Each of the toes terminates in a sharp, strongly curved claw. All true cats have retractile claws which can be extended or withdrawn at will by powerful flexor muscles. When not in use, the claws are retracted into their sheaths, which protect the needle-like points, leaving the paw soft and harmless with no indication of the concealed weapons. All the claws can spring into service in a split second as deadly weapons, but it is the great claw on the thumb, raised a little higher than the other four, which can inflict the greatest amount of damage and is often called the killer claw.

A member of the cat family *Felidae*, the cougar is one of the most specialized of the *Carnivora,* or flesh-eaters, and its teeth are especially adapted for a flesh diet. It has long, dagger-like canine teeth for piercing through skin and flesh. Even the functional cheek teeth are reduced to two pairs of cutting teeth, one on each side of the upper and lower jaws. These sharp-edged, shearing teeth are used like notched scissors for cutting tough muscle and sinews. Other teeth are present but they are so small that they serve no useful purpose. The tongue, another adaptation of this highly specialized flesh-eater, is rough and rasp-like, its surface coated with horny points directed backward for scraping.

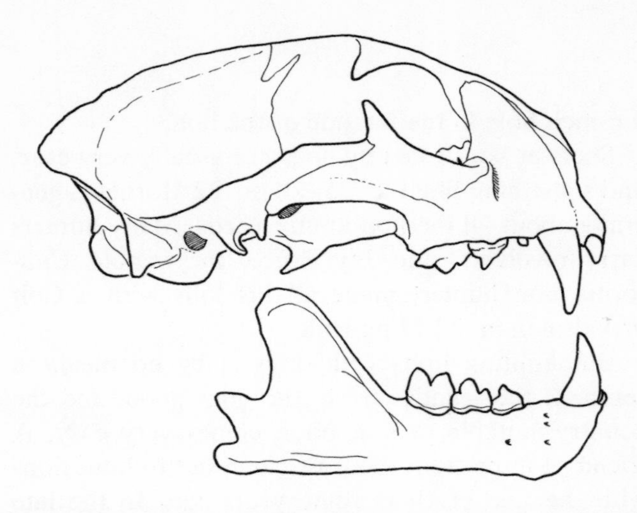

The cougar has long, sharp-pointed canine teeth, and cheek teeth with sharp, notched edges for shearing flesh.

## ORIGIN

The true cats are the most specialized of the *Carnivora* and are therefore a comparatively late addition to the big game animals of North America. They first appeared in numbers during the Pleistocene era and possibly to a lesser degree in the Pliocene era. The earliest known forms of American big cats were the American lion (*Felis atrox*) and the saber-toothed Smilodon. The cougar was also a member of the North American Pleistocene fauna but it never occurred in the Old World, nor has it any close relatives there. In general the cats are of Euro-Asiatic origin and are probably descendants of *Dinictis* stock (earliest true flesh-eaters) of the Oligocene and Miocene eras.

## RANGE

The original range of the cougar covered practically the whole of North America south of the Great Lakes, Maine, Nova Scotia and British Columbia, south through the United States, Central America and from coast to coast in South America south to the Straits of Magellan. Today the range of the cougar is mostly in western North America, from Alberta and British Columbia south in the United States to New Mexico and Louisiana, and in Florida. Normally the home range of an individual cougar does not exceed 12 square miles but during the mating season it may travel far afield and cover a distance of 30 miles in two days.

There are several named geographical forms of cougars recognized in North America. The Sierra Madre cougar, found in New Mexico, Arizona, and northeastern Mexico, is a medium-sized form with rather short, pale-tawny pelage. The Colorado desert cougar, found on the desert plains and low mountain ridges of the Colorado River valley, is a medium-sized pallid subspecies resembling the Sierra Madre, but paler in color. The California cougar, distributed over most of California except in the desert regions of the southeastern part, is similar to the Colorado but smaller and darker in color. The Florida cougar, native to Florida and Louisiana, is a rather large, tawny-colored subspecies with comparatively short pelage. The Central American cougar, restricted to tropical forested regions of Panama, Costa Rica, and Nicaragua is a small cinnamon-colored form that represents the connecting link between the North American and South American cougars.

The Eastern cougar, formerly located in the northeastern United States and eastern Canada, is now rarely found in most of its original territory. It was a rather large species with pelage a dark-fulvous or tawny color. The Rocky Mountain cougar occurs in the Rocky Mountains in Wyoming, Idaho, Colorado, and Utah. Largest of the North American cougars, it is rather pale in color with soft, full pelage, reaching a length of 8 feet and a weight of 227 pounds. The Baja California cougar, restricted to the desert regions of Lower California. Mexico, is a small, short-furred, pale-colored subspecies. The Kaibab cougar is found on the Kaibab Plateau north of the Grand Canyon of the Colorado River. It is a large, long-haired subspecies with pale, tawny pelage lightly overlaid with black. The Guatemalan cougar, found in the tropical, forested regions of southern Mexico and Guatemala, is a small, reddish subspecies, the smallest form of the North American cougars. Its total length is 5 feet, 6 inches.

The Montana cougar covers the Rocky Mountain region from Yellowstone National Park north to Jasper Park, Alberta, the Cassiar Mountains, British Columbia, and the Peace River District. The Cascade Mountain cougar ranges in the Cascade Mountains of Washington, Oregon, and southwestern British Columbia. It is a large, dark-colored subspecies with dark facial markings and a black-tipped tail. The Great Plains cougar is found west of the Mississippi to the Rocky Mountains in the north central United States. It is a large, rather pale, short-haired form. The Texas cougar, found in Texas and northeastern Mexico, is a moderately large form with pelage grayer than tawny. The Vancouver Island cougar is a large, dark cinnamon-rufous form and resembles the adjacent mainland subspecies but is darker and more rufous in color.

## HABITS

A big game hunter, the cougar's staple prey is deer, but it also kills wapiti, mountain sheep, and pronghorn. When there is a scarcity of big game it will feed on various kinds of rodents, rabbits, and hares. When stalking its prey, the cougar usually travels in circles, taking advantage of the darkest shadows and keeping hidden behind rocks and tree trunks. It approaches within striking distance, gathers its feet under its body, hunches its back, and catapults headlong at its quarry. In one or two bounds and a final spring the cougar is on the neck or shoulders of its prey. Always prepared for such a catastrophe, the deer is ready to bound away; if the cat does not overtake it in its first rush, it makes no attempt to follow.

A hungry cougar devours 6 or 7 pounds of venison at one meal, covers up what is left of the kill with sticks and leaves, and finds a comfortable resting place close by to sleep. When conscious of the need to feed again, the cougar returns to the kill for a second and third meal.

An extremely powerful animal, the cougar can drag a victim five times its own weight a hundred yards or more. Although curious about man and his activities, the cougar scarcely, if ever, makes an unprovoked attack on a human being. It is shy and elusive where people are concerned and is mortally afraid of dogs. Cornered by a pack of dogs, a cougar, with its tail swinging back and forth, its ears clamped down on its head, will sell its life dearly, and more than one dog is apt to be mortally wounded in the battle. Whenever there is a tree handy, however, the big cat will take refuge in its branches rather than fight.

The cougar depends on sight more than on its senses of smell and hearing. Sight is much faster, anyway, since it is based on light, which travels at 186,000 miles per second. Sound travels only at the rate of one mile a second and air-borne odors are governed by the direction of the wind. The big cat usually travels between sunset and sunrise, and its eyes are especially adapted for dim light. Although the cougar's eyes have a bright shine, they do not generate any light themselves but merely amplify the little light that is absorbed. This is due to particles of guanin that coat the eye's inner walls. Guanin has a metallic luster of silver and brightens a dimly lit picture reflected on the retina, providing better visibility. During daylight hours, when the big cat's eyes do not need a booster to brighten their vision, the guanin retreats into the so-called rods, or minute storage tubes. On a dark night, when a bright light is suddenly flashed into the cat's eyes, the guanin particles do not have a chance to retreat and they throw back the excess light as eye-shine which is pale greenish-blue.

Distribution of the races of the cougar *Felis:* 1. Sierra Madre cougar, 2. Arizona desert cougar, 3. California cougar, 4. Florida cougar, 5. Central American cougar, 6. Eastern cougar, 7. Rocky Mountain cougar, 8. Baja California cougar, 9. Kaibab cougar, 10. Guatemalan cougar, 11. Montana cougar, 12. Cascade Mountain cougar, 13. Great Plains cougar, 14. Texas cougar, 15. Vancouver Island cougar.

To supplement its sight in dark, dimly lit covers and corners during its nightly prowls, the cougar has long, bristle-like whiskers to feel its way around. The whiskers themselves are not actually sensitive, but each whisker has its root associated with minute raised points on the skin known as touch spots. The slightest touch on the tip of a whisker is transferred to a touch spot, automatically causing the animal to react accordingly. Thigmatropism, the impulse which causes a cat on its back to struggle to its feet, is directly associated with the sense of touch, which is highly developed in all cats.

It should not be assumed, however, that the cougar is hard of hearing. Actually, it is one of the most difficult animals to approach in the forest. The faintest crackle of a twig will alert the big cat and it will seek a vantage point to see who is approaching.

## LOCOMOTION

Among the most versatile of the mammals, a cougar can walk softly on cushioned feet, trot, gallop, climb trees, and swim, but its special achievement is its ability to spring. Don't ever underestimate the power of this big cat. Charged with high-tension muscles and a reservoir of stored-up energy, the cougar can, in a fraction of a second, change from a perfect example of complacency and relaxation to a catapulting streak of fighting fury. From an almost standing position, a cougar in one leap can cover a distance of 27 feet, rising to 11 feet before landing. In a high jump it can clear 18 feet

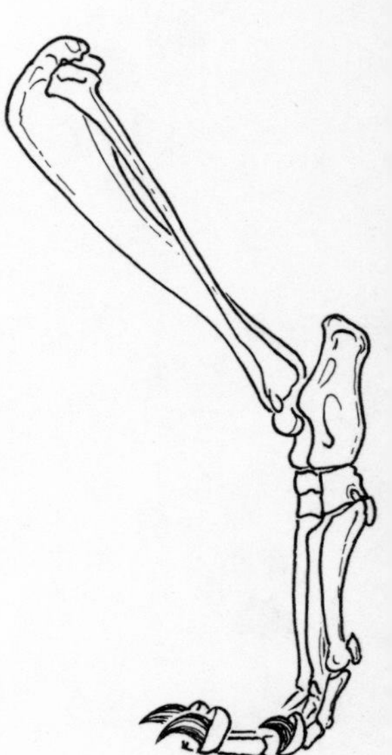

Like all cats, the cougar travels on the tips of its toes. Its sharply curved claws are retractable, and are only extended when the animal attacks.

and has been known to cover a distance of 60 feet in a downward plunge, the long tail serving as a balance to keep the animal on its course.

### TRACKS

The tracks left by the forefeet of the cougar are roughly semicircular in shape in front and consist of a broad, triangular central pad, with an oval toe pad on either side and forward of the triangle. In front are the two oval pads of the middle front toes. The impressions left by the hind feet are much the same as the front paws except that the toe pads are elongated and the central pad is narrower. Claw points are never in evidence. When walking, the cougar's hind foot usually falls into the impression left by the forefoot or close to it. Cougar tracks for an adult male average about 4½ inches wide and 4 inches long, but some of the Rocky Mountain cougars leave tracks 6½ inches wide.

### VOCAL

The cougar scarcely ever uses its vocal powers, and few people have heard a cougar scream, not even those living in districts where it is known to be plentiful. On occasion during the breeding season, some naturalists have heard the female emit a blood-curdling, hair-raising scream, described as resembling the screams of a woman being murdered. The toms are credited only with a soft, musical whistle.

### MATING

There is no fixed mating season for the cougar, and the family relations between the male and female are usually short. During the brief mating period the tom is exceedingly jealous and will fight any other male that may intrude on his domain. Usually both cats separate after mating. There are exceptions to these short-lived family unions; on very rare occasions a tom will stay in the company of a female until after the kittens are born and help supply the family with food.

### BIRTH AND EARLY DEVELOPMENT

Most cougar kittens are born in the spring, about twelve weeks after mating, and number from two to four in a litter. They measure about 12 inches long at birth, weigh about 1 pound, and their eyes are tightly closed and fully furred. At this time their tails are quite short, ringed with alternating dark and light-brownish bands, and their pale fawn-colored coats are dotted with numerous dark-brown spots. The nursery may be almost anywhere: a dense thicket on the forest floor, under an overhanging rocky ledge, or a sheltered cave. The kittens begin to open their eyes on the ninth day, cut their first baby teeth on about the eighteenth day, and are soon playing together like domestic kittens. When two weeks old the kittens play outside the den in the warm sunshine and are nursed for five weeks. At the age of two months they are 2½ feet in length, weigh about 10 pounds, and the dark spotting of the pelage is beginning to fade. The kittens grow rapidly and when eight months old are 5 feet long, weigh about 50 pounds, and are beginning to hunt for themselves. The grown kittens remain with the mother until toward the end of the second year at which time family ties are completely broken, the mother is ready to mate again, and the kittens are old enough to mate. The cougar has few natural enemies and has a life expectancy of about twelve years.

## Popular and Scientific Names of the Mountain Lion, or Cougar

**ORDER:** *Carnivora*

**FAMILY:** *Felidae*

**GENUS:** *Felis*

**SPECIES:** *concolor*

**SUBSPECIES**

|  |  |
|---|---|
| Sierra Madre cougar | *Felis concolor azteca* |
| Colorado desert cougar | *Felis concolor browni* |
| California cougar | *Felis concolor californica* |
| Florida cougar | *Felis concolor coryi* |
| Central American cougar | *Felis concolor costaricensis* |
| Eastern cougar | *Felis concolor couguar* |
| Rocky Mountain cougar | *Felis concolor hippolestes* |
| Baja California cougar | *Felis concolor improcera* |
| Kaibab cougar | *Felis concolor kaibabensis* |
| Guatemalan cougar | *Felis concolor mayensis* |
| Montana cougar | *Felis concolor missoulensis* |
| Cascade Mountain cougar | *Felis concolor oregonensis* |
| Great Plains cougar | *Felis concolor schorgeri* |
| Texas cougar | *Felis concolor stanleyana* |
| Vancouver Island cougar | *Felis concolor vancouverensis* |

The cougar's tracks can be identified by the rounded toe pads in a curved row in front of the large heel pad. The trail is a staggered line with the hind-foot track some distance behind that of the forefoot on the same side. The claws are retracted and do not register.

CHAPTER 13

# THE JAGUAR

I MET my first jaguar in Mexico as the result of a job I had with an adventurous uncle and an acquaintance I had with a blond, blue-eyed Indian boy. I was in my teens then, and my uncle was running a shoestring lumber outfit on the Fuerte River in Sinaloa, Mexico. He was a man of many ideas, vast industry, but little judgment and very poor luck. About 1909 he had sold a large tract of land in California because he thought that the California boom had run its course forever and the state was in for a population decline and a great drop in land value. The land he sold would now be worth millions. He invested in a silver mine somewhere in mountainous central Mexico, and a few months later the revolution broke out and he lost his mine and was lucky to escape with his life.

For some years he made a precarious living along the border, buying and selling cattle, and also (I suspect) running some guns and ammunition to revolutionaries. Once he tried to get rich raising winter tomatoes in the Yaqui River valley for the American market, but two armies decided to have a battle in his fields. To save themselves the exertion of digging graves, the victors dumped the dead into his wells. His house was ruined, his crop destroyed, and his livestock killed or stolen.

On the impulse of the moment, and through some vague feeling of good will, he invited me to spend the summer with his lumber outfit. His plan was to make a truck driver out of me, but the insides of the miserable old trucks were as mysterious to me as the laws of nuclear physics, and I was always getting stranded somewhere and having to walk back for help. It took me forever to change a tire, and the patches I put on the tubes had a way of falling off.

There were many small whitetail deer in the area, and to save the money he would otherwise have spent for beef, my uncle had employed a professional hunter to shoot deer for his crew. About the time my uncle had decided that for most purposes I was utterly worthless, his *cazador* got embroiled in an affair of the heart with a local maiden and had to take it on the lam.

There were three rifles in camp—a .30/30 Model 94 Winchester carbine, a Mexican Army 7 mm. Mauser, and a Model 99 Savage in .250/3000 caliber. The .30/30 and the 7 mm. had been salvaged from the battle in the tomato fields, but my uncle had bought the Savage in the United States and had smuggled it, along with a good supply of cartridges, into Mexico.

In the time I had been able to steal from my inept truck driving I had shot a couple of deer, so my uncle decided to try me as a hunter. I had patience, could get around quietly, and I had been going to a high school where I regularly took part in competitive shooting with a 1903 Springfield. However, without my pal Ignacio I would have been sunk.

Ignacio was an Indian boy of about my own age. He was as keen a hunter as I was, and much more skillful. He knew the habits of the deer, where they fed, what they ate, where they watered, and he could track, and his sense of direction was uncanny. I could shoot better than he could, but otherwise he was the leader.

The Mayos are a mysterious tribe. They speak a language akin to that used by the Papagos of northern Sonora and southern Arizona, and their culture is much the same. However, in this particular village about 10 per cent of the people were blond and blue-eyed. Most of them were fair-skinned, and over 50 per cent had light-colored eyes. Some had Indian features, coppery skin, and gray or blue eyes, but a great many of them, Ignacio included, looked no more Indian than I did.

The Mayos, I have been told, believe that their ancestors came to the Sinaloa coast by boat from a land far away. There are legends suggesting that Scandinavian whalers sired the blond strain, but an anthropologist of my acquaintance laughs at the notion. His idea is that, following the penetration of the Spanish in the area, a battalion of Castilian, Basque, or Catalan conquistadores was stationed in the Mayo country and that they left their genes behind them.

Whatever the explanation was for his blue eyes, his fair hair, and his freckles, Ignacio was a nice guy. He was not only completely illiterate but had only vaguely heard of reading and writing. But he knew the tracks of every animal, the call of every bird. He could build cunning traps for quail, bleat like a fawn in distress, and with the aid of a cow's horn he could roar like a jaguar, which like all Mexicans, he called a *tigre,* or tiger.

He and I used to leave camp at dawn every day riding a couple of skinny horses and leading a pack mule. We generally managed to shoot at least one deer every day, and somewhere I still have a picture of the mule with five deer packed on it. They were small deer, but on the other hand it was also a small mule.

There were *tigres* in the country. We often saw their tracks, and sometimes we found where they had killed deer, javelinas, or one of the half-wild cattle that ranged through the brush. Ignacio had never killed a *tigre,* and I had never even seen one. Our opportunity came when a *tigre* killed a colt at the far end of a *milpa* (field) not over half a mile from the village.

Ignacio owned a couple of dogs that looked as if they had a little hound in them, and which indeed had fair noses. As soon as we discovered the kill, Ignacio put his two dogs and half a dozen starving village mutts on the trail. We never saw the *tigre.* The dogs jumped it within a mile of the village. We did our best to follow on horseback, but the brush was so thick we couldn't quite keep up. Once, not over 200 yards ahead of us, we heard roars and yelps that told us the dogs had the *tigre* cornered, but by the time we got there the big cat was gone and one of Ignacio's hounds lay dead. A mile farther on we met the mutts coming back, all thoroughly whipped. The bowels of one were hanging out. We found Ignacio's second hound dead, and the wounded mutt died a few days later.

We decided that a *tigre* was a pretty formidable animal, and the villagers didn't look with approval on our borrowing any more dogs. Another time we sat in a tree all night waiting for a *tigre* to come to the carcass of a steer it had killed. It did not show up, and before the second night the buzzards had reduced the kill to hide and bones.

But we finally saw a *tigre.*

One morning just at dawn we had tied our horses and planned to hunt a long, brushy draw. Ignacio was going to wait at the foot of the draw while I circled around and got to the head. Then he was going to move up through the draw, and if a deer came out I was supposed to shoot it. I was about halfway to my stand when a big *tigre* walked quietly out of the brush and crossed an open space about 30 yards wide. The sight frightened me half out of my wits. I had the .250/3000 Savage in my hand. It was loaded and on safe, but it never occurred to me to use it. Instead I simply stood rooted to the spot and stared. As it happened, Ignacio too had been in a position where he could see the *tigre.* His reaction was the same as mine. He had stood there open-mouthed and let it walk away. His first remark was, "Very big, very formidable." Then he decided he had lost face. "You had the best rifle," he said. "If I had been carrying the *viente-cinco* (.25) I would have killed the *tigre.* With the *triente-triente* (.30/30) I was afraid."

Ignacio was a crack hunter but not a very good shot. He was likely to hit his deer in the middle, and when he did he found that the .250/3000 flattened the little deer (many didn't weigh more than 45 pounds) much better than did the slower, heavier .30/30 bullet.

We never did get a *tigre.* As the summer came to

a close I had to go back to the United States and to school. Ignacio drove me to San Blas in a two-wheeled cart. It took us two long days. We made a little camp late in the afternoon, and Ignacio went out and quickly shot a small buck. Our meal was what I had been living on all summer—venison, coffee, eggs, chilis, and tortillas. As we went to sleep a *tigre* was roaring back in the bush. It was drizzling a little, and for as far as we could see the dark bush was pulsating with the light of millions of fireflies.

The jaguar is the largest of the American spotted cats, and in the form of the large South American species he is the third largest cat in the world, being outranked in size only by the lion and the tiger. His Latin name is *Felis onca*. *Felis,* of course, means cat, and *onca* is the name the Portuguese gave the creature in Brazil. It, in turn, is simply a Portuguese term meaning a big cat, as is *onza* in Spanish. The name jaguar came from some South American Indian language, probably one from Brazil.

The American pioneers called the American whitetail a deer, after the very different red deer of the British Isles, and they named the wapiti, which is related to the red deer, an elk. Then when they actually ran into animals related to the Old World elk, they adopted an Indian name and called them moose. The Spanish called the puma or cougar a *leon,* or lion, and the jaguar a *tigre,* or tiger. They were as vague about the appearance of an Asiatic tiger as the British pioneers were about the appearance of the Scandinavian elk. Actually it would have made much more sense to call the jaguar a leopard, as superficially he is a large spotted cat which looks much like the leopard of Africa and Asia.

The principal superficial difference between the Old World leopard and the New World jaguar is that the jaguar tends to be a blockier animal with a shorter tail, and he does not carry his tail in an upcurve as does the leopard. It is also my impression that the leopard has a hide of richer gold and that the Mexican jaguar is more of a creamy-buff. The spots along the back of a jaguar hide are solid black and form a dark, broken line along the spine. Along the sides the spots, which are really in the shape of broken rosettes, often have a central dot.

Over his enormous range—from southern Texas and southern Arizona to northern Patagonia toward the tip of South America—the jaguar appears in wide variations of size and color. The jaguars of northern Mexico are the smallest and brightest. Those of central South America the largest and the dullest. The skin of a medium-size jaguar sent me by a friend in Brazil looks about like the hides of the Mexican cats I have seen except that it is not quite so bright. Two subspecies of the Mexican jaguar are recognized—*hernandesii,* from near Mazatlan on the west coast of Mexico, and *goldmani,* from the state of Campeche on the Yucatan peninsula.

Responding to Dale Lee's seductive calls on the hollowed-out cow horn, the big male *tigre* boldly swam to within 40 yards of the boat.

The famous cat-hunting Lee brothers of Tucson, Arizona, probably have had more experience with jaguars than any other Americans. They write me that in northern Mexico the jaguars weigh about the same as Southwestern lions. The average male weighs about 120 pounds. The Lees say they caught several large males in Mexico that weighed 140 to 150 pounds, and the largest they have ever taken in Mexico weighed 162 pounds. It was brought to bay in the mountains of Sinaloa near the town of San Ignacio. The female Mexican jaguars, the Lees say, run a good deal smaller and average about 80 pounds. The largest one they ever got weighed 90 pounds.

At one time, the jaguar was common in southern Texas, and apparently there were a few in southern California when the first Americans arrived. James O. Pattie, the famous mountain man and beaver trapper, reported seeing one on the lower Colorado River in Arizona back in the eighteen thirties.

The jaguar likes damper country, thicker brush, and less rocky areas than the mountain lion, but restless old male *tigres* are likely to be found anywhere. Every few years some lion hunter in southern Arizona catches a far-wandering *tigre*. Not long ago a jaguar was killed in southern Arizona not far north of the Mexican border. Several have been seen or killed in the immediate neighborhood of Tucson, in the Rincon, Santa Catalina, and Santa Rita mountains. There is a record of one killed at 7,000-feet elevation on the South Rim of the Grand Canyon in northern Arizona. There is also a record of a family of jaguars seen in the mountains of the Mojave Desert of Southern California, and living on mountain sheep.

Walking into the sacristy, the brother was attacked and instantly killed by the panic-stricken cat.

In 1955 a *tigre* was killed near the southern tip of the San Pedro Martir range in Lower California. It was an old male. To get where he was he had traveled across the deserts of northern Sonora and southwestern Arizona, had crossed the Colorado River, and had then wandered south a hundred miles on the peninsula of Lower California.

Jaguars are not naturally desert animals, but I know of several that have shown up in one of North America's driest deserts—that of northwestern Sonora. One stayed for about two months in the Sierra Picu, a low but rugged range within sight of the Gulf of California. It was living on mule and whitetail deer for the most part, but occasionally it killed a cow. The *tigre* was seen a few times by *vaqueros,* and twice it was chased but not caught by packs of dogs.

Another wandering male *tigre* made its headquarters around a spring that wells up at low tide on the shore near where the mountains rise out of the sea south of Port Libertad, Sonora. He killed several mountain sheep in the rough hills within a few miles of the water, and was in turn chased and killed by the late Charlie Ren, who had scratched up a pack of dogs for the purpose from some Mexican ranch. I saw fresh *tigre* tracks at the spring one time, but never saw the *tigre*.

I hunted whitetail deer on many occasions about 125 miles south of the border at the point where the Purgatorio River comes out of the mountains. A Mexican named Manuel Parades from whom I used to rent saddle horses showed me the skin of a *tigre*. He told me that his javelina dogs cornered the big cat and that he had waded in and beat it to death with a club. Manuel had an extensive arsenal, but he was chronically out of ammunition. When I went down I used to take him cartridges for his .30/30, his .32/20, and also for an old 7.62 mm. Russian Army rifle of mysterious origin.

*Tigres* found far away from regularly inhabited *tigre* country are always old males, probably decadent animals that have been run out of some favored hunting country by younger and stronger rivals. I do not believe I have ever heard of a female being killed in the northwest Sonora desert or in southern Arizona.

Some Mexicans in *tigre* country tell me that the home range of the mature male is very small, and that the average *tigre* lives and dies within a radius of 5 or 10 miles. They say they see the tracks of the same animals in the same area and are convinced that the big males drive rivals out. Females, they say, will wander between areas. Dale Lee does not agree with this. He says that several big *tigres* will use the same area in Mexico. In South America, however, he says that one big male will rule a large area inhabited by several females and perhaps two or three immature males. The big one, however, is the boss.

Like the mountain lion, the jaguar is almost entirely nocturnal. During the day he lies up in his brushy lair and does not come out to hunt until nightfall. Deer are everywhere the preferred prey of the mountain lion, but the *tigre* is more catholic in his taste. He will kill deer, but in some areas he is almost exclusively a killer of javelinas. In country where game is scarce, he is a great cattle killer, but he also will eat monkeys, tapirs, birds, fish, or about anything else.

The late Ernest Lee told me some years ago that in one area on the west coast of Mexico a *tigre* had become a man-eater and had killed about a dozen persons before he was followed up by dogs and shot. This is the only instance of a man-eating *tigre* that I have ever heard of, but I have heard vague stories of hunters being killed by wounded *tigres*.

A famous and well-authenticated story of a man-killing *tigre* comes from New Mexico. During the spring floods on the Rio Grande near Santa Fe in 1825, a *tigre* was driven from the flooded river bottom and took refuge in a monastery. A lay brother blundered into it in the sacristy and was immediately killed. Another man who heard the cries of the first rushed to his rescue and was also quickly killed. Shortly after the *tigre* killed another man in the sacristy and a fourth in an adjoining room. The *tigre* was not killed until someone bored a hole through the door and fired through it.

In this case, the jaguar was undoubtedly panic-stricken by the flood and felt himself trapped within the monastery. In his terror he killed blindly.

The *tigre* is a tougher, more truculent, and courageous creature than the mountain lion. In my chapter on the mountain lion I told how one was treed in Arizona by a little white dog about the size of a jackrabbit. This would never happen with a *tigre*. He would give such a dog one belt with his paw and that would be that. As I have told previously, my one attempt to chase a *tigre* with dogs resulted in the quick death of the only two in the pack that had any courage. Back in the late nineteen thirties or early nineteen forties, Ernest Lee had two famous and wonderful cat hounds for which he had been offered 1,500 dollars each. He turned down the offer, and on his next trip to Mexico both dogs were killed by the same *tigre*. One reason a *tigre* hunt is expensive is that the wear and tear on dogs is pretty grim, and many more are lost when hunting mountain lions. Apparently the *tigre* does not climb as well as the lion, and it generally comes to bay against rocks or in a thicket.

A guide I know had two Americans on a *tigre* hunt in Sinaloa. The dudes were middle-aged and well upholstered, and were very cautious horsemen. The *tigre*, an old male, led them on a long, tough chase in heavy brush and through rough country. As a consequence, the Americans couldn't keep up with the dogs and the cat. The guide, however, by riding hard, fast, and recklessly managed to stay close to the dogs. He left a second guide to accompany the sportsmen. Several times the *tigre* bayed briefly, but when he got his wind back he beat off the dogs and ran again. Finally, however, he bayed on top of a pile of boulders. He was completely surrounded by dogs, and after some minutes the guide decided the cat would stay put.

The guide was off his horse with his .30/30 carbine in his hands. He was cold, hungry, weary, and hoped that before long the other guide would come up with the dudes so they could shoot the *tigre* and get it over with. Minutes passed. The *tigre* seemed reconciled to the situation, so the guide decided it would alleviate his miseries if he smoked a cigarette. He put his carbine between his knees, got out his tobacco and papers, and built himself a smoke. Just as he applied a match to it the *tigre* came barreling off the pile of rocks and right at him. He dropped his cigarette and grabbed the .30/30. With a shot from the hip he managed to break one of the *tigre's* front legs. The cat went down and the dogs jumped it. The *tigre* shook himself free and tore off on three legs with the howling dogs right behind him.

At that moment the other guide and the dudes rode up, and the *tigre* and the dogs came swarming right at them. The horses bolted and both dudes got thrown off. The crippled *tigre* came to bay again about half a mile away, and this time the dudes got up in time to shoot it. The main event over, the guide managed to get his smoke, but it was far from a dull morning.

There are many jaguars in Mexico but apparently there aren't many packs of good jaguar dogs, and many hunts are unsuccessful. One prominent hunter I know of went on five expeditions for jaguars before managing to get one.

But some hunters get lucky. One I knew spoke Spanish, and when he was driving down the west coast of Mexico he made it a point to stop in at villages and ranches and gossip about hunting conditions. At one ranch in Sinaloa, he saw that the *ranchero* had a pack of reasonably good-looking hounds and asked him if he hunted *tigre*. The *ranchero* said he did and, as a matter of fact, he was planning to go out and see if he could catch a cattle-killing *tigre* the next morning. The American went along and got a big male by nine o'clock.

One time when I was going into Mexico for a sheep and deer hunt near the Sonora coast, I ran into a couple of hunters from Cleveland who were going on a *tigre* hunt. As luck would have it I saw them again when I was coming out three weeks later. They had three *tigres*. The dogs, they told me, were almost worthless. After they had spent a couple of fruitless weeks, they decided one day to explore a cave they could see from the bottom of a valley. Both were amateur archeologists, and they suspected that the cave might at one time have been inhabited by Indians. They climbed to the entrance of it, went in with their flashlights, and suddenly found themselves in the presence of a female *tigre* and two large cubs. Luckily they had their rifles with them and they shot all three.

The mountain lion is such a quiet and furtive animal that one of the oldest arguments in North America is whether he ever makes a noise or not. No such doubt about the jaguar. Like the other big cats, the jaguar is a noisy animal. On many occasions I have heard the roaring of lions in Africa, and I have been in camps where lions could be heard every few minutes from dusk until dawn. In India I heard the ooom-ooom-ooom of tigers calling, and the sawing, coughing noise made by leopards. It has been a long time since I have heard the roar of a jaguar, but as I remember it, the sound is something like the last phase of the roar of a hunting lion.

Like the Indian tiger, the jaguar will answer a call. The big cats can be located by calling, and one of the ways they are hunted is by calling them up at night and then turning dogs loose on their fresh tracks at daylight. Jaguar hunters generally use a cow's horn to give volume to their calls.

On a recent scouting trip to Bolivia, Dale Lee received three answers to his first call, and within half an hour he had a big male *tigre* swim to within 40 yards of the boat from which he had been calling. He says this area along the Yapacani River is the best *tigre* country he has ever seen, and that he was up to his ears in the great cats. Sometimes he'd have three and four *tigres* roaring and coming to his call at the same time, and once in the daytime a big male came within 20 feet of him on an open sand bar.

This calling-up method has been used on tigers with some success in India, and José Simoes, the famous white hunter of Portuguese East Africa, used it to hunt lions. I have never heard of its use in East Africa. In that area lions are usually taken by putting up a bait and then stalking the bait at dawn the next day. As reverse of that, however, I got my last lion in Southern Tanganyika, not by calling but by going to the roars.

Incidentally, in parts of South America, jaguars are incredibly plentiful. In 1952, the Lee brothers, hunting in Venezuela, got twenty-seven of the big cats in thirty days.

In northern Mexico, the young *tigres* are born in midsummer. Litters are generally two, sometimes three, rarely four. The gestation period is about one hundred days, so that would make the breeding period come in the spring. The male takes no part in the rearing of the young. The females are good and zealous mothers, and, from what those who live in jaguar country tell me, it is as dangerous for anyone to blunder between a female and her young as it is to run afoul of a grizzly sow.

One of these days I am going to have to finish the job that Ignacio and I started forty years ago and catch myself a *tigre*. Oddly, I have taken lion, tiger, leopard, and one not very impressive cougar. My never having shot a jaguar leaves a gap in my collection of the world's great cats. And it is quite a gap, since the jaguar is not only one of the world's largest cats, but it is one of the rarest in trophy rooms.

# The Natural History of the Jaguar

[FELIS ONCA]

**DESCRIPTION**

The jaguar is a big, spotted cat with a barrel-like body, a large, rounded head with low ears, and a short face with large, yellow eyes placed well forward. The coat of the typical species varies from shades of clear golden-yellow to tawny, depending on whether its home is the open woods of the arid, tropical upland country or the humid lowlands of the dense jungles. The black spots on its velvety fur are formed like rosettes—dark, broken circles with yellow centers containing one or two black dots—tending toward solid black lines on the throat and chest. Against its natural background of yellow light and shifting shadows, the jaguar defies visual detection until it moves.

Not all jaguars have spots shaped in the rosette pattern. Some have solid or ring-shaped spots similar to the leopard's, while other forms are black with barely visible markings and are called panthers.

The jaguar has a moderately long, thin tail, more heavily marked with black than its back. Its short, muscular legs terminate in large, rounded paws, with five toes on the forefeet and four on the hind, all armed with claws nearly an inch long. The claws are strongly curved, sharply pointed, and retractile. They can be instantly extended or retracted by powerful flexor muscles. As in all cats, the fingers and toes of the jaguar have been lengthened to raise the animal off the ground for faster speed and it walks digitigrade fashion on the tips of its toes.

Among the most specialized of the flesh-eaters, the jaguar has sacrificed its crushing molar teeth for the more formidable weapons suited for killing and cutting flesh. The short jaws are powered by strong cantilever massiter muscles so they can open excessively wide and snap shut with force. They are armed toward the front with sharp, piercing canine teeth and carnassial, or notched shearing teeth, which have knife-like edges specially suited for cutting tough muscle and sinew. The surface of its tongue is rough and rasp-like, coated with numerous fine, horny points directed backward for scraping. By merely licking the skin of a victim, the cat's tongue can erase the surface and cause it to bleed.

The jaguar is the largest, heaviest, and most powerful of all the American cats. Full-grown males range from 6 to 9 feet long, stand from 25 to 30 inches at the shoulder, and generally weigh between 100 and 160 pounds or more. Some of the South American forms are considerably larger, weighing 300 pounds, occasionally equalling the size of a small Asian tiger. Females are about 25 per cent smaller than males.

## ORIGIN

The jaguar is of South American origin but in recent times has moved north as far as southern Texas, New Mexico, and Arizona. The cat family *Felidae* can be traced back in geologic time to the common ancestors of all the *Carnivora,* the Creodonts of the Tertiary. Ancestral forms of the cats include the earliest true flesh-eaters, among them the *Dinictis* of the Oligocene and *Pseudaeclurus* of the Miocene, but the true modern cats *Felis* are not known to have existed before the Pliocene or Pleistocene eras.

## RANGE

The present range of the jaguar in the United States is restricted to the southern parts of Texas, New Mexico, and Arizona. In the past it was known to occur as far north as the Grand Canyon. Its distribution today extends southward through Mexico, Central America, and in South America as far south as central Argentina. The jaguar is found in its greatest abundance in the hot, humid forests bordering the lakes and rivers of tropical South America. Except during the breeding season, the jaguar travels alone and has a home territory of about 10 or 12 square miles. It favors the humid tropical lowland forests, but it also ranges into the arid upland wooded regions up to 8,000 feet and the broken jungle along the seacoast.

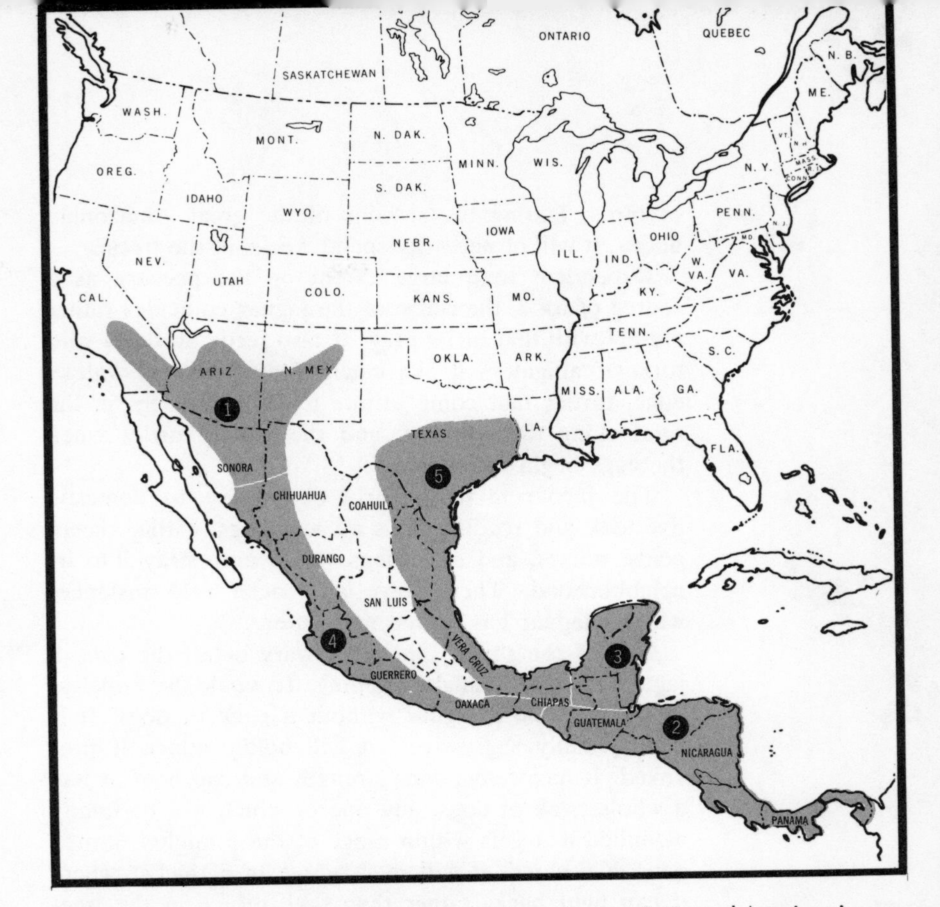

Distribution of the races of the jaguar *Felis:* 1. Arizona jaguar, 2. Central American jaguar, 3. Yucatan jaguar, 4. Pacific Coast jaguar, 5. Gulf Coast jaguar.

There are five named forms of jaguars (*Felis onca*) found north of the Panama Canal: The Arizona jaguar, native to Arizona, Sonora, and New Mexico, is an arid country form, pale buff in color with rosettes broken into spots. The Central American jaguar ranges from Colombia through Panama to Costa Rica, Honduras, and Salvador. It is a small jaguar with well-marked rosettes. The Yucatan jaguar, found in the Yucatan Peninsula, has an intense and bold color pattern. The black rosettes are very sharply set off from the golden-yellow background. The Pacific Coast jaguar, occupying a narrow strip along the Pacific Coast from Oaxaca to Sonora, has black rosettes that are so broken they are barely perceptible. The Gulf Coast jaguar frequents the forests bordering the Gulf of Mexico from southern Veracruz north to central Texas.

## HABITS

The jaguar is endowed with sight especially adapted for dim light. It also has a sharp sense of hearing and a reasonably good sense of smell. Like most cats it has a well-developed sense of touch and, by using its whiskers, can feel its way around in total darkness. Thus the cat does most of its hunting on the ground at night; occasionally it will climb trees after sleeping monkeys

or birds. During the seasons of the great Amazonian floods, it will of necessity spend weeks in the trees.

Dependent to a large extent on the peccary as a source of food, the range of the jaguar coincides rather closely with that of its prey. It also feeds on deer, wild turkeys, alligators it can catch away from the water's edge, turtles that come ashore to lay their eggs in the sand along the seacoast, and the young turtles when the eggs begin to hatch.

The jaguar is particularly destructive to domestic livestock and readily preys on any hogs, cattle, sheep, goats, horses, and even dogs which may stray into its neighborhood. There have also been rare instances when a jaguar has turned man-eater.

One of the shyest and most wary of all the cats, a jaguar is rarely caught napping. It would be hopeless to try and find a jaguar without a pack of dogs. It is not normally aggressive but will boldly attack if provoked. It has tremendous strength and can hold at bay a whole pack of dogs, any one of which will be fatally wounded if it gets within range of those mighty, armed paws. Cornered, it will seek refuge in a thicket where it can fight back, rather than take refuge in the treetops. The jaguar has a curious nature and will, for no apparent reason, follow a human being at a safe distance without any malicious intent.

## LOCOMOTION

Though not as fast as the cougar, the jaguar can muster enough speed in its first quick rush to overtake a deer. It travels mostly under cover of darkness and walks silently through the forest. It may spring at its prey from ambush but is more apt to charge with a series of short, quick bounds. Unlike most cats, the jaguar does not have an aversion to water. It swims well and may cross lakes and rivers for better hunting on the other side.

## TRACKS

The tracks left by a jaguar are larger than a cougar's, but otherwise are much the same. They consist of impressions made by the wide central pad, which is rounded in front, and the four oval toe pads, which are widely and evenly spaced forward of the central pad. The tracks left by the hind feet are smaller than those of the forefeet and the toe pads are closer together and more directly in front of the wide central pad. The tracks of the front paws are from 4¾ to 6 inches wide, while those of the hind feet are only 3 to 4 inches wide. The thumb or toe on the forefeet, bearing a large claw, is higher than the other four and does not touch the ground. The claws, though often an inch long, are carried in a sheath when the cat is walking and never show in the tracks. The jaguar has a fairly long stride—about 20 inches—and when the animal walks along, the hind foot almost always falls into the impression left by the forefoot.

## VOCAL

The call of the jaguar is a hoarse cough made up of a repetition of guttural notes sounding like uh-uh-uh-uh. The jaguar, like the African lion and the Indian tiger, has the hyoid appendages in the throat adjusted to utter deep guttural calls of great volume and therefore is unable to purr like a house cat. For this reason some authors have placed the four big cats—jaguar, leopard, lion, and tiger—in a separate subgenus called *Panthera*.

## MATING AND EARLY DEVELOPMENT

There is no fixed breeding season for the jaguar. Females probably breed once every second or third year. In the northern part of their ranges most jaguars mate in the early spring and the young are born about one hundred days later, in a nest scraped out in a dense thicket, or near the mouth of a cave. There are usually two kittens in a litter but there may be as many as four. At first their eyes are tightly closed and their bodies are covered with rather long, coarse fur marked with large, black spots instead of rosettes. The jaguar kittens progress slowly and it is two years before they are old enough to feed themselves. There is reason enough to believe that the male is a permanent member of the jaguar family and helps to keep his progeny supplied with food. He is not, however, allowed in the nursery while the kittens are small. The kittens are fully weaned when two years old and have a life expectancy of about fifteen years.

### Popular and Scientific Names of the Jaguar

**ORDER:** *Carnivora*

**FAMILY:** *Felidae*

**GENUS:** *Felis*

**SPECIES:** *onca*

**SUBSPECIES**

| | |
|---|---|
| Arizona jaguar | *Felis onca arizonensis* |
| Central American jaguar | *Felis onca centralis* |
| Yucatan jaguar | *Felis onca goldmani* |
| Pacific Coast jaguar | *Felis onca hernandesii* |
| Gulf Coast jaguar | *Felis onca veraecrucis* |

The jaguar leaves a staggered line of tracks with the hind foot registering behind the forefoot. The small, rounded toe pads form a curved row in front of the large heel pad, and the retracted claws do not show.

CHAPTER 14

# THE BLACK BEAR

IF THE black bear were as aggressive and ferocious a beast as he is often made out to be, it would hardly be safe to take a walk in the woods. This fearful reputation of all bears may be a dim racial memory of the days when our cave-dwelling ancestors battled with the cave bear of ice-age Europe—or it all may have started with the nursery tale of Goldilocks and the Three Bears. But for whatever reason, the average American looks upon the black bear as a formidable monster indeed. The situation of the bear hunting the bear hunter is a favorite cliché of the cartoonists, one that's as popular as the desert-island situation, the cannibals and their cooking pot, or the psychoanalyst and his couch.

The beginner who goes bear hunting generally is convinced that he's taking his life in his hands. I'm constantly surprised at how many letters I get asking me for advice on what sort of handgun a bear hunter should carry in addition to his rifle in order to make a last-ditch defense of his life in case he is attacked. This interest of sportsmen in bears is never ending; there is hardly such a thing as a poor bear story.

The size of the black bear is as much exaggerated as his ferocity. In reality, the average black bear is a shy, timid, eternally wary fellow who seldom weighs much over 200 pounds. In most areas, he's so shy that he is almost as difficult to see unassisted by dogs as is a mountain lion. One whiff of human scent will generally send the black bear off like a sçared rabbit, and he'd always rather run than fight.

And running has paid off for the black. He is found today from Alaska to Pennsylvania and from Maine to Arizona, and in many areas he is surprisingly plentiful. He has learned to cope with man and to survive, whereas the larger, more courageous, and more truculent grizzly is almost extinct in the United States, except for Alaska. The black bear, by his craft and wisdom, has conferred a priceless boon on the American hunter as his presence in many areas lends spice to hunting that would not otherwise be there. The chances of a hunter's being mauled by a black bear are about the same as his being struck by a meteor, but if he thinks he is afield in the haunts of a dangerous and mysterious monster, those woods will hold an excitement and magic for him that would under other circumstances be missing.

I'll never forget my first black bear. I was hunting deer and turkeys in the White Mountain area of Arizona when, early in the morning, I lucked onto one. He was rooting around for piñon nuts under a tree. I had the wind on him and had happened to approach without making a sound, as I'd been walking on soft pine needles.

That was the first wild bear I'd ever seen. For a moment I could hardly believe my eyes, and when it dawned on me that it actually was a real, live bear, my heart almost jumped out of my mouth. Shaking violently, I raised my rifle to shoot offhand, but in that condition I couldn't have hit a barn. A few feet in front of me lay the trunk of a long-dead pine. I wobbled over to it, my breath snorting so that it's a wonder the bear didn't hear me. I got down behind the trunk, laid my left hand on it, and put the fore-end of my .30/06 on my hand. I was still shaking, but gradually I cooled off, and the sight of the gold bead bright against the black bear's glossy hide steadied me. Finally I had calmed down to the extent that I felt it safe to shoot. I managed to squeeze the trigger, and the bear collapsed.

That was, I believe, the most violent attack of buck fever I have ever had—and I've suffered plenty from the malady. It's a wonder I didn't shake the fillings out of my teeth. When I got back to camp with the bear hide hours later, greasy, bloody, and dirty, chilled from excitement and exertion, I knew exactly how St. George felt when he killed the dragon, or how Stanley Ketchell must have felt when he had Jack Johnson briefly on the ropes. Since that magic day, I have shot my share of black bears, but never has one of them given me the thrill my first did. I was convinced that I'd taken a great chance and that if my bullet hadn't gone right, I would have been torn to bleeding fragments. When I related my adventure, I told my rapt listeners that my bear weighed 500 pounds. Later I was to realize that it probably weighed less than 200, and that its size had been exaggerated by my panicky eyes and jittery nerves.

Fear of bears is something that is apparently deeply atavistic in the human being. Many years ago I served on a naval vessel that had a black bear as a pet. My first night aboard, I hadn't been assigned a pair of hooks for my hammock, so I spread the hammock on the topside in the lee of a gun turret and went to sleep. Along about three a.m., I was dimly conscious that someone had moved in with me—someone that was very large and extraordinarily warm. Irritated by his effrontery, I put my hand out to push him away. He was large and hairy, and when I touched him he woofed. I shot out of that bed like a bullet, went below, and dressed. If that bear wanted my hammock, I was no one to argue.

The black bear is an entirely different animal from the American grizzly and the various Old World members of the genus *Ursus.* He has no near relatives in the Old World. His scientific name is *Euarctos americanus.* The average black bear is much smaller than the average grizzly. He doesn't have the shoulder hump characteristic of the grizzly, the brown bear, and the European bears. Nor does he have the grizzly's concave profile. The grizzly's claws are long and fairly straight. Those of the black are short and curved. He can climb a tree, whereas a mature grizzly cannot.

Most black bears are jet black, whereas the darkest grizzlies and brown bears are a medium to dark brown and never really black with the shiny stove-polish black of the black bear. One mysterious "black" bear, the so-called Kermode bear, has been called a subspecies of the black. It was formerly found on Gribble Island off the British Columbia coast, but now—according to reports—most have been seen on a neighboring island. It has also been reported that black sows have been seen with a white cub and a black cub, and white sows with black cubs. In that case, the Kermode is not a subspecies, but simply a rare and local color phase of the black. The taking of bears of this type is now illegal, I understand. Incidentally, snow-white "black" bears have also been reported from the mainland. There is a chance that these are albinos, which the Kermode bears are not. The *emmonsii,* or rare glacier bear, is a silver-tipped sort of blue-gray. In some areas, the "blacks" are mostly brown; in others the famous "cinnamon bear," which is a real blond, is common. The blond and brown bears are simply color phases of the blacks, and not separate species as some would believe. I have seen old sows with two cubs, one blond and the other brunette.

One time back in the nineteen twenties, an amigo and I went on a bear hunt on the Navajo reservation in the Four Corners country, where Arizona, Utah, New Mexico, and Colorado come together. There were many piñon trees that furnished rich, oily nuts for bear food in the area, and likewise many Navajo sheep. In addition, the bear is a sacred animal to the Navajo. The combination of plentiful food, good cover, and an absence of hunting resulted in tame and plentiful bears. Now progress has come to this wild and lonely country. Oil and uranium have been found there, and members of this generation of Navajos are undoubtedly far less superstitious than their fathers. What has happened to the bears I do not know.

But in those days, it was possible to see bears every day, and at night they would come into camp to steal ham and bacon. My companion and I rented horses from a Navajo who spoke some English. We split up, and about an hour out of camp before the sun was much more than over the mesas, I rode up to the rim of a canyon and got off to look around.

Almost at once I saw a bear on a wide bench below me. He was sniffing around, feeding on the piñon nuts that were plentiful that year. I sat down, waited until he was broadside, and shot him with a 150-grain .30/06 bullet right behind the shoulder. The sound of the shot echoed and re-echoed through the canyon, and before the noise had died down, another bear came hell-bent around a bend on the same bench, and headed in my direction. I piled him up within 50 feet of the first. One was the regulation brunette, but the other was almost as blond as Marilyn Monroe. The two bears were about the same size, and I doubt if either weighed over 200 pounds.

I'm not the speediest bear skinner in the world, and it was mid-afternoon before I had peeled the two hides off. I planned to put them on my horse and lead him back to camp. He was nervous anyway because of my revolting white-man smell, but the smell of blood and bears drove the horse crazy. I left the hides in a tree, and finally—by leading the horse well away—I calmed him down enough to get on him and ride to camp. When I got there I found that Bill, my companion, had likewise shot two bears and said he'd seen seven. The next day, the Indian and I led a burro over and got the hides. The philosophical little jackass took the bear smell in his stride.

I saw more bears in that Navajo country than in any other place I've ever hunted except along the shore of the Alaska mainland south of Juneau, and one time in a low, semiarid little range in northern Mexico. On that trip in the Navajo country, we saw as many brown and blond bears as we did blacks—perhaps more. The light-colored bears range all the way from a straw tan to a deep, dark chestnut. The lightest of them are sometimes called "silk" bears or "sun" bears. Sometimes they have straw-colored bodies but chocolate-colored faces and legs. For whatever the reason, light-colored blacks of all sorts are much more common in the West than in the East.

Like the blond and brown-black bears of the West, the glacier or "blue" bear is likewise a color phase, and the blue cubs are found in the same litter with black ones. They are found in the area along the Alaska coast from the Lynn Canal to Cape St. Elias, a region of great ice fields. I have seen only one hide, that of a small one.

How large does a black bear become? If my memory serves me right, I have shot sixteen black bears, and I have been in on the kill of about that many more. I am quite certain that none of them

Attacked unprovoked as he was cutting a trail, Wesley Brown split the black bear's skull with his ax.

would weigh over 300 pounds, and probably most of them would go much closer to 200 than to 300. There's a tendency to exaggerate the weight of bears. I have seen pictures published in newspapers and magazines of 500-, 600-, and even 800-pound black bears that I'm convinced would not have weighed over 300.

There is one report of a 900-pound black bear killed in 1921 by a Biological Survey hunter in Arizona. I do not believe it, particularly as about that time the same organization reported killing a mountain lion that weighed 300 pounds. I have never seen a black bear as large as a medium-size male grizzly, and the idea of a black bear the size of an enormous grizzly or a good big brown bear is simply fantastic. So, I might add, is the idea of a cougar as large as a heavy African lioness. Not one large grizzly in 100 would weigh 900 pounds.

But the fact that I have never killed a very large black bear doesn't mean that there is no such thing. Some years ago Andy Russel, Alberta guide, photographer, and writer, sent me a photo of a big male black he'd shot one spring. I have forgotten whether Andy had weighed it or not, but it was a perfectly tremendous bear and as large as many grizzlies. Another big black that was supposed to be nine feet long and to have weighed 633 pounds is supposed to have been killed in Pennsylvania. From ear tip to ear tip, this monster was supposed to have measured 19 inches. That's another bear story I do not believe, any more than I'd believe it if someone told me he knew a man 12 feet tall.

On the wall of my study, I have the mounted head of a large Alaska brown bear. When it was killed, the bear measured less than nine feet along the curves from the tip of the nose to the end of the tail. The mounted head is a fearsome thing. Children scream when they see it, and strong men turn pale. From ear tip to ear tip it measures 17 inches. An extremely large grizzly will measure about 8½ feet, and some may even measure 9, but the grizzly and the black bear are very different animals.

There is no doubt, though, that a black bear can put on a lot of lard under special circumstances. Twice I have seen black bears so fat that the hair was worn off their bellies from rubbing against down timber and stones. One was a garbage-fed bear in the Jasper National Park in Alberta, and the other was a bear shot during a good piñon year in northern Arizona.

Weights of many game animals are a source of endless arguments. The evidence doesn't remain long, because the carcass is perishable. Hides can be stretched. Sheep, deer, and antelope have horns that remain to be measured and which cannot be exaggerated—if they are measured by a neutral observer. The only thing about a bear that will do for argument-free records is the skull. Let's make some comparisons. The world-record brown-bear skull measures 17 15/16 inches long by 12 13/16 inches wide. The record grizzly skull measures 16 10/16 by 10. The record polar-bear skull 17 13/16 by 10 15/16. The record black (shot in Wisconsin in 1953, incidentally) measures 13 3/16 inches long by 8 12/16 inches wide (see "Biggest Black Bear Ever," *Outdoor Life,* April, 1958). Since the size of the skull is reasonably indicative of the size of the whole animal, I believe I can be forgiven for being skeptical about stories of 900-pound black bears, 9 feet long, and 19 inches from ear tip to ear tip. And while we're on the subject of large black bears, the records of skull size tend to show that on the average the bears grow somewhat larger in the West than they do in the East. Of the first ten listed in the latest edition of *Records of North American Big Game,* one is from Nova Scotia, one from Pennsylvania, and all the others from the Western or Midwestern states or Alaska.

The black bear is a creature of great adaptability, as shown by his enormous range. He is found from subarctic Alaska and the Yukon to the mountains of central Mexico, from the dry hills of Sonora and Chihuahua to the dripping rain forests of the Alaska panhandle. I once shot a black bear right at timberline and at an altitude of about 10,500 feet, and I shot another one that rolled into the salt sea. Generally the black is a creature of the forests, but if he has to, he can get along with pretty sketchy cover. He likes a country that produces nuts and berries, but he can, if he has to, get along with few of those.

A black is as omnivorous as a raccoon; there isn't much he won't eat. He will devour carrion, roots, berries, nuts. He will kill domestic sheep, raid pigpens and beehives, eat chocolate bars, garbage, fish. He will kill and devour the young of big game animals—even full-grown deer and elk. On the other hand, he does not disdain the lowly grub, grass, mice, green corn, or watermelons. For the most part, though, he is a vegetarian to a much greater extent than the more carnivorous grizzly, but anything edible is to the black an opportunity. Once, at the time the mule-deer fawns were dropping, I watched a black bear for almost an hour; if he wasn't trying to find a bedded fawn, I don't know what he was doing. Apparently there was a fawn close by, as a doe that was watching him was about to lose her mind. He never found the fawn, but it wasn't because he didn't try.

The bear is a skilled, bold, and resourceful thief, particularly after dark. Every fall in Idaho, where I live, the black bears steal many quarters of deer and elk, make away with hunters' groceries, and scare the wits out of many honest hunters. The havoc a bear can create in a trapper's cabin or with his cache is proverbial. Sheepmen hold no love for bears, and neither do those who have tried to raise hogs or keep bees in thickly inhabited bear country.

As the black will eat anything, it is an exceedingly wary and spooky animal, and is much more nocturnal than the grizzly. He is a very hard creature to exterminate, even when every hand is turned against him. For many years in most Western states, the law gave him no protection at all. He could be hunted twelve months of the year, chased with dogs, trapped. In many areas there was even a bounty on his head. Most Western states are run by sheepmen and cattlemen, and those who raise livestock do not love bears and generally exaggerate the damage they do, particularly to cattle.

Yet, over much of the West, the black bear is still relatively plentiful; in many areas he is increasing. Give him food and cover, and he'll pretty well take care of himself. The old and thickly settled state of Pennsylvania has good black-bear hunting and a substantial annual kill. Many are shot each year all through New York state's Adirondack Mountains, and black bears have been shot right in the city limits of Vancouver, British Columbia.

The black's eyes are poor, although it seems to me that he sees better than a grizzly. His nose is one of the best in nature, and he has ears like a bat. He is one of the most difficult of all animals to encounter in the woods, and a man might stillhunt for black bears for a lifetime and never see one. I know many persons who have spent their lives in black-bear country without having seen one that wasn't put up by dogs.

I'm no smarter and no more virtuous than anyone else, but for some reason I have blundered into a good many bears, generally when I wasn't hunting them. I still have a moldy old .30/06 that was my lucky bear rifle. Its second barrel is pretty well shot out. The stock is held together with a bolt and glue because a horse once rolled down a hill on it, and the scope is an obsolete German job most modern sportsmen have never heard of. But for years it brought me luck. Somehow, if I had that musket in my hands, I'd see bear.

Once I was hunting deer and turkeys in Arizona's Mogollon Rim country. It was windy that day, and for an hour or so I had occasionally heard hounds, and had made a mental note that someone was running a bear or lion. I was sitting down wondering what to do next when my startled eyes made out a black bear running as if the devil were after him and approaching at an angle and not much more than 100 yards away. I grabbed the .30/06 and shot the bear by pure reflex. He had hardly hit the ground when about a dozen hounds came tearing around a point and swarmed all over the bear. In about five minutes three of the maddest hunters you ever saw showed up, and for a little while I thought they were going to shoot me instead of the bear. I apologized, and we parted friends.

Park bears sometimes rip into tourists' locked cars to get at food.

I remember another odd-ball bear I shot. I was hunting in the Yukon in a fine grizzly country where there were very few blacks. A guide, a pal, and I were moving a jack camp to be nearer to a sheep mountain, and we were sitting on the bank of a creek boiling tea and eating sandwiches. Suddenly my horse snorted; I could see he was watching something in the woods across the creek. Through my binoculars I made out the head of a black bear looking at us from the other side of a log. I picked up my rifle and shot it right in the forehead.

In the West anyway, the surest way to get a bear is to run one with dogs and put it up a tree. I have been on hunts where dogs were used, but I have shot only one bear that had been treed by a dog. That was pure accident. I was coming back from a sheep hunt in Alberta and was almost back to the railroad when the camp dog tore into a patch of bushes by the trail and ran out an old sow and two cubs almost as big as she was. I plunked the sow as she ran, and then nailed a cub that had climbed a tree.

A fat black bear soon plays out and takes to a tree when run by hounds, but a thin one will travel longer, faster, and harder than a mountain lion and will give any pack of hounds a run for their money. Once I went on a hunt in some semiarid hills in northern Mexico. My host had a pack of mongrel dogs that he used to hunt javelinas for their hides. Those dogs put up several bears. I don't think one of them would have weighed much over 150 pounds. They had little heads and small bodies, but tremendously long legs. They were all skinny and could run like greyhounds. The dogs never did tree one, and actually the bears could run faster than the dogs. By putting down a barrage on them, we managed to knock over a couple. But as it happened we were together each time, and no one ever knew who hit what.

I wouldn't say for sure, but I think I have probably shot my last black bear. A man can use only so many bear trophies, and if I bring home any more bear meat I think my wife will take after me with a rolling pin.

Actually bear meat can be pretty good. It depends on the individual bear. In 1946, when I was hunting Stone sheep around the heads of the Muskwa and Prophet Rivers in northern British Columbia, my companion shot a young black that had got fat on berries. Our cook roasted a ham, and it was about as good a piece of roast as I've ever eaten. Another very fine chunk of bear meat I devoured was from a piñon-fattened bear in northern Arizona. Bear fat is useful for cooking, and it is also excellent for waterproofing shoes. However, bear fat will go right through leather, as those who waterproof their saddle-bags with it find out when they find their lunch sandwiches saturated. A thin bear, a fish-fed bear, or a carrion-eating bear is no good on the table.

Most of the opposition to bear meat as well as the Indian taboos against eating bears arise, I believe, from the appearance of a skinned bear carcass. It looks like the naked body of some poor derelict laid out on the slab at the morgue, and the sight of it will give a sensitive person the creeps. Our pioneer ancestors thought highly of bear meat, cooked with bear fat, slept on bear hides, and considered smoked bear hams a great delicacy. If we wishy-washy moderns gag at devouring bear, it's because we are made of less stern stuff.

Is a black bear ever dangerous? Only rarely. Around twenty years ago, the northern British Columbia guide and outfitter, Wesley Brown, was cutting trail at the head of a packstring when he happened to notice a large black bear off in the timber nearby. He paid no attention to it, expecting it to flee. Suddenly he was aware that the bear was coming at him, full of fight. He split its skull with an ax just as Edgar Dopp, another guide, shot it with a revolver. That is the only case of an unprovoked attack by a black bear in recent years that I can think of offhand.

In the early years of this century, a lumber-camp cook was killed in Canada by a black bear. Unprovoked, the bear swam a river, came right at the cook and two other men, chased them, and killed the cook. Another Canadian, years ago, was killed by a black bear with a head and muzzle full of porcupine quills, and evidently mad with pain.

Generally, if anyone has trouble with a wild black bear, it's with a wounded one or a mother bear with cubs. Back in the nineteen forties a man in Wyoming got in trouble with a small female black over cubs. Whether he was trying to take a cub or whether she thought he was, I don't know. At any rate the mother bear took after the man. She chewed him up a bit, but he managed to kill her with a club. At least that's the tale as I heard it in Jackson.

A park bear that's protected and has lost all fear of man is another thing. At any Western national park, it's routine to see people feeding bears right under signs that say, "Do Not Feed The Bears." Black bears are powerful creatures with sharp teeth and claws, and they panic easily. Some years ago a woman tourist was feeding a black bear in a park. She thought it was cute when the bear would stand up and rest its paws on her shoulders while she fed it. Then something frightened the bear. As it jerked away, its claws caught in her clothing and tore off one of her breasts.

Bold park bears are great pests. Many a tourist in Yellowstone has left his food in a locked sedan to wake up in the morning and find that bears have just about torn his car to pieces to get at it.

Some years ago a couple of hunters I know were camped near Sycamore Canyon in Arizona. They had a little sheepherder's tent, and when they went out to hunt they left their food in it. Returning about dusk, one of the hunters was astonished to see the rear end of a large black bear protruding from the door. He didn't want to shoot the bear in the hind end or to kill him in the tent, so he yelled to scare it out. The bear took off suddenly, draped in the tent and scattering grub, bedrolls, and spare clothing in every direction. The hunter opened up on the galloping tent, but bear and tent disappeared together. The hunters had brought a horse in by trailer to pack their deer out with. It was hobbled and peacefully grazing in a grassy mountain meadow about a quarter of a mile from the camp. The sight of the galloping tent unnerved the horse and it also took off. The hunter said he had no idea that a hobbled horse could move so fast. He finally retrieved the tent, the worse for wear and with several bullet holes in it, but he didn't find the horse until the next day. The sleeping bags were torn and covered with honey, broken eggs, and flour. All in all it wasn't a very successful hunt, and those chaps have been distinctly against anything that has to do with bears ever since.

Black bears become sexually mature when they are about three years old, and they mate in late June or early July. The young are born in January when the mother is in hibernation. When first born, the cubs are about the size of large rats, blind, and almost naked, but when the mother comes out of the den they are cute and recognizable little cubs. Litters run from one to four with two being the most common. A female black will produce young until she is about twenty years old and live to be twenty-five or more. Generally a sow will breed every other year. She is a good mother, and the survival rate of cubs is high.

Man is the principal enemy of the black bear, but it is also killed by the larger and stronger grizzly. Blacks are deathly afraid of their big cousins; where you see many grizzlies, you see few blacks. In 1943 when I was hunting around the Big Smoky in Alberta, my companion and I saw thirty-three grizzlies, but only one black. On several hunts in the Yukon I have seen many grizzlies, but only one black bear. There are no black bears on Admiralty Island in Alaska, as it is heavily populated by the giant browns. I have heard that wolves and mountain lions will attack black bears, but I have never run into a case where this has happened.

The darndest concentration of black bears I have ever seen was along the Alaska coast south of Juneau in 1956. In spite of days of pouring rain, I saw many bears every day I hunted, and my companion and I shot three bears within a half-mile radius in two days. As is the case with the grizzly, the black is easiest to get without dogs early in the spring when he's moving around restlessly and eating grass. Blacks are also hunted regularly and quite successfully by putting out horse baits.

Any gun editor gets a lot of questions about bear rifles. My notion is that black bears are little if any harder to kill than a deer, and that a rifle suitable for deer in a particular area is also good bear medicine. The .30/30 is entirely adequate for black bears under ordinary circumstances, and with proper bullets a .30/06 or .270 will almost always kill a bear in its tracks with a well-placed shot. I have killed more bears with a .30/06 than with anything else. Of those I have shot, I can think offhand of only three that moved more than 20 feet after they were hit. One that was hit with a 220-grain .30/06 bullet right through the heart ran about 50 yards before it collapsed. Another hit with the same kind of bullet started up a hill, fell, and rolled down. Another that was hit too far back—just forward of the diaphragm —with a .270 ran 100 yards, crawled into a windfall, and needed another bullet. The black is smaller than the grizzly and has always struck me as being much easier to kill and also easier to kill than an elk or a white goat.

Any way you look at it, the black bear is a fine game animal and one worth saving. With a little help, he'll save himself. If he and the whitetail deer ever become extinct, we might as well kiss big game hunting good-by.

# The Natural History of the Black Bear

[EUARCTOS AMERICANUS]

## DESCRIPTION

The inquisitive, intelligent American black bear (*Euarctos*) is medium in size for the bear family. Average weight for full-grown individuals varies between 200 and 300 pounds. Very large males may even tip the scales at more than 500 pounds, but this is exceptional. The head and body length varies from 4½ to 6½ feet; at the shoulder adult black bears stand from 25 to 40 inches. Females or sows are, on an average, 20 per cent smaller than males. The black bear has a straight profile, pointed head, small dark eyes, large erect hairy ears, and a very short bobtail. The outline of the back is straight and not humped at the shoulders like a grizzly.

The long soft fur of the typical black bear is uniform jet black broken only by the brownish muzzle and sometimes by a splash of white on the chest. Color phases and geographical variations do occur, usually on the western half of the continent, that vary from black through various shades of rusty-brown to pale-cinnamon, blue-gray or pure-white.

The forefeet of the black bear are armed with short, narrow, strongly curved, black, non-retractile claws; those on the hind feet are similar to those on the forefeet but not so strongly curved.

Scats or droppings of the black bear are usually about an inch in diameter and an inch or two in length; they may consist of tightly packed hair but more often grasses, root fibers, hard casings of beetles, ants, seeds of fruits, berries, shells, and casings of nuts.

## ORIGIN

The American black bear is a distinct kind of bear restricted to the North American continent and some of the neighboring islands such as Newfoundland and Vancouver. It first appeared on this continent during the Pleistocene period about half a million or more years ago and has continued down to the present time in numbers that far exceed those of any other kind of bear anywhere in the world. The earliest known true bears, however, lived in Europe some ten million years earlier during the Pliocene period.

## RANGE

From northern Alaska, Hudson Bay, and northern Labrador south through all of Canada, the United States and south to northern Mexico was once black bear country, wherever there were forests or cover, from the Atlantic coast west to the Pacific Ocean and from sea level to the limit of tree growth on the mountain peaks. Civilization has pushed back its range from populated areas but due to its nocturnal life and secretive habits, the black bear has continued in limited numbers over much of its former range.

The black bears of North America are separable into eighteen regional groups or recognized named forms. The typical black bear (*Euarctos americanus*) has the widest range and is the best known. Each of the other forms listed differ from each other in various specific characters. In some instances the differences would be apparent only to the zoologist. Others are, however, quite distinct. The Florida, or Everglades, black bear is one of the largest. It may weigh from 500 to 600 pounds and is wholly black. The opposite extreme is the Kermode bear, a very small, pure-white bear found on islands and coastal regions of British Columbia. The most handsome of the black bears is the Glacier, or Blue, bear, restricted to the glacier regions of the St. Elias Alps and southeast to Glacier Bay. It is a comparatively small race with a beautiful blue-gray pelt in typical specimens. The prevailing color in the Cinnamon bear is reddish-brown or yellowish-brown. Other species that vary in shades of color between cinnamon and black with different characteristics are: Olympic black bear, New Mexico black bear, California black bear, Queen Charlotte black bear, East Mexico black bear, Newfoundland black bear, Mackenzie black bear, Louisiana black bear, West Mexico black bear, Kenai black bear, Dall black bear, Yukon black bear, Vancouver black bear.

Some authors may consider the various named forms as local variations or color phases of the typical black bear *Euarctus americanus*. They are, however, recognized and listed as valid in the latest check list of black bears published by the Smithsonian Institution.

**HABITS**

Having no fixed abode and being a habitual nomad, when the black bear is tired it lies down to rest in a quickly scooped-out depression, wherever it happens to be. It does, however, have a home territory varying from 10 to 15 miles in diameter. Its travels are governed largely by the food supply; when there is an abundance of berries on a hillside one bear may use the same nest two or three times in succession before moving on. Several bears may congregate together where there is a bountiful harvest but they are attracted by the food and not for a social gathering.

One of the black bear's outstanding characteristics is its curiosity. It will investigate anything and everything it cannot understand. Things left hidden away in the north country will surely be investigated and ripped apart by a black bear. Leave a canoe out in the open and the chances are that you will find it intact on your return. To hide it in the treetops is to insure its destruction; somewhere in that canoe there must be food or why hide it, is the bear's philosophy.

Although a member of the great order *Carnivora,* or flesh-eating mammals, as indicated by its long, pointed canine teeth (shown in the illustration of a black bear skull), the black bear is more vegetarian than flesh-eater. Its back or molar teeth have broad crushing surfaces, well suited for milling an omnivorous diet. Almost anything edible is food for the black bear, but it prefers the easy way of making a living rather than the arduous job of hunting big game. Furthermore, it is too slow and clumsy to catch large animals.

When the black bear leaves its winter den in the early spring, its first impulse is to take a long drink of cool water. Still carrying a liberal coat of fat, the bear now feeds sparingly on various kinds of grasses, sedges and the juicy inner bark of pine and fir trees torn from the trunks of trees by the powerful canine teeth. A little later its diet is varied with the bulbous roots of various flowering plants that are dug up with the bear's strong hooked claws. The bursting fat buds of low trees and shrubs are also eaten with relish. As spring advances, logs are turned over, anthills ripped open for larvae and ants that are drawn into the bear's mouth by means of the long, pink flexible tongue. Occasionally a kid or fawn may fall an easy victim to the now hungry black bear, but such instances are rare. A newborn deer has no telltale scent to betray its presence and the sight of the black bear is rather poor. By the time the summer comes around and the berries begin to ripen our black bear feeds incessantly on manzanita berries, buffalo berries, wild cherries, raspberries, blueberries, and many other kinds in season. In the fall it fills its belly with acorns, beechnuts, and chestnuts by climbing into the trees and shaking the fruit down to the ground. It also pilfers the store of pine and fir seeds carefully gathered by the hard-working squirrels. Birds' nests are robbed for eggs and nestlings on the ground and in the tops of tall trees. The black bear also feeds on mice, larvae of wasps, hornets, and is especially fond of honey. It digs out ground squirrels and fat woodchucks; occasionally a black bear will become a habitual killer of sheep, goats, and calves.

By late fall when the cold weather begins to make itself felt, the black bear has converted its sumptuous feast into surplus fat which encases its body. This is the way a bear builds up a storage of food and energy that will be used during the lean months ahead spent in deep slumber beneath a blanket of protective snow. Wise and fastidious bears are particular about their winter quarters, which may be under a stone ledge, a cave in the rocks, a hollow tree stump, or even a self-excavated den underground. Usually a southern exposure is selected and the cold winds blowing from the north pile the snow deep over the den, making it snug and warm. Lazy and shiftless bears make little or no provision for winter quarters and pass the winter shivering uncomfortably in a thicket.

As the cold increases the bear becomes more drowsy and slumbers off into a deep, prolonged sleep which usually lasts until April or May. This winter sleep, though deep, is not so profound as that of a wood-

The black bear's large, powerful canine teeth and low, flat-crowned molars are suitable for the animal's omnivorous diet.

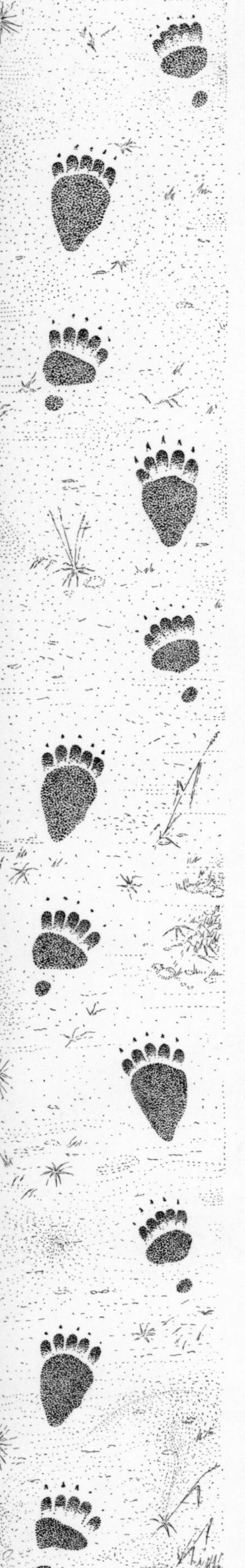

chuck that actually hibernates. Breathing and temperature remain normal. Very little provocation is needed to bring the bear back to life for the protection of its den from undesirable intruders. No food is eaten for several days before entering the winter den. The actual date of winter retirement depends on local conditions. In the northern parts of the black bear's range, the period of inactivity may extend from October until May; in the northern tier of the United States it is usually from November until April, while in Florida the bear may retire for only a week or a few days at a time.

## MATING

Life for the black bear begins once again in the spring when it comes out of the winter den. Once out, it does not return to the den until fall. When leaving the den, the bear is nearly as fat as it was the day in the fall when it went to sleep. Very little of its fat is used up during the months of inactivity. Forage in the early days of spring is scanty and the surplus fat is soon used up. The adult male and female show not the slightest interest in each other until some time in the early summer. During the mating season, however, there is a considerable amount of affection displayed between the sexes and males may fight fierce battles for possession of females, but it is all soon over. In less than one month the honeymoon is ended and forgotten. Males and females have gone their separate ways. For the next two years the female will not tolerate any attention from the opposite sex.

## BIRTH AND EARLY DEVELOPMENT

In January or February of the year after mating, the expectant female gives birth to her family. This would place the period of pregnancy at between seven and eight months. Development of the embryo is delayed, perhaps for one or two months, which may in part explain the extremely small size of the newborn bear cubs. They come into the world during the mother's "twilight sleep" in a winter den under a blanket of snow. The nursery is a soft couch of pine needles, dry grass and leaves. The first-born is a solitary cub but the number may be increased in later years to as many as four. At birth the cubs are tiny in comparison to the size of the mother, who may weigh between 200 and 300 pounds; each cub will weigh from 6 to 10 ounces and measure no more than 8 or 9 inches in length. Naked, blind, toothless, with tiny undeveloped ears, the cubs somehow manage to scramble under their own power to the mother's feeding stations.

In the first forty days of life the little sleepy bears grow black, downy coats and at the end of that period open their eyes for the first time and cut their first teeth. At that time they weigh about 2 pounds each and measure a foot in length. In April or early in May, the mother bear, fully awake, leads her family out into the warm sunshine. The cubs weigh about 4 pounds each when they leave the winter den. Life now begins for

The black bear's tracks reveal that it places its hind foot slightly forward of its front foot on the same side. As in all bears, the big toe is on the outer side.

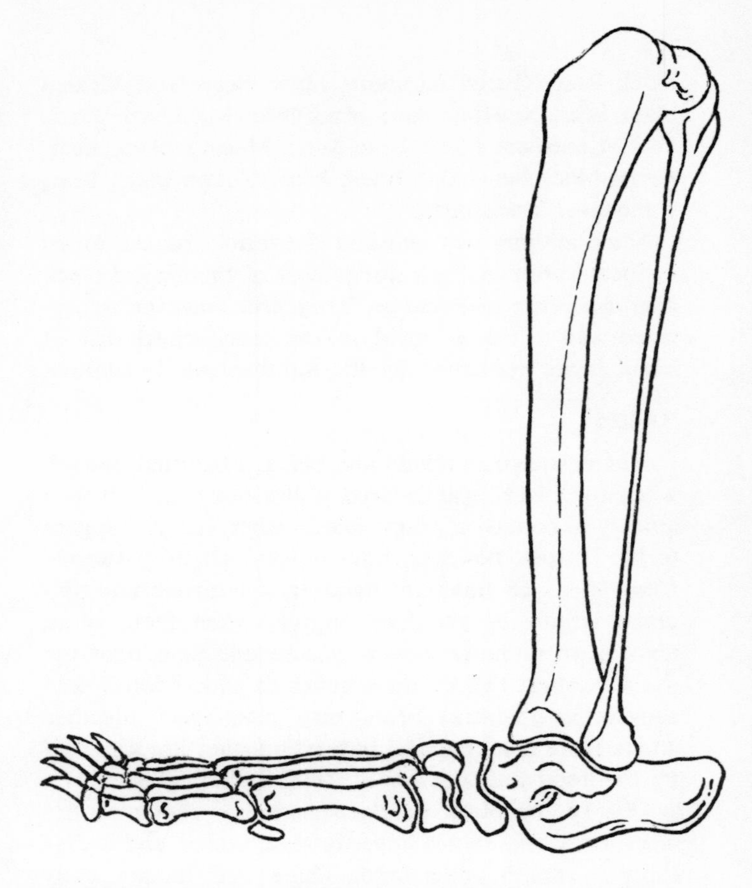

The black bear's foot lies flat on the ground from the tip of the toes to the heel. This is a primitive foot not adapted for fast travel.

the cubs and the mother must give them a liberal education; she is tolerant and sympathetic but a cub who persistently disobeys gets a swift cuff from the mother's paw. First the cubs must be taught to climb, and they soon learn to scramble up a large tree at the first sign of danger and to stay there until the mother gives her permission for them to come down to earth. The cubs love to frolic and wrestle and when tired may climb on the mother's back to steal a ride. By fall the cubs will weigh about 40 pounds each and must prepare for the long winter sleep. They may all crowd into one den with the mother or make separate dens in a group. By the following spring the cubs, now well grown, are old enough to hunt and forage for themselves. Family ties, however, are not entirely broken until the mother shows her willingness to accept the attentions of another male. Young bears are not sexually mature until three years of age, when they seek out mates of their own. A healthy female may bear young every other year until she is eighteen or twenty years old and often lives to the grand old age of twenty-five years.

## LOCOMOTION

Flat-footed, the black bear walks on the soles of its feet; this manner of travel is known as plantigrade, shown in the illustration of the bones in the foot of the black bear. The palms of its hands are also laid flat on the ground. Undisturbed, a black bear ambles along at a speed of 2 or 3 miles per hour, but frightened or in a charge it can muster a speed of 25 miles per hour and keep it up for a considerable distance.

The black bear is a first-rate climber and goes up a tree at a fast rate. It is a hand-over-hand action more like that of a school boy than of a squirrel, and it backs down the same way. Very young bears are more agile and do run up a tree in a squirrel-like fashion. The first lesson that the baby black bear has to learn is how to climb a tree. There does not seem to be a reason why this bear should be so proficient as a tree climber; to collect a few birds' eggs and nuts in season is not reason enough; perhaps it was the only safe retreat from the grizzly, its only natural enemy. A first-class swimmer, the black bear will cross swift rivers and lakes five miles across.

## TRACKS

Footprints or tracks of the black bear left in soft mud or sand are not altogether unlike those of a human being. There is one unmistakable distinction: the large toe on the hind and forefeet of a bear is on the outside and not on the inner side as is the great toe and thumb in man. A black bear makes a double row of tracks, one on each side of a given center line. Each track left by a bear represents an imprint of the naked pads on the soles of its feet with claw marks sometimes indicated. The footprint of the forefoot is shorter and rounder than that of the hind foot, about 4½ inches wide and 5 inches long. The impression left by the hind foot is 4 inches wide and 7 inches long. A bear leads with its right forefoot and brings the left hind foot forward at about the same time; the left fore and right hind feet now move forward. The hind foot comes down 3½ inches in front of the impression left by the forefoot on the same side of the center line; there is a space or distance stride of 11 inches between the back of the forefoot and the front of the hind foot, producing an overall effect of a staggered line of double prints, hind and fore right, hind and fore left.

## VOCAL

Most wild animals go their separate ways in silence without uttering a sound and the black bear is no exception. In fact, it does not even have a mating call or a cry of the chase. A mother bear may make a few grunts of pleasure or a growl of disapproval to her young and a bear in pain can utter a loud, bloodcurdling bawl that is almost human. Cubs separated from their mother for some time will often whimper.

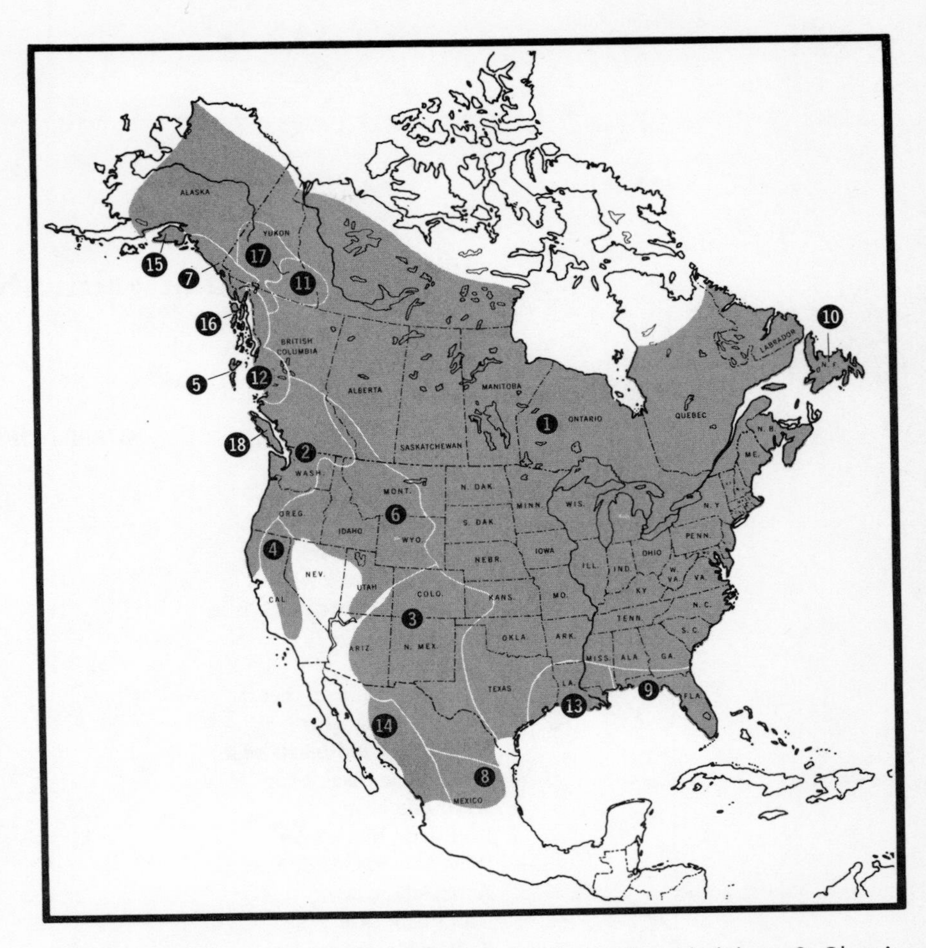


Distribution of the races of the black bear *Euarctos:* 1. American black bear, 2. Olympic black bear, 3. New Mexico black bear, 4. California black bear, 5. Queen Charlotte black bear, 6. Cinnamon bear, 7. Glacier bear, 8. East Mexico black bear, 9. Florida black bear, 10. Newfoundland black bear, 11. Mackenzie black bear, 12. Kermode bear, 13. Louisiana black bear, 14. West Mexico black bear, 15. Kenai black bear, 16. Dall black bear. 17. Yukon black bear, 18. Vancouver black bear.

## REACTIONS TO MAN

Inquisitive, intelligent, the black bear is not considered one of the dangerous animals, though it is not to be trusted implicitly. Pokerfaced, the black bear never reveals its feelings or intentions beforehand. Ninety-nine times out of a hundred, black bears will make a hasty retreat in the forest at the approach of man; when one gives a short, rasping cough it is time to take notice—this one is different and about to charge. A black bear can be trained and is smart enough to put up a good show for tidbits it expects to receive from spectators touring in zoos and national parks, but it can never be truly tamed or trusted. There are rare instances where a black bear has made unprovoked attacks on man, but it is more apt to carry off a small child than a full-grown man.

## Popular and Scientific Names of the Black Bear

**ORDER:** *Carnivora*

**FAMILY:** *Ursidae*

**GENUS:** *Euarctos*

**SPECIES:** *americanus*

**SUBSPECIES**

| | |
|---|---|
| American black bear | *Euarctos americanus americanus* |
| Olympic black bear | *Euarctos americanus altifrontalis* |
| New Mexico black bear | *Euarctos americanus amblyceps* |
| California black bear | *Euarctos americanus californiensis* |
| Queen Charlotte black bear | *Euarctos americanus carlottae* |
| Cinnamon bear | *Euarctos americanus cinnamomum* |
| Glacier bear | *Euarctos americanus emmonsii* |
| East Mexico black bear | *Euarctos americanus eremicus* |
| Florida black bear | *Euarctos americanus floridanus* |
| Newfoundland black bear | *Euarctos americanus hamiltoni* |
| Mackenzie black bear | *Euarctos americanus hunteri* |
| Kermode bear | *Euarctos americanus kermodei* |
| Louisiana black bear | *Euarctos americanus luteolus* |
| West Mexico black bear | *Euarctos americanus machetes* |
| Kenai black bear | *Euarctos americanus perniger* |
| Dall black bear | *Euarctos americanus pugnax* |
| Yukon black bear | *Euarctos americanus randi* |
| Vancouver black bear | *Euarctos americanus vancouveri* |

CHAPTER 15

# THE GRIZZLY BEAR

AMERICANS first encountered the grizzly bear when they ventured across the Mississippi River to the buffalo plains and into the Rocky Mountains early in the nineteenth century. They were shocked to discover that he was an entirely different creature from the shy and timid black bear of the Eastern woods.

Not only was the grizzly much larger than the black, but he was also a much more formidable animal. He was the king of the plains and mountains, afraid of nobody. Those other predators—the coyote, the wolf, and the mountain lion—he held in contempt, and he paid little attention to the Indians armed with their bows and spears. He was equally unafraid of white men, and was just as willing to take a kill away from a beaver trapper or an explorer as he was to take it away from an Indian.

Lewis and Clark, the famous trail blazers who opened up the West, were afraid of grizzlies and wrote that they'd rather face half a dozen hostile Indians than one of the big bears. The beaver trappers found them difficult to kill with their small-caliber, muzzle-loading Kentucky rifles, and demanded more power. The result was the heavy, large-caliber plains rifle such as the Hawken. They called the grizzly the gray bear, the white bear, the grizzled bear, and later—with respect and almost affection—"the grizzly." Later he was sometimes called the "grisly" or horrible bear, and that is his scientific name—*Ursus horribilis*.

A century ago the grizzly was found from northern Sonora and Chihuahua in Mexico to the Barren Grounds of the Arctic and from timberline and above in the highest mountains, to the open plains, tidal flats, and even along the rivers in the arid Southwest. California was famous for its very large and truculent grizzlies. In fact, a big bear of the species appears on California's state seal. As late as 1885, one hunter near Bakersfield, California, saw fourteen grizzlies in the foothills in one day. Years ago in Caborca, Sonora, a fine old Mexican who in his youth had been a smuggler told me that grizzlies were once very common in the river valleys of the Sonora and southern Arizona desert, and that they preyed constantly on herds of cattle.

But in the United States today grizzlies are just about things of the past. They're long extinct in the plains states where they once preyed on the great herds of buffalo, and the great California grizzly is only a memory. The last grizzlies were killed in Arizona along in the early nineteen twenties. There are a few in the isolated mountains of Chihuahua, and perhaps some in Sonora. They're gone in Nevada, Oregon, and Utah. There may be a few along the Canadian border in Washington, and in Idaho a track is reported now and then, but I don't know anyone who has seen a grizzly there in recent years. A newspaper story in the spring of this year said one had recently been seen in New Mexico. The estimate is that only about 800 are left in the United States, and most of these are in Wyoming and Montana in the neighborhood of Yellowstone and Glacier National Parks.

The guess is that there are around ten thousand in Alaska, and grizzlies are fairly plentiful all through the Canadian Rockies and tributary ranges from the U.S.-Canada border to Alaska. In 1943, when Jack Holliday and I were hunting around the Smoky River of Alberta with Roy Hargreaves as our guide and outfitter, we saw between us thirty-three grizzlies in thirty days. Once in the Yukon, before there was a limit on grizzlies, I shot three on one trip.

The grizzly is a tough, truculent, formidable animal that doesn't get along well with civilization. He preys on cattle if he has an opportunity, just as he used to prey on the buffalo herds. On rare occasions he has even been a man-eater. Bert Riggall, pioneer Canadian guide and outfitter, tells how in the early days in the Rockies of southern Alberta the Stoney Indians were so decimated by smallpox that they simply were unable to bury their dead. The grizzlies got used to eating dead Indians, and then found they could enter the tepees and devour sick Indians. The next step was hunting and killing live and healthy Indians. When he first came to that country, Riggall says, the Stoneys were so afraid of man-eating bears that they'd deserted the area.

The American grizzly is so closely related to the big Alaska brown bear that it would be pretty difficult to say where one species leaves off and the other begins. For purposes of record keeping, any bear shot along the Alaska coast within 75 miles of tidewater and north of Frederick Sound is a brown bear. If he is shot in British Columbia and south of the Sound, he is a grizzly.

The grizzly is likewise related to the European and Asiatic brown bears of the genus *Ursus.* When I was hunting in the Zagros Mountains of Iran in 1955, I was surprised to find that the Persian brown bear looks like a dwarf grizzly. All these bears are characterized by a concave profile that is unmistakable, by claws much longer than those of the black bear, and by a shoulder hump. I don't see how anyone could ever mistake a black bear for one.

In coloration, grizzlies vary enormously, even in the same area. In my trophy room I have two grizzly hides, both from the White River area of the Yukon. One hide is mostly a light yellowish-brown. The other is a rich medium brown with light-tipped hairs giving it a grizzled appearance. The largest grizzly I ever shot was dark brown with many long, light-colored hairs along his back—a true "silvertip."

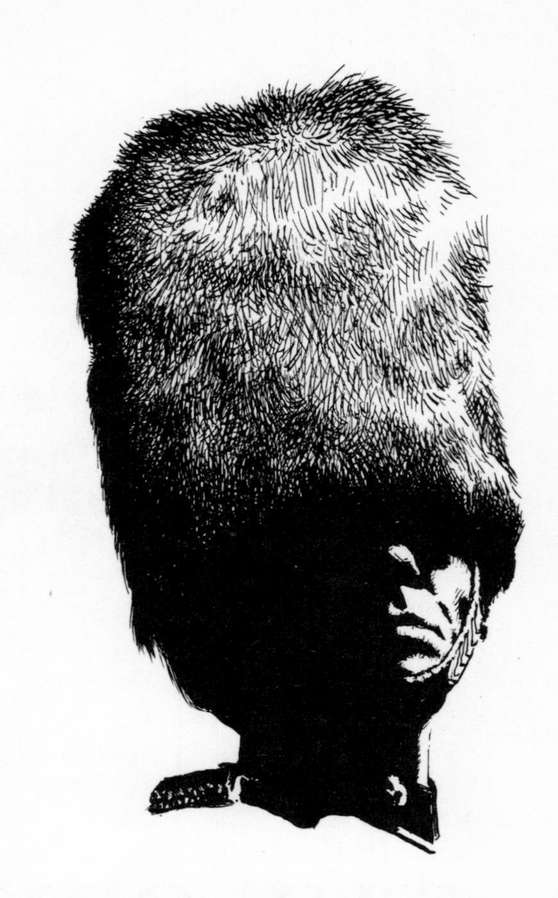

Many grizzly pelts were made into shakos for the British army.

I have heard of grizzlies so light in color that at a distance they appear white, but I have never seen one. On Admiralty Island most of the big browns are dark brown, but one female I saw shot by Lew Bulgrin was a typical silvertip. Now and then a grizzly will have a light-colored head and a dark body. These are the so-called bald-faced bears, and I have heard it argued that the grizzly, the silvertip, and the bald-faced bears are different species. This, of course, is not true. No grizzly is black in the sense that black bears are black, and their hair is much longer. I'll never forget the first grizzly I saw. It was walking along on the far side of a canyon, and as I watched it with binoculars its long hair rippled like a field of wheat in the wind.

How big is a grizzly? The average large bear will probably weigh around 500 pounds, although the very largest might go 800, and an enormously fat one in a zoo once weighed over 1,000. A grizzly hide that will square 8 feet 6 inches when spread out freshly skinned on the ground is enormous. The squared measurement of a hide, by the way, is taken this way: 1. Measure the length from tip of nose to tip of tail. 2. Then measure between the front paws. 3. Add the two measurements together. 4. Divide the total by two. A bear hide that measured 8 feet long and 6 feet wide, for example, would be said to square 7 feet.

The largest supposed grizzly I ever saw was shot in the northern Cassiar district of British Columbia, a collaboration between Vernon Speer, the bullet-maker, and the late Dr. E. G. Braddock. The bear was in its summer coat and the hide was poor, but it squared 9 feet. The bear was shot in grizzly country, but it was undoubtedly an Alaska brown or at least a bear from the coast, where the bears are considered to be browns rather than grizzlies. It was shot on the east side of the Coast Mountains but near a stream that cut through to the sea.

For many years the Hudson's Bay Company of Canada annually bought hundreds of grizzly skins to be made into the fur hats called shakos and worn by certain crack British regiments. Their records show that the largest hides came from the British Columbia coast south of the Alaska panhandle. The coastal grizzlies average a good deal larger than those found in the interior. It is a matter of food and hibernation. Along the west coast, winters are comparatively mild, and the bears are out longer, denned up less. They also have access to a plentiful supply of rich, nourishing salmon. In the interior, the grizzlies must seek their winter dens earlier, stay in them longer, and they have to scratch harder for food. Consequently they don't grow so large.

Any bear is omnivorous. The grizzly will devour just about anything, and his diet ranges from grubs to moose. It includes everything from grass to ground squirrels, from roots to berries, from carrion to the side of bacon in the trapper's cabin, and from salmon to skunk cabbage. In years when berries are plentiful, he feasts on the crop as long as it lasts, and his droppings look like the filling of a blueberry pie—something that has turned many hunters against blueberry pies. The grizzlies of the great plains followed the buffalo and lived largely on the herds, and no grizzly will turn down a piece of meat that offers itself.

A score of years ago in the Yukon, Bill Barthman of New York made movies of a pair of grizzlies stalking his Indian guide. The guide had extended his arms over his head so they would look like caribou antlers. The grizzlies, with their poor eyesight, were deceived and were making their stalk. I have been told by Indians and trappers that grizzlies kill great numbers of moose and caribou calves in the spring. When sheep and cattle first were brought into the West, the big bears feasted on them. In the Zagros Mountains of Iran it appeared to me that those small relatives of the grizzly—the Persian brown bears—must subsist largely on red sheep and ibex. I could see little else that appeared to be bear food.

The same grizzly that will kill a bull moose with one blow of his paw will spend half an hour digging out a gopher (Columbian ground squirrel) or a whistler (hoary marmot). Above timberline in squirrel country, the grizzlies will excavate large areas so that they look as if they'd been worked over by a steam shovel.

The smell of meat will bring a grizzly. One of the most popular ways to hunt grizzlies is to take a worn-out horse into the mountains, then shoot it and let it get high. The hunter conceals himself and watches, and eventually a bear will come to it. Many of the rhubarbs that natives of grizzly country get into with bears come over kills. An Indian shoots a moose, a bear smells the blood, and tries to drive the Indian off.

Twice I have had grizzlies come to me because they smelled blood. Once I'd shot a couple of bull caribou, and my Indian guide and I were starting to carry the heads out of a basin to our horses when a grizzly came rolling along upwind toward the kills. Another time I was carrying the meat and head of a fine Dall ram off of a Yukon mountain. My guide had gone ahead and I had stopped to change film in my camera. Suddenly I heard a growl behind me and was startled half out of my wits to see a grizzly about 30 yards uphill. Apparently I was the first man this wilderness bear had ever seen. He had smelled the sheep blood but had paid no attention to my man smell. Then when he'd got close, he thought I looked strange. He stopped and growled to see what would develop. Plenty did. My hair stood up so straight and stiff that it almost lifted my hat off. I dropped the sheep head, threw off the safety of my .30/06, and faced the bear. "Get out of here, you so-and-so!" I shouted. My yell was too much for the bear. The last I saw of him he was going over the next ridge at a dead run. The bear wanted no piece of me, nor I of him. I was cold and wet, and a little snow was falling. It was a long way to camp, and of all the things in the world I didn't want, one was a ruction with a grizzly. I was very lucky that time as I had no idea there was a bear within miles.

Once, a score of years ago, a native of the Yukon had shot a moose and was dressing it out. Suddenly he felt a tremendous blow on his backside, a blow that knocked him clear over the moose and 20 feet beyond. He scrambled to his feet and saw a grizzly running away. Apparently the bear had smelled the meat but not the hunter, and when he'd come up he thought the man was another bear. Just as he struck he got the man smell and fled.

The grizzly is a tough hombre. He and his cousins, the Alaska brown and the polar bear, are the only animals in North America that merit being called dangerous game. More people in North America have been killed or mauled by grizzlies than by any other animals. A few years ago a Montana hunter was killed by a wounded grizzly, and within the last year or two an Alaska hunter was killed by one. In the spring of 1957, one bear killed both a hunter and his guide. During the years when I was doing a lot of hunting in the Canadian Rockies and writing about bears, readers of *Outdoor Life* used to send me many newspaper clippings about killings and maulings by grizzlies. It is my guess that in Canada alone about a dozen people a year get into serious trouble with the big bears.

Compared with the hundreds of persons who are killed annually in India by tigers, and other hundreds that are killed in Africa by lions, this doesn't sound like much. It must be remembered, though, that both tigers and lions often live in heavily populated areas where they have many contacts with unarmed human beings. The grizzlies, on the other hand, live in thinly populated wilderness country, and the few people they meet are usually armed men. If grizzlies were plentiful in areas of great population, there would be plenty of trouble. In the national parks of Canada, I have been told, grizzlies are shot as soon as they start hanging around the garbage dumps where people congregate to watch the black bears. The authorities simply don't want the tourists chewed up.

Most people get into trouble with grizzlies by either wounding a bear and following it up, by encountering a bear on a kill, or by running into a female with cubs. Most of the trouble comes with wounded bears. However, now and then a bear will attack unprovoked.

A famous example is the experience of my guide and friend, Field Johnson, a Yukon Indian guide. One spring morning several years ago Field took his ancient and rusty .30/30 and went out from the village of Champagne to get himself a moose. He was slipping quietly along through the subarctic forest when suddenly a terrible blow knocked him down and wrenched his rifle out of his hand. The next thing he knew he was being mauled by a grizzly. He realized that the only thing for him to do was to feign death. He lay there. The bear, after batting him around and chewing on him tentatively, moved off. Presently Field heard him no more. He was in great pain, so finally he decided that he'd try to go back to the village.

But the bear had been lying quietly nearby watching him. As Field arose, the bear charged, knocked him flat once more, and began to maul him. This time Field lost consciousness. When he awakened he found that the grizzly had dragged him more than a mile, holding onto one foot, and had buried him in a shallow grave covered with brush and sod. Many hours had passed as it was then late afternoon. Field knew he had to get help or die, so he set off for the Alaska highway. One of his arms was broken, one foot and leg terribly lacerated, several ribs broken, and his scalp was hanging down over his eyes. He managed to make it to the highway, and got a ride into Whitehorse. Modern antibiotics and surgery saved his life, but the experience was too much for him and eventually he lost his mind.

When a grizzly makes a kill, or when he finds a choice piece of carrion that he cannot eat at one sitting, he will bury it and generally hang around nearby to look after it. His eyesight is poor and often he mistakes a man for another bear. A Yukon trapper I met was going into Burwash Landing on Kluane Lake one spring for cartridges and supplies when he stumbled onto a grizzly kill. The bear charged him in spite of his shouts, and he was lucky enough to kill it stone dead with the one cartridge he had in his .270.

A female grizzly who feels her cubs are threatened is likewise bad business. Some years ago a friend of mine and a companion were traveling with a packtrain when they chanced on a grizzly sow with a cub. By some trick of the wind she hadn't heard them, and the whole outfit came around a point and right on her. Apparently she thought she was surrounded. She took on the whole works. My friend was thrown from his horse and his arm broken, and the terrified packhorses were scattered all over the place. As I remember the story, someone finally managed to kill the bear, but it was quite a day.

Frank Golata, the famous Stone-sheep guide, told me this one. At one time he was guiding a tycoon for sheep and grizzly up around the head of the Prophet River in northern British Columbia. The packstring was winding along a trail beside a creek when someone spied a big grizzly rooting around on the steep hillside, about 250 yards above them. The tycoon decided that the grizzly was just the one he wanted, so he got off his horse, unlimbered—of all things—a .404 Jeffery, and took a shot at the grizzly. With both shoulders broken, the grizzly came rolling down the mountainside right into the midst of the packtrain. The terrified horses, squealing, bucking, and kicking, scattered in every direction. It took Golata and the wrangler until the next day to round them all up, and another day to gather the scattered gear and mend the broken pack boxes.

The grizzly is an animal of enormous power. It is said that in the days they preyed on buffalo, they could crush the skull of an adult bison with one blow of a paw. And my grandfather, who shot many grizzlies to protect his cattle when he pioneered in the mountains of New Mexico in the eighteen seventies and eighteen eighties, told me that a grizzly could kill a powerful range bull almost as easily as he could a rabbit. I once saw a small sow uproot a stump with one smooth, even pull. A grizzly digging for ground squirrels and marmots above timberline will move stones that would stagger a bulldozer. When a grizzly is skinned, its strangely manlike carcass shows one of the most magnificent sets of muscles in the animal kingdom—muscles that make a big lion or tiger look almost feminine.

The grizzly mates in mid-June in most areas, and young are born in midwinter when the sow is hibernating. They are tiny things when born, but they suckle the rest of the winter and emerge from the den in the spring as respectable looking little cubs. Generally two are born, but sometimes three, and rarely, four. When I was hunting brown bears on Admiralty Island, Alaska, in May, 1957, I saw a sow with four merry little cubs.

Males stay with the sows only during the rut. At other times the big males are solitary. Sows with families avoid them because the old bears will kill and eat their own young if they can. Sows breed every other year and the young stay with their mother until they're run off by a new lover when they are in their second year. Any time more than one bear is seen, they're almost surely a mother and her cubs. Often, however, several grizzlies can be seen at once—along a salmon stream, along a stretch of beach where they're eating sedge in the spring, or on a slide where they eat grass. Years ago around the head of Sheep Creek, a tributary of the Smoky in the Alberta Rockies, Roy Hargreaves and I could see five grizzlies at one time—a mother and two cubs above timberline in one direction, a lone bear of undeterminable sex in another, and below us in the timber an enormous bear turning over rotten logs to look for grubs.

A wounded grizzly charged at Dr. John Hammett just as he fired a shot from the hip. Then the bear was on him.

I lay no claim to being an expert grizzly hunter. I have made only one trip exclusively for bears, and that was to southern Alaska for a spring hunt. I shot a couple of the big browns and a couple of blacks. All of the grizzlies I've shot, helped to shoot, or have seen shot were by-products of general hunts for sheep, goats, moose, and caribou. In reality, that's a pretty good way to get a grizzly in the fall, as the big bears are then generally above timberline either working on berries or digging for gophers and marmots. A good, painstaking man with binoculars who spends a couple of weeks at and around timberline in sheep and goat country and who goes out early and comes in late is apt to see a grizzly. I have told how on one trip a companion and I saw thirty-three between us. That's a lot of bears for one hunt, and the answer is that the berry crop in the area had been excellent. On another trip I saw seven. On some, two or three, on others I have seen none.

Along the coast of British Columbia, grizzlies are hunted by going up the salmon streams in the fall and by trying to catch them along the tidal flats eating sedge in the spring when they first come out of their winter sleep. In the interior, the favorite ways to get them are to bait with dead horses or to watch for them to appear on grassy slides and then stalk them.

In wilderness areas where they've had little contact with man, grizzlies have never appeared to me to be very wary. They are the monarchs of the mountains and—except for men with rifles—there is nothing for them to be afraid of. They have good ears and very fine noses, but their eyes are poor. It has always struck me that as long as a hunter went quietly and kept the wind in his favor, they were easy to stalk. Once the late Johnny Johnson, a Yukon Indian guide, and I stalked a male grizzly in a big, open basin above timberline and finally shot it. The only precautions we took were to stay on one side of the bear so our scent would blow past him, and to remain stationary every time the bear turned our way.

If a hunter gets into trouble with a bear, it is almost invariably because of poor and hasty shooting. The only time one very thoroughly scared me was when I took a shot through a hole in the brush and didn't know what part of the bear I was aiming at. A wounded grizzly is bad medicine. He averages larger than either a lion or a tiger, and he is stronger. The famous African hunter and writer, F. C. Selous, came to North America for a couple of grizzly hunts and declared them to be tougher animals than African lions. Anyone hunting grizzlies should make certain never to fire the first shot unless he knows exactly where that bullet is going. Then he should shoot as long as the grizzly moves.

A Montana hunter who was killed by a grizzly a few years ago had wounded it with a hasty shot, and he and a companion followed it up. One of the hunters killed most recently in Alaska wounded the bear, but then couldn't stop the charge.

About ten years ago in the Yukon, Dr. John Hammett of New York followed up a wounded grizzly shot by a companion, and suddenly came upon it lying in some brush at short range. Recognition was mutual and the bear charged Hammett just as he fired a shot from the hip. Then he was knocked down by the blow of the great paw and the bear was on him and mauling him. I talked to Dr. Hammett not long after the incident, and he told me that at one point the bear had his hand in his mouth. Dr. Hammett is a surgeon and he said that he knew the bear would damage his hand so much that he'd never be able to operate again. As he lay there he wondered what specialty he could take up that didn't require the use of hands. His Indian guide ran up and killed the bear, and the two men had a good deal of trouble rolling the carcass off the doctor. Luck was with him that day. He was covered with the bear's blood, and one thigh was so bruised that Moose Johnson, the guide, said it was as black as his hat. Dr. Hammett's hand was skinned but not otherwise injured. His shot had broken the grizzly's jaw.

As I count up, I can remember shooting eight grizzlies, helping to shoot two, and being in on the death of two more. I have shot or helped to shoot eight with a .30/06, one with a .270 and one with a .300 Weatherby Magnum. Of the two I saw killed, one was downed with a .270 and one with a .300 H. & H. Magnum. Both of the allied Alaska brown bears I have killed were taken with a .375 Magnum. Of all these bears, only three were killed stone dead in their tracks with one shot—one with a 130-grain Silvertip bullet from a .270, one with the 180-grain Silvertip from a standard .300 H. & H., and the other with a 180-grain Remington Bronze Point bullet from a .300 Weatherby. Another grizzly (a large male) was hit twice with the tiny 41-grain bullet from a .22/250. The first shot blew up on a rib. The second slipped between two ribs and killed the bear in its tracks.

Of the two bears I've killed instantly with one shot, both were lung hits, one with the .270 and one with the .300 Magnum. The other one-shot kill by Red Earley was with a neck shot. About half the grizzlies that I've killed with the .30/06 and the 180-grain bullet have been hit the first time in the shoulder. They were knocked down and rendered helpless, but I continued to shoot as long as they showed life. My own notion is that a .30/06 is enough for a grizzly, but if anyone is happier with a .375 he should use it.

The best shot on a grizzly (or on any dangerous game animal) is the shoulder shot, preferably at an angle to break both shoulders. If one shoulder is broken, a large grizzly is generally helpless; if both are broken, it is absolutely helpless. Many experienced hunters like neck shots, but the vertebrae are easy to miss, and if they're missed far, the only result is a wounded bear. The lung shot is a good one, particularly if a high-speed, quick-opening bullet is used, but the lung shot cannot generally be counted on to kill instantly. I once shot a grizzly three times through the lungs at around 175 yards with a .30/06 before it went down and stayed. I then took another shot for luck. Above all, the hunter should see that his shots are well forward so he will avoid hitting the bear in the guts. It's the gut shot grizzly that kills people. Under most circumstances, head shots should be avoided; there's a lot of head to aim at but not much brain.

A hunter's first grizzly is one of the high points of his life. The hunter knows that he's shooting at an animal that can shoot back. Generally there's plenty of action. A hit almost anywhere will knock a bear down, but a wounded grizzly can go down and get up faster than anything I've ever seen.

I think I have probably shot my last grizzly. It's not that grizzly hunting bores me, but I've taken my share and will leave the others for someone else. The grizzly will be with us a long time in Canada, and he can be brought back in wilderness areas in the United States that are closed to cattle and sheep.

The last grizzly I got close to was also in the Yukon. I was hunting white sheep when my guide spied the bear digging for gophers about a mile away. We rode to within a quarter of a mile of the bear, and then made a quiet, easy stalk. We wound up on a ridge overlooking a little canyon, and the old boy wasn't more than 125 yards from us. He was a big male with a beautiful coat of long, silvered hair and a head that looked as wide as a bushel basket.

A couple of times I put the cross hairs right on his shoulder. All I had to do was to put a little pressure on the trigger and the 150-grain .270 bullet would knock him down. But I couldn't apply that pressure. I preferred to watch him work, and I bitterly regretted that I'd left my movie camera in camp.

"Why don't you shoot?" the guide whispered.

"I don't want to."

"Big bear," he said. "Pretty hide."

"I still don't want to," I told him.

So we quietly backed down the ridge and walked back to our horses preparing to hunt sheep again. But before I mounted, I watched the bear for a couple of minutes with my binoculars. He was still digging for gophers. I hoped he found a lot of them. I likewise hope he left a lot of descendants. To me a mountain with grizzlies on it is ten times as interesting as one without.

# The Natural History of the Grizzly Bear

[URSUS HORRIBILIS]

### DESCRIPTION

The grizzly has a massive, thick-set body with a distinct hump on its shoulders. Its huge head, with its broad muzzle, is supported by a short, muscular neck. Its forehead is strongly elevated above the face line, producing a somewhat concave profile, and its small, rounded ears are placed wide apart and well back on its head.

Although the grizzly is not as large as the Alaska brownie, it is a powerful bear. Males reach a head and body length of 6 to 8 feet, stand from 3 to 4 feet at the shoulder, and weigh from 500 to 750 pounds. Females are much smaller than males.

The grizzly's long, thick hair varies from dark brown to brown tipped with white, producing a grizzled effect. In some forms the color is pale yellowish-brown. The bear's long, narrow mouth is armed with sharp

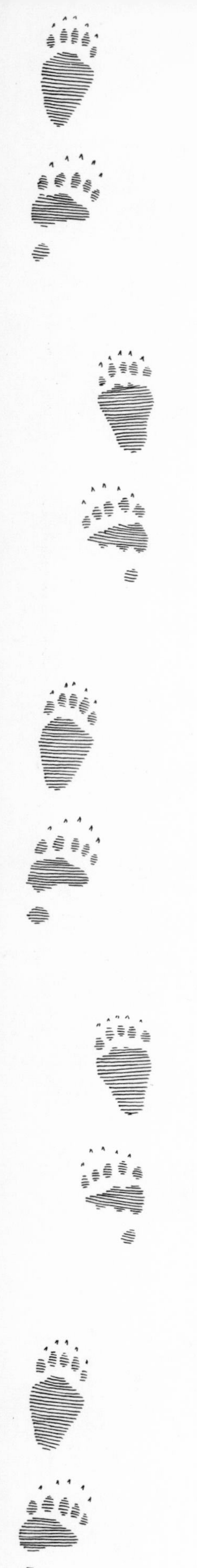

canine teeth and broad-crowned, crushing molars. Its jaws, powered by strong muscles, have enormous strength, but they cannot open as wide as, for instance, a cat's or a wolf's. Although the animal is a carnivore and feeds at times on big game and rodents, it also devours plants and vegetables.

**ORIGIN**

The grizzly is a member of the *Ursidae,* the most recent group of animals granted family rank, which first appeared in the Miocene period of Europe. Typical bears of the genus *Ursus,* such as the grizzly, appeared in the Lower Pliocene, spread across Asia and reached North America over the Alaska-Asiatic land bridge some time during the Pleistocene era. The bears were derived from canid stock, the most primitive of modern flesh-eaters. Grizzly bears were present in England at the time of the Roman invasion and were transported to Rome to combat the gladiators in the arena games.

**HABITS**

With the exception of the polar bear, the grizzly is the most carnivorous of the bears. Included among its victims are elk, moose, deer, bison, and sheep, usually the aged, sick, and dying. After feasting on a kill, the grizzly lugs the carcass away into the forest, covers it with sticks and leaves, and stays close by to protect the cache from robbers. With its strong claws the grizzly digs out of the earth quantities of ground squirrels, marmots, and mice. Nevertheless, as a hunter the grizzly cannot kill sufficient animal life to support its huge frame, and it must depend on vegetable matter for the major part of its sustenance.

In the early spring, when the animal comes out of its winter quarters, it takes a long drink of water and then, grazing like an ox in the upland meadows, proceeds to fill its belly with grasses and sedges. Later, it devours roots, tubers, and sprouting buds. It searches under rocks and down timber for ants and ant eggs, beetles, and insect larvae. When the many kinds of berries begin to ripen the grizzly is there to get its fill, and in the fall it feasts on nuts and acorns. Near the Pacific Coast, the grizzly knows just when the salmon begin to run up the rivers to spawn. The great bear strides into the swift-running river and with a mighty swipe of its paw sends a big salmon sailing onto the beach. It also thrusts its head under the water and frequently comes up with a fish impaled on its great fangs.

Some time in August, a wise grizzly in northern climes selects the place for its winter quarters and cleans out the chosen den. It may choose a natural cavern in the rocks, a hollow under the roots of a giant tree, or a self-excavated den on the mountainside with dry grasses or mosses on the floor and a southern exposure.

With the first days of really cold weather, the bear gets drowsy and, after fasting for a few days, retreats to its winter den, curls up into a ball, and slips off into a long, unbroken slumber which lasts until some time in April. When the snow falls, winds from the north pile the drifts deep on the den's south entrance and the bear's body heat keeps it snug and warm inside.

For some reason the grizzly makes its appearance before the winter is really over, apparently wanders over the snow and retreats to the den again until warmer weather comes. This winter sleep of the bear is not a state of hibernation. Its temperature and heart action are not greatly reduced. With very little provocation a bear will come to life in a remarkably short time.

The grizzly has a surprisingly well-developed sense of hearing and an unsurpassed sense of smell. It depends on the latter for guidance and for its livelihood. It has a narrow range of sight, due to the narrow placement of its eyes, but it can see moving objects at a considerable distance.

A grizzly usually does not attack without some provocation but its behavior is unpredictable. In the wild it will usually retreat if given sufficient warning, but surprised at close quarters a grizzly will charge. It is resentful of intruders in its domain. A female with cubs is always dangerous; to come between a bear and her cubs is to court certain disaster. It just is not safe to travel in grizzly-bear country without some kind of armed protection.

A full-grown grizzly can pick up and lug away into the hills the carcass of a big bull elk. With a single blow of its mighty paw, a grizzly can kill a horse or break the neck of an ox. When it roamed the Great Plains, the grizzly preyed regularly on bison. On one occasion a grizzly was seen to approach a group of four bull bison; singling out one at a time, it broke the animal's neck with a single stroke of its huge paw. The fourth bull was more alert and put up a brave battle, mortally wounding the bear with its sharp horns before it succumbed.

The grizzly bear may be a ferocious animal, but it also seems to have a sense of humor and playfulness. An observer tells of a grizzly, out of its winter quarters early, enjoying a slide on the packed snow of a mountainside. It would sit down, human fashion, wiggle to get started, then use its forepaws to put on the brakes. At the bottom of each slide the grizzly would roll head over heels in the snow, get up and survey his tracks, and climb to the top again for another coast.

**LOCOMOTION**

Despite its short legs, huge body, flat feet and great strength, the grizzly is surprisingly agile. Though built to travel at a seemingly careless walk, it can break into a bounding gallop that it can sustain for five miles over steep mountain slopes. On level ground a grizzly can travel at 30 miles per hour and can reach 35 in a charge. Almost as much at home in the water as on

The typical pattern of the grizzly's tracks is a staggered line with the hind foot track a little forward of the forefoot on the same side. Sometimes the hind foot is placed squarely in the forefoot track.

land, it is a strong swimmer and will cross swift rivers and lakes several miles wide.

### TRACKS

The trail left by a grizzly constitutes a double row of staggered tracks wider than a man can comfortably straddle. A bear always steps in the impressions left by its predecessor on the trail. Thus, a regularly used bear trail appears as a series of large, rounded holes in a staggered line. On soft mud or sandy soil the impression left by the hind foot is about 5½ inches wide and 10 inches long, the sole of the foot showing as a triangular pad narrowing at the heel, the rounded pads of the toes forming a slightly curved line in front. The small dots in front of the toe pads are made by the long, sharp nails. The imprint of the forefoot is shorter and slightly wider than the hind foot with the toes somewhat more widely separated. The length of the forefoot is about 5¼ inches. The great toe is always on the outer side of the paws and not on the inner side as in man. Walking on fresh ground, the bear brings its hind foot down a little farther forward of the impression left by the forefoot on the same side, but on a well-worn trail the hind foot falls exactly into the hole left by the forefoot. At a fast gallop the hind feet come down well in front of the forefeet and the space between the groups of tracks is about 50 inches, more or less.

### VOCAL AND COMMUNICATION

The grizzly utters various sounds as a means of expressing its feelings; it may grunt, growl, cough, roar, or snort. When it is hurt, the grizzly—especially a cub—may let out a loud bawl.

The grizzly has a unique way of conveying messages to its own kind. Bears follow regular trails through the mountain passes, and at various intervals along the trails there are "bear trees." On coming to a "bear tree," a grizzly sniffs up and down the trunk, then stretches its paws upward as far as it can reach, sets its big canine teeth into the bark of the tree and yanks off several chunks, which fall to the ground. The bear now continues his travels and repeats the same performance at the next marked tree. In the course of the time quite a pile of chunks accumulate.

### MATING

During the bears' courtship, which begins toward the end of May and continues until the last of June, there is considerable affection between the sexes. The pair are inseparable and inclined to be unfavorably disposed toward strangers—both animal and man. They fondle each other with their paws, feed side by side, playfully hug and wrestle. Once the romance is over, they separate and travel their individual ways. The male may seek a new mate the following year but the female does not enjoy male society for the next two or three years.

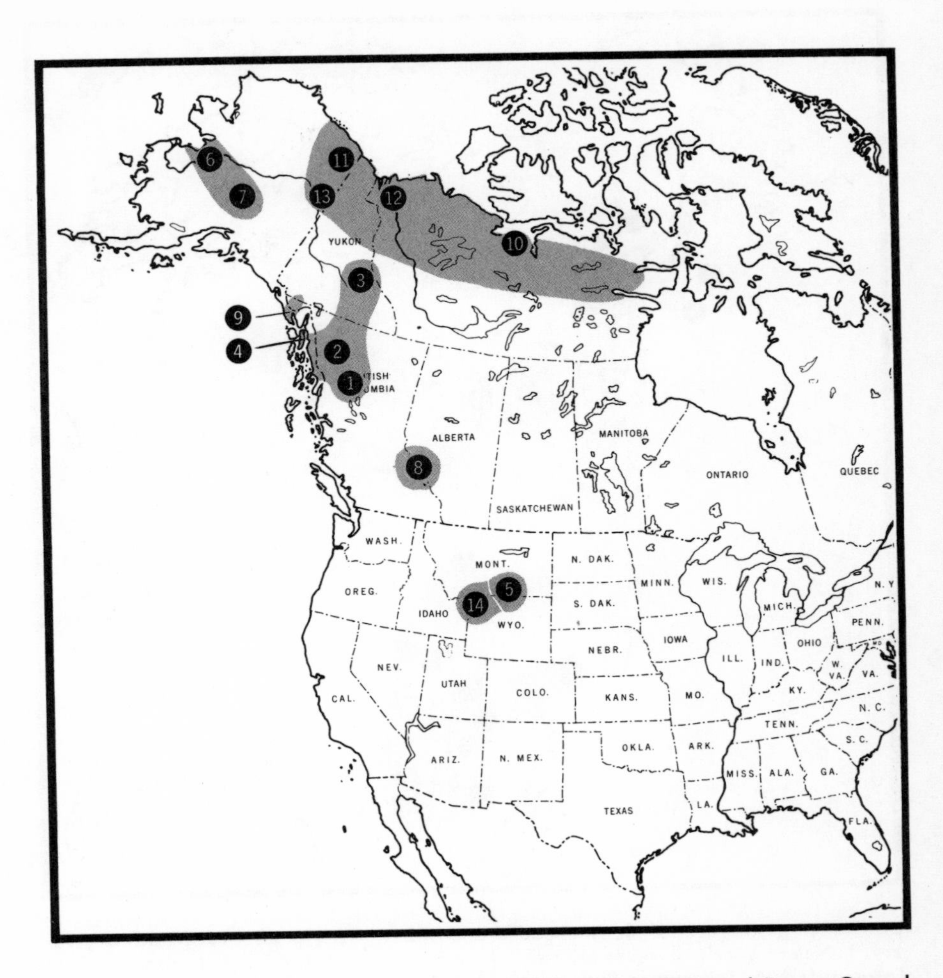


Distribution of the races of the Big-toothed, Alaska, Small-toothed, and Barren Ground grizzly *Ursus*. **Big-toothed grizzly:** 1. Stikine grizzly, 2. Big-toothed grizzly, 3. Thickset grizzly, 4. Strange grizzly, 5. Absaroka grizzly. **Alaska grizzly:** 6. Alaska grizzly, 7. Toklat grizzly, 8. Broad-fronted grizzly. **Small-toothed grizzly:** 9. Townsend grizzly. **Barren Ground grizzly:** 10. Barren Ground grizzly, 11. Alaska Boundary grizzly, 12. Mackenzie Delta grizzly, 13. Tanana grizzly. 14. Washakie grizzly.

Females breed every two or three years. The cubs, generally twins and occasionally four, are born in the winter den during January or February, six months after mating season. The cubs come into the world toothless, with their eyes closed, and are covered with a short coat of fine, downy hair. They weigh less than 1 or 2 pounds each and are about 10 inches long. They open their eyes for the first time when about six weeks old. The cubs are nursed for about six months and may stay in the company of the mother for a longer period. Young grizzlies are good climbers but when they reach maturity are too heavy and clumsy to climb trees. Full growth and maturity are reached in the eighth or tenth year but the females may breed before this. The grizzly bear has a long life expectancy and may reach an age of twenty-five or thirty years. Some, it is claimed, live to the half-century mark.

### RANGE

The overall range of the grizzly extends from the peninsula of Alaska east to Hudson Bay and south to northern Mexico. It is found from the Barren Lands in the arctic regions and the Great Plains up to and

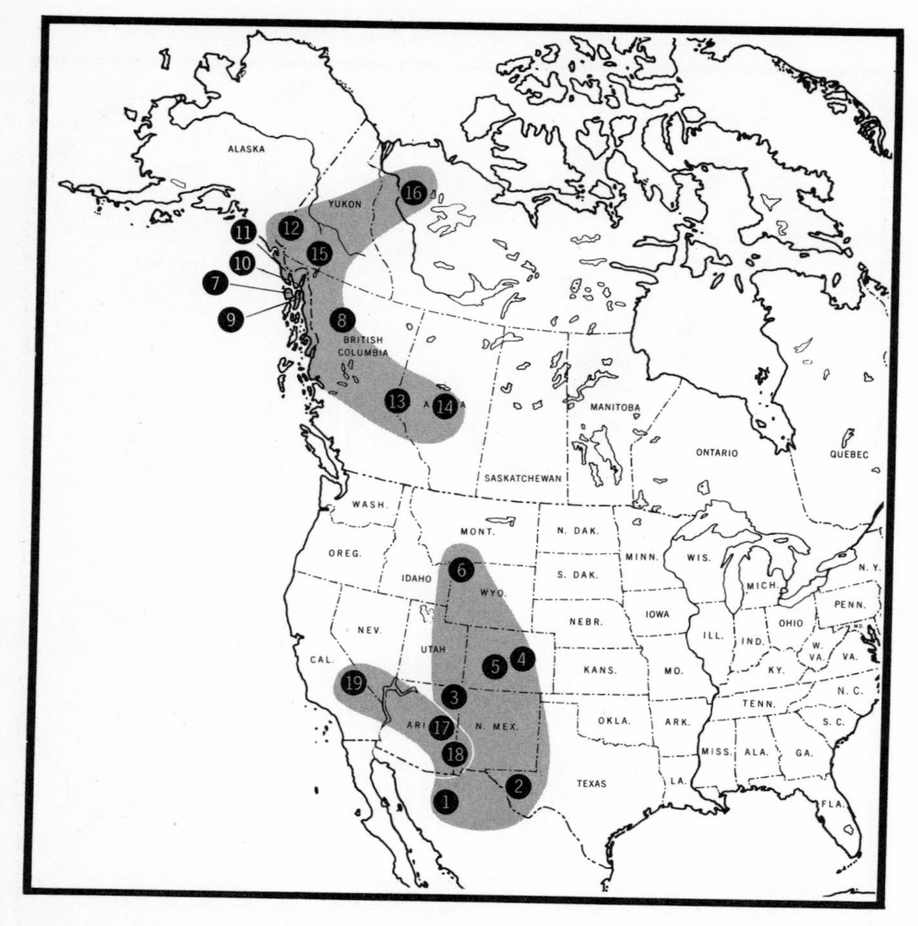

Distribution of the races of the Flat-headed and Desert grizzly *Ursus.* **Flat-headed grizzly:** 1. Nelson grizzly, 2. Texas grizzly, 3. Navaho grizzly, 4. Flat-headed grizzly, 5. Twin Lakes grizzly, 6. Yellowstone Park grizzly, 7. Sitka grizzly, 8. Tahltan grizzly, 9. Island grizzly, 10. Glacier Bay grizzly, 11. Alsek grizzly, 12. Pallas grizzly, 13. Canada grizzly, 14. Rungius grizzly, 15. Crested grizzly, 16. MacFarland grizzly. **Desert grizzly:** 17. Apache grizzly, 18. New Mexico grizzly, 19. Henshaw grizzly.

above timberline in the Rocky Mountains. In the early pioneer days grizzly bears were common in most parts of western North America, their range being almost continuous from northern Mexico northward through the western United States and western Canada to northern Alaska. With the exception of a few isolated areas in national parks, the grizzly is rare or nonexistent in the eastern portions of its range in the United States south of the Canadian border. The individual range of a grizzly is governed largely by its feeding habits. It may travel considerable distances to berry grounds and the rivers that salmon ascend to spawn. On the other hand a grizzly may be satisfied with a home range of from 5 to 10 miles or less for short periods of time.

Outside the national parks there are not more than six hundred grizzlies in the United States today. The grizzly, however, still ranges in fairly large numbers in extreme western Canada, the Yukon, and Alaska.

The species and subspecies of the grizzly bear are as follows:

Plains Grizzly (*horribilis*) Group

Big Plains grizzly *Ursus horribilis horribilis*. Range: Great Plains bordering Missouri River from western Kansas to plains region of southwestern Manitoba, Saskatchewan, and Alberta.

Baird grizzly *Ursus horribilis bairdi*. Range: Southern Rocky Mountain region from San Juan Mountains, southwestern Colorado, northward through Wyoming to Montana, and perhaps to southeastern British Columbia.

Rindsfoos grizzly *Ursus horribilis dusorgus*. Range: Rocky Mountain region of western Alberta and eastern British Columbia.

Yellowstone grizzly *Ursus horribilis imperator*. Range: Yellowstone National Park.

Jervis Inlet grizzly *Ursus chelidonias*. Range: Jervis Inlet, British Columbia.

Atnarko grizzly *Ursus atnarko*. Range: Mountains inland from Bella Coola area.

Kwakiutl grizzly *Ursus kwakiutl*. Range: Burrard Inlet, Howe Sound, Jervis Inlet northwesterly to or beyond the lower Bella Coola.

Yakutat grizzly *Ursus nortoni*. Range: Coastal plain on southeastern side of Yakutat Bay, Alaska.

Warburton Pike grizzly *Ursus warburtoni*. Range: Coast region of southeastern Alaska and adjacent parts of British Columbia.

Admiralty Island grizzly *Ursus neglectus*. Range: Admiralty Island, southeastern Alaska.

California Coast grizzly *Ursus californicus*. Range: Humid coast region of California from San Francisco Bay south about to San Luis Obispo.

Tejon grizzly *Ursus tularensis*. Range: Dry chaparral hills of interior coast ranges between San Joaquin Valley and Los Angeles plain.

Sacramento Valley grizzly *Ursus colusus*. Range: Sacramento Valley and adjacent foothills.

Flat-headed Grizzly (*planiceps*) Group

Nelson grizzly *Ursus nelsoni*. Range: Southwestern New Mexico and Sierra Madre of Mexico from northwestern Chihuahua and northeastern Sonora south to southern Durango.

Texas grizzly *Ursus texensis texensis*. Range: From Davis Mountains, Texas, to southwestern Colorado.

Navaho grizzly *Ursus texensis navaho*. Range: Chuska Mountains.

Flat-headed grizzly *Ursus planiceps*. Range: Mineral County, Colorado.

Twin Lakes grizzly *Ursus macrodon*. Range: Lake County and Routt County, Colorado.

Yellowstone Park grizzly *Ursus mirus*. Range: From lower levels of Yellowstone National Park down Snake River Valley over southern Idaho to lava bed region of southeastern Oregon.

Sitka grizzly *Ursus eltonclarki*. Range: The Sitka Islands, Baranof and Chichagof.

Tahltan grizzly *Ursus tahltanicus*. Range: Middle and upper Stikine-Skeena region, British Columbia, Canada.

Island grizzly *Ursus insularis.* Range: Admiralty Island, southeastern Alaska.

Glacier Bay grizzly *Ursus orgilos.* Range: Bartlett Bay, east side of Glacier Bay, southeastern Alaska.

Alsek grizzly *Ursus orgiloides.* Range: Coast strip southeast of Yakutat Bay, Alaska.

Pallas grizzly *Ursus pallasi.* Range: Central and eastern Yukon.

Canada grizzly *Ursus canadensis canadensis.* Range: Northeastern Washington and southeastern British Columbia.

Rungius grizzly *Ursus canadensis rungiusi.* Range: Southwestern Alberta, Canada.

Crested grizzly *Ursus canadensis sagittalis.* Range: Champagne Landing, southwestern Yukon, Canada.

MacFarland grizzly *Ursus macfarlani.* Range: Arctic coastal region of Mackenzie District from Coronation Gulf and eastern parts of Mackenzie River delta, Canada.

Southern Grizzly (*arizonae*) Group

Arizona grizzly *Ursus arizonae.* Range: Eastern Arizona and Mogollon Mountains of southwestern New Mexico.

Idaho grizzly *Ursus idahoensis.* Range: Northeastern Oregon, Blue Mountains of southeastern Washington, and Idaho.

Upper Yukon grizzly *Ursus pulchellus pulchellus.* Range: Central and southern Yukon, Canada.

Kootenay grizzly *Ursus pulchellus ereunetes.* Range: Beaverfoot Range, Kootenay District, British Columbia, Canada.

Liard River grizzly *Ursus oribasus.* Range: Upper Liard River, Yukon, Canada.

Chelan grizzly *Ursus chelan.* Range: Cascade and Cassiar Mountains from northern Washington to upper Stikine River and Dease Lake, British Columbia.

Shoshone grizzly *Ursus shoshone.* Range: Mountains of Colorado and Wyoming.

Sonora grizzly *Ursus kennerleyi.* Range: Mountains near Los Nogales, Sonora, Mexico.

Utah grizzly *Ursus utahensis.* Range: Southern Wasatch and Pine Valley Mountains, Utah.

Mount Taylor grizzly *Ursus perturbans.* Range: Region lying between Mount Taylor and Datil Ranges, New Mexico.

Rogers grizzly *Ursus rogersi rogersi.* Range: Greybull River, Absaroka Mountains, Yellowstone National Park, Wyoming.

Black Hills grizzly *Ursus rogersi bisonophagus.* Range: Black Hills of South Dakota and adjacent northeast corner of Wyoming.

Lillooet grizzly *Ursus pervagor.* Range: Interior of southwestern British Columbia.

Lynn Canal grizzly *Ursus caurinus.* Range: Coast of mainland of southeastern Alaska from Chilkat River Valley and Lynn Canal.

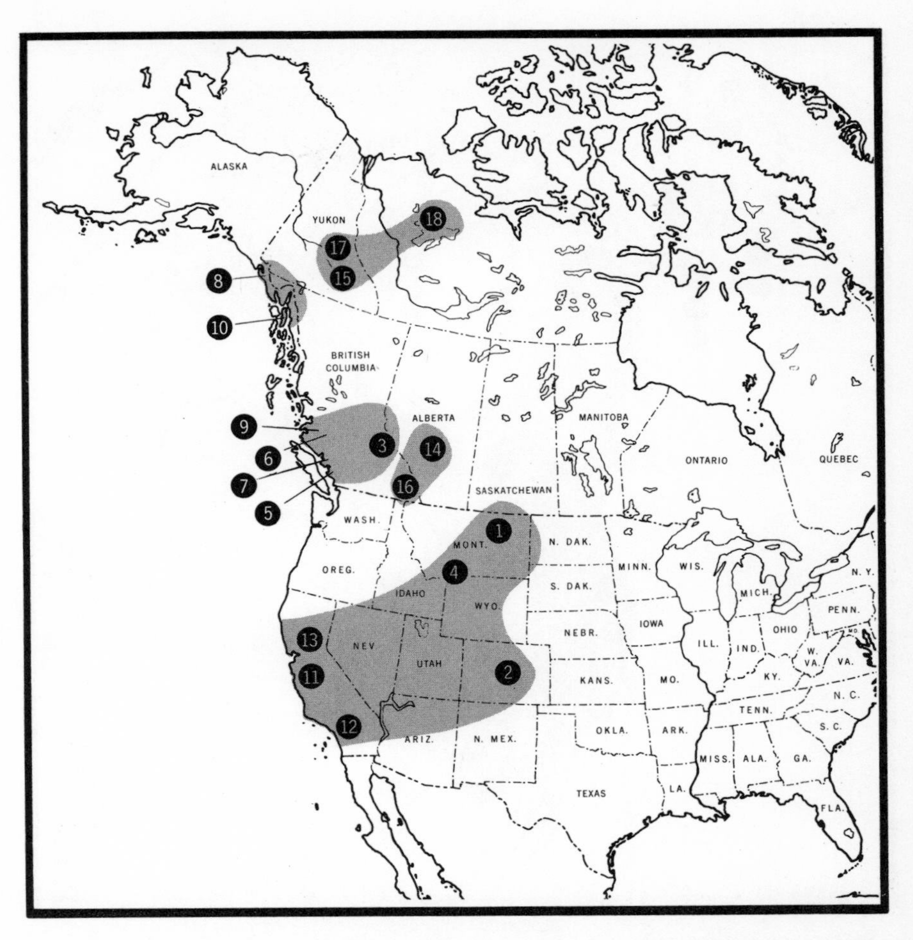


Distribution of the races of the Plains and Forest grizzly *Ursus.* **Plains grizzly:** 1. Big Plains grizzly, 2. Baird grizzly, 3. Rindsfoos grizzly, 4. Yellowstone grizzly, 5. Jervis Inlet grizzly, 6. Atnarko grizzly, 7. Kawakiuti grizzly, 8. Yakutat grizzly, 9. Warburton Pike grizzly, 10. Admiralty Island grizzly, 11. California Coast grizzly, 12. Tejon grizzly, 13. Sacramento Valley grizzly. **Forest grizzly:** 14. Forest grizzly, 15. Kluane grizzly, 16. Industrious grizzly, 17. Pelly grizzly, 18. Anderson grizzly.

Admiralty Island Crested grizzly *Ursus eulophus.* Range: Admiralty Island, Alaska.

Klamath grizzly *Ursus klamathensis.* Range: Siskiyou Mountains of northern California and southern Oregon.

Mendocino grizzly *Ursus mendocinensis.* Range: Northwest coast belt of California.

Southern California grizzly *Ursus magister.* Range: Trabuco Mountains, Cuyamaca and Santa Rosa Mountains, California.

Forest Grizzly (*hylodromus*) Group

Forest grizzly *Ursus hylodromus.* Range: Rocky Mountain region of western Alberta and eastern British Columbia.

Kluane grizzly *Ursus kluane kluane.* Range: Southwest corner of Yukon Territory east of St. Elias Range.

Industrious grizzly *Ursus kluane impiger.* Range: Western Montana, western Alberta and southeastern British Columbia.

Pelly grizzly *Ursus pellyensis.* Range: Pelly and Ross Mountains, northwest to Dawson region, Yukon.

Anderson grizzly *Ursus andersoni.* Range: Barren Grounds along northern edge of Hudsonian Zone from Eskimo Lakes east and southeast to east end of Great Bear Lake, Canada.

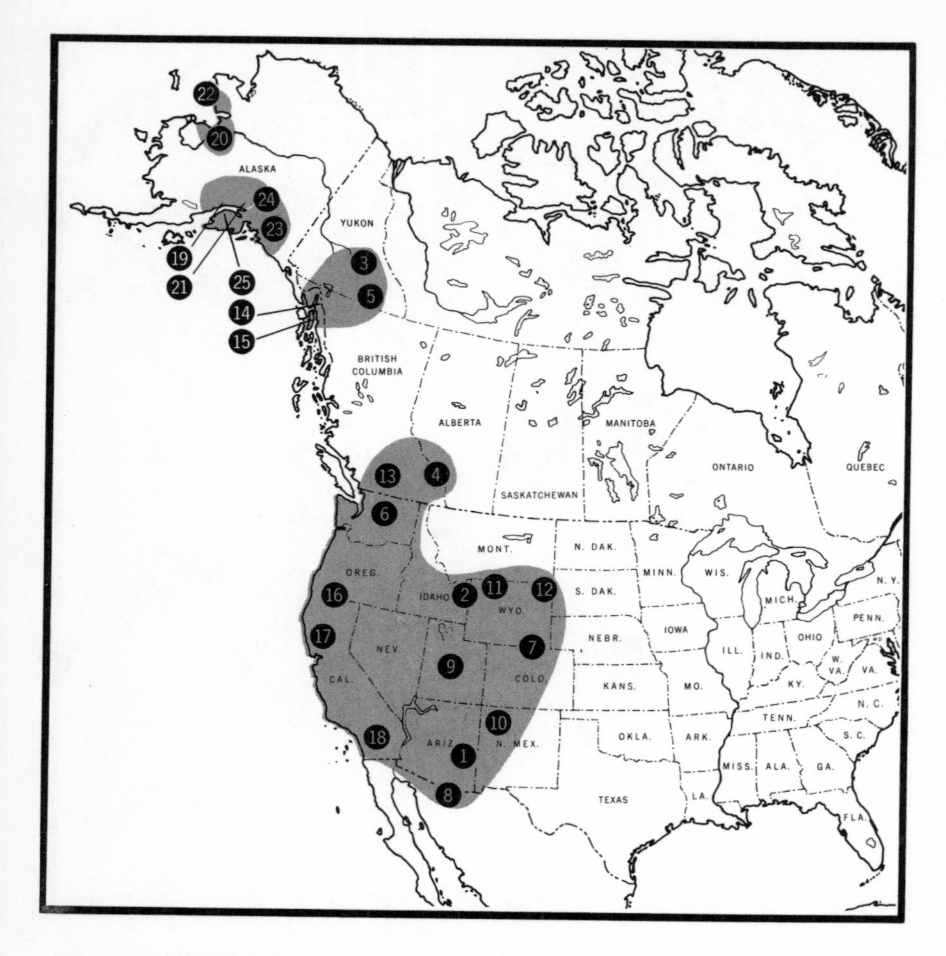


Distribution of the races of the Southern, Tundra, and Yukon grizzly *Ursus*. **Southern grizzly:** 1. Arizona grizzly, 2. Idaho grizzly, 3. Upper Yukon grizzly, 4. Kootensy grizzly, 5. Liard River grizzly, 6. Chelan grizzly, 7. Shoshone grizzly, 8. Sonora grizzly, 9. Utah grizzly, 10. Mount Taylor grizzly, 11. Rogers grizzly, 12. Black Hills grizzly, 13. Lillooet grizzly, 14. Lynn Canal grizzly, 15. Admiralty Island Crested grizzly, 16. Klamath grizzly, 17. Mendocino grizzly, 18. Southern California grizzly. **Tundra grizzly:** 19. Kidder grizzly, 20. Tundra grizzly, 21. Knik grizzly. **Yukon grizzly:** 22. Innuit grizzly, 23. Chitina grizzly, 24. Holzworth grizzly, 25. Alexander grizzly.

Desert Grizzly (*horriaeus*) Group

Apache grizzly *Ursus apache*. Range: From White Mountains, Arizona, to Sangre de Cristo in northern New Mexico.

New Mexico grizzly *Ursus horriaeus*. Range: Foothills and valley country around Mogollon Mountains to Rio Grande Valley of southern New Mexico, south to Casas Grandes, Chihuahua, Mexico.

Henshaw grizzly *Ursus henshawi*. Range: Lower slopes of southern part of Sierra Nevada, California.

Big-toothed Grizzly (*stikeenensis*) Group

Stikine grizzly *Ursus stikeenensis*. Range: Headwaters of Skeena River, head of Finlay River, and Dease Lake region, northern British Columbia and northerly in Yukon.

Big-toothed grizzly *Ursus crassodon*. Range: Headwaters of Skeena River, head of Teslin Lake, and Tatlatui River in northern British Columbia.

Thickset grizzly *Ursus crassus*. Range: Eastern Yukon to northern Mackenzie District, Canada.

Strange grizzly *Ursus mirabilis*. Range: Admiralty Island, Alaska.

Absaroka grizzly *Ursus absarokus*. Range: Laramie and Bighorn Mountains, eastern Wyoming, Black Hills region, South Dakota.

Alaska Grizzly (*alascensis*) Group

Alaska grizzly *Ursus alascensis*. Range: Norton Sound region, Alaska.

Toklat grizzly *Ursus toklat*. Range: Alaska Range.

Broad-fronted grizzly *Ursus latifrons*. Range: Rocky Mountains of western Alberta and eastern British Columbia, Canada.

Barren Ground Grizzly (*richardsoni*) Group

Barren Ground grizzly *Ursus richardsoni*. Range: Along Arctic coast from Kent Peninsula on coast and islands of Bathurst Inlet, Canada.

Alaska Boundary grizzly *Ursus internationalis internationalis*. Range: Region near Arctic coast along Alaska-Yukon boundary.

Mackenzie Delta grizzly *Ursus internationalis russelli*. Range: Outer part of Mackenzie delta region as far east as Richards Island and west side of delta, Canada.

Tanana grizzly *Ursus phaeonyx*. Range: Tanana Mountains between Tanana and Yukon Rivers, Alaska.

Washakie grizzly *Ursus washake*. Range: Shoshone River, Absaroka Mountains, between Bighorn Basin and Yellowstone National Park, Wyoming.

Tundra Grizzly (*kidderi*) Group

Kidder grizzly *Ursus kidderi kidderi*. Range: Entire length of Alaska Peninsula.

Tundra grizzly *Ursus kidderi tundrensis*. Range: Tundra region of northwestern Alaska from Shaktolik River on Norton Sound, southerly across lower Yukon, Kuskokwim, and Nushagak Rivers to Bristol Bay and north side of base of Alaska Peninsula.

Knik grizzly *Ursus eximius*. Range: Head of Knik Arm, Cook Inlet, Alaska.

Yukon Grizzly (*innuitus*) Group

Innuit grizzly *Ursus innuitus*. Range: Coastal region of Norton Sound, Alaska.

Chitina grizzly *Ursus cressonus*. Range: Chitina River Valley and adjacent slopes of Skolai and Wrangell Mountains, westerly through Chugach Mountains to west side of Cook Inlet.

Holzworth grizzly *Ursus holzworthi*. Range: East slope of Talkeetna Mountains, near headwaters of Oshetna or Black River, Alaska.

Alexander grizzly *Ursus alexandrae*. Range: Kenai Peninsula, Alaska.

Small-toothed Grizzly (*townsendi*) Group

Townsend grizzly *Ursus townsendi*. Range: Mainland of southeastern Alaska, probably between Cross Sound and Alsek River delta.

*See Range category for scientific names of subspecies*

CHAPTER 16

# THE BROWN BEAR

THE COAST and islands of southern Alaska form the greatest bear country in the world. The climate is relatively mild. There is plentiful vegetable food for bears, and the streams are full of salmon. In addition, most of the country is wilderness that can be reached only by boat or plane. On the mainland there are many brown bears and multitudes of blacks, and on some of the islands the great brown bears are found in numbers that seem fantastic to those hunters used to the relative scarcity of the interior grizzly.

It is a wonderful country of quiet, blue-gray estuaries, of thick hemlock and spruce forest, of narrow sandy beaches, of brawling salmon streams, of glaciers, of cloud-sheathed peaks, of hillsides clothed in tangles of willow and alder. It is a land of muted colors—gray sea, dark forests, and heavy, gray sky. It is a quiet country, where you hear only the slap of the waves, the cry of the sea gulls, and often for days on end, the drumming of the rain.

The mainland from the mouth of the Stikine north and west in a great semicircle along the coast, plus islands such as Baranof, Chichagof, and Kodiak, and ending on the long, barren Alaska Peninsula, is the home range of the Alaska brown, the world's largest bear, the world's largest predator, and, according to some, the world's most dangerous game animal.

Like the grizzly, the Alaska brown bear is distinguished by the hump on his shoulders, by his concave profile, and by his long claws. Also like the grizzly, he comes in numerous shades of brown. The big male bears I saw and shot on Admiralty Island were a uniform medium-brown, but a female killed by my companion had a coat for all the world like that of a silvertip grizzly. In some areas the great bears are a light brown, almost a tan. I have seen hides like that from the Alaska Peninsula.

A brown bear that died at a Washington, D. C., zoo when it was about 13 years old weighed over 1,000 pounds at the time of its death, and was estimated to have weighed about 1,200 pounds three years earlier. He wasn't large for a brownie and was never allowed to get unduly fat. Probably the largest browns will weigh 1,500 and possibly 1,600 pounds. That's a lot of carnivorous animal when you stop to think that the very largest lions of South Africa weighed about 500 pounds, and the average big lion shot today is closer to 400, and that the very largest Indian tigers weigh at the most about 600. A predator nearly four times as heavy as a large African trophy lion is quite an animal.

A very large brown bear will stand a bit over 4 feet high at the shoulder, and his hide will square from 9 to as much as 11 feet. A hide that squares 9½ feet is very good, one that squares 10 is excellent, and one that squares 10½ is just about at the top of the list. In some areas, really big brown bears are getting hard to come by, as it takes a long time to grow a really big bear. Consequently many sows and young bears are shot, and many of the trophies taken by bear hunters are not large, even compared with grizzlies. One fall in Juneau, Alaska, when I was returning from a Stone-sheep hunt just below the Yukon border in northern British Columbia, I ran into a party of three men who had hunted Alaska browns. The grizzly that one of my companions had killed in the interior was a good deal larger than any of the brown-bear trophies those hunters had.

The correct way to measure a bear hide is to lay it out fresh and flat on the ground, fur side down, and then measure from nose to tail and across the paws. Its "square" size is the total of these two measurements divided by two. If, for example, the hide is 9½ feet long and 10½ feet wide it is said to square 10 feet. Bear hides are invariably wider than they are long.

Guides have been known to hang up green hides with heavy weights attached. It is no great trick to stretch a hide that is 8 feet long into a 9-footer or to stretch a 10-footer until it measures 11 feet. The 12- and 13-foot bear hides one hears about but never sees could have got that way only by being stretched. But let us not fret. Even a hide that squares only 9 feet wraps up a lot of live bear meat—more than I would want to blunder into in the tangled brush of some Alaska salmon stream. I have the hide of a fine tiger that now, after it was tanned, measures flat 10 feet 7 inches. The animal it was peeled off of measured 9 feet 9 inches from the tip of his nose to the last joint of his tail on a straight line between pegs. But the bear has little tail, and the tiger has a long one.

Ranking animals as trophies by their hides is a pretty unsatisfactory business, as hides can be stretched. It is also unsatisfactory in the case of some species like lion, tiger, or leopard because a medium-sized animal may have a long tail and a large animal a short one. An animal may even have lost some of his tail. The last lion I shot in Africa (a very respectable trophy lion for these days) had lost about 6 inches of tail. Although he was a large lion, his lack of tail would handicap him in an over-all length measurement against a lesser lion.

Because of such variables, there is no really satisfactory and foolproof way to rank any of the game animals that lack horns and antlers. Bears particularly are seldom shot where they can be weighed, yet the weight and bulk are the things that make the great brown bear impressive. So brown and grizzly bears are ranked by their skull measurements, an odd situation as the hides—not the skulls—are the trophies. This is also not very satisfactory, as smallish bears can have large heads, and large bears can have small heads, just as human beings can. Among my acquaintances are a little guy who wears a 7½ hat and a chap who is well over 7 feet tall and has a fighting weight of about 250 pounds, yet who wears a 6⅞ hat. Ralph Young, the famous brown-bear guide of Petersburg, Alaska, tells me that many of the largest bears he has seen have comparatively small skulls, just as in Africa some of the largest bull elephants have indifferent ivory, or sometimes none at all.

Be that as it may, the way to measure a bear skull is to take the greatest length without lower jaw, the greatest width, and add the two. That's the score. The largest bears in the record book (or at least the bears with the largest skulls) come from Kodiak Island and the Alaska Peninsula. Of the first ten, nine are from Kodiak and one from the peninsula. Of these, four were killed in the trophy-conscious nineteen fifties. One of the four, incidentally, is the world record. It was shot on Kodiak in 1952.

Because bears grow large on Kodiak and the island was the locale of many early hunting expeditions for the big bear, the terms Alaska brown bear and Kodiak bear have become almost synonymous in the minds of most people. Actually this is incorrect. Kodiak bears are Alaska brown bears, but not all Alaska brown bears are Kodiaks.

But call him what you will, the great brown bear of Alaska is one of the world's most impressive trophies. In bulk alone, he overshadows the lion and the tiger, and he makes the tough and dangerous leopard look puny. A really big Alaska brown bear dwarfs even the grizzly. In sheer bulk, the only things that top him are the big wild cattle like the Cape buffalo of Africa, the gaur of India, the giraffe, and the pachyderms.

Some hunters would put the big brown bear right at the very top of the list of North American trophies, and some would put him as number one of all the trophies of the world. I doubt if I would. I would rather shoot a bighorn ram with a 16-inch base and a heavy, broomed head with horns 44 or 45 inches long than the biggest brownie on Kodiak. At the top of the world's list of trophies I'd put one of the great wild sheep of Central Asia. Never-

Sprawled on the beach in a driving rain, O'Connor zeroed in on the brownie lumbering toward him.

theless, a really big brown would come toward the top, no matter who was compiling the list.

The Alaska brown is simply a specialized form of grizzly, and it is difficult to say where the brown leaves off and the grizzly begins. For purposes of record-keeping, any bear shot along the Alaska coast north of the Taku River and within about 75 miles of tidewater is a brown. A bear shot farther south along the coast or in the interior of Alaska, British Columbia, or the Yukon is a grizzly. Occasionally an animal that is plainly a brown will wander up a stream well into the interior. The late Jean Jacquot of Kluane Lake, Yukon, showed me the pictures one time of an enormous bear he said was a coastal brown that had wandered into the Yukon. And when I was hunting sheep in the Atlin country of northern British Columbia, a companion shot a very large bear that had all the characteristics of a brown and probably was one.

American biologists have always been hairsplitting classifiers, and as a consequence brown bears have been divided into several different subspecies. The divisions are largely based on skull form, and this is something most sportsmen would know or care little about. Since the type specimen of the Alaska brown came from the Alaska Peninsula, the peninsula bears are *Ursus gyas gyas.* Those of Kodiak are *Ursus gyas middendorffi,* and those of Admiralty Island are *shirasi. Ursus,* of course, means bear and *gyas* is Greek for gigantic, so the Latin handle for the Kodiak means Middendorf's gigantic bear.

The big browns are great wanderers; they range from the sedge flats at sea level to the tops of the highest peaks. During the salmon runs they set up business on a stream and fatten up on the big silver fish. One of my most thrilling memories of a brown bear hunt on Admiralty Island is that of one of the great bears climbing slowly and purposefully to the top of a snowy peak at a time the setting sun was painting it with rose.

In the spring when the big bears come out of their winter sleep, many of them go down to the shore to eat sedge, and in most areas it is at this time that they are mostly hunted. Later, when the snow is off the high mountain basins above timberline, they eat various roots and grasses. Along the sea and in the lowland woods they clean up the carcasses of winter-killed deer and eat dead fish, seaweed, dead seals, defunct whales, and—on the mainland—even winter-killed goats.

The salmon runs start in June and with them comes the soft part of the bear's life. According to some writers, the big bears put their paws under the salmon, flip them out onto the bank, and then devour them. Ralph Young says this is fiction, that the bears pounce on the salmon and grab them in their mouths.

Mating occurs in mid-May and June. An old male finds a female and stays with her as long as she is in a receptive mood. Then he leaves her. At other times the old males are always alone and have no interest in the females. The sows breed every other year—or possibly every third year. When they're not in season they avoid the old males, as papa bear would just as soon as not kill his cubs and eat them. If a feeding mother and cubs see an old male show up in the spring, they usually vamoose out of there. Sows have been killed defending their young from big bears.

The cubs are born in the winter dens, tiny creatures for an animal that will eventually grow so huge, generally weighing about a pound and a half. They are naked, blind, and helpless, but get warmth and sustenance from their mother's body. Litters run from a single to quadruplets. One sow I saw late one afternoon on Admiralty had four merry little teddy bears with her, but when a big male came out onto the sedge flats about a quarter of a mile away, she quickly herded her brood back into the timber.

At the end of their second year, mamma chases the young bears off to shift for themselves. Sometimes, the cubs apparently stay with their mothers until they are long two-year-olds, which would mean that some sows breed only every third year.

A bear is mature by his seventh year, but continues to grow heavier thereafter until old age and his final decline set in. He lives to be about thirty.

The bears go into their winter sleep in September and the big males come out sometime between early April and late May. By early May many of them are down on the sedge flats by the sea. They lie up in the middle of the night and also during the middle of the day, doing their feeding early in the morning and late in the afternoon. The late-spring days are long in Alaska and usually the hunting time begins about four or five o'clock and lasts until ten.

It is fortunate that the brown bear has lived until now in country that has not been heavily used by man. In southeast Alaska the main business is fishing, and the salmon packers hate the bears because they eat some salmon. At various times the packers have agitated to have the bears shot down. How the new Alaska Department of Fish and Game will resist the agitation of the salmon packers now that statehood has been achieved, I don't know. The decrease in the salmon runs was not caused by the bears, which have been eating salmon for hundreds of thousands of years, but by overfishing. Fish eaten by the bears are spawned-out salmon that are dying anyway.

There is a naval station on Kodiak, and some of the personnel take bears. But the island is a tough place to get around in, and they probably don't shoot very many. Some cattle are raised on Kodiak, and like cattlemen everywhere those on Kodiak hate bears and would like to see the brownies reduced in numbers.

As the supply of timber suitable for pulpwood diminishes farther south, there will be more lumbering on the coast and islands. Already there is a pulp mill at Ketchikan, and lumbering is in progress along the coast. All of the bear country in southeast Alaska is in national forests, and most American foresters these days are timbermen rather than game managers. Many of them cannot see a ripe tree without wanting to cut it down. Plans are underway to cut timber on Admiralty Island, the greatest brown-bear country in the world. Timbering there will, of course, reduce bear habitat and cut down the number of bears. Chichagof Island also supports a lot of timber—and bears—but the whole island will be timbered for a Japanese-owned pulp mill at Sitka. In the future, the timber of southeast Alaska will probably come first. But if the Alaska Peninsula has any economic use, I don't know what it is.

Actually the big brown is an economic asset of no mean proportions. A bear on the paw is worth a lot of money, and the sportsmen who come from "outside" leave many hundreds of dollars in Alaska for every bear they bring out. They spend this money for commercial and charter planes, hunting licenses, boat hire, and guide fees. Some come simply to see and photograph the great bears. Tourism and big game hunting are among Alaska's major assets. If properly managed, the brownie should be with us for a long time, but short-sighted and greedy policy could just about exterminate him in a generation.

How dangerous is this great bear? There are two schools of belief. One holds that he is not dangerous at all, and that unless he is wounded he never causes trouble. Another holds that he is a wicked and ravening monster ready to attack at the slightest pretext.

I do not set myself up as any authority on brown bears, and my own personal experience with them is slight. From what I can learn by talking to Alaskan hunters and from what I can read, I'd say that the big brown mauls and kills fewer people than the grizzly. This is not because he is a less-formidable or better-natured animal, but because he lives around fewer people. The more contact there is between bears and people the more there is likely to be trouble. Much of the brownie's territory is completely uninhabited.

Like the grizzly, the big brown was—for countless thousands of years—the undisputed king of his country, and the only thing he feared was a bigger and tougher bear. Even now the only enemy he has is man. In wilderness areas where man seldom penetrates, the grizzly is not a wary animal, and over much of his range the brownie isn't either. In the continental United States and in southern Canada, where grizzlies have been much hunted and associate the smell of man with the roar of rifles, pain, and danger, they are far more timorous than they are in areas where they've never been shot at. Once, in a much-hunted area where the grizzlies knew all about men, I stalked a female grizzly with two cubs so I could photograph them. When the wind shifted and the sow caught my scent, she rushed away in abject terror and left the cubs to follow as best they could. Under similar circumstances in a little-hunted area in the Yukon, a female grizzly forced me to choose between turning tail and shooting her. I turned tail.

Both the brown and the grizzly have very poor eyesight, as I had demonstrated to me one time when I stalked and shot a grizzly in an open basin above timberline where I had no cover at all. The only precaution I took was to stop and stand still whenever the bear looked my way.

I think that in many cases of attack by brown bears, the bear hasn't the faintest idea what he's attacking. He hears a noise in his stretch of salmon stream, thinks it's another bear, and comes barging in to scare the interloper off. Under these circumstances the man mauled by the bear is mauled all right, but the bear didn't know he was attacking a man until he smelled him.

The brown, because of his great size and strength, is potentially one of the most dangerous animals in the world, and it pays to be circumspect with any potentially dangerous animal. It is not wise to fool with any female bear with cubs, even the usually timorous black. Nor does it pay to take chances with any feeding bear, whether it's a brownie eating salmon or a grizzly on a moose kill.

When a man is after any dangerous game, he should carry a rifle of adequate power and take great pains to place his bullet absolutely right. I have never had a ruction with a wounded brownie, but I have followed up two wounded grizzlies. One ran like a rabbit; the other scared me half to death and made me resolve to be a good boy and be careful in the future where that first shot went. I think anyone who prowls around unarmed in brown-bear country is foolish, just as anyone is foolish who does the same in heavily populated rhino country.

Brownies are hunted in several ways, but all of them depend on locating the bear and stalking it. Some outfitters fly their hunters into lakes where they've set up camp. Then they glass the surrounding mountains for bears and make the stalk when a suitable bear is seen. Others set up camp on the shore and hunt along it in a small boat with an outboard motor. Cushiest way to hunt is from a small yacht cruising along the coast with a lookout to spot bears on the beaches.

When I hunted with Ralph Young in the spring of 1956, we ate and slept on a converted salmon boat and then went by skiff to some place where we could overlook good country and spot the bears as they came out of the heavy woods to feed on sedge by the shore. When a bear was spotted, we approached for a better look or for a stalk by rowing. In the fall, Ralph hunts bear by walking up the salmon streams where the bear are then feeding on salmon.

I have never hunted the interior of Kodiak Island or on the peninsula, but from all I hear, this must be pretty tough going. The man stalking a bear has to plow through soft silt and muskeg and climb steep mountains through snow and tangled alders. It sounds like a grim and exhausting chore.

Hunting bears in the spring along the beaches is pretty soft. The hunter doesn't have to do much walking in making the stalk, and what walking he does is generally over level beach. The bear hunter in Alaska often has to clothe himself in rubber from head to foot—a rubber pull-over raincoat that hangs to the knees. One thing the bear hunter can count on is rain, and when I hunted bear it rained at least

The cushiest way to hunt brownies is from a yacht cruising along the coast, with a lookout watching for bears.

six days out of seven, and for as long as three days straight. But clad in rubber from head to foot, the hunter gets used to rain, and if he has a snug, warm boat to eat and sleep on, he doesn't mind the chill and the dampness. I wore long wool underwear, khaki pants, wool shirt, and down jacket under my rubber. The longest walk I had was to a good black-bear area, about 4 miles each way through tidal muck. I didn't enjoy the tramp in those hip boots, but it didn't kill me. Actually a bear hunt with headquarters on a boat is fine sport.

When we were on Admiralty, the weather was awful, and bears don't move as much in the rain as they do in good weather. Nevertheless, we saw a great many bears. I didn't keep count, but we must have seen forty or fifty in all. The trouble was not in seeing bears, but in seeing the right ones. We saw our quota of females and young, and many of the big males we saw were so badly rubbed that their hides wouldn't have been good trophies. As the bears wander through the heavy forests in the summer and fall they get their hides full of the wicked spines of the devil's club. In their dens during the winter they rub the itching places until the hair is off in great patches.

Ralph Young and I made several stalks that brought us close to bears we decided not to take. We saw one perfectly gigantic bear with a fine, unrubbed hide. The younger bears are rangy, and the females have narrower heads than the males; this old boy had an immensely broad head, and looked as massive as a Cape buffalo. When he walked slowly off into the woods, he moved with the ponderous power of a bull elephant. Never have I seen a more impressive animal. He was the finest bear we saw, but he didn't give us a chance for a stalk. He couldn't have smelled us and I doubt if he saw us across a quarter of a mile of salt water. Perhaps he'd eaten enough and simply wanted to go into the woods and lie down.

On another occasion, Ralph and I were hiking to our skiff. I was in the lead by about 20 feet and walked around a wooded point to come face to face with a brown. I could have shot him as he plunged for the woods, but I was doubtful that he was big enough. Let me assure you, though, that viewing a big brownie within 20 feet on a lonely Alaska beach is an entirely different thing from looking one over behind the bars in a zoo.

At that time, two bears were allowed on Admiralty. I shot my first when Ralph had to stay in the skiff to keep the tide from carrying it out to sea. The bear was feeding on sedge along a beach only about 40 feet wide, and a couple of jumps would take him out of sight into heavy woods. I sneaked along the edge of the timber, taking cover

Rounding a wooded point, O'Connor ran into a brown bear unexpectedly at close range.

behind rocks and driftwood until I was about 250 yards from the bear. From there on, there was no cover whatsoever. Since the bear was still feeding, I decided I'd be smart to take a good shot at him at fairly long range rather than to attempt getting closer and risk a running shot.

I dropped into a prone position, held high on his shoulder, and squeezed off the shot. The bear dropped but was still threshing around, so I shot again and he lay still. The 270-grain .375 bullet had broken the shoulder.

My second bear was a thriller, a hunting experience I'll never forget. It was raining cats and dogs that afternoon, and Ralph and I rowed ashore from the boat to sit under the dripping hemlocks and spruces and watch a long semicircular stretch of silver beach between the dark, heavy forest and the gray and sullen sea. Along late in the afternoon we saw a bear walking rapidly in our direction along the beach, and Ralph pronounced him a big one. He said he was traveling and if I got across a shallow tidal arm he would walk right to me.

The water and muck came almost to the top of my hip boots as I struggled across. Ralph went to the right to get a better look at the bear. He found the going even worse and had to remain quiet there in the water, the muck, and the pounding rain while I fought my way across and lay down on the beach to await the bear. Being prone made me inconspicuous, and it also gave me a good steady position to shoot from.

I saw the bear come around a headland, still walking rapidly in my direction. Then he disappeared. When he came into view again, he'd be a little over 100 yards away. About 60 yards from me a piece of driftwood lay on the beach in the drumming rain, and I made up my mind that when the bear reached that point, I'd let him have it. I wiped the raindrops from the ocular lens of the scope on the .375, found I could see through it, and waited.

Then the big bear came around the point and straight toward me. I put the intersection of the crosswires on his left shoulder, and when he reached the driftwood I squeezed the trigger. The 270-grain soft-point bullet broke his shoulder and tipped him over bawling and roaring. I jumped to my feet, fired offhand into his chest, and he lay still. He was a large bear, but larger ones have been shot on Admiralty. He did, however, have an enormous head, and the shoulder mount I have in my trophy room is satisfactorily impressive.

Where and when should the sportsman anxious to add a brownie to his trophies go after one? I'd say the easiest and surest hunts are the spring hunts made by boat or yacht along the mainland and off the islands of southeast Alaska. Admiralty and Chichagof islands are probably the most densely populated brown-bear territory in the world, and the hunter should be sure of a good bear there. However, in the spring the hunter will see a great many female and small bears, and many of the large ones he'll see will be badly rubbed.

A fall hunt in the same area will produce fewer bears, but those the hunter will see up the salmon streams are apt to be large males and their hides will be good. The largest of these island bears compare very favorably with the largest anywhere.

Kodiak Island is hunted rather hard, but there are big bears in the interior of the island if the hunter is willing to work for a good trophy instead of just taking the first bear that comes along. As the record book shows, the man who gets a big Kodiak gets the best.

There may be a larger percentage of very big bears on the peninsula than anywhere else, but hunting there is hard work. And because a lot of flying is involved, the trip is expensive.

What about rifles?

Probably more brownies have been shot with .30/06 rifles than with anything else, and there isn't any doubt but that a good shot using proper bullets in the .30/06 can kill any brownie that ever walked. The late Hosea Sarber, a warden for the Alaska game commission who was for years stationed at Petersburg, used mostly the .30/06 with a handload of the 172-grain Western Tool & Copper Co. bullet in front of 51 grains of No. 4320 powder. Velocity was about 2,750 feet per second. Before his mysterious death (his empty boat was found, but his body was never recovered) he shot several big bears with a .270 with a handload of the 160-grain Barnes bullet and 54 grains of No. 4350. He wrote me that he thought it killed just as well as the .30/06.

Ralph Young holds that the .30/06 is plenty of bear medicine in the hands of a good shot, but when he's guiding he always carries an iron-sighted .375 Magnum, a Winchester Model 70. He wants plenty of powder in case he has to go into the brush after a wounded and indignant bear—something he has to do every year. He also wants plenty of power and bullet weight in case of an unexpected encounter. He wrote me that although one of his dudes had recently killed a big brownie very neatly with a .270, he considers the .270 on the light side for brownies, just as he considered the .458 Winchester on the heavy side.

For most dudes he thinks the .338 with the 250-

grain Silvertip, the .375 with the 270-grain soft point, or the 300-grain Silvertip about ideal. Many of his hunters have used the .300 Weatherby Magnum with the 180- and 220-grain bullets and have done very well. No matter what caliber is used, the bullets should be heavy and strongly constructed, as a brownie's bones are heavy and you have to shoot through a lot of meat to get to the vitals.

From my own limited experience I'd say that the .375 is just about ideal, and the .338 should likewise be very good. Sometime I'd like to take a crack at a big brownie with a .416, and in case anyone owns a double like the .450/400, it should also be about right with its 400-grain bullets at about 2,150. I think the average hunter tackling his first big brown will feel less nervous if he carries a powerful rifle in which he has complete confidence. But whatever caliber he takes, his rifle should have iron sights available. My .375 has a scope on a Griffin & Howe side mount. I shot both bears with the scope, but I had a Lyman 48 available in case the scope got fogged. Mine did not, but it was a close call. Chances are 50-50 that the bear will be shot in the rain. Particularly if the rifle is scope-mounted, it should be carried in some sort of a waterproof case and kept there until needed.

Wherever he is shot and whatever he is shot with, a big brownie is one of the world's top trophies, the largest flesh-eater on this earth, and one of the most dangerous animals. Never take him lightly.

# The Natural History of the Brown Bear

[URSUS GYAS]

## DESCRIPTION

The Alaska brown bear is the largest terrestrial, flesh-eating mammal in the world today. Although the polar bear may equal the big brownie in overall dimensions, the white bear is a slender, long-bodied animal compared with its big, brown cousin. A full-grown male Alaska brown bear measures up to 4½ feet at the shoulder, has an overall length of from 8 to 9 feet, weighs up to 1,600 pounds, and has a skull 18 inches long. Standing on its hind feet, a large brownie may have a reach of 12 feet.

The brown bear has long, thick hair varying in color from blackish-brown to pale yellowish-brown. Its huge body is humped at the shoulders and its massive head is supported by a short, muscular neck. Its low, rounded ears are placed wide apart, well back on the head; the eyes are small and set close together well forward on the face. Broad and rounded on top, the head terminates in a rather long, heavy muzzle.

Like most true bears the brownie has short, stout legs and mighty paws. It has five toes on each of the fore and hind feet, armed with long, slightly curved claws, which are not retractile like those of a cat. The big brown bear is terrestrial, though the cubs can and do climb trees. It is plantigrade, and walks flatfooted on the palms of its hands and the soles of its feet. The brown bear has long, sabre-like canine teeth, and broad, low-crowned molars. However, it is more omnivorous than carnivorous and is about at all hours of the day and night.

## ORIGIN

The brown bear is a member of the *Ursidae,* the most recent group of animals granted family rank. The bears were derived from canid stock, which is the most primitive of the modern flesh-eaters. The *Ursidae* became distinct as a family well along in the Miocene era or, according to some authors, not until the beginning of the Pliocene. Typical bears of the genus *Ursus* first appeared in the Lower Pliocene of Europe, spread across Asia and reached North America when Alaska and Siberia were connected across the Bering Straits. Today there are big brown bears on both sides of the straits and some of the Siberian specimens are almost, if not equally, as large as the Alaska brownie. In the Amur region, bear tracks have been seen that were 10 inches long. Primitive bears, not direct ancestors of our modern species, were present in North America from the Middle Pliocene well into the Pleistocene. Particularly worthy of mention was the presence of the huge Arctothere, a bear that stood over 5 feet tall at the shoulder.

## RANGE

There is something rather strange and mysterious about the home range of the big Alaska brown bear. It is restricted to a narrow coastal strip of land and shore islands from the tip of the Alaska Peninsula south along the Alaska coast to northern British Columbia. Nowhere does its range extend beyond the influence of the salt sea air. It is at home almost anywhere from the flat, sandy beaches and alder swamps up into the rocky, forested mountain slopes to and above timberline. A bear's individual range, governed largely by the food supply, may extend in a radius of 1 or 2 to 10 miles between berry crops and spawning salmon.

There are eleven species of Alaska brown bear recognized by science. The Peninsula giant bear is perhaps the largest of the Alaska brownies, though the Kodiak bear may approach or equal it in size. The color varies from brown lightly mixed with fine, white-tipped hairs

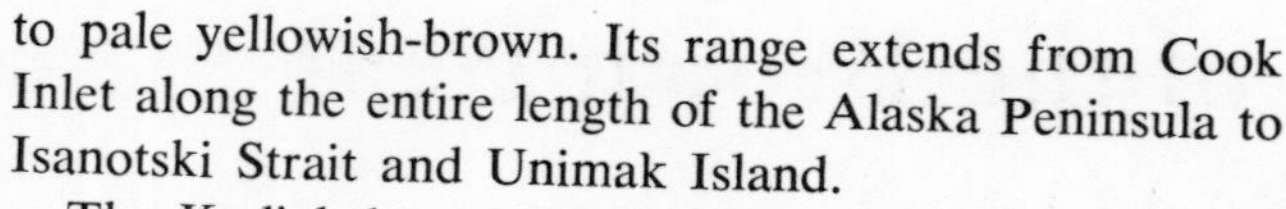

to pale yellowish-brown. Its range extends from Cook Inlet along the entire length of the Alaska Peninsula to Isanotski Strait and Unimak Island.

The Kodiak bear is generally considered the largest of all the bears found on Kodiak Island and the adjacent islands of Afognak and Shuyak, but does not occur on the mainland. It is colored much like the Peninsula bear.

The Kenai giant bear is a large brown bear approaching the Peninsula bear in size, but resembling the grizzly in many respects. It has moderately curved claws and in fresh pelage has a whitish wash over the brown coat. This species is restricted to the Kenai Peninsula.

The Alaska brown bear is another large species with a very dark-brown coat mixed with white-tipped hairs. Its known range includes the Malaspina Glacier and the region northwest of Yakutat Bay, Alaska.

The Sitka brown bear is a large bear but smaller than the Alaska brownie. Generally its color is very dark brown or sooty, but its summer pelage becomes yellowish or golden on head and neck. The Sitka bear is found on Baranof Island, Chichagof Islands and the Sitka Islands off Alaska.

The Sheldon brown bear, a large brown bear allied to the Kenai bear, is restricted to Montague Island, Prince William Sound, Alaska. The Stikine brown bear, a medium-sized brown bear allied to the Alaska brown bear, is only known from the vicinity of the Stikine River, British Columbia. The St. Elias brown bear, a medium-sized species allied to the Alaska brown bear, is known from Prince William Sound easterly to Mount St. Elias. The Asiatic brown bear, a large brown bear, is restricted in North America to St. Lawrence Island, Bering Sea, Alaska. The Shiras brown bear is bigger than the Sitka bear, coal black in color except for some brownish markings on the head. The Shiras brown bear is restricted to Admiralty Island.

The Patriarchal bear, the last and only known specimen of this strange and peculiar bear, was killed over one hundred years ago and was considered a lone survivor of a race of bears that belonged to a bygone era. Robert R. Macfarland, a famous naturalist and arctic explorer, killed the animal at Rendezvous Lake northeast of Fort Anderson Mackenzie and sent it to the Smithsonian Institution in Washington, D.C., where it remained unnoticed for fifty years. It was named *inopinatus,* the unexpected. It was a large bear with a heavy coat of soft, full fur varying in color on the body from grayish-brown to buff. The head was yellowish but the muzzle was a golden-brown, shading to fulvous around the eyes and reddish-brown on the ankles and feet. The Patriarchal bear is not one of the typical brown bears and it is quite distinct from the grizzlies, but belongs in a group of its own.

## HABITS

In the early spring, the brown bear feeds almost exclusively on grasses and sedges, grazing on the meadows like an ox. Later it digs up roots and bulbs of plants. When the berry season comes around, the brown bear is there to get its share, stripping the bushes of fruit, twigs, and leaves, swallowing them all together. It also excavates large holes in the ground to find squirrels and other rodents. In June when the salmon ascend the rivers to spawn, the brownie becomes a fisherman. Naturalists have seen many a bear wade out to the gravel bars and flip passing fish onto the bank with a swift stroke of its paw. Or a bear may plunge its head into the water and come up with a fat salmon hanging from its dripping jaws. In many cases more salmon are flipped ashore than the bear can consume at one time. They are not wasted but help to feed the foxes, crows, and seagulls. With its keen sense of smell, the brownie finds and devours any animals that have been killed during the winter, and dead whales that have been washed ashore. A bear, like all other mammals, requires a considerable amount of salt in its diet to maintain a healthy condition. About three quarts of body fluid, a salt solution, is lost daily by a bear through perspiration, respiration, and excretion. This loss of salt is replaced in part or altogether by the food, especially animal matter, that it eats.

Winter comes early in the northwest and a fussy brownie begins the preparation of a winter den some time late in August. The winter home may be a cavity in the rocks, a small cave, a hollow under a tree stump, or a self-excavated burrow on a mountain slope. The brownie is choosy about its winter home. It should have a southern exposure so that the driving winds from the north will pile the snow high over the den to keep it warm. The bear takes care that its home is free from drafts, that the ceiling is not too high, creating too great a loss of body heat. Some bears are particular about having a bed of dried leaves, mosses, and pine needles. With the first really cold snap of winter, sometimes in late September, the brown bear, now fat and lazy, becomes drowsy and retires to the winter den. After a few days' fast, it goes into a deep slumber and does not see the light of day again until some time in April. The sleep may be deep and long, but it is not a state of hibernation; body temperature and respiration are only slightly reduced and the bear will come to life with very little provocation. Just why some brown bears leave the den in April is difficult to explain. It is still winter in the north country and food is scarce. The chances are that these early risers return to their dens and sleep for another month.

While not endowed with outstandingly sharp eyesight, the brown bear hears well. It also has a remarkable sense of smell, and appears to be constantly testing the breeze and listening for the approach of an enemy. However, there are times when the great hairy giant shows a lack of caution, permitting man to approach at close quarters before taking off. On the other hand, it sometimes will retreat at full speed at the first whiff of human scent.

The tracks of the brown bear walking are in a staggered line; the hind foot imprint is a little forward of the forefoot on the same side. However, when walking slowly, the bear places its hind foot squarely in the forefoot track.

The superstition that, when attacking, the brown bear hugs and squeezes its victim to death gave rise to the proverbial phrase, "bear hug." It is doubtful if a bear could accomplish such a feat. A bear attack is far from a hug. The animal strikes with its paws with a round swing and drives its claws into the body of its victim. One such blow would be sufficient to reduce any enemy to a lifeless, mangled mass.

## LOCOMOTION

Unless disturbed, the brown bear ambles along at a lumbering walk, leaving two rows of footprints. It leaves trails that are usually nearly straight, regardless of the roughness of the country or the steepness of the mountain slope. It may cross rivers, pass through dense alder thickets, and ascend straight up steep mountain slopes. These trails are usually used by many bears, who wear holes in the ground 8 to 10 inches deep. When disturbed, a brown bear will take off at a light, bounding gallop and continue at a fast rate for 4 or 5 miles without pausing to rest. It can travel for a short distance at a speed of 30 miles per hour.

## VOCAL AND COMMUNICATION

Normally going its own way in silence, the brown bear can growl, grunt, roar, and sniff. It also may cough, a sound that usually indicates that it is about to charge.

The brown bear leaves "bear trees," or signposts, along its trails. On approaching one of these markers, a bear sniffs around, then rises 6 feet or more off the ground, yanks off a chunk of bark with its teeth, and continues on its journey. Some of the slashes in the bark are made 12 feet above the ground.

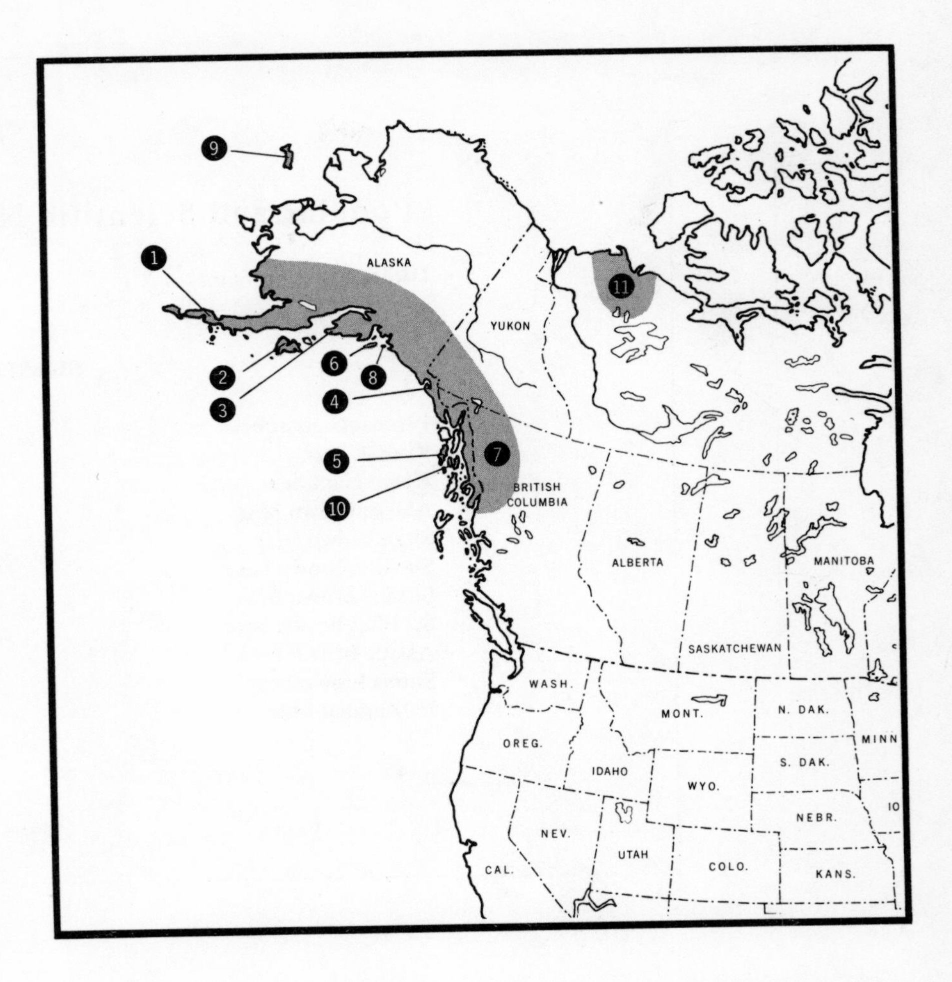


Distribution of the races of the brown bear *Ursus:* 1. Peninsula giant bear, 2. Kodiak bear, 3. Kenai giant bear, 4. Alaska brown bear, 5. Sitka brown bear, 6. Sheldon brown bear, 7. Stikine brown bear, 8. St. Elias brown bear, 9. Asiatic brown bear, 10. Shiras brown bear, 11. Patriarchal bear.

## MATING

During the mating season a male may share a female with another male, provided they are equally matched. However, a big male will drive away a smaller male that meekly accepts his fate. The breeding season lasts about one month for each individual. It starts about the middle of May and continues until the end of June. Females mate once every second or third year. During this period there is a considerable amount of affection displayed between the sexes, which travel together in pairs. They frolic, wrestle, and nuzzle one another with great ardor. Should another male join the party, he may even be accepted without opposition; if he is big enough he may decide to appropriate the female for his own. Once the honeymoon is over, the sexes separate and the female does not seek social relationship again for at least two years.

## BIRTH AND EARLY DEVELOPMENT

The cubs, numbering from one to four, are born in the winter den some time during January or February, six months after mating. At birth the cubs are small and helpless, weighing about 1½ pounds. They are toothless and hairless and their eyes are closed. For the first three months the female continues to doze, and the cubs stay in their warm bed of grasses and leaves to feed and sleep. They grow rapidly, open their eyes in about forty days, and cut their first teeth at about the same time. About the tenth of May the female leads her cubs out of the winter den. The cubs are nursed for nearly six months but family ties may not be broken until June of the following year. The female has a great parental feeling for her cubs and will permit no one to harm them or come between her and her offspring. When the small cubs are tired, they ride on their mother's back. When crossing a river, she picks up each one in her mouth and deposits it safely on the opposite bank. The cubs reach maturity in size and weight in about eight years and have a life expectancy, barring accidents, of about thirty years. Some bears live to the age of forty.

## Popular and Scientific Names of the Brown Bear

**ORDER:** *Carnivora*

**FAMILY:** *Ursidae*

**GENUS:** *Ursus*

**SPECIES:** *gyas*

**SUBSPECIES**

| | |
|---|---|
| Peninsula giant bear | *Ursus gyas* |
| Kodiak bear | *Ursus middendorffi* |
| Kenai giant bear | *Ursus kenaiensis* |
| Alaska brown bear | *Ursus dalli* |
| Sitka brown bear | *Ursus sitkensis* |
| Sheldon brown bear | *Ursus sheldoni* |
| Stikine brown bear | *Ursus hoots* |
| St. Elias brown bear | *Ursus nuchek* |
| Asiatic brown bear | *Ursus arctos beringianus* |
| Shiras brown bear | *Ursus shirasi* |
| Patriarchal bear | *Ursus inopinatus* |

DOUGLAS ALLEN

CHAPTER 17

# THE POLAR BEAR

NANOOK, the great white ice bear of the polar seas, is one of the strangest, most interesting, and romantic creatures on the face of the earth. A land animal that has adapted himself to the water and ice of the freezing northern ocean almost as completely as the seal, he still looks like a bear—not something like a fish. The seal, the walrus, the whale, and other mammals that have forsaken the land for the sea have developed many of the external characteristics of the fish. On land they range from clumsy to almost helpless. Nanook is still uncompromisingly a bear.

Nanook is no doubt descended from bears that were living in the Northern Hemisphere when the first of the several great ice ages that marked the Pleistocene era began. These ancient bears had the choice of moving south before the encroaching ice or of learning to live with it. The ancestors of the ice bears decided to stick it out. As the ages passed, the bears developed thick, white pelts for camouflage and warmth, hairy paws to keep their feet from freezing, and a streamlined shape to get them through the water with a minimum of effort.

In addition, the polar bear is one of the largest predators on earth, and likewise one of the largest bears. For years a mild controversy has been going on as to whether the polar or the giant Alaska brown is the larger bear, but that is an argument I'll stay out of. The world-record brown-bear skull is both wider and longer than the world-record polar skull. Weights are something else again. Few trophy bears are actually weighed. Getting the accurate weight of a brown bear shot in dripping, head-high alders on some Alaska hillside, or the weight of a polar bear killed out on an ice pack, is a problem to stagger Hercules. Many estimates have been made, but estimates, particularly with bears, have a way of being on the generous side.

However, polar bears have been shot from ships, then hauled aboard and accurately weighed. Some have been found to weigh 1,600 pounds, and one shot in 1935 went over 1,700 pounds. The heaviest brown bears, from what I can find out, weigh about the same.

Brown bears and polar bears are entirely different creatures. They do not even belong to the same genus. That of the brown, the grizzly, and many old-world bears is *Ursus*. The ice bear, on the other hand, is the sole member of the genus *Thalarctos*. The ice bear has a longer, snakier-looking neck than the brown, and the average polar bear gives the impression of being a longer, lither animal, less blocky and massive than the brown. However, there is no getting around the fact that a big polar is a

One way to get a trophy is to fly over the ice, spot the bear, land, and stalk him.

tremendous animal. I have seen movies friends have made on polar-bear hunts, and the bodies of some of those large bears look as bulky as those of beef cattle.

The average male polar bear is from 8 to 9 feet long from tip of nose to tip of tail, and weighs 800 to 900 pounds. That is still a lot of bear.

The polar bear is one of the three large mammals of the world that is white the year around. The others, of course, are the Dall sheep and the Rocky Mountain white goat. Actually, it would be more correct to say that the polar bear is just off-white, as the hair is actually a pale cream. It is dense and oily to shed water, and it covers the soles of the bear's feet. Besides his warm, waterproof coat, the polar bear in good condition is also kept warm by his insulating layer of fat. The nose of the big bear is black, and so are the pads of the feet. The cubs are less yellowish than the mature bears—almost snow white in fact.

The polar bear is a circumpolar animal, an inhabitant of the great arctic ice pack and the shores of the northern mainlands and islands. He is found in all the arctic seas—those adjacent to Greenland and Iceland and to Siberia as well as to Alaska and arctic Canada. Because the bears live largely on seals, they are most plentiful where the ice is broken and there are numerous leads where there is open water. This would mean that the bulk of the bears are found around the edges of the arctic ice pack. However, they have been found far to the north. A wandering polar bear got entangled in the wires of the runway lights on the drifting ice station called Alpha in late 1957. The bear wrecked the lighting system just as a plane was coming in to land. The bears come south with the drifting ice. They have been seen and shot in all parts of Hudson Bay—even as far south as James Bay, only about 500 miles north of Ottawa. They commonly are seen off the coast of Labrador and have been killed off the coast of northern Newfoundland.

The American polar bears are found off the coast of northern and northwestern Alaska along the edges of the arctic pack. The ice moves and drifts with the currents of the ocean, and it may well be that an Alaska bear is a Siberian bear one year, a Greenland bear the next.

Data gathered from airplane flights over the ice within 75 miles of the Alaska coast would seem to indicate that there are, in any one season, about 2,500 polar bears in Alaskan waters. A projection of the same figures over the habitat of the whole arctic pack would indicate that there are about 19,000 in the world. This would mean that the great white bear is a comparatively rare animal, much rarer than the tiger, probably rarer even than the lion, an animal which is extinct over a great part of his former range.

But in spite of the comparatively small number of polar bears in the world, there is probably little danger of their becoming extinct or even being depleted seriously. They live in as bitter and hostile an environment as exists on the face of the earth. In the foreseeable future man will have but little use for these frozen seas, and the bears should have them pretty much to themselves.

The white bears are only incidentally land animals. The females come ashore on the arctic mainland or to some of the numerous arctic islands to give birth to their young, and all bears feed on dead whales that have been washed up along the shore. Sometimes they will wander 20 or 30 miles inland in search of food, and one went inland to Ft. McPherson from Hudson Bay, a distance of over 100 miles.

In areas where food is plentiful, they are often seen in large numbers. One explorer has written of seeing the great white bears along the coast of Greenland like "flocks of sheep." Another tells of seeing a score of them feeding on the carcass of a stranded whale. Still another tells of having seen more than one hundred along the coast of Greenland. When conditions are right along the coast of Alaska, bear hunters commonly see several bears a day from planes, and they can pick their trophies.

In the past few years the hunting of polar bears by planes has become popular, and some conservationists have expressed fear that the animals were being shot out. According to a paper given at the twenty-fourth North American Wildlife Conference, there is little danger of this. The estimate is that the annual kill of polar bears over the world runs from 900 to 1,350. Somewhere between 100 and 200 are taken in Alaska, from 400 to 500 in the Canadian arctic, 150 to 200 in Greenland, from 150 to 300 by Norwegians, and from 100 to 150 by the Russians.

The hunting of the great bears by the use of airplanes may be esthetically displeasing, the paper says, but there is no evidence that the practice is biologically harmful. More males than females are taken because plane hunters are trophy hunters. They are looking for big bears, and the males are larger than the females. Since the animals are polygamous, no damage is done by killing off excess males. However, this is a tentative conclusion because decreases in the population of white bears have been reported from the Siberian coast and from Greenland.

Any control over bear hunting would have to be international, since the animals themselves are international, and a bear that is on the American side one week might be on the Siberian side the next. In addition, most of the bears are killed outside the 12-mile limit, and hence local authorities theoretically have no control over the hunting.

The great bears are powerful animals, with all the traditional strength of the bear. It is generally believed that they do not hear too well, something which would be odd indeed, as both the grizzly and the black bear have very keen hearing. Explorers credit the polar bear with exceedingly keen vision, however. If this is so, it is likewise odd, as bears do not generally see well.

But there is no argument about the keenness of the polar bear's nose. Ernest Thompson Seton says the animal can smell a stranded whale from 10 to 20 miles away. I have seen deer give evidence of having caught human scent downwind a half a mile away, and a few times I have seen pointing dogs catch the scent of pheasants under favorable conditions, go straight to them, and pin them down from 300 to 400 yards. If the polar bear can, indeed, smell even a ripe whale at 10 miles and more, he must be good.

However, the big white bears do have keen noses—no doubt of it. A favorite way of luring the bears within range as used by Norwegian hunters is to burn a herring. If there is a bear downwind, he soon shows up. Many an arctic explorer has been scared half out of his wits by discovering that he has inadvertently lured in a bear by cooking bacon.

The bears are tremendous swimmers and have often been seen swimming strongly out at sea, miles from land and even miles from an ice cake. Bears have been known to outswim whaleboats rowed by crack crews. That would mean a steady speed of 4 or 5 miles an hour. It is said that the bears can travel in the water at 6 miles an hour for short distances. The bears propel themselves in the water by the use of their front feet. On land they can come on with surprising speed, just as the big, lumbering grizzly or brown bear can.

It is believed that, like other large bears, the polars breed only every other year, as it takes a couple of years for the mother to teach the youngsters enough to get by in the cruel world in which they must exist. The female gets rid of her long-yearling cubs in the fall, wanders along through the winter until she meets a male, and then breeds in the spring. Evidence is that the bears are semi-monogamous, the male staying with the female as long as she is in a romantic mood. When she no longer is, he takes off, possibly to find himself another lady. The mating season probably begins in March and may last as late as June.

The female comes ashore to have her cubs. She finds some spot sheltered from the wind and digs herself a den in the snow. Then she curls up, goes to sleep, and lives on the fat her body has stored up. Like the young of all bears, the baby polars are very small, no larger than rats and nearly naked. Almost always there are two of them. They snuggle against the mother's warm body, burrow into the long, warm fur, nurse, and grow. Now and then Eskimo dogs scent the den from its air vent, and then the arctic hunter gets an easy bear.

Along in March, the cubs have grown until they are well furred and as large as hares. Then mamma, hungry by that time, leads them down to the shore and begins to hunt along the ice.

I have been told that one reason hunting bears by plane is less damaging to the brood stock than hunting by dog sled along the coast and close to shore is that the plane hunters are out in the domain of the big males and seldom see a female. Eskimos and other shore hunters, however, generally see and kill more females and young.

The female polar bear is a devoted mother. She teaches her cubs to swim, to stalk the seal. Explorers have testified that when the bears are pursued in water, the cubs ride on the backs of their mothers or cling to their tails. Like the females of any other large bears, polar mothers will fight to the death to preserve their young cubs.

The polar will eat just about anything he can find or catch, just so long as it has some nourishment. Dr. E. W. Nelson, the American biologist for whom the California desert bighorn (*Ovis canadensis nelsoni*) is named, found hundreds of polar bears on islands in the Bering Sea in 1881. He said they were eating grass like so many cows in a meadow, digging up roots like so many grizzlies.

The big white bears will also eat the eggs of waterfowl, bushwhack ducks if they get a chance, devour carrion washed ashore, or knock off a fish if the opportunity offers. But their staff of life is the seal, which they stalk while it is resting on the ice. Often the hunting polar bear is followed by arctic foxes, just as lions in Africa and tigers in Asia are followed by jackals that clean scraps from the big predators' tables. Occasionally a white bear, driven by hunger, will tackle a herd of giant walruses in the hope of getting a young one, just as the African lion will occasionally raid a herd of elephants.

A female polar is a devoted mother and often gives her young a free ride when pursued.

In the old days, the polar bears that were killed were largely got by Eskimos, whalers, fishermen, and arctic explorers. What little sports hunting there was for the white bears was done by very wealthy men who chartered special ships. One such hunter was Dr. Richard Sutton of Kansas City, Missouri, who hunted all over the world and who did considerable writing for *Outdoor Life* back in the nineteen thirties. Taking his wife, his son, and his pretty daughter, he embarked on his arctic hunt from northern Norway and hunted at the edge of the ice pack between Iceland and Greenland. The family killed perhaps a dozen white bears, as well as seals and ducks. The doctor wrote a book about the trip and called it *An Arctic Safari*.

Such a hunt sounds like a dream hunt. The food was excellent and there was plenty of it. The hunters slept in warm, comfortable cabins and were waited on by the crew. Most of the bears were shot from the deck of the ship or on the ice after short stalks. Then they were hoisted aboard and skinned. Such hunts were, of course, very expensive and time-consuming. One does not hire a small steamer and a crew of twelve for peanuts. One firm in Norway puts on similar hunts even today, but several hunters go along to share the expense.

A few adventurous Americans have gone right out on the ice with Eskimo guides and their dog teams to hunt polar bear. This, I am sure, is a tough and often uncomfortable way to hunt, but it is a sporting way and one which should be a never-to-be-forgotten experience for anyone who attempts it.

The surest way to get a good polar bear trophy, and in many ways the best, is by flying out over the arctic ice in a small plane, finding a good bear, then landing and stalking it. Since the technique has been worked out, there has been a great increase in sport hunting for polar bears in the Alaska portion of their range. A polar bear rug is now a fairly common trophy, but only a few years ago the big white rugs were seen only as decorations in the homes of the very rich, or were used as props for photographs of glamour girls reclining in the seminude.

I have never been on a plane hunt for polar bears, but I can see that this method would rob the experience of much of its sense of adventure and its atmosphere. To me, even flying to a far-away country to hunt takes some of the romance out of it. The first time I went to the Yukon I spent four days on a steamship going through the cold, foggy Inland Passage to Skagway, Alaska, and then another day going by narrow-gauge railway from Skagway to Whitehorse. When I arrived, I felt in my bones that I was really around 2,500 miles from my Arizona home, that I was actually in the mysterious subarctic. I have been to the Yukon three other times by ship, and always I have the feeling of mystery, romance, and distance.

I have also flown up from Seattle. The planes leave in midmorning and get to Whitehorse in time for lunch by local time. When I fly up, my feeling when I arrive in Whitehorse is that I am just somewhere else and that Seattle, where I had breakfast, is just over the hill.

Nowadays, it is possible for the safari-bound American to fly from New York to Rome in a few hours by jet, then hop aboard a Nairobi-bound plane at Rome and see the African veld beneath him when it grows light the next morning. He is in Nairobi not long after breakfast. Then Africa is just somewhere else. In the old days, the American bound for an African shoot went by boat to London, by train to Marseilles, then through the Mediterranean, the Suez Canal, and the Indian Ocean to Mombasa. When he arrived at Nairobi after a day's train travel he felt that he was really half a world away.

Not long ago, a correspondent wrote me that one of the outfitters in the Stone-sheep country is scratching out a landing field up near the head of the fabled Prophet River in British Columbia. The sheep hunter will be able to eat breakfast in Fort St. John, hop out to the airport, and jump into a plane. In less than two hours he'll be able to land on the Prophet, and maybe that afternoon he'll get his glasses on a 40-inch Stone ram.

When I hunted the Prophet and Muskwa back in 1946 and was with the first party to camp at the head of the Muskwa since 1939, I rode and walked two weeks just to get there. But I knew that I'd covered some country.

It is the distance and the hardship that makes far-away game worth going after. If the sheep hunter could land by helicopter on a ram mountain, stroll down a ridge, and pick off a big ram at the head of a canyon, the great ram would have no more value than a whitetail buck bushwhacked in the hunter's apple orchard.

And so it is with polar bears. In the days when the taking of a polar meant a hunt with Eskimos or a long voyage on a chartered steamer, the white bear was one of the world's great trophies. Nowadays it is too cut and dried. I know one chap who flew up to Anchorage, then on to Point Barrow. He went out the next morning. His pilot landed him close to a fine bear. He killed it, and the next day

Many an arctic camper has been horrified that the smell of his cooking bacon has lured a bear.

he was back in the States. He was home and at his desk before anyone had missed him. When he told pals who had seen him at the 21 Club in New York a few days before that he had been to the Arctic and had shot a polar bear, they looked at him as if he'd lost his marbles.

But be that as it may, this hunting polar bears by plane is the easiest, most comfortable, and surest way to get a trophy. The hunters stay in hotels at Point Barrow and Kotzebue and eat in restaurants. They fly out in small cabin planes. For the sake of safety, the planes hunt in pairs. If a plane goes through the ice, cracks up its skis, or has motor trouble, a rescue plane is soon out.

This hunting is relatively, but not absolutely, safe. After all, the planes are fairly fragile things, and they fly over and land on one of the most hostile pieces of the earth's surface. Four or five years ago, a pal of mine hunted with a famous arctic pilot. They spied a fine polar bear and shot it. But while they were skinning it, a sudden storm came up. They had no choice but to tie the plane down with blocks of ice (or whatever one ties planes down with in the Arctic), get out their sleeping bags, their little emergency tent, their canned food, and their primus stove, and wait for a three-day to blow itself out.

Another friend of mine, a chap in his late sixties, was in a plane that cracked up its landing gear. He and his pilot had to sit on a cake of ice for several days during bad weather, wondering when it was going to break up, and when, if ever, it would clear enough so they could be rescued.

A few years ago I had made arrangements to hunt polar bears out of Point Barrow with a couple of friends, but I couldn't make it as I had to attend an editorial conference in New York. On the trip, one of the planes went through thin ice. The plane was lost, the pilot drowned, and one of my amigos, who, by heroic efforts, made it to ice thick enough to hold him and was rescued, was in the hospital for many weeks and was months recovering from frozen hands and feet.

Like the wilderness grizzly, the polar bear is the monarch of his strange and terrible habitat of leads and pressure ridges of floating ice islands. The only thing the old male bear far out at sea has to fear is a man, and he does not see many of them. The history of arctic exploration is full of tales of explorers stalked by the great white bears, of bears attacking dog teams, or bears even coming aboard ship and trying to tear the doors off the galley to get to the source of the odor of frying bacon.

The polar bear is one of the world's largest predators—an animal as strong as a bull—but from talking to those who have hunted him, I get the impression he is not a very dangerous animal. When he is wounded, he seems to have no idea what happened and simply wants to get away. I have talked to several persons who have wounded and followed up the big white bears, and in no case has anyone reported a charge. Grizzlies and brown bears are probably more dangerous animals, and so are the big cats—lions, tigers, and leopards.

Nor do polar bears, from what I hear, seem particularly difficult to kill. Most of my friends who have gone after them have used .300 Weatherby Magnums and have got one-shot kills when the bullets were placed right. Many have used .30/06's and have reported ample killing power with the 220-grain bullet. Some have used .375 Magnums, and if I should hunt polar bears I think that's what I would take. I doubt if I would need that much bullet weight, but when I am after dangerous game the sight of the big hole in the end of the .375 barrel and one look at one of the big cartridges fills me full of euphoria. Long experience has taught me that the man full of self-confidence at the butt end of a rifle is worth a dozen or so men full of misgivings.

With good management there is no reason why we can't have this strange member of the bear tribe —this sea bear, this ice bear—with us for the foreseeable future. After all, there isn't much use to which man can put its home of bleak arctic islands, of frozen shore, of frigid sea, and of shifting ice. He has claimed and conquered it. He should keep it.

# The Natural History of the Polar Bear

[THALARCTOS MARITIMUS]

## DESCRIPTION

The polar bear is a close competitor of the giant Kodiak bear for the rank of biggest carnivorous land mammal in the world. A full-grown male polar bear measures about 9 feet long, stands from 4 to 4½ feet high at the shoulders, and weighs about 900 pounds, with exceptionally large individuals weighing up to 1,700 pounds. Females are about 25 per cent smaller than males.

A long-bodied bear with a long neck, the polar bear has a comparatively small, slender head, small, rounded ears, long, massive limbs, and a short tail. Like all other bears, it has strong, non-retractile claws and is plantigrade, or flat-footed. As a protection against cold and for friction on slippery ice, its soles and paws have a protective covering of hair. Except for the black tip of its nose, the lips, eyes, and foot pads are covered with a warm coat of dense, long hair. The pelage is snow white the year round, usually tinged with a yellowish shade, due to immersion for long periods in salt water. The white coat serves a dual purpose: to conserve body heat, and as concealing coloration to enable the bear to stalk its prey in a land of perpetual snow and ice.

## ORIGIN

The polar bear (*Thalarctos*) is the most recent addition to the bear family and appears for the first time in the geological formations of the late Pleistocene era. The bear family *Ursidae* was a comparatively late arrival and is unknown before the beginning of the Pliocene. The bears represent a branch that springs from the primitive canids (early flesh-eaters) developed during the Upper Eocene and Lower Oligocene.

## RANGE

Few white people have seen a polar bear in its native habitat, a barren land of extreme cold, perpetual snow and ice. The polar bear is circumpolar in distribution; its range in North America extends from the northwestern coast of Alaska to northern Labrador, Hudson Bay, and the islands and pack ice of the Arctic Ocean, but it is not found in the Antarctic.

The polar bears have been divided into four geographical varieties: The typical polar bear of West Greenland, Ellesmere Land, Hudson Bay, and the Arctic coast to northwestern Alaska; the Ungava polar bear of the Ungava region of northeastern Canada; the Greenland polar bear, of eastern Greenland; and the Labrador polar bear.

Distribution of the races of the polar bear *Thalarctos:* 1. East Greenland polar bear, 2. Greenland polar bear, 3. Labrador polar bear, 4. Typical polar bear, 5. Ungava polar bear.

## HABITS

A great traveller by land and sea, the polar bear is at home on the edge of the ice pack where seals are frequent visitors. At times a white bear will stray a long distance inland and travel a hundred miles up large rivers, swimming most of the way.

A powerful swimmer, it may swim with all four feet, but more often uses only the forefeet for propulsion, leaving the hind feet trailing behind. This peculiar trait seems to indicate that the polar bear is in some sort of transitional stage, perhaps similar to that through which the seals passed when they first took to the water. Polar bears have been seen swimming in the open sea more than a hundred miles from substantial ice packs or land. They ride on the floating ice, following the seals on their way to the breeding grounds, and as the ice melts and breaks up, they swim back toward the north.

Most bears in the northern regions spend the cold, long winter asleep in the shelter of a well-protected den—but not the polar bear. During the long, arctic night which begins in September and lasts until March, lit only by the flickering flashes of the Northern Lights, the white bear travels over the ice and snow in search of food. It visits the breathing holes in the ice where the seals haul out to rest and breathe. Polar bear males, yearlings, and females with their cubs born during the first of the year remain active all winter, but the gravid female dens up for the winter like the bears that live farther south.

The polar bear is the most carnivorous of all the bears. Seals are its staple food, supplemented by crustaceans and fish. Although it is a fast swimmer, it cannot keep up with the seals and must hunt them by stealth. A stranded whale will provide a feast for many polar bears and is about the only place where several of the white bears will be seen together. On one occasion twenty polar bears were seen together feeding on a whale. In the spring the polar bear feasts on the eggs and young of ground-nesting birds and takes a spring tonic of grasses and roots. During the lean days it may attack man, if it does not get the human smell until at close range.

Having excellent eyesight, the polar bear can see a moving object a mile or more away, and its well-developed sense of smell can detect a herd of seals even at a greater distance. Living in a land of grinding ice packs, where ice may split with a loud roar, the polar bear is not alarmed by most sounds.

## ENEMIES

With the exception of the Eskimo, the polar bear has practically no enemies living in its domain. Caught in the open sea, it probably would be doomed if a pack of killer whales came along, but we have no way of knowing what happens at such times.

## MATING

Some time in mid-March, during the late arctic spring, the male polar bear embarks on the romantic mission of finding himself a mate. Just what transpires during the courting days, or if there is fighting between the males, we do not know. By the end of June the sexes have separated and each has gone its separate way. The male bear goes back to his hunting on the ice packs. The female bear also continues to feast on the bountiful supply of food available during the short arctic summer and puts on a thick protective layer of fat for sustenance during the coming winter. In the early fall she turns her back on the sea and makes her way inland to a high, dry, sheltered nook. Here she scoops out a den beneath a snowdrift and digs down until she reaches earth. Or she may find a cavern in the pressure ice formed by huge ice piles.

The sun now sinks below the horizon as the long unbroken winter night sets in. The snow, driven by the bitter winds, piles deeper and deeper over the den, but the heat from the bear's body keeps it warm and comfortable. The rising warm air melts a small chimney through the roof and keeps it open for ventilation. Now, curled up and contented, the female drowses off into a deep slumber and sleeps until spring without food or water. This state of inactivity is nothing more than slumber and should not be confused with hibernation, a condition that occurs in the woodchuck and some other animals.

## BIRTH AND EARLY DEVELOPMENT

Early in February or sometimes late in January, about nine months after mating, the cubs, usually twins, are born while the mother is still drowsy with sleep. They are naked, toothless and their eyes are tightly closed. At first the tiny, chubby cubs are no more than 10 inches long and weigh less than 2 pounds. They lie close to the mother's side for warmth, and sleep and nurse on the mother's rich, warm milk until spring. Soon after birth the cubs are covered with a soft coat of downy, white hair, but they do not open their eyes until they are six weeks old. About the time that the warm March sun begins to melt the wall of the den, the mother breaks out of her ice-encrusted winter quarters and leads her cubs back to the sea. The trek back to the water may be a distance of 10 or even 20 miles, but the mother, ever solicitous for the welfare of her cubs, permits them to ride on her back when they get tired. For their first summer the cubs are dependent on the mother's milk, and woe to any unsuspecting stranger—man or beast—that may come between them. By fall the cubs are learning to hunt for themselves, beginning with small crustaceans in shallow water. Watching and imitating their mother, they soon learn to hunt bigger game.

In the fall the female does not den up as she did the previous year but hunts with her fast-growing cubs over the ice fields. Family ties are not actually broken until spring when the cubs, now seventeen months old and weighing about 200 pounds each, are driven away to forage for themselves. Twins may stay together for a while longer, but soon disperse. The two-year mating cycle is approaching for the female, and she is reaching the time when she will be ready to accept a new mate and begin again to raise another family.

### Popular and Scientific Names of the Polar Bear

**ORDER:** *Carnivora*

**FAMILY:** *Ursidae*

**GENUS:** *Thalarctos*

**SPECIES:** *maritimus*

**SUBSPECIES**

| | |
|---|---|
| Typical polar bear | *Thalarctos maritimus maritimus* |
| Ungava polar bear | *Thalarctos maritimus ungavensis* |
| Greenland polar bear | *Thalarctos maritimus groenlandicus* |
| East Greenland polar bear | *Thalarctos maritimus eogroenlandicus* |
| Labrador polar bear | *Thalarctos maritimus labradorensis* |

The tracks of a polar bear walking may vary: usually the hind foot oversteps the forefoot, as shown here; sometimes the hind foot falls into the forefoot track.

DOUGLAS ALLEN

CHAPTER 18

# THE WOLF

IF EVER there was an animal with a bad reputation, it is the wolf. The very word is the epitome of evil and greed. He who is as cunning as a wolf is a bad actor indeed, and anyone who says he is as hungry as a wolf is in desperate circumstances. The wolf in sheep's clothing is evil hiding behind innocence. The groups of German submarines that ganged up on Allied shipping during World War II were wolf packs, and the villain in literature commonly regards tender maidens with a wolfish glitter in his eye. A human wolf is a reprobate against whom all nice girls should be warned, and a wolf whistle is more insult than compliment. In tradition and literature, the wolf is an unmitigated villain, and the symbol of a terrible death is to be torn to pieces and devoured by wolves.

The wolf is indeed an ancient enemy of man. Our fur-clad, spear-carrying ancestors of ice-age Europe had to compete with packs of wolves for their reindeer and horse meat. During the hungry winters of ancient and medieval Europe, packs of wolves not only killed sheep, horses, and cattle, but also pulled down and devoured peasants in their fields. Even in recent times wolves have killed human beings in Russia and Siberia, and many are the tales from northern Europe and packs of wolves chasing sleighs across the snow in bitter cold.

Yet we forget that not only is the wolf one of the oldest enemies of man, but one of his most ancient friends. The dog is nothing but a tamed wolf altered and twisted into odd sizes and curious shapes by selective breeding. The hunting instinct that we so admire in sporting dogs is but the hunting instinct of the wolf. The friendliness of the dog, his attachment to a master and to a family, and his willingness to co-operate in the hunt are manifestations of the gregarious instinct of the wolf. Just as wolves will co-operate in pulling down a moose or an elk, or in taking turns in running an antelope to exhaustion, the fine bird dog co-operates with his master. The two of them, in the dog's mind, form a pack. The intelligent pointing dog that circles and pins a running pheasant in wheat stubble is simply employing a tactic used by his ancestral wolves 1,000,000 years ago.

Dogs and wolves interbreed, and many of the sled dogs of the far north are part wolf. Dogs allowed to run wild form packs, chase and kill game and domestic stock, and, in effect, become wolves. Even the most pampered lap dog is at heart a wolf and, given a chance, will revert to type. One deer-killing pack of semi-wild dogs I saw in Mexico contained a preposterous little Chihuahua. At heart he was a wolf—maybe a small wolf, but still a wolf. The tracks of wolves and large dogs cannot surely be told apart. I once shot an animal identified by several observers as certainly a wolf. It turned out to be a large mongrel dog with some German police dog in his ancestry.

The wolves that made an alliance with the human race and became dogs have increased and prospered, but those that remained wolves now live only in the wild and desolate regions of the earth. In the continental United States, excluding Alaska, they are just about extinct, and the few authentic wolves that are reported now and then are generally migrants from across the Mexican or Canadian borders. The other wolves that are reported are generally coyotes or dogs gone wild.

Dogs and wolves have many habits and attributes in common. Just as dogs always investigate fireplugs and leave their calling cards, so do wolves have their signposts. By going to them they can tell what other wolves are in the country, their sexes, their states of mind, and possibly their sizes. I once saw a charming camp dog named Tango trot up to a wolf signpost, sniff, and back away growling. For the next several miles he stuck close to the packtrain with his tail between his legs. His hair stood up on the back of his neck. Now and then he'd glance around apprehensively and growl. The wolf that had left his calling card must have been a very tough cookie indeed.

Actually, wolves can often be converted into dogs without too much trouble. Generally, a wolf raised in captivity by his wolf mother is apprehensive, furtive, and mean. Those captured young and raised by dog mothers are much more tractable, and now and then a wolf pup grows up that is indistinguishable in disposition from an ordinary dog.

There's no doubt that from such friendly wolf pups domestic dogs are descended. Our primitive, fur-clad ancestors would probably dig a litter of wolf pups out of a den and raise them. The friendly pups they would keep. The mean ones they'd kill or drive away.

The North American wolf is a much less specialized creature than the dog, but in many ways he is superior. No wolf can smell as well as the specialized bloodhound or run as fast as the greyhound. He is, of course, without the retrieving instincts of the Labrador, and if put in harness he might not be as enduring as a sled-dog breed such as the Siberian husky.

Nevertheless, this magnificent wild creature has a wonderful nose, good eyes, tremendous strength, and keen intelligence. He is a large animal, and depending on his age, his condition, and where he is taken, he will weigh from 85 to perhaps as much as 170 pounds. No dog has the strength of jaw the wolf possesses. He will chew up a bone a dog would only gnaw on. One time when I was hunting sheep in northern British Columbia, I caught several glimpses of a pack of wolves that hung around a salt lick much frequented by sheep. About 50 yards from the lick was a steep bluff where the sheep could take refuge from the wolves. Twice, as I was riding out of camp to the high country, I saw two ewes and two lambs on the bluff staring down at the hungry wolves below them.

Then one morning when I rode by I noticed fresh blood and sheep hair at the foot of the bluff. That time a couple of the sheep had not quite made it. The wolves had really cleaned up the carcasses. All the evidence left of that wilderness tragedy was blood, a little hair, stomach contents, and the skull plate and horns of one ewe. Every other scrap of hair, bones, and internal organs had been cleaned up by the wolves. The only other animal that could have done the job so thoroughly is the African hyena.

I have seen only two wolves south of the Canadian border. Both were of the southern variety which the Mexicans call lobos. Both were males. The one which I watched carefully with binoculars was certainly a large animal, probably larger than a big police dog. The one I shot would have weighed, I believe, about as much as an Arizona whitetail deer —somewhere between 85 and 100 pounds. Both of these animals were a light gray.

In the Canadian north, where I have seen a good many wolves, they vary amazingly in color, ranging from almost white to pure black. Some hides are a gray-blue, and some are an interesting combination of blue and dark gray.

The hide of a winter-killed wolf is a beautiful thing, to my way of thinking. The fur is rich, soft, and almost luxurious. Wolf hides make up into warm and handsome robes and warm sleeping bags, but for whatever the reason they have never had much value as fur. From what trappers tell me, about ten dollars is as much as one can expect to get, even for a prime wolf hide. I have seen the tanned hides displayed for sale at Whitehorse in the Yukon and at little backwoods trading posts. They are generally priced at around fifteen dollars. Most trappers aren't willing to bring a frozen wolf carcass into their cabins to skin it for what they can get out of it. Wolf hides are used to some extent as trimming for women's coats. When I was in college, long-haired furs were exceedingly collegiate. There were hundreds of coonskin coats and a few of wolf hide. I thought the latter were handsomer.

O'Connor and guide came across seven wolves on a river bar in the Yukon. The author dropped three.

If the ranking of trophies were objectively done, a wolf fairly stalked and shot would come high on the list of North American big game trophies. Over most of North America the wolf is rare. He is a big, impressive animal with keen senses, great caution, and enormous intelligence.

His wonderful nose, his good ears, his fine eyes, his alertness, coupled with the fact that he is largely nocturnal, make him one of the most difficult of all animals to see in the course of a big game hunt. There may be twenty wolves in a piece of country for every grizzly bear, but in a thirty- or forty-day hunt the sportsman may see half a dozen grizzlies and not one wolf. On many occasions I have hunted for weeks in country that was all tracked up by wolves. I have heard their howling every night, but seldom have I seen one.

There are still some wolves in Mexico, and I have often seen wolf sign there. I am sure that if I added up the time I've spent on Mexican hunting trips, I would be able to say that I have spent years in country where there were some wolves. But in all that time I have seen only one wolf in Mexico. That was late one afternoon about twenty years ago and about 125 miles south of Nogales, Arizona. I had been hunting whitetail deer and had paused to rest. Suddenly the Mexican *vaquero* who was with me whispered, "Lobo!" and pointed.

About 500 yards away I saw a light-gray wolf trotting diagonally toward us right on the top of a grassy ridge. He was apparently following a trail of some sort, as every now and then he'd put his nose close to the ground. When the wolf was about 200 yards away, the *vaquero* started whispering, "Shoot him! Shoot him!" But this, the second lobo I had ever seen in my life, was too rare and beautiful an animal to blast down willy-nilly. Intent on whatever he was following—possibly a female wolf—the lobo trotted up the ridge and disappeared into some oaks. The *vaquero* was a bit put out. He told me that all lobos killed cattle and should be shot.

The only other lobo I have ever seen was near Van Horn, in the Big Bend of Texas. With me in the car I had a little Remington trombone-action .25/20 with a Lyman 1-A, tang peep sight. I regret to say that I shot the wolf. It was the only one I have seen in the United States, and in all probability it was a migrant from Mexico.

As I was writing this I telephoned a friend in the Idaho game department. Idaho is a thinly populated state with probably more wilderness area in it than any other in the continental United States except Alaska. It abounds in wolf food—elk, bighorn sheep, goats, and deer. But in this great rugged land of rough ridges, high peaks and wild, lonely canyons, the wolf is gone. The game department report is that in many years there has been no authentic report of a wolf seen, shot, or trapped. If there are any in Idaho, they are those that have slipped over the Canadian border.

In my youth in Arizona, wolves were fairly common but by no means abundant. During the last twenty years I lived there, however, the killing of a wolf was always news. Now and then one would be trapped or shot near the Mexican border, but such animals had wandered across from Sonora.

Wolves have been reported in recent years from Montana, Minnesota, the Dakotas, and even from New York, but in most cases these were surely Canadian wolves. Now and then one wanders across into Texas. Elsewhere, I believe, the wolf reports are based on the sighting of coyotes or dogs that have gone wild.

The hand of every man has been raised against the wolf. He has been trapped, shot, and poisoned. A bounty has been placed upon his head, and specialists have made their living hunting him. Sportsmen have shouted for his extermination because he kills deer, elk, bighorn sheep, and antelope. Cattlemen hate him because he is destructive to their herds.

And indeed the wolf and civilization do not get along well, as the wolf is a hungry carnivore and a fine hunter. When the Western prairies swarmed with buffaloes there were tens of thousands of the big gray wolves hanging around on the outskirts of the herds. They preyed on the old, the young, the sick, the wounded, and the foolish, and they also raided the herds to pull down the strong and well.

When the buffaloes were shot off in the late sixties and early seventies and cattle were introduced into the plains, the wolves turned to this new source of food. Pioneer cattlemen took heavy losses from the wolves, but the wolves in those days were fairly unsophisticated and they were shot, trapped, and poisoned until the remnants were driven back into the mountains and badlands. Then knowledge of traps and poison seemed to spread among the surviving wolves. They became more difficult to see, more difficult to trap, and by the late eighteen eighties or early eighteen nineties they were on the increase again and causing great losses to cattle and sheepmen.

In 1918, the President of the New Mexico College of Agriculture estimated that wolves killed in New Mexico about 34,000 head of cattle and 165,000 sheep annually. One wolf was believed to have killed about five thousand dollars' worth of stock in six months. One Wyoming wolf killed 30 head of cattle during one spring.

Touch a man in his pocketbook and you have made an enemy. Associations of cattlemen and game departments put bounties on wolves. In some cases rewards of as much as one thousand dollars were offered for individual wolves. Many men made their living as wolf hunters. They worked out careful and cunning methods of trapping. They used deadly poisons. Gradually they whittled down the number of wolves, and by the late nineteen twenties the animals were just about extinct.

Not only were the wolves killed off by traps and poisons, but the fact that they were continually harried probably kept them from breeding normally. Wolf hunters located dens by following adult wolves carrying game to their young, then dug out and killed the pups.

Even continual harrying alone will make a pack of wolves leave the country. The late Bert Riggall, the dean of Alberta sheep hunters in the days when the Alberta Rockies were the greatest bighorn country in North America and the guide who led Martin Bovey to the world record bighorn ram, told me this one. A troublesome pack of wolves was killing cattle and game in southwestern Alberta, he said, and the animals were so smart that they were almost impossible to trap, shoot, or poison. A German immigrant guaranteed to get the wolves out of the country for a price. The desperate ranchers agreed, but with the provision that there would be no pay unless all the wolves were gone.

The German took up the tracks of the pack in the winter when snow was on the ground. A tough hombre, he carried his little camp on his back. Always he was after them. Never was he far behind them. From dawn to dusk the wolves knew this implacable human being was on their trail. He seldom saw them; he didn't kill a one. But the knowledge that they were constantly pursued was too much for them. They left the country, and for years there was not a wolf in the area.

Hunters and outfitters hate the wolves almost as much as ranchers do, and every few years they raise a great hue and cry that the wolves are destroying the game of the wilderness areas. For years a very good friend of mine who guided in the Alberta and British Columbia Rockies—in writing me a sort of annual report—told me that his country had gone to pot because of the great increase of wolves.

Ten or twelve years ago, guides and hunters over the Yukon, northern British Columbia, and Alaska were saying that the game of this wild, wonderful country was doomed unless there was more wolf control. Some even recommended wolf extermination.

The relationship of wolves to game is a complex question, and one on which I am surely no authority. Undoubtedly there are cycles of wolf abundance and scarcity in wilderness areas, and it is also an undoubted fact that at certain times in the cycles the wolves prey heavily on the game. An intelligent and observant trapper who had lived for many years among the game of the north told me that he thought wolf abundance followed the abundance of arctic hares. When these hares were on the upper portion of their cycles and plentiful everywhere, the wolves subsisted largely on them. They had no trouble procuring food for their young and they raised large litters. Then when the rabbits died off, as they do every few years, the wolves did more hunting of the larger game.

The primary victim of the wolf in the far north is the caribou, and there are always wolves in good caribou country. Wolves always follow the large caribou migrations. Moose are also heavily preyed upon by wolves, and in the snow a pack can pull down the largest bulls.

Although wolves kill many sheep and are surely a factor in limiting sheep numbers, I doubt if the wolf is a natural predator of sheep. In first-class sheep country, the soft-footed wolf would have a great deal of trouble following sheep into the rocks.

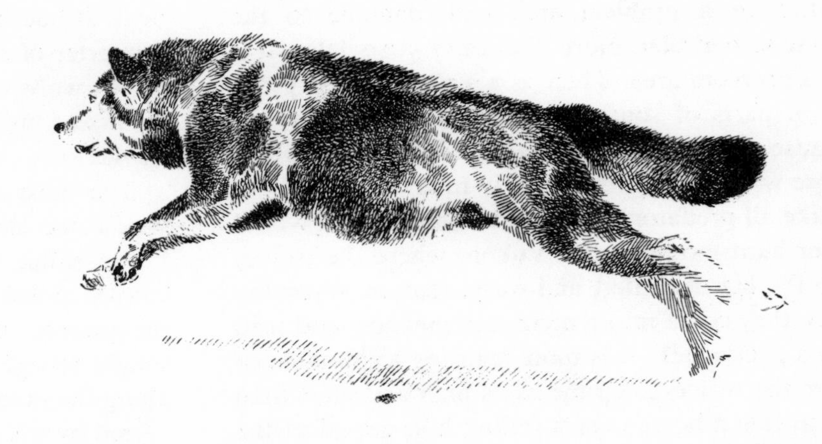


Bush pilots help to control the wolf population in Alaska by shooting the animals from planes.

I have seen wolves try to catch sheep running up shale and rockslides, and it is simply no contest. The wolf is quickly outdistanced and gives up. The sheep know that once they gain the cliffs and slides they are safe, and when they are in their refuge country they do not seem to be afraid of wolves.

I believe the bulk of wolf predation on sheep occurs around licks, around streams and springs where they water, and in fairly level country when the wolves catch a band feeding low or migrating from mountain to mountain. In times of plentiful wolves, the sheep are driven back into rough, steep country where they can escape. There some may perish from deep snow or from lack of winter feed. When there are few wolves, or none at all, the sheep increase and greatly extend their range, often moving into low, rounded mountains that are marginal sheep country and where they would have little chance to get away from wolves. In the Yukon and in northern British Columbia, I have often found many sheep on low, rounded hills where all but the final stalk could be accomplished on horseback and where wolves could catch sheep easily. I have never seen much wolf sign when I have found sheep in such country. Where I found a great deal of wolf sign and heard wolves howling every night, the sheep have generally been high and in rough country.

A certain amount of wolf predation is probably necessary for a healthy sheep herd. It has been the history of the wild sheep that whenever the herds get too large they contract disease and die off. I remember one area in northern British Columbia where there were many Stone sheep and where a favorite bedding ground on level country right at the edge of high cliffs was as deep in sheep dung as a domestic sheepfold. I saw no wolf sign in the area, and probably the sheep would have been in better shape if there had been some wolves around to scatter them, stir them up, and pick off the laggers.

Wolves perform the same function with caribou and probably moose. Any breed of animal tends to increase until he endangers his food supply. I am told that wildlife experts in Alaska, where there has been a great deal of wolf control, are now worried over the possibility that the caribou are becoming too plentiful and that the caribou moss is being depleted. The presence of the wolf makes for livelier and more interesting game. In British Columbia and the Yukon, where there are a good many wolves, the moose is a wary and cautious animal, difficult to hunt. In Wyoming, where there are no wolves, the moose are almost as tame as cows.

Nature does a pretty good job of seeing that wolves do not become so plentiful as to exterminate the game. A big wolf population means that wolf diseases like rabies, scab, and distemper spread easily. As wolves become plentiful and game scarce, the bitches have difficulty in raising pups. Frank Golata, the famous guide with whom I hunted Stone sheep in 1946, told me he has seen evidence that starving adult wolves eat their own young. Nature has ways to prevent overpopulation.

Untrained sportsmen, trappers, and ranchers are seldom good observers, and as a consequence they generally blame any decrease in game on the predators. But the predator is part of the precarious balance of nature. Remove him and the game is generally in trouble. Killing off the mountain lions in the Kaibab National Forest in northern Arizona prior to World War I, while allowing the deer to increase, resulted in a problem area with damage to the browse so bad that, more than forty years later, it is still a problem area. There is a serious moose problem in parts of southern British Columbia. Why? Because there are not enough wolves to keep the moose within the limits of their food supply.

Like all predators, the wolf has his place. I would rather hunt moose in the Yukon, where the wolves keep the big deer alert and wary, than in Wyoming where they come into a mountain meadow and feed with a pack stock. It is more sporting to hunt sheep where the wolves keep the rams high and alert than it is to ride a horse over a rolling hill, get off at the crest, and shoot a ram below.

Wolves are generally too hard to see nowadays to afford much sport hunting, but occasionally the riflemen will blunder into them and then there can be some fast action. One time in the Yukon, my guide and I were riding across a wide river bar. We had just emerged from some willows that fringed one of the channels when, right out on the open sands, we saw a bunch of seven wolves. I jumped off my horse, started shooting, and with considerable expenditure of ammunition I managed to get three down—the last a very lucky shot at a running animal a good 400 yards away. This was apparently a family party, as one of the wolves was an old male and the others were youngsters of the year. For two reasons I regretted I had shot the wolves. For one thing, it was August and the hides were worthless. For another, my shooting spooked an enormous grizzly bear. It had been feeding on berries on a bar about a quarter of a mile away, and if I hadn't opened up on the wolves we would have ridden right up to him. As it was, we only saw him running at about a half a mile.

The ram reached safety on a ledge and then peered down calmly at his panting and frustrated pursuer.

The most satisfaction I ever got out of killing a wolf came about when I caught one chasing sheep. I was riding along a creek in a British Columbia canyon. Some sheep watered in the creek, fed up on the plateau through which the canyon ran, and sought refuge in the cliffs and rockslides. The sand along the creek bottom was all tracked up by sheep—and by wolves.

I rode around a bend in the canyon and saw, about 300 yards off, a ram about four or five years old humping up a rockslide with a wolf right behind him. For about 50 yards the race looked even. Then the ram began to gain, and finally it jumped up on a ledge and stood there facing the wolf about 15 feet below. It was a lovely sight to see the crosswires in the 4X scope settle right behind the wolf's shoulder. Neither ram nor wolf had seen me. The wolf's mouth was open, his tongue was hanging out, and he was panting heavily. The ram, on the other hand, seemed hardly bothered by the run. When my rifle went off, the 130-grain .270 bullet cracked that wolf right through the ribs, and the animal was flattened as if by a giant hammer. The startled ram put on about as nice an exhibition of mountaineering as I have ever seen, leaping from ledge to ledge and finally disappearing over the top.

An exciting way of hunting wolves, and one that I have never tried, is shooting them with buckshot from light planes. This is widely done by Alaskan bush pilots, and it is not only sporting, but a very effective means of wolf control.

The mating season of the wolf begins in January and lasts through early March, and wolves are presumed to pair for life. As animals go, the male wolf is a good husband and father. He helps guard the den, baby-sits while mamma is out hunting or stretching her legs, and brings game for the pups to eat.

The den is often in a crevice in the rocks, in a cave, or dug into a creek bank. The gestation period is a bit over sixty days. The average number in a litter is about seven, but litters vary from three to thirteen. The young are suckled for about three weeks and later are fed on food swallowed by the mother and then disgorged. When the pups are a little older, the parents, I've been told, bring rabbits and other game to the dens for the pups to eat.

Most of the pups, however, probably do not survive their first year. If they did, wolves would soon outnumber the game. Wild sheep, by comparison, usually have but one lamb. Eagles pick off the small pups as they play around the den, and the young wolves are subject to disease. Probably the greatest killer is starvation time of the first winter.

When the pups are old enough to follow their parents, they leave the den and range out on the hunt. The wolf packs seen in the late summer and early fall by big game hunters in the Canadian Rockies are almost always these family groups. The large packs are formed only in winter.

The parents teach the young to hunt, to fear man, and to avoid poison and traps. When the wolves mate again, the pairs go off by themselves, but the young wolves do not breed until their second spring.

The howl of a wolf is like that of a large dog and nothing like that of a coyote. I have been told that the animals howl when a storm is approaching, just as dogs do, and that they also howl during the mating season.

The extermination of the wolf in areas of civilization has been both necessary and inevitable, as the toll taken by wolves on domestic stock is too great to be borne. But it saddens me that, with the exception of Alaska, the wolf is gone in the United States. Back in far, wild country there still should be a place for him, and in areas of too many deer, too many elk, and too many moose he would be a very useful addition to the wildlife.

I rejoice that there is still a place for him in the northern wilderness. Not only is he part of nature's plan, but his presence helps lend mystery and enchantment to that lovely country. When one no longer sees wolf tracks and wolf droppings along the trails, when his howls no longer ring through the frosty wilderness beneath the glowing northern lights, it will be a sad day to those of us who love wild places and far countries.

# The Natural History of the Wolf

[CANIS LUPUS]

## DESCRIPTION

The wolf is a typical carnivorous mammal, or flesh-eater, which resembles a large German shepherd dog. It has a heavy frame, a large, massive head, long limbs, and large forefeet. The wolf's skull is especially large and heavy, with strong, powerful jaws armed with long, sharp canine teeth, massive carnassial, or scissor, teeth, which have sharp edges for cutting muscle and sinew, and broad, low-crowned molars for crushing bone. Living in a land of severe winter frosts, it has small ears which are not apt to freeze at the tips.

A full-grown dog wolf measures up to 7 feet in length, stands as high as 38 inches at the shoulder, has a 16-inch tail, and weighs about 100 pounds. The largest wolves are found in the arctic regions where some weigh as much as 175 pounds. Females average about 20 per cent smaller than males.

The wolf is a runner and travels on the tips of its toes. The bones of the toes on all four feet have been lengthened for increased speed, but the five digits on each of the fore and hind feet have been retained. The claws are strong and suitable for digging in the earth but are non-retractile. The fur is moderately long,

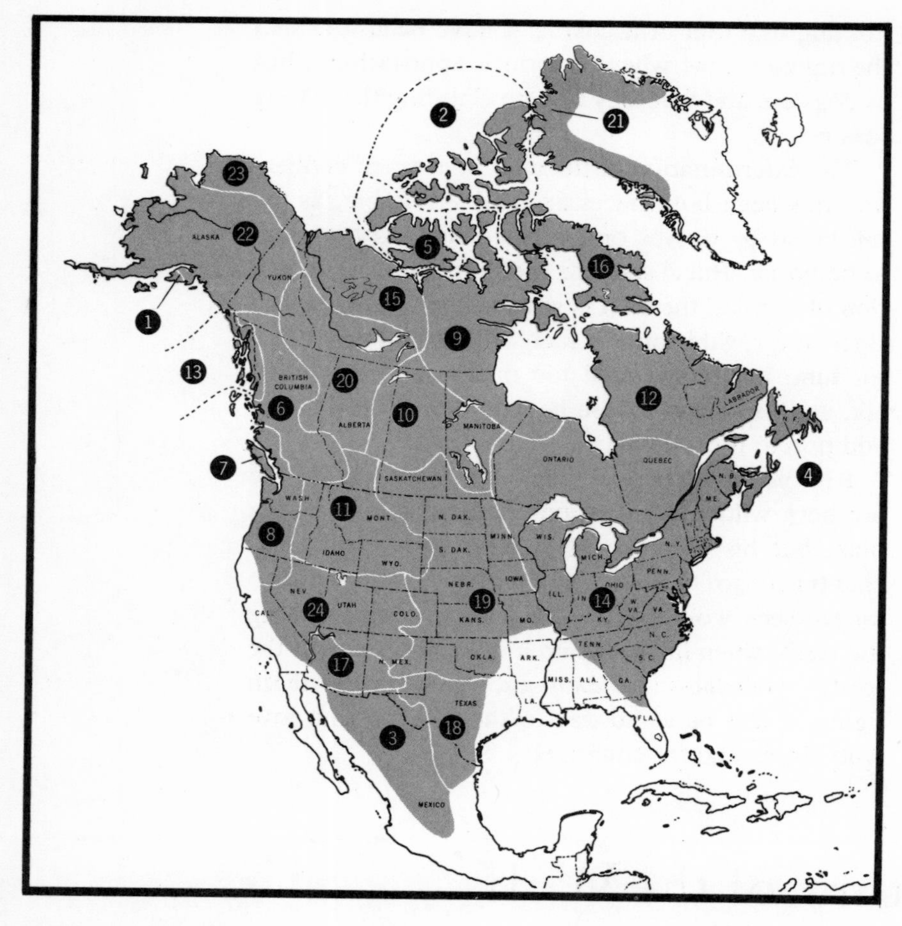


Distribution of the races of the gray wolf *Canis:* 1. Kenai Peninsula wolf, 2. Melville wolf, 3. Mexican wolf, 4. Newfoundland wolf, 5. Banks Tundra wolf, 6. Columbia wolf, 7. Vancouver wolf, 8. Cascade wolf, 9. Hudson Bay wolf, 10. Saskatchewan wolf, 11. Rocky Mountain wolf, 12. Labrador wolf, 13. Alexander Archipelago wolf, 14. Eastern wolf, 15. Mackenzie Tundra wolf, 17. Mongollon Mountain wolf, 18. Texas gray wolf, 19. Great Plains wolf, 20. Mackenzie River wolf, 21. Greenland wolf, 22. Alaska black wolf, 23. Alaska Tundra wolf, 24. Blue Mountain wolf.

thick, and varies in color with the species from almost white through various shades of gray and brown to black. The lighter shades are predominant in the northern part of its range. Since the tip of a wolf's nose and all the pads on its feet are naked, nature has provided it with a long, bushy tail which serves as a sleeping wrap. Curled up, with its nose and feet covered by the encircling tail, the wolf's warm breath helps to keep its entire body warm when temperatures drop to as low as 75 degrees below zero.

The three major senses are well developed in the wolf. It has sharp eyesight and detects anything that moves within a reasonable distance. A wolf will recognize air-borne sounds long before they are audible to the human ear, but its sense of smell is the major guiding factor in its life. By its sense of smell a wolf can follow a trail through deep forest on a dark night as accurately as a human being can find his way along a well-posted highway in broad daylight.

## ORIGIN

The wolf is the common ancestor of our domestic dogs. With an unbroken ancestral lineage, the wolf can be traced back to the Creodonts of the late Eocene and early Oligocene eras. Of the living carnivores, the wolf is the most like its primitive ancestors. Immediate ancestors of our modern species were present in North America along with the Great Dire wolf during the Pleistocene and were apparent emigrants from Asia, but the famous Titian wolves of the Pliocene were completely absent in the Pleistocene.

## HABITS

The wolf loves company but its social life is centered around family ties. A so-called pack includes a male, female, their young of the year and possibly some yearling cubs. Strangers are not usually accepted.

The wolf feeds largely on rabbits, ground squirrels, gophers, and mice. It also preys on large game such as deer, caribou, moose, bighorn sheep, antelope, and bison, most of which are usually sick, weak, or dead, but the wolf will run down a healthy animal when hard pressed for food. As with other large carnivorous animals, the wolf often has long fasting periods between meals and may go for a week without food. After such a fast one 110-pound wolf devoured over 19 pounds of meat at one meal, or nearly one-fifth of its weight. At times a wolf will forage on beaches for crustaceans and other kinds of animal life.

## LOCOMOTION

The top speed for a wolf is about 28 miles per hour for about a quarter of a mile; 24 miles per hour for a distance of up to 2 miles; after this the speed drops to 10 or 12 miles per hour. However, if necessary the wolf can lope along at this speed all night. Most animals can run faster but few have as much endurance. The wolf is a great traveller and when not bound by family ties may have a hunting range of 60 or even 100 miles. A wolf usually travels in great circles, and, strangely, nearly always in a counter-clockwise direction. It swims well, but cannot overtake a deer in the water.

## VOCAL

The wolf makes four different vocal utterances, each with a particular significance. Its most significant call is a long-drawn-out tremulous cry. Then there is a soft, plaintive cry in a high key, one of the most stirring sounds ever heard in the arctic wilderness and northern forests. The dog wolf has a lusty, throaty mating call, and a loud, guttural cry uttered in the chase. The latter is strangely ventriloquial and it is difficult to determine the direction from which it comes or the number of animals involved.

## MATING

The wolf has a special scent gland located on its back near the base of the tail. When two wolves meet, their tails rise rigidly almost to a right angle with their bodies, causing the glands to function. Urine is extensively used by the wolf for marking signposts. Should a strange wolf pass along and use the same trail, his scent would be immediately recognized as that of an outsider.

The wolf retains one mate for life or until a pair is forcibly separated. Mating takes place in late winter or early spring. The nursery, or den, is usually located at a high point where there is a view of the surrounding country. The dog wolf and the she wolf join in excavating an underground tunnel to the den which may cover a distance of thirty feet. The den itself is a roomy chamber big enough for the wolves to stand upright and may have more than one entrance. The dog wolf is not permitted to remain in the den but stations himself on rising ground nearby where he can keep a watchful eye on the entrance. It is his duty to supply the family with food.

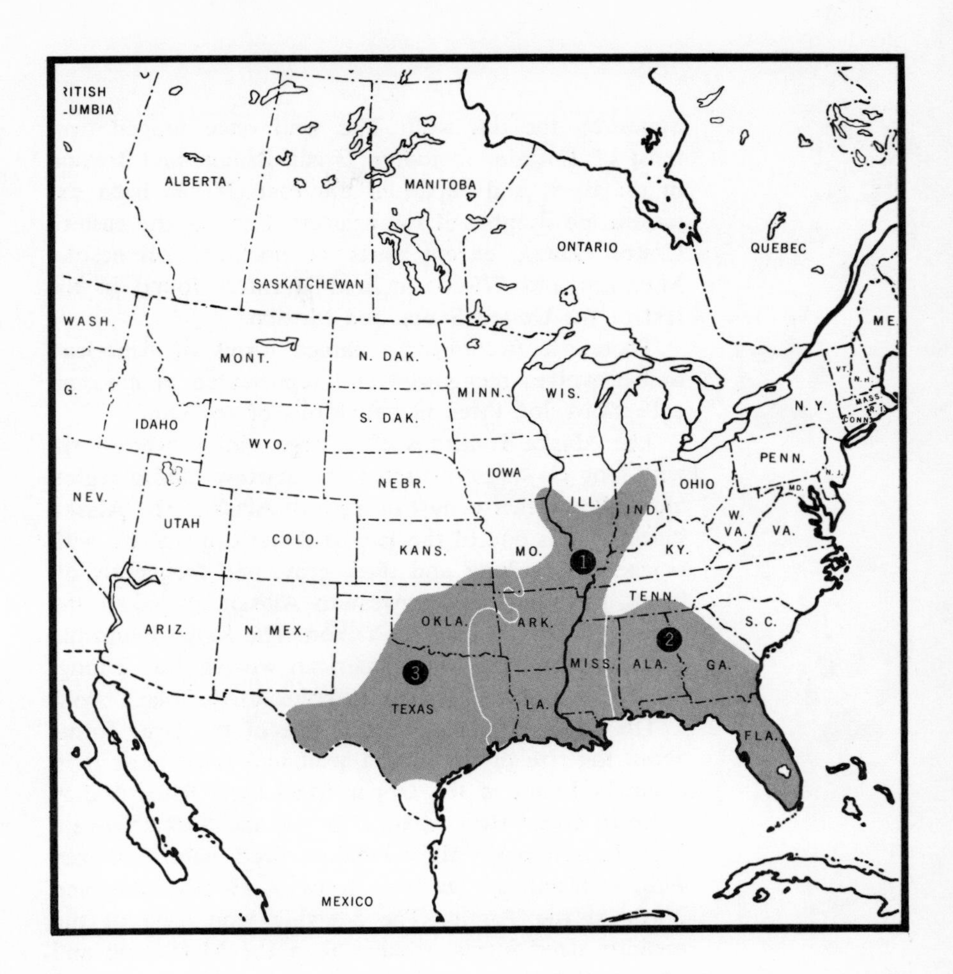


Distribution of the races of the red wolf *Canis:* 1. Mississippi Valley red wolf, 2. Florida red wolf, 3. Texas red wolf.

## BIRTH AND EARLY DEVELOPMENT

From sixty to sixty-three days have elapsed after mating when the pups are born in April, May, or June. There are usually six in a litter but there may be as many as fourteen. At first the pups' eyes are tightly closed and they are covered with fine, blackish-brown hair. Between the fifth and the ninth day, the pups open their eyes, which are deep blue and remain so for two months after birth, finally turning grayish-brown. They are nursed on the mother's milk for three weeks; later the mild diet is varied with partly digested food disgorged by the mother. By the time the pups are eight or ten weeks old their teeth are developing and chunks of solid meat are added to their diet. Should any misfortune happen to the mother, the dog wolf will take over and feed the pups with partly digested food. Young wolves grow rapidly and during the early stages appear to be all head, legs, and feet. When five months old a pup measures 2 feet high at the shoulder and before it is a year old will be almost as big as the parents. In about the ninth week the family moves out of the underground den and from then on lives on the surface of the ground. The pups are grown when two years old. Males are sexually mature at three; females are old enough to mate at two. A wolf has a life expectancy of from fifteen to twenty years.

The wolf is a powerful and capable animal, a fast breeder, and has practically no natural enemies, yet it never overpopulates any region to the extent of being a serious danger to local game such as deer and caribou.

It is generally believed that during a hard winter a pack of wolves will attack man; most of these stories are of Russian origin and may or may not be true, but such reports about American wolves have never been substantiated.

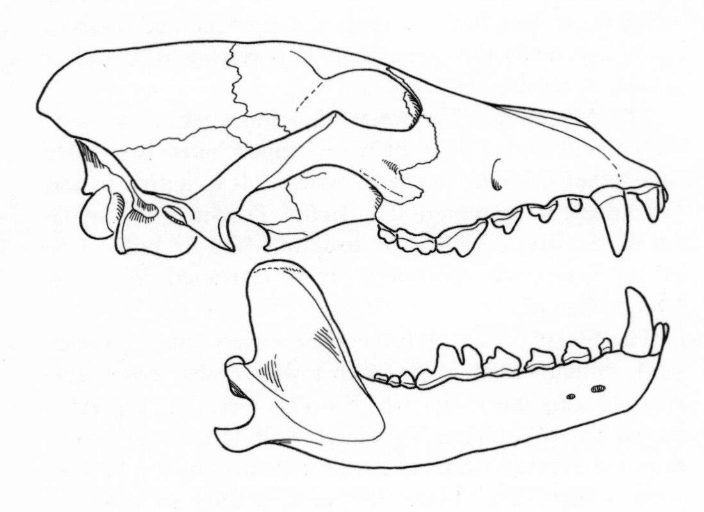

A primitive type of flesh-eater, the wolf has sharp-pointed canine teeth for piercing and tearing, sharp-edged cheek teeth for cutting, and low-crowned molars for crushing.

## RANGE

The true wolf *(Canis lupus)* is known by a number of colloquial names such as timber wolf, lobo, gray wolf, loafer, Buffalo wolf, and brown wolf. It should not be confused with the brush wolf or coyote, a much smaller and inferior animal. The original range of the true wolf in North America covered all of Canada and Alaska, most of the larger islands of the Arctic, parts of Greenland and Newfoundland. It ranged over most of the United States, except west of the Sierra Nevadas in California, south to the end of the interior plateau in Mexico, but was replaced in Florida and the Gulf

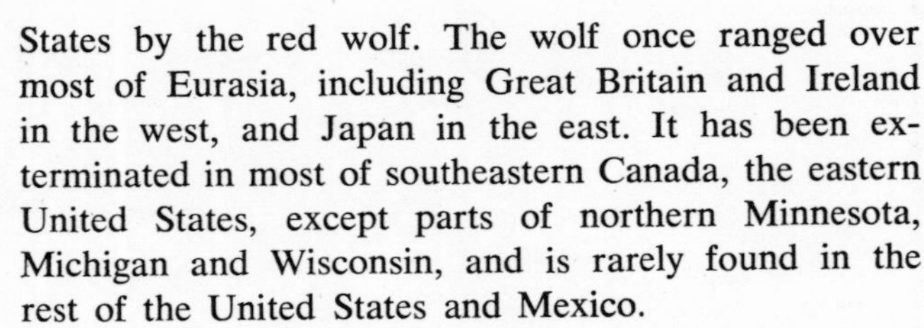

States by the red wolf. The wolf once ranged over most of Eurasia, including Great Britain and Ireland in the west, and Japan in the east. It has been exterminated in most of southeastern Canada, the eastern United States, except parts of northern Minnesota, Michigan and Wisconsin, and is rarely found in the rest of the United States and Mexico.

There are twenty-three named forms of American timber wolves recognized and represented in museum collections and three named forms of red wolf.

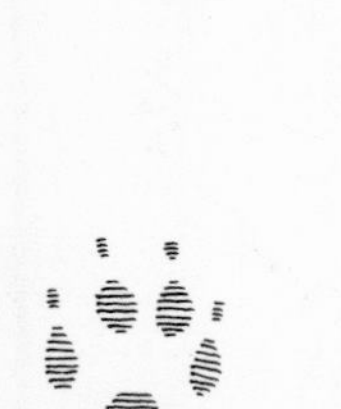

The Alaska Tundra wolf, a large, almost white form with long claws, is restricted to a narrow tundra region along the northern coast of western Alaska. The Alaska black wolf is one of the largest American wolves, with pelage that is long and dark gray, and frequently all black, is found in southwestern Alaska, including the Seward Peninsula and the Yukon. The Kenai Peninsula wolf, the largest of the American wolves, has a long, broad head and is similar in color to the black wolf.

The Mackenzie River wolf, one of the large forms about the size of the tundra wolf and resembling it in color, is found in the Upper Mackenzie River Valley north to Great Bear Lake, Alberta, and Saskatchewan. The Hudson Bay wolf, a medium-sized, pale, buff-gray wolf, is found on the west coast of Hudson Bay and north to the Arctic. The Melville wolf, one of the medium-sized forms, smaller than the Mackenzie and almost white in color, is found on Melville Island and east to Ellesmere.

The Greenland wolf is a comparatively small form, smaller than the Melville wolf, and white or grayish-white in color. It is found in northern Greenland. The Labrador wolf, a medium-sized, pale-gray wolf with a broad head, is found in Labrador and northern Quebec. The Newfoundland wolf is nearly pure white with a tinge of yellow about the head and limbs. The pelage has deep, woolly underfur. It is about the size of the Labrador wolf. The Eastern wolf is a small form with dark-grayish pelage heavily overlaid with black. Its original range extended from southern Quebec and the middle Atlantic states west to Minnesota and Ohio. The Great Plains wolf, Buffalo wolf, or loafer, is a medium-sized wolf with light-buff pelage grizzled with black, and a short, broad head. It was originally widely distributed on the Great Plains from southern Canada to New Mexico.

The Rocky Mountain wolf, a rather large, pale, buff-colored wolf, was originally found in the northern Rocky Mountain region. The Columbia wolf, a large wolf with dark-grayish pelage and buff ears, is found over most of British Columbia. The Alexander Archipelago wolf, a medium-sized wolf with buff pelage heavily overlaid with black, and tawny ears, is found on the Alexander Archipelago and the adjacent parts of the Alaska mainland. The Cascade wolf has dark-cinnamon pelage heavily overlaid with black. A medium-sized wolf with a rather short head, it was formerly found in Oregon and Washington. The Vancouver wolf is a medium-sized grayish wolf with its upper parts heavily overlaid with black and has large teeth. It is restricted to Vancouver Island, British Columbia. The Blue Mountain wolf, a rather large, light-colored form, larger and more buff-colored than the Great Plains wolf, was formerly found in the southern Rocky Mountain region.

The Mogollon Mountain wolf, a small, dark-brown wolf, varying to almost white in some individuals, was formerly found on the Mogollon Plateau in New Mexico and Arizona. The Texas gray wolf, medium-sized, dark-grayish or yellowish in color with rather coarse, thin pelage, formerly ranged over most of western Texas and eastern New Mexico. The Mexican wolf is the smallest of the true American wolves. Its dark-brownish color is heavily overlaid with black-tipped hairs, and it has a broad head with a sharply pointed nose. Its range is the Sierra Madre and table-land of western Mexico. The Banks Tundra wolf is whitish with a buff tinge, a rangy form, long limbs, a narrow, long head and massive teeth, especially the carnassials. It is restricted to Banks Island, Canada.

The Mackenzie Tundra wolf, almost white in color with a buff dorsal band of black-tipped hairs, is smaller than other extreme northern wolves. It is native to the Mackenzie delta region. The Baffin Tundra wolf, smallest of the arctic wolves, is usually white or buff-white in the immature specimens. It is restricted to Baffin Island, Canada.

The Florida red wolf is a comparatively small, slender wolf, cinnamon in color, with tawny limbs, nose, and ears. Its original range was Florida, Georgia, and Alabama. The Mississippi Valley red wolf, larger and grayer than the Florida wolf, was once common in the Mississippi Valley. The Texas red wolf, similar in color to the Mississippi Valley form but about the size of the Florida red wolf, is now restricted to central and eastern Texas, but formerly ranged from Arkansas and Oklahoma south to the Gulf Coast in central Texas.

The tracks of a wolf at a gallop show the four feet bunched together and the claws, which are not retracted, in front of the toe pads.

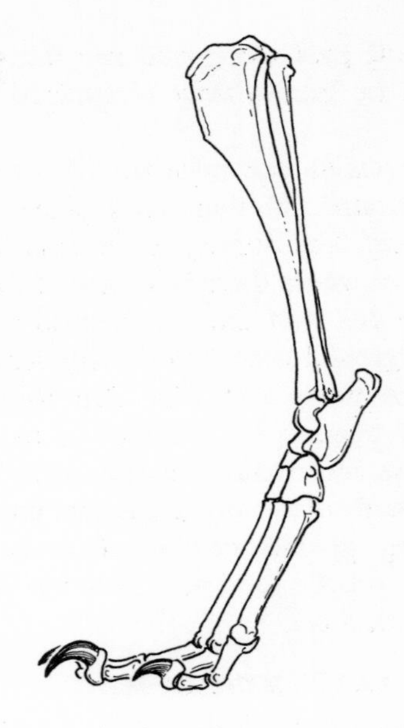

The wolf's hind-leg bone sructure illustrates its habit of walking on the tips of its toes. Its curved, nonretractable claws are used only for scratching and digging, not for seizing prey.

## Popular and Scientific Names of the Wolf

**ORDER:** *Carnivora*

**FAMILY:** *Canidae*

**GENUS:** *Canis*

**SPECIES:** *lupis, niger*

**SUBSPECIES**

| | |
|---|---|
| Alaska tundra wolf | *Canis lupus tundrarum* |
| Alaska black wolf | *Canis lupus pambasileus* |
| Kenai Peninsula wolf | *Canis lupus alces* |
| Mackenzie River wolf | *Canis lupus occidentalis* |
| Hudson Bay wolf | *Canis lupus hudsonicus* |
| Saskatchewan wolf | *Canis lupus griseoalbus* |
| Melville wolf | *Canis lupus arctos* |
| Greenland wolf | *Canis lupus orion* |
| Labrador wolf | *Canis lupus labradorius* |
| Newfoundland wolf | *Canis lupus beothucus* |
| Eastern wolf | *Canis lupus lycaon* |
| Great Plains wolf | *Canis lupus nubilus* |
| Rocky Mountain wolf | *Canis lupus irremotus* |
| Columbia wolf | *Canis lupus columbianus* |
| Alexander Archipelago wolf | *Canis lupus ligoni* |
| Cascade wolf | *Canis lupus fuscus* |
| Vancouver wolf | *Canis lupus crassodon* |
| Blue Mountain wolf | *Canis lupus youngi* |
| Mongollon Mountain wolf | *Canis lupus mongollonensis* |
| Texas gray wolf | *Canis lupus monstrabilis* |
| Mexican wolf | *Canis lupus bailey* |
| Banks Tundra wolf | *Canis lupus bernardi* |
| Mackenzie Tundra wolf | *Canis lupus mackenzii* |
| Baffin Tundra wolf | *Canis lupus manningi* |
| Florida red wolf | *Canis niger niger* |
| Mississippi Valley red wolf | *Canis niger gregoryi* |
| Texas red wolf | *Canis niger rufus* |

CHAPTER 19

# The Natural History of the Muskox

[OVIBUS MOSCHATUS]

## DESCRIPTION

The muskox is a sturdy, hoofed mammal which looks larger than it really is because of its long, shaggy coat of hair. The entire skin of the animal is covered with a thick coat of deep wool. Over this is an overcoat of long, silky hair that falls to the ankles and sweeps the top of short grass when the animal moves along. The hair reaches a length of 6 inches on the back, and as much as 2 to 3 feet in length on the neck and shoulders—the longest body hair for any animal.

An average full-grown bull stands about 4 feet high at the shoulder, and a very large one about 5 feet. The average length is somewhere between 6 and 7 feet. A large 7-foot bull may weigh as much as 900 pounds, but 500 is nearer the average. Cows are about 25 per cent smaller than bulls.

For the most part the muskox is dark chocolate-brown or almost black in color. Some species are somewhat lighter-colored on the back and whitish on the feet. The short tail, scarcely 4 inches long, is practically lost in the long coat. The short, sturdy limbs terminate in broad, evenly paired hoofs with hair in between the horny casings, and small lateral hoofs.

Even stranger than its long coat are the massive horns that form a protective helmet for the short, broad head. The horns, which consist of a tough, horny covering that grows over a bony core, are never shed, and grow bigger and more effective every year. They rise close together on top of the head between the eye and ear and sweep abruptly downward close to the head, then make a rounded curl upward to a sharp, vicious point. The horn of a large male ranges from 7 to 10 inches wide at the base and may reach a length of 28 or 29 inches. The average length for adult bulls is nearer 25 inches. Both sexes have horns, but those of the female are not as broad at the base as those of the males.

The hind foot of the muskox is smaller than, and comes down in the rear half of the track left by, the forefoot.

Despite the implication of its name, the muskox is a member of the goat-antelope group although it does resemble the ox, especially the yak of the Tibetan highlands. Its scientific name, *Ovibos,* comes from *Ovis* (sheep) and *Bos* (cow), and was given to this arctic inhabitant under the misapprehension that it was some kind of wild ox.

## ORIGIN

Living in the barren Arctic, where the summer seems like one long day and the winter an endless night, the muskox has survived through the ages far from the habitations of civilized man. Except for the Eskimo and Indian, few people have seen a muskox outside a zoological park.

Over a million years ago the muskox was native to northern Asia. It emigrated to America over the land bridge which once connected Siberia and Alaska. Contemporaries of the muskox in the early Pleistocene era were the mammoth, woolly rhinoceros, and two big muskoxen, *Symbos* and *Bootherium,* which were extinct by the end of the era. In Europe the muskox lived at the same time as the Neanderthal and the Cro-Magnon men. When the great glaciers began to move south during the ice age, the creeping ice fields kept pressing suitable conditions and climate for the arctic animals farther and farther south until the muskox reached as far as New Jersey in the western hemisphere and Southern Europe in the Old World. When the ice melted and the glaciers retreated, the American muskox followed in the wake of the disappearing ice, always living in an arctic climate with arctic vegetation. The woolly mammoth and the muskoxen's contemporaries which had moved south did not return and for some unknown reason died out: nor did the muskoxen of Europe and Asia return. The little lemmings seem to be the only arctic residents that returned with the muskox to their original home in the far north.

## RANGE

At home in the vast wilderness that stretches from the last stand of timber to the polar seas, the courageous, plucky little muskox does not migrate south in the fall like the caribou for shelter from the hardships of wintry snows and extreme cold. Its overall range extends west from the northern and eastern coasts of Greenland on a number of arctic islands such as Prince of Wales, Melville, Bathurst, Cornwallis, Axel Heiber, the Ellesmere Islands, and Devon Island. On the mainland its range extends from Chesterfield Inlet to Great Slave Lake and North Coronation Gulf and Great Bear Lake. Greenland muskoxen have been introduced on Nunivak Island, Alaska.

There are three recognized geographical forms of muskoxen. The black-faced muskox ranges from west of Hudson's Bay to Coronation Gulf north to 60° north latitude. The Hudson's Bay muskox ranges from Wager Inlet westward to Baker Lake and to Hudson's Bay. The white-faced muskox is native to northern and eastern Greenland, westward to Grant Land and Banks Land.

Distribution of the races of the muskox *Ovibus:* 1. Black-faced muskox, 2. Hudson Bay muskox, 3. White-faced muskox

## HABITS

Having a sociable nature, the muskox travels in herds or groups ranging from three or four individuals up to a hundred or more. The small groups consist of a few bachelor bulls, the large herds include cows, a few herd bulls, calves, and yearlings.

During the pleasant, short Arctic summer the muskox grazes knee deep in lush grass and varies its diet with shoots of willows, sedges, alders, moss, lichens, and many kinds of Arctic herbs and plants.

With spring come the trickling streams, banks gaily decked with flowers. The warm sunshine soon hatches swarms of black flies and mosquitoes which bite with savage persistency. Fortunately, scattered over the tundra are cold spring lakes, havens free of insect pests where the muskoxen can feed and rest in the summer sunshine with ease and comfort.

## ENEMIES

In appearance a muskox seems to be mild, passive, and inoffensive, but when cornered or molested it swiftly takes the offensive and becomes a tough fighting ball of fury capable of routing any single foe, even the Barren Ground grizzly bear.

The archenemy of the muskox is the great white arctic wolf. It often happens that a family group of these northern predators, numbering ten or fifteen hungry mouths that have not eaten for a week or more, closes in to attack a herd of muskoxen. No walls of rocks, cliffs, or even trees offer the herd protection from the rear. But all is not lost; the muskox solved this problem in the dim ages of the past. As the pack of wolves approaches, the herd forms a tight circle with the calves locked inside. The mature bulls and cows lower their heads, presenting a bristling array of sharp horns. To communicate their fighting mood the bulls rub their noses against their forelegs, releasing a strong musky smell which can be recognized a hundred yards away. From time to time a wolf in the pack driven by hunger may close in and try to stampede the herd, but it is met half way by an infuriated, charging bull who will gore and trample it to death if it does not retreat in time. The bull now backs up and the formation opens to let him take his place once more.

## LOCOMOTION

Nimble and swift on its feet when necessary, the muskox is not usually a fast runner, though its white-stockinged feet can carry it along at 15 or 20 miles per hour for a considerable distance without tiring. It also swims well and readily takes to the water. Herds of twenty or thirty animals, including small calves, will cross lakes a mile wide with little or no provocation, just the top of the head and the hair of the high shoulders showing above water.

## VOCAL

Except for a few snorts and grunts made when the competitive bulls are battling for supremacy during the rut or fighting predators, the muskox goes through life in virtual silence.

## MATING

During the spring, when the arctic wastes are covered with masses of blooming flowers, the sexes tend to sepa-

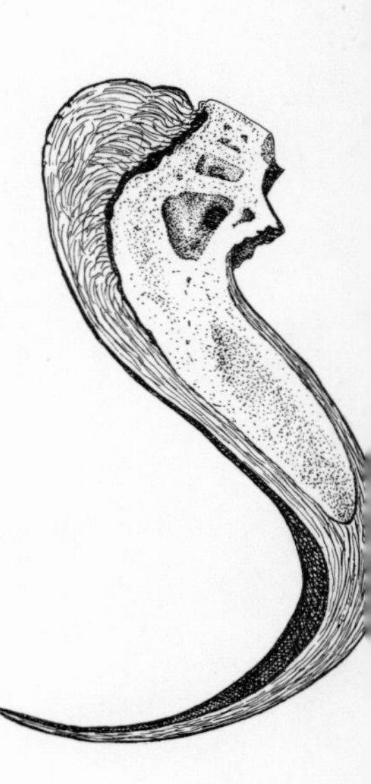

The cutaway longitudinal section of a muskox's horn shows the bony horn core, horn sheath, and heavy deposit of horn at the base.

The muskox has a small scent gland, which opens at the front corner of its eye, and a heavy concentration of horn on top of its head.

rate into groups. There are large herds of cows, calves and half-grown bulls. The mature bulls live in small bachelor groups of about four or six individuals, with a few solitary old bulls on their own.

As July and August approach, when the days are warm and pleasant, the tempers of the adult bulls become taut. Battles for possession of the cows are furious, unmerciful and unrelenting. Two evenly matched bulls will eye each other with hatred, then back off and charge, their heads coming together with a resounding thud. Only the massive shield of horns saves them from smashing their brains in. During the battle a bull always faces his adversary; to turn to one side would court disaster because the other bull would plow in with his sharp-pointed horns and rip the first to pieces.

When an enraged muskox about to charge rubs its nose on its forelegs, it is actually pressing the musk gland situated 2 inches below each eye. Despite the fact that the muskox does at times release a strong, musky odor, there are no well-developed scent glands to be found anywhere on the animal's body.

These competitive combats last until one of the bulls runs, or is too weak to stand and is gored to death. By September the passions of the bulls have faded and they again live peacefully together.

**BIRTH AND EARLY DEVELOPMENT**

The chubby, newborn calves in their snug, curly, brown coats come into the world in April or May when the days are beginning to lengthen but are still so short that there are only a few hours of daylight between the rising and setting of the sun. The cold, bleak winds still blow across the tundra from the arctic seas. The herds of cow muskoxen accompanied by a few bulls now forage on the open windswept spaces where there is little or no snow. Low, rolling hills and shallow valleys afford some slight shelter for the newborn calves. The herd keeps close together for protection from chance predators.

For the first few hours after the calves are dropped (from 9 to 9½ months after mating), they cuddle close to their mothers' sides for warmth and protection from the bitter cold winds.

At birth the newborn muskox calf measures 18 inches high at the shoulder, is 20 inches long and weighs from 15 to 25 pounds. As a sort of ritual never omitted by any of the hoofed animals, the mother muskox's first duty is to lick the newborn calf completely from head to foot to tip of tail. This not only cleanses the calf but puts the mother's mark on it so that she will recognize her own from the other calves in the herd. The newborn calf is able to stand and nurse within the hour.

For two or three months it flourishes on the rich fat milk of the mother, but is soon feeding on the fresh tender grasses and shoots of herbs. By the time the calf is four months old it is foraging largely for itself.

The mortality rate among the muskoxen calves is high, and when they are born during extremely cold, windy weather, some may freeze to death. Herds of muskoxen numbering twenty to thirty cows rarely have more than four or five calves in attendance. There is usually only one calf to a cow, rarely twins.

A cow may breed each successive year but more frequently on alternate years. There are no statistics on the ages of muskoxen but cows are believed to breed when three years old and to have a life expectancy of about fifteen years.

## Popular and Scientific Names of the Muskox

**ORDER:** *Artiodactyla* | **GENUS:** *Ovibus*

**FAMILY:** *Bovidae* | **SPECIES:** *moschatus*

**SUBSPECIES**

| | |
|---|---|
| Black-faced muskox | *Ovibus moschatus moschatus* |
| Hudson Bay muskox | *Ovibus moschatus niphoecus* |
| White-faced muskox | *Ovibus moschatus wardi* |

CHAPTER 20

# The Natural History of the Walrus

[ODOBENUS ROSMARUS]

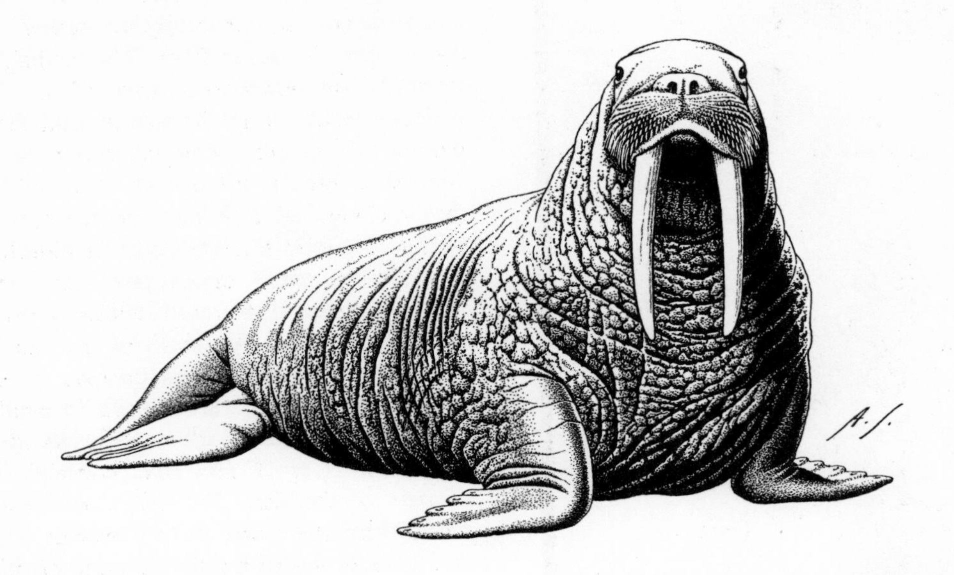

## DESCRIPTION

Were it not for the redeeming feature of a handsome pair of ivory tusks, the walrus would be one of the ugliest creatures in the animal kingdom. Its huge, ungainly body is covered with rough, wrinkled skin practically devoid of hair and dull yellowish-brown in color. A large bull walrus measures 10 to 12 feet in length and weighs from two to three thousand pounds. Its head is small compared with the massive bulging neck. It has small nostrils placed well up on the broad, blunt muzzle which is set with thick, short bristly whiskers. It has small eyes, no apparent external ears, and no external tail. Its limbs are fashioned like long fins or paddles with toes fully webbed for swimming. The fore flippers have five toes bearing flat nails; the hind flippers also have five toes with nails but the fifth toe is the longest.

The upper canine teeth are long yellowish-white tusks which extend straight downward from the corners of the animal's mouth, giving it a regal appearance. The tusks are present in both sexes but in the cow they are more slender and are usually bowed outward in the middle. Tusks range from 15 to 25 inches in length for the average bull, and weigh from 6 to 9 pounds pounds each. Exceptionally large tusks have been known to measure 39 inches, not including the root embedded in the jaws.

## ORIGIN

The *Pinnipedia,* or fin-footed marine mammals, such as the walrus, are generally recognized as an offshoot from an Eocene and Oligocene stock which is the common ancestor of the dogs, bears, cats, seals, and sea lions. Little is known about the early history of the *Odobenidae,* or walrus family. There were primitive forms during the Upper Miocene and Pliocene eras that date back over eleven million years, but these, like our modern species, had already become adapted for an aquatic life. Typical walruses, much the same as the ones living today, were present from the dawn of the Pleistocene era about one million years ago.

The early Norsemen hunted the walrus from the beginning of recorded time. The Norsemen's name for the animal was Volross or sea horse, which became walrus in English. The Eskimos have traditionally hunted the walrus with harpoons for its hide to cover their igloos and boats, for its flesh to eat, for its fat or blubber for oil and food, for its ivory tusks to fashion into implements, tools, and ornaments. Even civilized man took part in their slaughter and hunted the walrus for its oil, which provided a lucrative trade until excessive hunting depleted the big walrus herds.

## RANGE

Inhabiting the most desolate and coldest parts of the world, the walrus is at home on the ice packs and floating ice of the polar seas of the Arctic, but not the Antarctic. It is found as far south as the coast of Newfoundland, Spitzbergen, the Pribilof Islands in the Bering Sea, Point Barrow, Alaska, and the Amur River in Siberia. During the early sixteen hundreds, the walrus ranged as far south as Nova Scotia, where a colony bred each year on Sable Island, but all were exterminated there by 1650. There are also records of an occasional walrus seen during the early colonial days in Massachusetts Bay. During the ice age some one million years ago, when the spreading arctic ice cap moved south, the walrus ranged at least as far south as Georgia.

There are two species of walrus now recognized: The Pacific walrus, found in the Bering Sea and north into the Arctic Ocean and west to the Amur River, Siberia, is the largest species. The Atlantic walrus,

Distribution of the races of the walrus *Odobenus:* 1. Pacific walrus, 2. Atlantic walrus.

found on both sides of the North Atlantic Ocean in the arctic regions, from Newfoundland east to Spitzbergen, is similar to the Pacific walrus but smaller.

**HABITS**

Having a strong social instinct, the walrus travels in herds, sometimes numbering up to several hundred individuals. Along with some of the true seals, they are the herd animals of the eternal ice fields of the Arctic, just as the buffalo and pronghorn are the herd animals of our western plains. In the fall the walrus herds migrate southward with the drifting ice almost to the southern limit of their range, and migrate northward again in May or June during the breeding season.

Despite its formidable-looking gleaming white tusks, the walrus is a peace-loving and inoffensive animal—unless threatened with danger. It feeds well and loves to spend hours sprawled asleep on the ice. The thick layer of fat or blubber encasing the body acts as an insulation to conserve body heat and prevent loss of body fluids in the water. Walruses that have been killed and immersed in icy water for twelve hours are still warm inside the body.

Clambering out of the icy water onto the floating ice is no easy feat for a walrus, and it is accomplished only after much clumsy maneuvering. A herd may climb out of the water and congregate on one side of a sheet of floating ice, overweighting it so it turns turtle and the entire herd is unceremoniously dumped in a scrambling, loudly protesting mass into the water. Sometimes a sleeping herd will drift fifty miles out to sea before the animals wake up and start the journey back to shallower water.

The walrus is a hearty feeder. Clams, mollusks, and other kinds of shellfish make up the diet and its huge tusks are not used primarily for fighting but for digging clams from the ocean floor. The feeding grounds range from shallow water to a depth of some 300 feet. The walrus cannot use its flippers to stuff the clams into its mouth. There are, however, muscular pads on each side of its muzzle fitted with short, stiff bristles about the thickness of a kitchen matchstick with which it sweeps the food sideways into its mouth. There are no teeth in the front upper jaw, but behind the tusks there is a series of round, flat-crowned molars which are used to crush the shells of the fish. Strong gastric juices in the stomach soon dissolve the meat from the shells and the latter are ejected in small piles on the ice or in the water. After eating, its stomach may be distended 2 or 3 feet and contain three or more bushels of shellfish. The Eskimos consider the clams taken from the stomach of a walrus a great delicacy, and after a walrus-hunting expedition have a chowder feast on the half-digested shellfish.

Occasionally a bull walrus will make a drastic change in its feeding habits. Instead of standing on its head digging cold clams with its tusks 300 feet below on the ocean floor, this individualist hunts and feeds on the warm-blooded seals. It rips open the seal and tears the flesh to pieces with the spike-like bristles at each side of its mouth.

In the fall, as the creeping ice spreads out from the shores, the walrus keeps breathing holes open by visiting them regularly. It can burst a hole with its muzzle through ice four inches thick. Later, as the colder and faster freezing weather makes it more and more difficult to keep the breathing holes open, they are eventually abandoned and the walrus heads for the open seas farther south.

**LOCOMOTION**

In the water the walrus can travel at a fast rate after it gets its huge form moving, but no one has checked its rate of speed. It propels itself with both fore and hind limbs, the hind flippers, acting as twin screws, developing the greater propulsion force. With its heavy bones and huge, solid body the walrus dives easily and goes down 100 feet or more. Being a true warm-blooded mammal, it must rise to the surface to breathe air and climb out of the water to rest and sleep. On land or ice the walrus hauls its huge form along by means of the fore and hind flippers and, like the sea lions, the hind limbs can be rotated forward. The true seals are incapable of this action and can only use the front flippers when travelling on land.

**VOCAL**

The walrus is the noisiest animal living in the polar regions. It roars and bellows at the least provocation and when attacked has a habit of blowing loudly through its nose or snorting. Its roars and bellows vary from the mooing of an ox to the deep braying of a mastiff dog. It also has a short staccato bark.

### ENEMIES

The huge size of a walrus along with its formidable tusks are sufficient in themselves to discourage attack by most predators. Not even a polar bear would be foolhardy enough to attack a grown walrus and would scarcely get away with its life if it did. A hungry polar bear will attempt to maneuver into position to grab a young walrus in an unguarded moment and make a quick getaway before being discovered by the mother. Once aroused, she will fight to the finish and for days afterward will attack any stranger that happens to be in the vicinity.

The greatest natural enemy of the walrus is the killer whale, the most ferocious flesh-eater of all time. At the approach of a pack of these rapacious killers, a herd of walrus will flee in abject terror. Their fear of whales is so great that they have been known to flee down the main street of an Eskimo village. Once a large herd, in its mad scramble to escape a whale and get on shore, trampled and smothered a hundred of its members to death.

### MATING

There seems to be a short segregation of the sexes during the fall migration. The bulls, cows, yearling calves along with the gravid cows are together again when the herds return north in the spring. The bulls begin to show an interest in the submitting cows in April and May. Usually there is little serious competition between the bulls for the favors of the females and there are few vicious battles fought by aspiring males over the females. Many loud and vociferous objections are always raised when a male is deprived of one of his female companions by a larger and stronger bull. On occasion fights start that may end in splintered tusks, ripped shoulders, and even a broken neck. The short mating season comes in May and probably lasts less than a month. Females become sexually mature during the fourth year but few mate until they are five or six years old. Bulls mature in the sixth year and usually breed when seven years old. Mature cows usually mate every other year but sometimes cows raise a calf every third year. The walrus continues to grow throughout life and has a life expectancy of from twenty to twenty-five years and may live to be thirty.

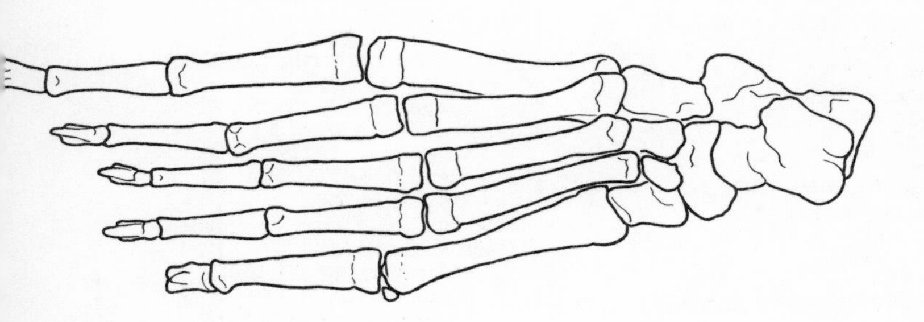

The walrus' hind-foot toe bones are lengthened to support a leathery covering of resilient skin, the combination forming a powerful turbine for propulsion in the water.

### BIRTH AND EARLY DEVELOPMENT

Late in May or early in the month-long day of June, 380 days after the mother has mated, the baby walruses are born. On its couch of cold floating ice of the Arctic, the newborn calf snuggles close to the mother's side for warmth. The mother strays a short distance from the herd which might injure her offspring before it has learned to maneuver on the ice.

At birth the baby walrus has a slate-gray skin covered with soft, ash-blond fur. This prenatal cloak is shed during the first few days after birth. Until the baby walrus grows a new coat of coarser and browner hair it is practically naked. At birth a calf measures about 47 inches in head and body length and weighs from 75 to 100 pounds.

The mother walrus bestows great affection on her single young; twins are unknown. She will defend it with her life against almost any foe. As a matter of fact, every grown walrus in the herd is concerned about the well-being of the babies, regardless of the relationship. During the early stages of its development, the young walrus stays close to its mother's side, often riding on her back holding tightly with its flippers. The two are inseparable and, when the mother descends to the ocean floor to feed, the baby tightens its grip on her back and goes down with her. Nursed on its mother's milk, rich in butter fat, the young walrus grows rapidly. It is dependent on its mother's milk for nourishment for almost two years, until its tusks have reached a length of about 4 inches and are serviceable enough for the walrus to forage for itself.

## Popular and Scientific Names of the Walrus

**ORDER:** *Pinnipedia*

**FAMILY:** *Odobenidae*

**GENUS:** *Odobenus*

**SPECIES:** *rosmarus*

**SUBSPECIES**

| | |
|---|---|
| Pacific walrus | *Odobenus rosmarus divergens* |
| Atlantic walrus | *Odobenus rosmarus rosmarus* |

# INDEX